Praise for Shackleton

'As a buccaneering Edwardian adventurer, as chaotic and hapless in his private life as he was dynamic in his public exploits, [Shackleton] is rescued by Michael Smith's genial biography as a flawed, enduring inspiration.' *The Times*

'A rich volume, written in a passionate, engaging style that makes it a compelling read, full of nuanced conclusions about many of Shackleton's formative life moments, and meticulously researched, as with all of Michael Smith's work.'
The Irish Times

'Absorb[ing]... a fair and rounded picture of a man who was a great companion and leader in a tight corner but possibly better viewed across an iceberg than across a boardroom table or a marital bedroom.' *Country Life*

'Fast-moving and gripping... Michael Smith's biography shows us a complex multi-faceted man.' *Scottish Review of Books*

'Diligently researched with extensive quotation... a welcome addition to the library of the polar aficionado.' *Literary Review*

Also by Michael Smith

An Unsung Hero: Tom Crean – Antarctic Survivor
I Am Just Going Outside: The Tragedy of Captain Oates
Tom Crean – Ice Man: The Adventures of an Irish Antarctic Hero
Polar Crusader: A Life of James Wordie
Shackleton – The Boss: The Remarkable Adventures of a Heroic Antarctic Explorer
Captain Francis Crozier: Last Man Standing?
Tom Crean: An Illustrated Life
Great Endeavour: Ireland's Antarctic Explorers

About the author

Michael Smith, a former journalist, is an established authority on polar exploration. He has written a number of books including *An Unsung Hero: Tom Crean Antarctic Survivor*, which was shortlisted for the Banff Mountain Book Festival 2002. The illustrated version was shortlisted for the Irish Published Book of the Year 2007. He contributes to TV and radio documentaries and lectures on polar history.

Shackleton

By Endurance We Conquer

MICHAEL SMITH

ONEWORLD

A Oneworld Book

First published in North America, Great Britain & Australia by
Oneworld Publications 2014
This paperback edition published 2015

Shackleton: By Endurance We Conquer is published
by permission of The Collins Press, Cork, Ireland, www.collinspress.ie

A CIP record of this title is available from the British Library

ISBN 978-1-78074-707-1
eISBN 978-1-78074-573-2

Typesetting by Carrigboy Typesetting Services
Printed and bound in Great Britain by Clays Ltd, St Ives plc

Oneworld Publications
10 Bloomsbury Street
London WC1B 3SR
England

To Barbara, Daniel, Nathan, Lucy and Zoe

Contents

Acknowledgements

This book arose from a lifelong interest in the history of polar exploration and it would be impossible to thank everyone who has helped me over the years. Some have long since passed away, though their assistance, guidance and sound advice will never be forgotten.

Equally, it would be impossible to thank all the archives, libraries, museums and personal collections I have benefited from over the years to inspect many records, papers and photographs relating to polar history. I am grateful to them all and any omissions are unintentional.

Special thanks must go to: Athy Heritage Museum, Ireland; British Library, London; British Library Newspaper Archive, London; Canterbury Museum, New Zealand; Dulwich College, London; Edinburgh University Library, Scotland; Kerry County Museum, Tralee, County Kerry; Library and Museum of Freemasonry, London; National Archives, London; National Library of Scotland, Scotland; National Maritime Museum, London; Oldham Local Studies & Archives, Lancashire; Royal Geographical Society, London; Scott Polar Research Institute, Cambridge; Alexander Turnbull Library, New Zealand.

I am especially grateful for the help given by: Mervyn Bassett, Beadle, The Skinners' Company; Sheila Donaldson, Bingley & District Local History Society; Calista Lucy, Keeper of Archives at Dulwich College; Peter Aitkenhead and Captain David Swain, the Library and Museum of Freemasonry; Del Styan and Alistair Murphy of the Cromer Museum; Angela Heard-Shaw at the Hull History Centre; Aubrey Jones for access to Koettlitz Family Papers.

My thanks go to Alexandra Shackleton, the granddaughter of Sir Ernest Shackleton, who allowed me access to material in the family possession. Jonathan Shackleton was also very helpful and willingly answered my questions. I am very grateful.

Robert Burton has been an enthusiastic and generous source of information about polar affairs and especially South Georgia. Anne Savours willingly shared her voluminous knowledge of polar history. I am hugely grateful to them both.

I must pass on a very special thanks to Seamus Taaffe for generously sharing his knowledge and information about polar history. Thanks must also go to Margaret Walsh at the Athy Heritage Museum for her patient and valued support. Joe O'Farrell was a source of wisdom and encouragement for which I am very grateful. I owe a particular debt of gratitude to Richard Green who generously allowed me access to Kilkea House and gave me a fine insight in the place where Shackleton was born. I am very grateful for the much-valued assistance of Dr Jim McAdam. Mary O'Connell was a source of inspiration.

I am indebted to Dr Cathy Corbishley for her very valuable help with medical matters. Dr Ursula Rack, Adjunct Fellow, University of Canterbury was especially helpful regarding Felix König. Nan Keightley was an important help with my research and I am very grateful.

Charles and Christine Dorman provided useful knowledge of Emily Dorman's family. I also appreciate the help given by Rev. Heidi Huntley and Michael Kingston of St Bartholomew's Church, Sydenham. I was also given generous assistance by Angie Butler on Frank Wild and by Helen Carpenter on John Quiller Rowett. Walter Hodder was generous with his understanding of the Dorman family connection with Wadhurst.

Thanks are also due to the following for sharing their knowledge on a variety of matters: Ulf Bakke; Mike Barry; Caroline Bone; Con Collins; Arthur Credland; Rosemary Fulton-Hart; Eugene Furlong; Richard Graham; John James; Sarah Lurcock; John Mann; Maureen E. Mulvihill; Alistair Murphy; James Nethery; Frank Nugent; Robb N. Robinson; Peter Wordie.

Where possible, I have identified all known sources of material used in this book and provided full accreditation where it can be properly established. Any omissions are purely unintentional and I would be pleased to correct any errors and oversights.

Families play a vital supporting role in producing a book and I am proud and delighted to say that I have received enormous support from those closest to me. Daniel and Nathan, my sons, were always there when I needed them. Lucy and Zoe, my grandchildren, were simply ... Lucy and Zoe! The help, patience and understanding of Barbara, my wife, has been supreme and I could not have coped without her.

Author's Note

The original units of measurement for distances, temperatures and weights used at the time have been used in this book. Where appropriate, the modern conversions are shown.

In some cases, distances were measured in both statute and geographic miles. For reference, a statute mile is 5,280 feet (1.61 kilometres) and a geographic mile is 6,080 feet (1.85 kilometres). For the purposes of consistency, distances are given in statute miles and any reference to geographic miles is explained. In both cases, a conversion to the modern metric equivalent is given.

Temperatures are shown in Fahrenheit, the measurement widely used at the time. Approximate conversions to the more modern Celsius scale are shown where appropriate. For reference, water freezes at 32 °F (0 °C) and 0 °F is equal to -18 °C. The normal body temperature of 98.4 °F is equal to 36.9 °C.

Weight measurement is generally shown in the avoirdupois scale common at the time and approximate conversions to metric are shown where appropriate. For reference, 100 lb is equivalent to 45 kilograms and 1 ton is equal to 1,016 kg.

Places names are generally given as they were used in the Victorian/Edwardian era. The Ross Ice Shelf, for example, is referred to as Great Ice Barrier or simply the Barrier.

The conversion of old money values into an estimated modern equivalent is provided by a formula supplied by the UK National Archives. For reference, £100 in 1900 would have the approximate spending value of £5,800/€7,000 today.

The punctuation, spelling and grammar used in original documents are faithfully reproduced, irrespective of the vagaries.

Introduction

From first to last the history of polar exploration is a single mighty manifestation of the power of the unknown over the mind of man … Nowhere else have we won our way more slowly, nowhere else has every new step cost so much trouble, so many privations and sufferings, and certainly nowhere have the resulting discoveries promised fewer material advantages …
FRIDTJOF NANSEN (1861–1930)

Fortitudine Vincimus
(By Endurance We Conquer)
SHACKLETON FAMILY MOTTO

The pallid twilight of daybreak hung over the still waters of King Edward Cove in the early hours of 5 January 1922. Dawn was minutes away on the remote island of South Georgia and the emerging daylight was slowly illuminating the magnificent natural amphitheatre of snow-capped mountains and grassy slopes surrounding the grubby, foul-smelling whaling station at Grytviken.

From shore, it was possible to glimpse the outlines of *Quest,* a small wooden ship anchored in the bay. On board *Quest*, as night gave way to day, Sir Ernest Shackleton succumbed to a massive heart attack and died.

It was a passing which simultaneously marked the loss of the greatest British explorer of the age and the moment when the celebrated era of Antarctic exploration, which was epitomised by the exploits of Shackleton, came to an end.

The final setting, a distant outpost on the edge of the Antarctic wilderness, could hardly have been better staged for Shackleton, a man synonymous with the icy regions. Shackleton, part adventurer and part romantic, was the Edwardian pioneer who made four epic voyages of discovery in what became known as the Heroic Age of Antarctic exploration, was feted as the consummate leader of men and today, nearly a century after his death, remains a lasting inspiration to new generations.

Outstanding historic figures are easily defined by their rank or title or by their association with places on the map. Captain Cook or Lawrence of Arabia spring to mind. However, Shackleton was – and remains so – just Shackleton.

Shackleton today is a cult figure who has assumed a mythical, almost saintly status. He occupies that peculiar place reserved for very few historical characters who can seemingly do no wrong. It is an unusual spot where critics tread carefully and where even rational debate is often made difficult by unswerving hero worship. Every detail of his life, including the most remote and tenuous connection, is pored over, dissected and analysed with an obsessive vigour.

The cult status is alive and well and grown men and women make pilgrimages to Grytviken and weep at Shackleton's graveside, overlooking the waters where *Quest* was moored in 1922. It is unlikely that tears are shed over explorers with equally impeccable credentials, such as Roald Amundsen, Christopher Columbus, Vasco da Gama, Meriwether Lewis and William Clark, Ferdinand Magellan or Henry Morton Stanley.

However, it may surprise Shackleton's modern disciples, many of whom are late converts to the cause, to discover that the current feverish popularity is a relatively new phenomenon. Indeed, Shackleton has spent longer in the shadows than in the spotlight. It is a situation which chimed with the fitting comment of Professor Stephen Jay Gould who said: 'The most erroneous stories are those we think we know best – and therefore never scrutinise or question.'

For over half a century there was room for only one popular polar hero: the tragic figure of Captain Scott. It is as though polar history could cope with only Scott or Shackleton in the ascendancy – not both.

Scott was applauded as a martyr who bravely sacrificed himself in the quest to reach the South Pole for King and country. Improbable though it may seem to modern audiences, images of Scott's disastrous South Pole expedition in 1912 were sent to the slaughterhouse of the Western Front during the First World War to rally the troops and demonstrate how to die nobly.

Every schoolchild was taught about the glorious failure of the South Pole expedition, dozens of memorials were erected to Scott and his four dead companions and a regular flow of books about the disaster poured off the presses for decades after. *Scott of the Antarctic*, the classic film drama, was released to popular acclaim fully 36 years after the tragedy and consolidated Scott's special place in history.

In contrast, Shackleton was a marginal figure for decades. During life he struggled for acceptance by the establishment of the day and even in death he was respected rather than adored. Where Scott, the gallant naval officer, was seen as a courageous ambassador for a dying age of imperial endeavour, Shackleton was a single-minded adventurer in pursuit of his own cause.

The prevailing attitude to Shackleton was demonstrated in the late 1920s when friends sought to erect a statue in London to honour his memory. Some thought St Paul's Cathedral was the appropriate location beside memorials to Nelson, Wellington and so many other notable Britons. A committee of associates and old companions eventually raised over £3,000 (about £100,000/€120,500 today) and a statue was finally unveiled outside the Royal Geographical Society in 1932, precisely 10 years after his death. It stands in a niche, high above the street and badly placed for anyone to see.

Nor was it possible for Shackleton to be commemorated in Ireland, the country of his birth. Shackleton, without question, was Ireland's greatest explorer but Irish independence from British rule was formally approved by Dáil Éireann on 7 January 1922, only two days after his death. Any association with Britain was highly dangerous in the post-independence years, even for famous explorers. Shackleton was from Anglo-Irish stock, the small, select and privileged group who had largely owned and governed Ireland for centuries, often as absentee landlords. After independence, the Anglo-Irish were effectively classless, considered too British in Ireland and too Irish in Britain.

Men like Shackleton, Francis Crozier from County Down and the others who ventured to the ice in the 19th and 20th centuries were especially vulnerable since their expeditions, though not military in flavour, had sailed under the ubiquitous Union Jack. Explorers were caught in the cross-currents of the changing political order and were soon either airbrushed from Irish history or forgotten. Tom Crean, the petty officer from Kerry and veteran of three Antarctic expeditions with both Scott and Shackleton, saw his elder brother shot dead during the War of Independence and subsequently never spoke to a soul about his exploits. Patrick Keohane from Cork, who marched to within 350 miles of the South Pole with Scott in 1912, fled Ireland to protect his family. Others simply kept their heads down.[1]

It would be 80 years and into a new century before any explorer from the Heroic Age of Antarctic exploration was formally commemorated in Ireland. Even today the only official memorial to Shackleton in Ireland is the small plaque on the wall of a house in Dublin where he lived briefly as a child.

The apathy towards Shackleton extended far beyond his own personal popularity or political differences. *James Caird*, the iconic small boat and outstanding surviving artefact from Shackleton's great endeavours on the *Endurance* expedition, spent many years in dusty corners of either Dulwich College or the National Maritime Museum in London. It was a half-forgotten remnant of a half-remembered explorer.

The number of books about Shackleton and his companions over the years was a mere trickle compared with the steady stream of works about almost every aspect of Scott and his colleagues on the South Pole venture. Hugh Robert Mill, Shackleton's best friend, published a fine biography in 1923 which, though insightful and an important work for all scholars, inevitably reflects the very close relationship between the two men.[2] The first fully impartial biography of Shackleton, written by Margery and James Fisher, did not appear until 1957, some 35 years after his death. Writing in the 1950s, the Fishers noted how to many Shackleton had become 'a surprisingly vague' character.[3]

The pendulum of popularity began to swing in Shackleton's favour from the 1980s onwards, partly as a result of Roland Huntford's brutal demolition of Scott in *Scott & Amundsen* which prompted a drastic reappraisal of a national icon and aroused a furious debate about what, by modern standards, constitutes a polar hero. At a time when Scott's stock was plunging dramatically, Shackleton enjoyed a sudden resurgence, helped by Huntford's fine biography of the man in 1985 and by *Endurance*, Caroline Alexander's book which leant heavily on the outstanding historic photographs of Frank Hurley to record just one of Shackleton's four expeditions to the ice.

The abrupt role reversal saw Shackleton catapulted to celebrity status as the flawless adventurer who never lost a man and Scott demoted to the role of bungling amateur whose failure symbolised the wider national decline of British pomp and power in the Edwardian era. Neither claim is wholly true.

It was the *Endurance* expedition, the greatest story of survival in Antarctic history, which became the principal focus of attention for those drawn to Shackleton for the first time. More books followed, mostly around the theme of *Endurance*, while new generations of followers were drawn to related exhibitions or television documentaries. Interest was maintained by a sudden flow of books about Shackleton's comrades on *Endurance*, notably Crean, Orde Lees, Wild, Wordie and Worsley. Shackleton's Irish roots were successfully explored by Jonathan Shackleton and John MacKenna.[4]

Picking over the finer points of 'Shackletonia' became a popular pastime for a new breed of devotees and his fame spread to some unlikely areas. For example, Shackleton's inspirational style of leadership, once deployed in the grim struggle to survive in the freezing Antarctic wilderness, are now taught in earnest management schools and adopted in the slick, air-conditioned corporate tower blocks of big business. One 21st-century observer even speculated that had Shackleton been in business today he would rank alongside tycoons like Bill Gates, without appreciating the irony that Shackleton was a spectacular failure in every business venture he ever attempted.

Modern-day adventurers, inspired by his feats, regularly make their own personal pilgrimages to the same hostile regions where, with all the trappings of modern equipment and technology, they honour Shackleton's memory by recreating the epic journeys and hardships of a century earlier. Tourists queue to visit Shackleton's old haunts and experience a flavour of life on the edge a century ago. Everyone returns from the ice with increased admiration and even deeper respect for Shackleton.

And men and women weep at his graveside in Grytviken.

A new comprehensive biography of Shackleton is overdue. Remarkably, a generation has passed since Huntford produced the last all-embracing biography in 1985.[5] Much has changed in the three decades since, including the appearance of new historical information and a more modern perspective on the history of Antarctic exploration. Shackleton, like the Heroic Age, is viewed differently today than he was 30 years ago.

Fortunately, any biographer has a rich source of material to assist in assessing the story of Shackleton's rich, often controversial and contradictory life. This includes personal diaries and correspondence, family records and a vast collection of official and semi-official records held in a variety of archives, museums and other institutions. In addition, there is a large selection of personal journals and papers kept by Shackleton's companions and his many associates, plus a substantial collection of published material spanning a century of writing about Shackleton and the Heroic Age of Antarctic exploration. Any biographer of Shackleton also faces the challenge of untangling the myths from the reality of a complex man's packed life.

There were two different Shackletons. One was the charismatic, ambitious, buccaneering, Edwardian explorer with a love for poetry who touched greatness combating unimaginable hardship and depths of adversity in the most unwelcoming region of the world. On the ice, he created history, inspired his men to almost superhuman peaks of human endurance and loyalty. It is a testament to his natural abilities that Shackleton's skills of leadership are still relevant in the 21st century. Those seeking the source of Shackleton's genius should look no further than his unerring ability to inspire others. He possessed a remarkable capacity to understand his men and judge their shifting moods. In many respects, he understood men better than they themselves did. Shackleton's unflagging spirit and unshakeable optimism in the direst circumstances were crucial to men clinging to the wreckage of their predicament. It was Napoleon who memorably said: 'A leader is a dealer in hope.' Shackleton was such a man, giving hope to men who feared they were beyond redemption.

Apsley Cherry-Garrard, a member of Scott's last expedition, offered an especially persuasive assessment of Shackleton. In the preface to his fine book *The Worst Journey in the World,* Cherry-Garrard wrote: 'For a joint scientific and geographical piece of organization, give me Scott; for a Winter Journey, Wilson; for a dash to the Pole and nothing else, Amundsen: and if I am in the devil of a hole and want to get out of it, give me Shackleton every time.'

The other Shackleton was the complex, flawed, restless, impatient and hopelessly unproductive character on dry land who struggled to come to terms with the civilising forces of day-to-day routine and domestic responsibilities. His private life was often chaotic and messy and he limped from one hopeless commercial venture to another without ever finding the riches he so eagerly sought. Shackleton's only notable achievement in business was that he was a failure at virtually everything he tried. It says much for his dreamy, far-fetched understanding of business that he maintained a childlike longing to search for buried treasure. El Dorado, though, always remained beyond his grasp.

Some have likened Shackleton to a Drake or a Raleigh, a throwback to the great Elizabethan adventurers and explorers. But Shackleton was a one-off, a unique and compelling character who wrote his own history. He raced through life, rarely glancing sideways and never looking back. Shackleton was a gale of humanity.

Amundsen, the most accomplished polar explorer, was in no doubt about Shackleton's qualities and declared: 'Sir Ernest Shackleton's name will for evermore be engraved with letters of fire in the history of Antarctic exploration.'

chapter 1

Touching History

The fingerprints of history can be found in the deep family roots of Ernest Henry Shackleton. Tracing the line back almost 1,000 years, the Shackletons emerge as an intriguing mixture of religious pioneers and aristocrats, adventurers and rebels, blended with a stock of respectable folk drawn from the ranks of doctors, teachers and writers.

The name Shackleton is almost certainly derived from the old Anglo-Saxon English word *scacol* or *scacoldenu* meaning 'tongue of land'. It was combined with *tun*, the Anglo-Saxon for enclosure or settlement, and is believed to spring from a hamlet now called Shackleton near Heptonstall, West Yorkshire.

The earliest recorded inhabitants were socage (feudal) tenants and yeomanry who were mentioned in the Wakefield Court Rolls from 1198 onwards. It is believed they held land in the area and may have been foresters and local law enforcers on the wooded estates of the Earl of Surrey, a descendant of the Norman nobleman William de Warenne who fought at the Battle of Hastings.[1]

Early variations of the name from the 12th century included Scachelden, Scackleton, Shackletun, de Shakeldene and Shakeltune. Richard Shackylton of Keighley was a bowman at Flodden in 1513, the largest ever battle between the English and Scots. The modern version appeared more consistently by the 15th and 16th centuries and, in 1588, Henry Shackleton of Darrington, near Pontefract, married into the family of Martin Frobisher, the colourful Elizabethan pirate-explorer from Wakefield made famous by three early attempts to navigate the icy waterways of the North-West Passage.

The immediate line to Ernest Shackleton can be traced to communes around the West Yorkshire settlements of Heptonstall and Keighley where in 1591 members of the family bought a home at Harden, a richly forested vale of land close to the town of Bingley. The property was subsequently called Shackleton House and was to remain in the family's hands for some 200 years.

In 1675, during the decades of political and social upheaval after the English Civil War, Shackleton House passed to Richard Shackleton. It was an age of aggressive religious dissent which produced factions such as the Diggers, Puritans and Ranters who defied the established Church and sought enlightenment in their own assorted and often extreme spiritual sects. Richard Shackleton, a deeply religious man, was swept up in the fervour and became an early convert to the Society of Friends, better known as the Quakers.

Formed in 1647 during the Civil War, the Quakers were the radical wing of the Puritans who provided the spiritual backbone to Cromwell's armies pitted against King Charles. But re-establishment of the Church of England in 1660, following the death of Cromwell, left the obdurate Quakers isolated and their refusal to pay tithes and take oaths inevitably brought them into conflict with mainstream society. Persecution and harassment were commonplace and Quaker meeting houses were attacked by mobs and many followers imprisoned for their beliefs.

Richard Shackleton was among the casualties, once serving three years in York prison for not attending church and holding Quaker meetings at Shackleton House. It was at Shackleton House in 1696 that Richard's wife, Sarah Briggs, produced the last of their six children. Named Abraham, he went on to establish the Shackleton dynasty in Ireland.

Abraham, a pious young man, was orphaned by the age of eight and drifted into teaching at David Hall, a Quaker school in Skipton. He was later invited to teach in Ireland where the Quaker movement was in the early stages of spreading the Nonconformist message at a new settlement formed at Ballitore, County Kildare.

Ballitore, founded in 1685 by Abel Strettel and John Barcroft, was the first planned Quaker settlement in Ireland and the nascent community flourished in the open fields beside the River Greese, developing the rich farmland, building flour mills and laying the foundations for a thriving merchant class. It was the ideal setting for aspiring teacher Abraham Shackleton and his new wife, Margaret Wilkinson.

Abraham, now 30 years old, opened the Ballitore School for boys in March 1726. The school, about 40 miles to the west of Dublin near the border of Kildare and Wicklow, was subsequently run by generations of Shackletons and emerged as a beacon of learning that became synonymous with the ideals of the Quaker brethren.

Ballitore's success – it was non-denominational at times – also helped dilute some anti-Quaker prejudice in Ireland during the 18th century and the school's illustrious pupils included the statesman-philosopher Edmund Burke and the revolutionary James Napper Tandy. Richard Shackleton, the son of Abraham, who took over the running of the school, became close friends with Burke. It was said that Ballitore helped shape Burke's strong civil and religious libertarian values. 'If I am anything,' Burke said, 'it is the education I had there [Ballitore] that has made me so.'

Other notable predecessors of Ernest Shackleton included the prolific writer and historian Mary Shackleton Leadbeater who was a friend of Burke and memorably chronicled the affairs of the Ballitore community in late 18th and early 19th centuries. Another member of the Leadbeater line was the pioneering mountaineer Charles Barrington, the Quaker merchant from Wicklow who in 1858 made the first ascent of the Eiger, the most notorious of the Alpine peaks.

A century passed before the Shackleton family parted company with the Quakers and moved onto more traditional religious ground. Ebenezer Shackleton, the great-grandson of the school's founder, became disenchanted with the Quakers in the early years of the 19th century and ushered the family into the mainstream Church of Ireland. It was a step which took the Shackleton family from one tiny and unpopular minority to the larger and most loathed minority of all – the powerful Anglo-Irish landowners and aristocrats who dominated Ireland, often as absentee landlords, for centuries.

Successive generations of landowners – the Protestant Ascendancy – flourished in the area known as the Pale, the ancient and rarefied enclave which marked the old territorial boundaries extending out from Dublin where the ruling class of Anglo-Irish lived apart from the wholesale poverty existing elsewhere. They owned Ireland's banks, businesses and legal offices and turned out a succession of prominent soldiers, statesmen, politicians, businessmen and writers – including Wellington, Swift, Parnell and Arthur Guinness – in blissful isolation from the majority.

Survivors by nature, the ruling minority successfully withstood repeated rebellions and even the horrors of the Great Famine of the 1840s when an estimated 1 million died and another 2 million fled the country. Some of the detested landlords exported food at the height of the humanitarian crisis in what one observer called an 'epic of English colonial cruelty'. A.J.P. Taylor, the distinguished English historian, said: 'The English governing class had the blood of two million Irish people on their hands.'

After withdrawing from the Quaker fold, Ebenezer Shackleton developed a life away from the immediate sphere of Ballitore. He opened a mill at nearby Moone and in 1831, at the age of 47, married his second wife, 25-year-old Ellen Bell from Abbeyleix. It was a fertile union which produced nine children and, at Ellen's wishes, the children were brought up as Anglicans, the first Shackleton children in well over a century to be raised outside the Quaker faith.

The eighth child, born at Moone on 1 January 1847 – at the height of the Famine – was named Henry. By the time Henry reached the age of nine, his father was dead and his widowed mother decided that the youngster should pursue a career in the army. Henry was subsequently sent to Old Hall School, Wellington, in England, but his studies were interrupted by illness and he returned to Ireland. After abandoning plans for a military career, Henry went to Dublin's Trinity College where in 1868 he earned a degree in the Arts.

Henry Shackleton was 25 in 1872 when he married Henrietta Laetitia Sophia Gavan, the 26-year-old daughter of Henry Gavan from nearby Carlow. Together they had 10 children, including Ernest Shackleton.

Shackleton's parents. Dr Henry Shackleton came from Anglo-Irish and Quaker roots and Henrietta Shackleton (née Gavan) was a member of the long-established Fitzmaurices from Kerry. COURTESY: ATHY HERITAGE MUSEUM

Henrietta, a bubbly, good-humoured woman, came from deeply rooted Irish stock which provided a strong Irish bloodline to the Anglo-Irish and Quaker lineage of Henry Shackleton. As an adult, Ernest Shackleton would proudly boast of his Irish heritage and usually listed his nationality as Irish. However, as one of his sisters later observed: 'We were never Irish till Mother [Henrietta Gavan] married into the family.'[2]

The link to old Irish ancestry came from Henrietta's mother, Caroline Fitzmaurice, who was descended from the long-established Fitzmaurice clan whose Irish origins can be sketched back to the Norman invasion and may have links to medieval kings Louis VIII of France and John of England. It was a lineage which featured an assortment of aristocratic dukes and earls, eminent politicians and flamboyant landed gentry. Luminaries included the first Earl of Kerry in the 13th century and some who rebelled against English rule and others who supported the Crown.

One notable figure among the Fitzmaurices was the multifaceted Sir William Petty, a founding member of the Royal Society and physician general to Oliver Cromwell, whose skilful surveying of Ireland in the 1650s – the controversial Down Survey – was instrumental in the wholesale confiscation of Irish lands in the 17th century. Another was William Petty-Fitzmaurice who, as Prime Minister in 1782, signed the peace treaty which ended the War of Independence and British rule in America. Through the Huguenot Daniel Boubers de Bernatre, the Fitzmaurice line shared a common ancestor with Sir Leopold McClintock, the prominent 19th-century Arctic explorer who lived long enough to witness Ernest Shackleton depart for the ice at the opening of the 20th century.

Henry Gavan, Henrietta's father, came from more modest stock. His father was Rector of Wallstown, Cork. Henry qualified as a doctor but abandoned medicine in favour of a commission in the Royal Irish Constabulary and was dead soon after.

Henry and Henrietta Shackleton settled in the familiar landscape of Kildare. The couple rented a 500-acre farm from the Duke of Leinster at Kilkea, a remote hamlet in the lush, fertile pastures a few miles south of the old market town of Athy. It is among the richest farmland in Ireland. Through the trees could be seen the 12th-century stronghold of Kilkea Castle and on a clear day it is possible to pick out the gentle curves of Wicklow's mountains. Ebenezer's mill at Moone was a handful of miles away and Henrietta's family home lay a short distance to the south. Ballitore, the ancestral home of the Shackletons of Kildare, was within easy reach.

The house at Kilkea, near Athy in Kildare, where Shackleton was born on 15 February 1874. MICHAEL SMITH.

The comfortable family home was a substantial Georgian farmhouse called Kilkea House, overlooking the easy slopes of Kildare. Henry and Henrietta Shackleton's first child, Gertrude, was born at the end of 1872. The second child was born at Kilkea House on 15 February 1874. The blue-eyed boy was named Ernest Henry Shackleton. He shared a birthday with Galileo.

chapter 2

The Lonely Sea and the Sky

Ernest Shackleton grew up in a rural idyll, surrounded by open countryside and close to the meandering waters of the River Greese. It was a happy and secure household on the upper slopes of Irish society. While Henrietta radiated kindness and good humour, Henry Shackleton was a cultured man with a fashionably full beard who provided stability, warm benevolence and a solid income. The rapid procession of six new children – Gertrude, Ernest, Amy, Francis, Ethel and Eleanor were born in a seven-year spell at Kilkea House – added to the sense of well-being in the Shackleton household.

Unfortunately for Henry Shackleton, circumstances elsewhere were disturbing the idyllic milieu. Irish farming faced critical economic problems in the 1870s. Incomes were in decline and, for the first time in centuries, the Catholic majority had begun to chip away at the bedrock of the Ascendancy's power base – the land. Major democratic reforms gave more power to tenants from the old peasant class and the mostly Anglo-Irish landlords received a significant blow to their privileged status with the disestablishment of the Church of Ireland in 1871.

Ernest Shackleton aged 11, in 1885, at around the time the family moved from Ireland to London. As a child he dreamed of sea-going adventures.

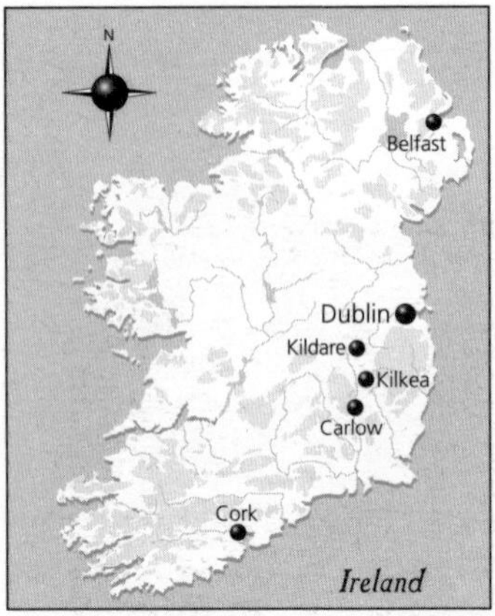

Where rebellion had failed, basic economics and creeping democracy were fomenting a revolution in land ownership and political agitators seized the opportunity to press for more far-reaching reforms to end the dominance of the landlords. The revolt gained fresh momentum in 1879 with the onset of another famine – the last significant famine in Ireland – and the founding of the rebellious National Land League, which sparked the bitter and bloody Land War.

In the changed political climate, farming suddenly looked unappealing to Henry Shackleton who looked around for a career in a safer, more stable field. An uncle, Dr William Bell, practised medicine nearby and had developed an interest in alternative remedies like homeopathy. Within a year of the formation of the National Land League, Henry took the radical step of abandoning the farm at Kilkea. Even more radical was the decision to return to Trinity College and become a doctor.

In 1880, the 33-year-old medical student with six small children moved to 35 Marlborough Road, a sturdy red-bricked terraced house in what is today the fashionable Donnybrook district of Dublin. During four years in Dublin, Henry Shackleton qualified from Trinity and three more children – Clara, Helen and Kathleen – were added to the brood.

Dr Shackleton found medicine far more satisfying than farming and, sensing that the old order was changing, he took another major decision. In December 1884, Henry moved the family to England and set up his own practice. He never moved back to Ireland.

Croydon, then an undistinguished suburb on the outskirts of London, was chosen as the site of his first practice. However, the practice was a failure, partly because of resistance to Dr Shackleton's interest in promoting unorthodox alternative medicines. After only six months, he withdrew from Croydon and in late 1885 opened a new surgery a few miles away in Sydenham, where he could run a general practice and develop his skills in homeopathy. Although trained as an orthodox physician and a member of England's Royal College of Surgeons, he joined the British Homeopathic Society, worked at the Homeopathic Hospital in London's Great Ormond

Aberdeen House, the Shackleton family home in the London suburb of Sydenham. The French impressionist, Camille Pissarro, once painted it. COURTESY SOPHIE KETTLE SMITH

Street and wrote articles on alternative medicine for a number of specialist journals.

The family set up home at Aberdeen House, 12 West Hill (now St David's House, Westwood Hill), a large three-storey detached home down the hill from the glittering Crystal Palace, with a small place in artistic history. Aberdeen House, which stands alongside St Bartholomew's Church in Westwood Hill, is a focal point of *The Avenue, Sydenham*, an acclaimed work by French impressionist Camille Pissarro, who worked in the area more than a decade before the Shackletons arrived.

Sydenham, which was enjoying rapid development on the back of Crystal Palace's increasing popularity, was more to Dr Shackleton's liking than Croydon and his practice thrived. Henrietta, now 42, gave birth to her tenth child – Gladys – in 1887 but was immediately struck down by a mysterious and debilitating illness. Henrietta, once a vivacious woman who provided a lively spark and passion to the family, would spend the remaining three decades of her life largely confined to bed.

Responsibility for the household fell solely onto the shoulders of Henry Shackleton, helped in part by assorted nannies and Caroline

Gavan, Henrietta's elderly mother. Somehow Henry managed to operate a successful general practice, pursue his interests in alternative medicine and maintain the firm but compassionate care of 10 children with ages ranging from toddlers to teenagers. In between, he methodically cultivated roses and reviewed medical books.

Dr Shackleton's other passion was literature, especially poetry, which he eagerly passed onto the family, either by reading aloud from his favourite Tennyson or by involving the children in word games to name the poet or complete a line of verse. The children were enthusiastic participants, but it was young Ernest who displayed the keenest interest and he quickly developed a remarkable ability to recall lengthy lines of verse or the names of poets.

He never lost the knack and years later a colleague remembered that Shackleton could 'quote [poetry] by the yard'. A friend, Mrs Hope Guthrie, recalled asking Shackleton if he ever needed to read a page from Shakespeare twice to commit the lines to memory. He replied: 'Sometimes to make sure of the punctuation!'

Aberdeen House was a typically Victorian household, where a sometimes grave Dr Shackleton maintained strict discipline and drummed strong moral and religious values into the children and servants. He read aloud from the Bible, frowned on parties and other indulgences and actively encouraged his flock to campaign against the evils of alcohol. Servants were asked to sign the 'pledge' against intoxicating drink and the children joined the Band of Hope, a temperance movement for the young. On occasions, assorted Shackleton children congregated outside the pubs of Sydenham to sing solemn songs about the wickedness of drinking.

Ernest was a likeable, cheery child who was worshipped by his sisters. He revelled in the female attention and called the girls his 'Harem'. He once persuaded them that the Monument, the 300-year-old column commemorating the Great Fire of London, had been erected in his honour. Charming the girls, even at an early age, came naturally to Ernest Shackleton.

Influenced by his father's taste for books, Ernest was an avid reader. He developed an early fascination with tales of adventure and journeys of discovery to distant places and was captivated by anything relating to the hunt for buried treasure. At Kilkea House he had played out the adventures in a 'ship' fashioned from a rotting tree and did the same at Sydenham. 'The unexplored parts of the world held a strong fascination for me from my earliest recollection,' he recalled years later.

The Boy's Own Paper, whose eye-popping serials nourished the imaginations of countless youngsters in the Victorian age, was a particular favourite. He was also fascinated by Jules Verne's *20,000 Leagues Under the Sea* which left a lasting impression. In later life Shackleton occasionally referred to himself as Nemo, in reference to the enigmatic sea captain in Verne's classic work.

Another much-thumbed book was Charles Francis Hall's *Life With the Esquimaux*, the record of an eccentric and obsessive American explorer from the 1860s. Hall's images of ice floes, igloos and strange native costumes fired the young man's imagination and, like Verne's book, it left a permanent impression. In 1909, about 25 years after first picking up Hall's memoir, Shackleton recalled: 'I have always been interested in Polar Exploration. I can date my interest in the subject to the time when I was about ten. So great was my interest that I had read almost everything about North and South Polar Explorations.'[1]

Soon after the move to Sydenham in 1885, Henry Shackleton formalised Ernest's education which up to this point had been handled at home by a series of governesses. At the age of 11, he was enrolled at Fir Lodge School, a preparatory school for the prestigious Dulwich College, close to Aberdeen House.

After a gentle, sheltered upbringing, the bustle of the classroom was a shock. In particular, his Irish background and distinct accent singled him out from the rest of the boys. Almost inevitably, he was called Mick or Mike, but was saved from being tagged Paddy only because a Patrick existed elsewhere at Fir Lodge.

Two years at Fir Lodge confirmed that, whatever else Ernest would achieve in life, he was no academic. Instead, he was remembered as doing very little work and as someone often involved in scraps with other pupils who poked fun at his Irish brogue. Much the same applied in 1887 when he was enrolled as a day boy at Dulwich College, the impeccably sound and highly regarded public school, where after three years of undistinguished plodding he left barely a trace. He excelled at little.

Dulwich, a brisk walk of a mile over the hill from Sydenham, was founded in 1619 during the reign of James I and by the late Victorian era was another cog in a wheel dutifully turning out respectable middle-class boys to serve as civil servants, clergymen and lawyers. Dulwich had earned the reputation as the nursery for the breed of men who administered colonial territories – particularly India – on behalf of the Empire. Matthew Arnold said Dulwich was the type of school he had 'long desired, and vainly desired, to see put at the disposal of the professional and trading classes throughout this country'.

Over the years, Dulwich College also produced a number of distinguished writers, including Raymond Chandler, P.G. Wodehouse and A.E.W. Mason. Mason, who left Dulwich a few years before Shackleton arrived, wrote *The Four Feathers*, the popular Edwardian adventure yarn, which resonated with the imperial age and the school's core values of serving God, monarch and country. The ambition of many young boys from the era was simply to serve the Empire as administrators or soldiers.

None of this carried any appeal for young Ernest. He found classical studies of Greek and Latin, which accounted for a large chunk of the basic teaching, unbearably dreary. His flaw was not lack of intellect. Ernest was impatient, drifting idly through lessons and rarely able to apply himself. He was easily bored and far more in tune with the dashing patriotic heroes created by Mason than with the classic ideals of Matthew Arnold. Teachers grumbled about his daydreaming and lack of effort, while his marks, particularly for the classics, were invariably bad. One report said he 'had not fully exerted himself' and another plainly exasperated master concluded: '... wants waking up, is rather listless.'

To the masters at Dulwich, he was a rolling stone who was unlikely ever to appear on the school's roll of honour. However, as one biographer noted, the 'masters failed to touch the spring which controlled his ambition'.

Not even the commanding presence of Arthur Gilkes, the notable Dulwich headmaster of the time, could reach young Ernest. Physically and intellectually, Gilkes towered over Dulwich for almost three decades and was an inspirational head to generations of boys. He stood 6 feet 5 inches tall, was a Double First at Oxford and revered as Dulwich's finest head. Gilkes lived by a code of 'respectful kindness' to the boys and was a father figure to many youngsters, especially the boarders whose parents, posted to far-flung corners of the Empire, were rarely seen. Gilkes, it was said, existed 'very near to God'. But even Gilkes found Shackleton 'backward for his age' and hard to motivate. Hugh Robert Mill, Shackleton's close friend and first biographer, summed up Ernest's undistinguished years at Dulwich with this observation: 'He was certainly a poor scholar ... and in the class lists his name was almost always far south of the equator and sometimes perilously near the pole.'[2]

Almost two decades later, Shackleton, by now a celebrated explorer, returned to Dulwich to preside over the school's prize-giving ceremony. Watched by Gilkes, who was well into his 60s, Shackleton remarked that the occasion was the nearest he had ever been to a prize at Dulwich College.

Ernest had no special hobbies as a child, unless it was reading or telling stories. Although he played and enjoyed the typical assortment of school sports, he never made the breakthrough to the forefront of team games like cricket or rugby, which embodied the typical character-building 'Muscular Christianity' of Victorian public schools like Dulwich. The only flicker of sporting prowess came where, one-on-one, he could pit his wits against a single foe in events like boxing.

However, he was generally popular with his fellow pupils who warmed to his lively temperament, cheerful banter and never-ending stream of stories. John Quiller Rowett, a fellow student, recalled that Shackleton was 'always full of life and jokes but was never very fond of lessons'.

Ernest's unease at Dulwich inevitably blossomed into truancy. On occasions he recruited two or three others to hide amidst the trees and undergrowth of the local Silverdale Woods, fortified by scraps of food smuggled from the kitchen and a few cheap cigarettes. Shackleton, with his gift for spinning a good yarn, kept the truants engrossed with tales of great sea journeys culled from the pages of *The Boy's Own* or by reciting heroic poems, such as the *Wreck of the Hesperus* or *Ye Mariners of England*. Shackleton, much the youngest of the truants, was notable as being leader of the gang.

Inspired by the rhetoric, the youngsters resolved to become sailors and once took a train to London Bridge where they roamed the docks gazing longingly at the ships coming and going in the busy Thames waterway, aching for the chance to run away to sea. Hoping to sign on as cabin boys, the lads optimistically approached the chief steward on a steamer who smiled fondly and told them to go home before they were missed.

The setback only delayed Ernest's ambition of becoming a sailor. As he approached his 16th birthday, Ernest was driven by an increasing desire to flee the monotony of Dulwich College. The sea, with all its adventurous appeal, was the obvious escape route.

The problem was how to make the break, particularly as Dr Shackleton nurtured hopes that his eldest son would follow him into the safe and respectable field of medicine. His father, Ernest later remembered, was 'very much against' him going to sea, with its assorted dangers and hardships and modest rewards.

However, Henry Shackleton was a realist, a positive man who had shown his decisive touch by changing career and country to provide a better life for his family. It was also apparent that, after three mediocre years at Dulwich, Ernest was not academically gifted and lacked the commitment to study for exams and qualify as a doctor.

Shackleton aged 16, embarking on a career at sea.

The unknown factor was Ernest's capricious nature. Dr Shackleton feared that the sea might be a passing fad for the youngster who, so far at least, had never shown devotion to any specific cause. In addition, the fees for the Royal Navy's Britannia College were beyond Henry's means.

Dr Shackleton's solution was to test his son's ambition to destruction. He decided to send Ernest on a trial voyage, hoping that the rigorous everyday reality of life at sea would cure the youngster's ambition once and for all. He reckoned without his son's inbuilt determination.

Dr Shackleton approached Rev. G.W. Woosnam, a cousin in Liverpool who was Superintendent of the Mersey Mission to Seaman and well connected in merchant shipping circles. Woosnam's choice was the North

Western Shipping Company of Liverpool and the young man was duly signed on to serve the first year of an apprenticeship at the rank of Boy.

Ernest Shackleton, barely 16 years of age, was paid 1s a month (about £3/€3.60 in today's terms) and was under no illusions about the challenging test his father had set him. He later explained: 'My father thought to cure me of my predilection for the sea by letting me go in the most primitive manner possible as a "boy" on board a sailing ship at a shilling a month. Twelve shillings a year for working hard, facing all kinds of weather, beating round the world against every wind that blew – that's the sort of school I swopped Dulwich for.'[3]

Joining North Western Shipping had an immediate impact on the young man's school work. Ernest suddenly became the ideal scholar, displaying abilities and dedication that idle indifference had obscured for years. He leapt to third in both chemistry and mathematics, second in history and his form master reported a 'marked improvement' in both work and behaviour. Gilkes, no doubt wishing the lad had shown the same application throughout, wrote: 'I hope that he will do well.'

Ernest Shackleton left Dulwich College at Easter 1890, not waiting for the full school year to finish. He travelled alone to Liverpool to meet Captain Partridge, skipper of *Hoghton Tower*, one of the impressive clippers in North Western Shipping Company's fleet, for his maiden voyage. As Dr Shackleton expected, it was to be a ferocious baptism.

Hoghton Tower, an elegant but ageing reminder of the fast-disappearing age of sail, was primed for a voyage around Cape Horn in the depth of southern-hemisphere winter. Launched during the great age of ocean-going clippers, the graceful three-masted craft boasted a displacement of 1,600 tons and measured 240 feet (72 m) in length. *Hoghton Tower* could carry 2,000 tons of cargo and offered select accommodation for 16 first-class passengers, a special ladies' cabin and a stylish saloon featuring polished teak panelling, gold mouldings and a piano donated by Sir Henry de Hoghton, the Lancashire baronet after whose ancestral seat the ship was named. The vessel, once described as a 'magnificent specimen of iron shipbuilding', was five years older than Shackleton.

Shackleton's maiden voyage began on 30 April 1890 as *Hoghton Tower* was towed out of Liverpool bound for Valparaiso in Chile. It was a classic sea-going journey which could easily have been plucked from the pages of *The Boy's Own* and would take him on a year-long passage more than 20,000 miles (32,000 km) across the Equator to the South Atlantic, around the Horn and into the Pacific.

Shackleton, who had never spent longer than a week away from the subdued surroundings of a suburban family home, quickly discovered that life at sea was an alien world. The drunkenness of the crew appalled the former member of the Band of Hope and the habitual swearing and blaspheming was a shock to the ears of a lad more accustomed to reciting lines of poetry or Biblical verses. *Hoghton Tower*'s quarters, he discovered, were packed with unwashed humanity and the food was unfamiliar and unappealing. He was badly sick as soon as the ship broke into open water.

But Shackleton adapted quickly, despite the demanding work and occasional drudgery of scrubbing decks or polishing brass. The key was the novelty of it all and Shackleton's eagerness to learn. The willing apprentice savoured the learning curve of unpicking the principles of sailing or mastering the bewildering names and functions of the myriad of ropes and wire stays criss-crossing the ship. Everything was new and, while it remained fresh, Shackleton retained a passionate, uninhibited interest.

Shackleton stood out in the first days, a slightly built fresh-faced novice who seemed hardly cut out for the challenge of the high seas. The crew laughed when he said his prayers at night or opened the Bible but his innocence had a peculiarly disarming effect on some. Before long, a few shipmates began to follow his example and could be found poring over the Bible as the *Hoghton Tower* drove south towards Cape Horn.

Making friends, even among the hard-boiled crew, came easily to the apprentice. His easy-going manner and gift for telling a good yarn was well received and Captain Partridge, a considerate man who kept a watchful eye on the young boys under his command, spotted something else about Shackleton. He was, said Partridge, the 'most pig-headed obstinate boy' he had ever encountered.

Shackleton relished what he called 'pretty hard and dirty work' and even the perils of climbing 150 feet aloft in a storm released an exhilarating mixture of fear and excitement. John Masefield, another of the North Western Shipping's trainees of the same era, most memorably captured the thrill felt by Shackleton and other apprentices. In what became an anthem for sailors everywhere, the future Poet Laureate wrote:

I must go down to the seas again, to the lonely sea and the sky,
And all I ask is a tall ship and a star to steer her by,
And the wheel's kick and the wind's song and the white sail's shaking,
And a grey mist on the sea's face, and a grey dawn breaking.[4]

Rounding the Horn, the sort of encounter Dr Shackleton believed would kill or cure his son's sea-going whim, was a terrible ordeal. *Hoghton Tower*, sailing east to west against the strong prevailing winds, was assailed by storms and men were on constant alert for marauding icebergs creeping up from the southerly reaches of the Drake Passage. Two boats were lost and spars were smashed, injuring several crewmen. Shackleton narrowly escaped being struck by falling tackle in one pounding storm. He now understood more clearly why old hands swore the deck of a clipper was 'about as close to God as man is ever likely to come'.

Hoghton Tower survived the battering and sailed into Valparaiso in mid-August after 15 weeks at sea. As a small reward, Captain Partridge took Shackleton to dinner with the local Consul, where he dutifully refused to drink wine. However, he found time to pursue the pretty young daughters of a local family.

Hoghton Tower began the return journey in October 1890, stopping first at the Chilean port of Iquique to pick up a cargo of nitrates. After another testing voyage around the Horn, the ship docked at Falmouth in March 1891 with water supplies almost exhausted. The ship re-entered Liverpool in late April, completing a round trip of almost 40,000 miles (64,000 km) in exactly one year at sea.

It was, Shackleton later recalled, 'one of the stiffest apprenticeships' that a boy ever experienced. 'My first voyage taught me more geography than I should have learned had I remained at school to the age of 80,' he added. By the end of the voyage Shackleton was smoking regularly.

Captain Partridge reported back to Rev. Woosnam that there was 'no real fault to find with him and he can do his work right well'. If it was little less than a ringing endorsement, Partridge added that he was 'quite ready' to take him back, if the apprentice wished to go.

Shackleton was mobbed by his eight sisters and quizzed by his father, who was eager to discover if a year at sea had ended his son's ambition of going to sea. It had not. Within months of returning to Sydenham, Shackleton was formally indentured as an apprentice to North Western Shipping.

Shackleton's apprenticeship took him into the heart of a Victorian institution, the mighty shipping empire of Thomas Ismay and William Imrie Jr, whose Oceanic Steam Navigation Company embraced White Star Line and North Western Shipping. Two of Oceanic Navigation's influential shareholders were Edward Harland and Gustav Wolff, creators of the Belfast shipbuilders Harland & Wolff who would later build *Titanic* for the White Star Line. While Ismay ran luxury ocean-going steamers under the White Star flag, Imrie managed North Western's graceful sailing ships like *Hoghton Tower*, which by the 1890s were still managing to defy, at least briefly, the advance of the steam engine and eke out a living of sorts on routes with favourable winds.

Shackleton was back on board *Hoghton Tower* by June 1891, sailing from Cardiff with a cargo of fuel bound for Iquique. The perilous trip around the Horn was made without the thoughtful influence of Partridge who had been replaced by the more disciplinarian Captain Robert Robinson. The hard work and high seas, though much the same as before, seemed more arduous and much less exhilarating under Robinson's authoritarian command and Shackleton felt more alone. He seemed less willing to cope with the foul language and bawdiness of his shipmates and retreated further into himself, comforted mainly by his books. He was struck by occasional bouts of homesickness and entered Iquique with the added distress of dysentery.

Hoghton Tower returned to England in May 1892 with Shackleton showing the first signs of uneasiness about the sea. Another two years of apprenticeship seemed daunting to the impatient 18-year-old, but the sailing schedules left little time to dwell. A month later, *Hoghton Tower* headed to India with a cargo of salt. Amidst the stress of a very rough passage around the Cape of Good Hope, Shackleton grew ever more restless and long stints hefting cargo sacks in the sultry heat of the Bay of Bengal suddenly seemed a long way from the romance of the sea.

From India, *Hoghton Tower* went to New South Wales in Australia, where the ship was ordered to cross the Pacific to Chile. Ferocious storms struck in mid-ocean and Shackleton barely escaped with his life during one gale when bits of rigging crashed to deck. 'It is a miracle I was not killed,' he reported. 'Nature seemed to be pouring out the vials of her wrath.'

Patched up and carrying fresh cargoes, *Hoghton Tower* again navigated Cape Horn before completing the voyage in July 1894. At the end of a two-year journey around the world Shackleton had finally reached the end of his apprenticeship.

Shackleton, now 20 years old, had grown up and filled out during four years of indenture on *Hoghton Tower*. He emerged as a brisk and assured young man of about 5 feet 10 inches with golden-brown hair, whose broad shoulders, barrel chest, firmly set jaw and glint in his eye radiated self-confidence. He was ruggedly handsome and his smile could light up a room. Months at sea had given Shackleton the typical rolling gait of a sailor and the characteristic flow of lively chatter was delivered in attractively rich

The 10 Shackleton children pictured around 1894. (Standing, l–r) Clara (1881–1958), Ernest (1874–1922), Eleanor (1879–1960); (seated, dark dresses, l–r) Ethel (1878–1935), Amy 1875–1953), Alice (1872–1938); (seated front, l–r) Kathleen (1884–1961), Frank (1876–1941), Gladys (1887–1962), Helen (1882–1962). COURTESY: SHACKLETON FAMILY

dark-brown tones. Shackleton was easy to like and in turn he seemed at ease with everyone from captains to cabin boys. Rank meant little to him. His family also noticed that Shackleton rarely went to church any longer.

Four arduous years on a clipper left him unsure about the sea, but he had no obvious alternative career in mind. Without any firm conviction either way, he elected to take the next step upwards.

It was common for young seafarers who were progressing towards qualification as ship's master to serve time on tramp steamers and Shackleton followed the custom. He passed the Board of Trade examination as Second Mate without too much difficulty and in October 1894 he took a posting as Third Mate on *Monmouthshire*, a tramp steamer in the Shire Line. His first voyage took *Monmouthshire* down the same waters of the Thames where as a truant schoolboy he had unsuccessfully tried to run away to sea.

The posting to *Monmouthshire* was no fluke for a young officer who had discovered that breezy charm was a useful asset in the search for work. Instead of pacing around the shipping offices in search of a berth,

Shackleton canvassed Owen Burne, an old school friend whose job in the wine trade provided useful contacts in the shipping lines. Burne introduced Shackleton to Shire Line's managing partner who offered him the position as Fourth Mate on *Monmouthshire*. On seeing the quarters available, Shackleton said cheekily he would only sail as Third Mate. The manager surprisingly agreed because, as he later admitted, 'I rather liked the chap.'

Shackleton served Shire Line – called Welsh Shire to distinguish it from the Scottish Shire Line – for almost five years and truly found his sea legs. Shire's biggest markets were in China and Japan which meant a regular succession of long voyages to the other side of the world. *Monmouthshire* was far more comfortable than *Hoghton Tower* and the welcome luxury of his own cabin allowed Shackleton to spend his off-duty hours reading in peace. He seemed to be immersed in books and was increasingly drawn to the poetry of Tennyson and Swinburne. At times he wrote his own verse.

Promotion followed and in early 1896, he passed the examination for First Mate and was posted to *Flintshire*, a larger steamer in the Shire fleet. Soon afterwards, Shackleton fell in love.

chapter 3

Love and Ambition

Shackleton, now 23, came home to Aberdeen House in June 1897 with sufficient time at sea under his belt to have lost all romantic notions about the life of a sailor. Long journeys around the Cape of Good Hope to the Far East or Australia on a tramp steamer were unrelentingly hard and the wages no more than moderate. The future held only more of the same. Shackleton wanted a great deal more than the certainty of mediocrity.

It was the rose-growing season at home and Dr Shackleton was as busy as ever as Shackleton strode into Aberdeen House. His arrival coincided with Queen Victoria's Diamond Jubilee celebrations, the lavish spectacular of pageantry which marked the high tide of the British Empire. But what caught Shackleton's eye was Emily Dorman, a friend of one of his sisters, who lived nearby in Sydenham.

Emily Mary Dorman was slim, elegant and blessed with striking blue eyes. She was well educated, articulate and especially keen on books and the arts. The playful smile and gentle flirting were risqué enough to make her interesting. Shackleton was aroused by the chase, especially when Emily showed only passing interest in a modest ship's officer. At 29, she was six years older than Shackleton and her sights may have been set elsewhere.

Tall, dark and wholesome, Emily Dorman came with a classically solid middle-class pedigree embedded in the Church and the Law. She was one of six children born to Charles Dorman, a senior partner in London solicitors Kingsford, Dorman, and Jane Swinford, who was brought up in the sheltered cloisters of the ancient Minster Abbey. Close family and friends called her Emmy.

The Dormans were well-off pillars of the community and the model of Victorian respectability who could call upon four servants to look after their every need. Now in his late 60s, Charles Dorman was widowed and combined his solid work in the legal profession with a restrained passion for plants and philanthropy. He played a prominent role at The Skinners' Company, one of the City of London's ancient guilds with a long interest in raising education standards. Dorman became Master of the 600-year-old guild and in 1890 laid the foundation stone for the new Skinners' School for Girls in London.

The three Dorman sons took the predictable steps of entering the Church or law. Arthur Dorman, the eldest, was curate at St Bartholomew's next door to the Shackletons' Aberdeen House. Another son, Charles, followed his father and became Master of The Skinners' Company. The Dorman daughters – 36-year-old Julia, Emily and 23-year-old Maud, known as Daisy – enjoyed all the benefits of a good education, comfortable lifestyle and a loving family. But marriage had somehow eluded all three women.

Although marriage was always on the agenda, Emily was determined not to be rushed into anything hasty or unsuitable. She was an independent-minded woman who rejected the convention of the day that a daughter's sole ambition was to find a husband. An unhappy affair had only recently ended when Shackleton first glimpsed her in the drawing room of Aberdeen House but she consoled herself with the knowledge that men invariably found her attractive. It was said Emily had entertained 16 proposals of marriage but as she approached her 30s, marriage seemed as far away as ever.

Shackleton took an instant liking to Emily Dorman, although he was allowed only a few weeks to pursue her before *Flintshire* embarked on another lengthy trip to the Far East. His feelings deepened and the pursuit was resumed with fresh vigour after Shackleton returned to Sydenham in early 1898.

Common ground was soon established. Both came from large, affectionate families and their respective fathers, well-to-do professionals and respected members of the community, shared an interest in gardening and plants. Dr Shackleton was a keen rose grower and member of the Royal Horticultural Society while Charles Dorman owned a well-appointed farm in East Sussex where he became one of the earliest private orchid growers in England.

The relationship struck another chord with reading, especially poetry. Emily, it emerged, shared Ernest's passionate interest in the poets and he was happy to impress her with lengthy quotations from his favourites. He also discovered that poetry was a convenient means of expressing his own feelings.

Emily's favourite was Browning, to whose work she introduced Shackleton. At the time he preferred Swinburne. Shackleton was no easy

Emily Dorman. Shackleton fell in love with the elegant, cultured woman who was six years his senior and they married in 1904 after a long courtship. COURTESY: ATHY HERITAGE MUSEUM

Charles Dorman, Emily's father, was a prosperous solicitor. COURTESY: CHRISTINE AND CHARLES DORMAN

convert but Emily gave him two books – a pocket volume of *Poetical Works* and the recently published biography of Browning by William Sharp – to take away to sea. 'Ernest loved Browning from that time onwards,' she remembered.

Shackleton discovered a liking for what he described as Browning's 'never say die' attitude and the 'grand way which he faces the future'. In addition, he found the passionate language gave words to his own feelings for Emily, while the burning sense of optimism in Browning's poems were echoed in Shackleton's own positive outlook and natural self-confidence.

Leonard Hussey, the meteorologist who served on two Antarctic expeditions with Shackleton, saw the connection between Browning's poetry and Shackleton's strong character. 'Shackleton held with Browning that "we fall to rise again" and every defeat stirred him to further efforts,' Hussey wrote.[1]

'Prospice', the powerful verse Browning wrote after the death of his wife, had a special appeal for Shackleton and Emily, particularly the underlying theme of defiance. (A translation of the Latin *prospice* is 'look forward'.) Emily explained: 'Prospice! means just everything, if only it is the truth.'

The poem's title became a private watchword between the pair and he frequently signed off letters or telegrams to her with the single word 'Prospice', each knowing the special meaning of lines such as:

I was ever a fighter, so – one fight more,
The best and the last!

Both also wrote a little. Or, as Emily recalled, they had 'small literary aspirations' in common. (Emily's aspirations were later fulfilled with the publication in 1902 of a minor book on the monarchy, entitled *The Corona of Royalty*.)

Shackleton was in love for the first time in his life and contemplated marriage. However, the measured pace of promotion at Shire Line and even the longer-term prospects of an officer on a tramp steamer were dismally short of what the affluent Emily might expect in a future husband. Or, by custom, what a prosperous solicitor might expect for his daughter.

It made little substantial difference to his prospects when Shackleton reached what for many young men was the pinnacle of the sea-going profession. In April 1898, while in Singapore, he collected his Master's Certificate – signed by Colonial Secretary, Winston Churchill – which conveyed the power to take command of any ship in the world's merchant service. He felt instinctively that it would not be enough to impress Emily.

A colleague on *Flintshire* recalled a conversation at around the time of Shackleton's promotion. Ship's engineer James Dunsmore cheerfully speculated that Shackleton would soon be elevated to captain of *Flintshire* and was told in reply: '"You see, old man," he said, "as long as I remain with this company I will never be more than a skipper. But I think I can do something better. In fact, really, I would like to make a name for myself – he paused for a moment – and for her." I noticed his face seemed to light up at the mention of her. In my bunk that night I felt convinced that the ambition of that man's life was to do something worthy – not only for himself, but for her.'[2]

According to Shackleton's version of events, it was around this time that he first contemplated becoming a polar explorer. Apocryphal or not, he recalled that while crossing from New York to Gibraltar, he claimed to have dreamt of standing on the bridge in mid-Atlantic gazing northward. 'I seemed to vow to myself that some day I would go to the region of ice and snow and go on and on till I came to one of the poles of the earth, the end of the axis upon which this great round ball turns,' he said. 'After that I never had any doubt that sooner or later I should go upon a polar expedition.'[3]

Shackleton's ambition was one thing. Emily's uncertainty was another. She was unsure about Shackleton and seemingly unable to commit herself. At times he sensed there was someone else in her life and her mood swings played havoc with his emotions, particularly during the long, lonely days at sea when he brooded over the relationship in the solitary confinement of his small cabin. On occasions her letters offered encouragement and on others she dashed his hopes. In one note to her, Shackleton wrote that the future was 'so uncertain that I dare hardly shape a hope ...'

Emily's apprehension about becoming a sea captain's wife was underlined on Christmas Day 1898 when Shackleton had to report for duty on *Flintshire*. Less than 24 hours later *Flintshire* ran aground in a storm off the Yorkshire coast. Shackleton, making the excuse that he wanted to celebrate his father's birthday on New Year's Day, rushed south to meet Emily.

Shackleton went straight to the Dorman household where he and Emily spent the evening in the billiard room, locked in deep discussion around the green baize, heavy drapery and ornate furnishings. Throwing caution to the wind, Shackleton told Emily he loved her and pledged to make a name for himself in preparation for marriage. Emily was deeply moved by his earnest conviction. For the first time she began to accept the possibility of marriage. It was a turning point in their relationship.

The conversation was so intense that Shackleton forgot about a lighted cigarette left on the oak chimney piece which slowly burnt a small black dent in the wooden frame. He kissed her hand and left through the conservatory at 10.30 p.m. But the memory of the special evening would always be summoned by a knowing glance at the black mark on the chimney piece.

Shackleton was greatly encouraged, helped with the knowledge that he was also winning the charm offensive with Emily's father. Charles Dorman, like most people of casual acquaintance, initially found Shackleton amiable and likeable. But he was less convinced the more he looked beyond the pleasantries and small talk. Dorman needed to know that Emmy's welfare was in safe hands.

To help satisfy himself, Dorman put Shackleton on probation. Shackleton was invited to a few of the regular dinner parties. On occasions, he spent weekends at Towngate, Dorman's farm overlooking the rolling pastures of Tidebrook Valley at Wadhurst, East Sussex where he successfully grew orchids and could take the measure of a prospective son-in-law. 'My father liked him and was very kind to us both,' Emily said. Others, she recalled, thought the relationship 'foolish'.

Shackleton was now a driven man and a week after absent-mindedly burning a dent in Dorman's chimney frame, resigned from Shire Line in search of a posting which carried more prestige and better prospects. Helped once again by Owen Burne, he took a job as Fourth Officer on *Tantallon Castle.* Prospects suddenly seemed brighter.

Tantallon Castle, an impressive 5,000-ton passenger liner in the Castle Line, was a significant step up for an ambitious young officer on the make and a prominent enough posting to make an impression.

Castle Line held a place among the elite of the British merchant fleet whose ships like *Tantallon Castle* provided the link between England and the colonial outpost of South Africa. Castle, with a timetable which ran like clockwork, carried passengers and cargo to the Cape with metronomic regularity and was one of only two shipping lines permitted to carry the Royal Mail. By repute, Castle's voyages across the equator created a new word in the English language – 'posh', meaning Port Out (coveted shady cabins on the left on voyages to the Cape and India), Starboard Home (shaded right-sided cabins on the northerly homeward leg).

Shackleton made three 12,000-mile (19,000 km) round trips from Southampton on the mail run to South Africa in 1899, with the added bonus that the regular sailing schedule made it easier to meet Emily. The stylish surroundings of *Tantallon Castle* were also more convivial and Shackleton, with his easy manner and engaging personality, had developed a distinct knack for picking out and impressing the more influential passengers. For someone trying to make a name it was a handy skill.

Gerald Lysaght, a prosperous steel manufacturer, was typical of those who were captivated by Shackleton's winning and eloquently amusing style. But Lysaght also saw beyond the blarney to spot a rugged determination and innate power in the young officer. He recognised in Shackleton what another acquaintance described as his 'inexhaustible animal spirits and explosive energy'. In time, Lysaght became one of Shackleton's most generous patrons.

Others found a more complex character. John Hussey, a captain with the Line, said he was 'several types bound in one volume'. Shackleton, with his shoulders hunched, square jaw set and his eyes cold and piercing, could suddenly switch from quoting Keats or Browning to being a 'determined, self-reliant, fearless, and dominant personality,' Captain Hussey found. 'When he was on a subject that absorbed his interest or appealed to his imagination, his voice changed to a deep vibrant tone, his features worked, his eyes shone, and his whole body seemed to have received an increase of vitality, he added. 'At such a time he might have been likened to a bull at bay.'[4]

The outbreak of war between Britain and the Afrikaans-speaking settlers in South Africa in October 1899, which was initially viewed as a minor scrap, brought new challenges and opportunities for Shackleton. He was appointed Third Officer on *Tintagel Castle*, a 3,500-ton Castle liner which was commissioned to carry troops to the Cape to quell the rebellious farmers and irregular Boer guerrillas. (Coincidentally, Castle was simultaneously negotiating a merger with the Union Line, the other shipping line permitted to carry the Royal Mail to the Cape.)

In a mood of near celebration and heady patriotism, *Tintagel Castle* sailed from Southampton on 14 December with a complement of 1,200 soldiers who, like the officers and crew and cheering well-wishers on the quayside, shared the widespread belief that the revolt would be crushed in a matter of weeks. Some feared the fighting would be over before the troops reached the Cape.

The optimism soon had a hollow ring since *Tintagel Castle*'s departure from Southampton coincided with Black Week, the ignominious opening episode of the war when the Boers inflicted three heavy defeats on British forces in the space of a week. Almost 3,000 soldiers were killed, wounded or captured in Black Week, forcing a rapid change of strategy and a call for extra troops to be sent to the Cape. Among those who answered the call was Frank Shackleton, a 24-year-old member of the Royal Irish Fusiliers and younger brother of *Tintagel Castle*'s Third Officer.

Tintagel Castle returned to Southampton carrying lurid details of the humiliations of Black Week and after a rapid turnaround sailed for the Cape again in early March 1900 with a convoy of fresh troops. The merger of Castle and Union, creating the powerful Union Castle Mail Steamship Company, took effect on the same day. It was a journey that also changed the course of Shackleton's life.

As unofficial entertainments officer, Shackleton was the effervescent soul of the crowded ship, breaking up the dull days at sea by arranging a flurry of sporting activities or concerts to entertain the troops. He taught semaphore to some officers and then, in an attempt at something new, tried his hand at publishing.

Shackleton with Emily Dorman (left) and her sister Daisy in 1900.
Courtesy: Athy Heritage Museum

The new diversion arose when Shackleton helped produce a small *souvenir de voyage* to commemorate the passage south which in a vague way he hoped might generate a profitable future sideline in books or journalism. The book, which was compiled with the ship's doctor, William McLean, and others, was entitled *OHMS or How 1200 Soldiers Went to Table Bay.* Shackleton, it seemed, had discovered a previously unknown flair for publishing.

The book included patriotic poems to chime with the popular mood, an article on the workings of the Maxim machine gun for armchair soldiers and a roll-call of every regiment and the peace-time occupations of the troops on board. About 2,000 subscribers were assembled, enough to print a limited edition. Shackleton, with an audacious display of self-confidence and feel for the value of good publicity, sent a specially bound copy to Queen Victoria.

Enlivened by the thrill of something new, he gave another copy to Emily with an inscription that hinted at the prospect of delving further into journalism or publishing. He scribbled in the book: 'E to E July 1900 The First Fruits.'[5]

Shackleton moved easily around *Tintagel Castle*, enjoying his moment as centre of attention and networking with those who caught the eye or who he thought might be useful. 'A vision in white and gold' said one witness who watched as Shackleton played the crowd and deftly filtered the interesting from the uninteresting.

One man who caught his attention was Lieutenant Cedric Longstaff, a young army officer with an immaculate connection. Longstaff's father was Llewellyn Longstaff, the wealthy industrialist. Almost single-handedly, Longstaff's generosity had provided the money to launch the proposed new expedition to explore Antarctica.

The expedition, the most ambitious attempt to explore the last unknown continent, would open Britain's programme of Antarctic exploration for the next two decades. The chance meeting also began the transformation of Ernest Shackleton from anonymous ship's officer to the country's most acclaimed living explorer.

chapter 4

Laying the World at Her Feet

Shackleton celebrated his 26th birthday in February 1900 while on the high seas somewhere between England and South Africa. If the celebrations were muted it was because he could not shake off the uneasy feeling that life was passing him by.

A colleague said he feared that the routine of weeks and months at sea might eventually 'strangle his individuality' and that his 'virility [was] passing away in weary waiting' for some unseen opportunity to arise. The sea, after 10 years of hard labour, had lost its appeal.

What the restless mariner lacked was a cause which would achieve the near impossible task of stimulating his interest, making a fortune and securing a respectable future with Emily. In the cursory chat with the young officer Longstaff on *Tintagel Castle* Shackleton found a calling which appeared to match his ambitions.

Shackleton seized the moment and asked Lieutenant Longstaff to arrange a meeting with his father. Through Longstaff senior he saw the chance to join the Antarctic venture and somehow make a name for himself. Beyond that lay the prospect of marrying Emily.

Going to the ends of the earth to impress Emily was a typically flamboyant gesture by Shackleton. Many years later his daughter Cecily would explain: 'he was going to lay the world at her feet ... He wanted to pour something out round her feet and say "there you are you see, you've married a man who's making his own way in life and I've brought you back the goods."'[1]

Exploration had been on his mind for some time, though Antarctica was something new. Shackleton's interest in exploration had been cultivated through the pages of *Boy's Own* and the Arctic exploits of Hall. He took his interest a little further in 1899 when he became a Fellow of the Royal Geographical Society, whose very essence was to promote discovery and expand horizons. (Shackleton also offered an article on Atlantic winds and currents for the Society's *Geographical Journal*, which was politely rejected because it contained nothing new.)

Shackleton's version of events, which he recalled in an interview many years later, carried the rose-tinted hue of man with a gift for spinning a good yarn. Speaking in 1910, long after he had learned the value of self-promotion, Shackleton claimed to know about 'everything and everybody' before first going to the Antarctic and even told a story of how in his dreams he was 'strongly drawn towards the mysterious south'. The magazine interviewer, sensing a trace of colourful embroidery, noted that 'for all his fame he [Shackleton] is still little more than a big schoolboy'.[2]

Others were equally sceptical about Shackleton's motivation. Mill, his first biographer, wrote that Antarctica was 'an opportunity and nothing more' and that Shackleton had 'no natural affinity for the polar regions, no genius for scientific research'. Mill, who understood Shackleton better than most, concluded that he might just as eagerly have joined a ship searching for buried treasure on the Spanish Main.[3]

Louis Bernacchi, the physicist on the proposed expedition, was another who contradicted Shackleton's claim to 'know everything and everybody' connected with the continent. Bernacchi recalled that Shackleton 'evinced no interest' in any previous Antarctic expeditions.

Yet there was no denying Shackleton's lust for adventure, and opening up the unknown Antarctic continent was a quest which echoed with the late-19th-century mood. This was the age of 'New Imperialism', a period of great empire-building when many European nations, America and Japan plunged into a headlong scramble to occupy new territories in Africa, the Far East and the Pacific islands. After more than two decades of global recession from 1873 to 1896, governments were eagerly trying to develop bigger markets elsewhere and annexing other territories was common. Imperialism was fashionable.

Britain of the time luxuriated in leading the world and in fostering a belief that almost anything was possible to smart Victorians. During the 'Imperial century' from Waterloo in 1815 to the outbreak of the First Word War, Britain assumed control over vast new territories in Africa, Asia and the Middle East and became a truly global power built on the solid foundations of imperial power. In 1897, as Queen Victoria celebrated her Diamond Jubilee, one in four of all people on earth were her subjects.

Empire-building was a work-in-progress for the Victorians. While much of the world had been mapped, the two Poles remained untouched and by the 1890s, explorers were taking the first tentative steps towards the remote

'Third Pole', Mount Everest. Antarctica, in every sense, was a vacant white space waiting for discovery and occupation.

Shackleton, like most children of the age, was brought up with the belief that Britain governed by divine right and that the British were in the vanguard of human advancement on earth. Cecil Rhodes, the swashbuckling standard-bearer of the Empire, captured the mood of self-righteousness and national superiority when he claimed: 'I contend that we are the first race in the world and the more of the world we inhabit, the better it is for the human race.'

Such sentiments rang true for Shackleton, a man whose upbringing within the Protestant Ascendancy was living proof of the value of the Empire for those born on the right side of the social order. Shackleton, immersed in the public school doctrine of unquestioning patriotism and *noblesse oblige*, could hardly be anything other than another staunch ambassador for the imperialism of the age.

Exploration was in vogue in Victorian times and explorers were its cast of celebrities. Explorers were the adventurers who led the way, opening up new territories and bringing 'civilisation' to millions across the globe in the name of the Empire. Legendary quests like navigating the North-West Passage or finding the source of the Nile were the imperialists' battle cries.

Men like Livingstone, Burton and Stanley were household names and rivalled great soldiers and statesmen for popular acclaim. Shackleton, with his restive ambition and untapped energy, possessed the same maverick qualities as a Burton or a Stanley and the persona of the explorer as a national hero sat far more happily with Shackleton's streak of fiery ambition than the more measured qualities needed for statesmanship or military strategy.

The popular appeal of heroic explorers was sustained by stirring books such as Rider Haggard's *King Solomon's Mines* or the many adventure stories for young boys flowing from the prolific pen of R.M. Ballantyne. Mainstream publications like *Illustrated London News* and *The Strand Magazine* poured out graphic accounts of great journeys and the growing phenomenon of popular newspapers for the increasingly literate working classes introduced legions of new readers.

James Gordon Bennett, the ebullient American newspaper proprietor, sent Henry Morton Stanley into the heart of unknown Africa in the 1870s to search for Dr David Livingstone in the hope of a sensational scoop which would sell more copies of his *New York Herald*. In Britain the success of mass-circulation newspapers was typified by the launch of the *Daily Mail* in 1896. Within a few years it was selling over 1 million copies a day.

Explorers, too, quickly realised that the popular press provided an ideal platform and might propel them onto the lucrative lecture circuit where the sponsors of future adventures could be unearthed. Hall, whose journeys had fascinated Shackleton as a child, was among the first to exploit the link between explorers and the media with a series of florid tales for magazines about his exploits in the Arctic wastes.

Shackleton, perhaps following the lead of Hall, would later fine-tune his relationships with the press and develop a very modern style of media strategy which linked the financing of his Antarctic expeditions with newspapers, books and even the latest advance of film-making.

Shackleton's most significant step towards becoming an explorer was to meet Llewellyn Longstaff. They met in the summer of 1900 at Longstaff's home in the London suburb of Wimbledon and the pair immediately clicked. Longstaff warmed to his cheerful, engaging guest and listened sympathetically when Shackleton talked enthusiastically about his ambition and asked for help to join the planned National Antarctic Expedition.

Llewellyn Longstaff, who was 59 years old, came from the liberal wing of Victorian England's industrial hierarchy. He made his money from the successful Blundell Spence paint company of Hull and took his liberal principles onto the shop floor as early as 1887 by introducing an innovative profit-sharing scheme for his workers. A newspaper of the time said he was 'a quiet, pleasant business-like man'.

He was considerably more. Longstaff's interests ranged from literature to zoology and from philosophy to meteorology. He was active in Hull's Chamber of Commerce and Shipping, a keen traveller and Fellow of the Royal Geographical Society for almost 50 years. Longstaff was also a retired colonel in the Brigade of East Yorkshire Volunteers and his philanthropic leanings made him a generous supporter of causes such as the Red Cross. (Tom Longstaff, his son, became an acclaimed mountaineer and his ascent of Trisul (23,385 ft/7,128 m) in the Himalaya in 1907 was a record altitude at the time.)

Longstaff, with his trim physique, sharp, darting eyes, close-cropped beard and bronzed complexion, looked more like a veteran explorer than a successful businessman. In the eager, energetic Shackleton he saw a man after his own heart. Longstaff was also a prominent member of the Freemasons. Within 12 months of their first meeting, Shackleton was also initiated into the shadowy domain of Freemasonry. Without hesitation Longstaff agreed to help in getting Shackleton to Antarctica.

Antarctica had lived in the imagination for centuries before it was even sighted. The ancient Greek scholars postulated its existence without

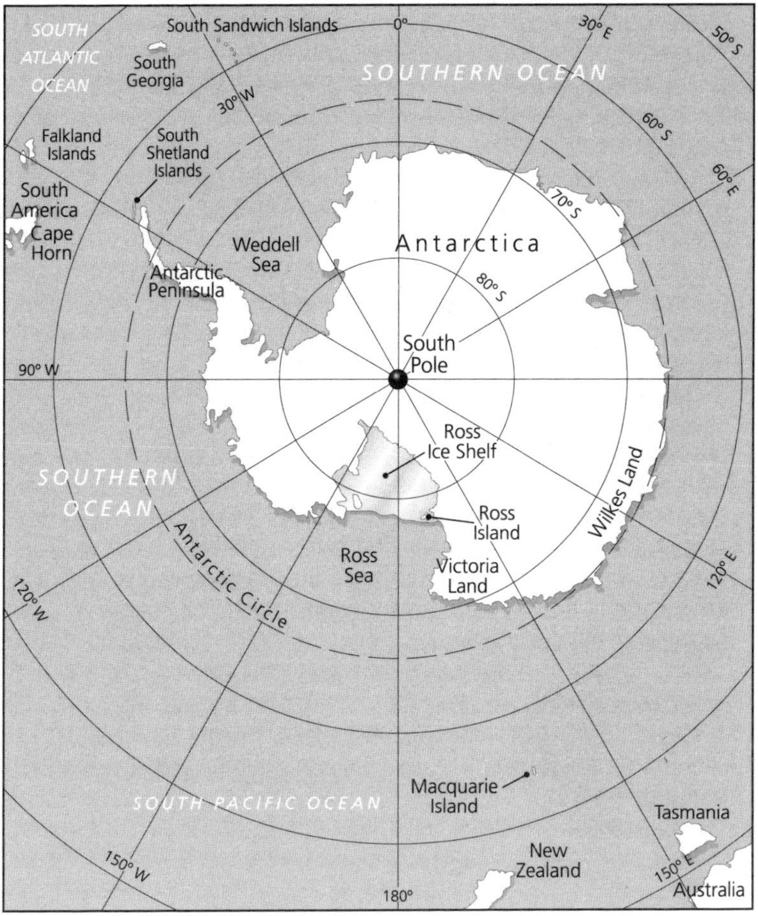

Antarctica

setting eyes on the continent and in 1773 Captain James Cook crossed the Antarctic Circle for the first time. Cook never saw the continent and doubted whether the frozen seas, which blocked the path for his ships, were even worth exploring. Land was not sighted until 1820 during the separate voyages of the Russian Thaddeus von Bellingshausen and Edward Bransfield from Ireland. Soon afterwards, the Scots whaling captain James Weddell took his ships into the sea that would later bear his name and John

Biscoe, another proficient sailor from the whaling fleet, circumnavigated the continent in the early 1830s.

The most significant breakthrough came in the early 1840s with the four-year voyage of James Clark Ross and Francis Crozier, the 19th century's most outstanding voyage of discovery at sea. Ross and Crozier's ships, *Erebus* and *Terror*, penetrated the pack ice surrounding the continent and mapped large tracts of territory for the first time, including the Ross Sea, McMurdo Sound and the huge Ice Barrier today known as the Ross Ice Shelf.

Yet Ross and Crozier returned to find that Antarctica had faded from the spotlight and public support for major polar expeditions began to evaporate in the 1850s, largely because of the calamitous Franklin expedition. Sent to find the North-West Passage in 1845, the entire expedition disappeared in the Arctic at a cost of all 129 lives – including Crozier – and an estimated £700,000 (about £40 million/€48 million today) spent in years of vain searching for the missing men.

Over three decades passed before *Challenger* crossed the Antarctic Circle – the first powered vessel to do so – during the mammoth oceanographic expedition of 1872–76. By the early 1890s a few doughty whaling ships, intent solely on making money rather than geographical discovery, re-entered Antarctic waters in search of fresh hunting grounds.

As the 19th century drew to a close, Antarctica remained as much a mystery to the Victorians as it did to the Greeks. No humans had penetrated beyond the coastline and it was still not known if the continent was a single land mass, a collection of islands or whether open seas ran all the way to the South Pole. Victorian scholars knew more about the moon than Antarctica.

The campaign to explore the Antarctic was effectively launched in 1893, the same year that imperial adventurers Charles Bruce and Francis Younghusband produced the first plan to climb Mount Everest. Dr John Murray, the distinguished scientist, posed the question to the Royal Geographical Society (RGS) in London: 'What is the nature of the snow and ice-covered land observed at so many points towards the South Pole?' Murray, a much-respected figure who served on the *Challenger* expedition and was among the founders of modern oceanography, advocated sending an expedition south to solve what he regarded as the biggest scientific challenge of the day.

It was a challenge picked up with relish by Sir Clements Markham, President of the RGS and godfather of early-20th-century polar exploration. It was Markham, a resolutely determined and Machiavellian character with an incurable fondness for plotting, who ultimately drove Britain to explore Antarctica.

Markham, crusty, manipulative and ambitious, was a mixed bag of gifted visionary and diehard reactionary. He was an empire builder who pushed exploration to the furthest extremes but ultimately stumbled because his grand schemes were too often rooted in old-fashioned ideals. Mill, an authority on polar affairs, summed up Markham's strengths and weaknesses with the observation that he was 'an enthusiast rather than a scholar'.

Born in the small Yorkshire village of Stillingfleet in 1830, Markham entered the navy at 14 and gained his first taste of the ice during the search for Franklin in 1850. Although he later developed a passion for polar exploration, his first love was Peru and the ancient Inca culture. During distinguished service in the India Office, he smuggled the native cinchona plants and seeds – a vital source of quinine – from Peruvian forests into India to help in the fight against malaria.

Markham was an inveterate traveller, prolific writer and secretary at the Royal Geographical Society for 25 years, a period which saw the RGS pushed to the centre stage of national geographical affairs and cement its status as one of the great Victorian institutions. Knighted in 1896, Markham was a man of formidable aspiration and classic 19th-century jingoism who was cursed by an unstoppable desire to control and dominate the committees and institutions he served.

After becoming President in 1893, Markham saw exploration of the Antarctic as a useful means of reviving interest in the organisation and preventing other nations establishing a foothold on the continent. In 1895, two years after Murray threw down the gauntlet, Markham presided over the Sixth International Geographical Conference in London and approval was given for exploration to begin. Exploration of the Antarctic, the Congress resolved, was the 'greatest piece of geographical exploration still to be undertaken' and would advance knowledge in 'almost every branch' of science.[4]

Even while delegates were talking, the first tentative steps had been taken. In January 1895, six months before the Congress sat, a Norwegian businessman, Henrik Bull, sent a small party ashore at a windswept Cape Adare and made the first documented landing on the Antarctic mainland. One of the most eagerly sought papers at the Geographical Congress a few months later was submitted by Carsten Borchgrevink, a pushy opportunist from Norway who leapt from the rowing boat coming ashore at Cape Adare and would always claim to be the first man to set foot on the Antarctic continent.

However, Markham's own polar ambitions soon became bogged down in bureaucracy, political infighting and an uphill struggle to persuade a reluctant government to provide money to finance the expedition. The government was lukewarm to Markham's overtures, mainly because the navy's most pressing need on the eve of the 20th century was the costly modernisation of the fleet in the face of Germany's heavy shipbuilding programme. Besides, the damaging failure of Franklin remained a clear memory.

In an attempt to sway government opinion, Markham gambled on inviting the Royal Society, the prestigious body representing the scientific establishment whose influential members had the ear of ministers, to join the expedition. But the gamble backfired, largely because of sharp differences between Markham and the Royal Society over whether the venture's main focus should be geographical discovery or the advance of science. The network of joint committees, involving scientists from the Royal Society, top naval figures from the Admiralty and Markham's clique from the RGS, soon ground to a halt in a quagmire of bureaucracy and bickering.

In 1899, after four years of wrangling and a poor response to appeals for money, Markham's ambitions had stalled and he was running out of options. The vision of a government-funded national undertaking of imperial endeavour was seemingly at an end.

Markham, now approaching his 70th birthday, was left with the huge task of generating up to £100,000 (almost £6 million/€7 million today) to launch a private expedition to replace a government-funded undertaking. By early 1899, only £14,000 had been raised. The RGS gave £5,000, but the Royal Society, to Markham's fury, did not provide a penny, aside from some personal donations by private individuals.

The quickening pace of developments elsewhere only added to Markham's mounting frustration. The Belgian ship *Belgica* sailed south under Adrien de Gerlache in 1897 and was trapped in the Bellingshausen Sea. *Belgica*'s party, which included the young Norwegian Roald Amundsen, earned the unexpected distinction of being the first to overwinter in the Antarctic.

Newspaper magnate George Newnes enraged the combustible Markham even further by giving Borchgrevink the substantial sum of £40,000 to fund his private *Southern Cross* expedition. The expedition, which landed again at Cape Adare in 1899, became the first party to spend the winter on the Antarctic mainland. At the moment when Markham's plans were dissolving, the German government delivered a fresh blow by agreeing to finance the *Gauss* expedition, a largely scientific undertaking led by Dr Erich von Drygalski.

Markham was at a low ebb in the spring of 1899 when Longstaff suddenly surfaced with a startling offer to donate around a quarter of the funds needed to mount the expedition. Markham, with a model of understatement, said: 'On March 24, 1899 Mr Longstaff asked me if £25,000 would enable the expedition to start.' Curiously, Longstaff asked for nothing in return and was never given adequate recognition for his outstanding generosity.[5]

Longstaff's generosity, worth around £1.5 million/€1.8 million in today's terms, was the catalyst. The Prince of Wales, the future King Edward VII, agreed to become patron of the expedition and his son, the future George V, vice-patron. The government, under intense pressure to support the expedition, performed a swift volte-face by agreeing to provide £45,000 if Markham could match the funds from private sources.

By August 1900, at around the time Shackleton first met Longstaff, the combined total of public and private money stood at £93,000. Markham's dream, the National Antarctic Expedition, was becoming a reality.

However, the welcome advances in fund-raising were overshadowed by the worsening relationship between Markham and the Royal Society, which came to a head over the vexed question of who should lead the expedition. Leadership, in turn, would dictate whether the expedition's main aims should be Markham's preference of discovering and mapping new territories or the Royal Society's insistence on expanding the scientific knowledge of the continent.

The Society's choice of commander was Professor John Walter Gregory, an experienced explorer and accomplished geologist with impressive credentials. Gregory, who had made the first crossing of Spitsbergen with Martin Conway in the early 1890s, had explored many unknown parts of Africa and coined the term Great Rift Valley in Kenya. He was initially appointed scientific director of the expedition and scheduled to take charge of the small party – mostly scientists – to land and overwinter in the Antarctic.

Markham's choice was Robert Falcon Scott, a 31-year-old torpedo lieutenant from the Royal Navy who, it was said, had caught Markham's eye more than 12 years earlier as a young midshipman. It hardly mattered to Markham that Scott had no experience of the ice and had never commanded an expedition. Markham wanted Scott to follow the tradition of naval explorers like Franklin, Parry and Ross. His one essential qualification, in Markham's words, was 'youth.' Gregory, at 36, was just five years older than Scott.

Advocating a naval-led enterprise was no whim on Markham's part. The navy was the beating heart of the Victorian Empire, protecting vast national interests in every corner of the world and keeping the arteries of global trade, the source of the country's great prosperity, flowing freely. All imperial endeavours, sooner or later, involved the navy and the Antarctic was no exception.

Scott's task, under the Royal Society's proposals, was to be the humble master of the ship and to ferry men and supplies to the south and cede all authority to the shore team under Gregory. Markham was unequivocally opposed, dismissing the scientific case with the lofty claim that 'geography is the mother of all sciences'.

Markham condemned the Royal Society's distinguished team of scientists on the joint committees as 'mud larkers' who wanted to turn the expedition into a cruise. Among those on the receiving end of Markham's insults were the pioneering surgeon Sir Joseph Lister, acclaimed oceanographer Sir John Murray and Sir Joseph Hooker, one of the outstanding botanists of the 19th century and veteran of the *Erebus/Terror* expedition to the Antarctic.

After months of acrimonious arguing, Markham skilfully outmanoeuvred his opponents, Gregory resigned and Scott was given sole command of the expedition.

Despite his money, Longstaff was not able to promise Shackleton an immediate place on the expedition. In September 1900, Shackleton formally applied to join the National Antarctic Expedition (NAE) and visited the offices in London where he found that preparations were already well in hand. A skeleton staff was deeply embroiled in the complex task of selecting personnel from thousands of eager applicants, arranging countless supplies of stores and equipment to sustain around 50 people for up to three years and managing the stifling bureaucracy. At the Stephens shipyard in Dundee construction of the expedition's specialist ice-ship, *Discovery*, was well under way.

At the centre of the frenetic activity was Scott, newly appointed and struggling to cope with the mountainous workload and an endless chain of interlocking official committees slowly strangling all efforts. Among Scott's first decisions as commander of the NAE was to turn down Shackleton's application for a posting.

While Shackleton waited to see whether Longstaff's influence carried any potency, he was called back to duties with Union Castle. In October 1900 he joined *Gaika* as Third Officer for a routine six-week trip to the Cape and back, and in January 1901 he sailed from Southampton in the liner *Carisbrooke Castle*. It was the last voyage he would make under Union Castle colours.

At a moment when Shackleton was somewhere at sea, Longstaff met Markham to press the case for Shackleton to join the expedition. Markham was in no position to argue, particularly as the expedition was likely to need more money in future and Longstaff was the obvious source. The request was passed back to Scott, who with far more urgent tasks at hand, asked Albert Armitage, his second in command, to examine Shackleton's application.

Armitage, a 36-year-old career officer in the merchant fleet with P&O, was ideally equipped to assess Shackleton's credentials. After enlisting at 14, Armitage had already accumulated over 20 years' experience at sea. In addition, he spent three years on the Jackson–Harmsworth expedition to the Arctic in the mid-1890s and knew more about the ice than most on *Discovery*. The Arctic encounter, he wrote, was 'one of the worst and one of the best' of his life.

Armitage understood the sea and immediately recognised that Shackleton's years on *Hoghton Tower* gave the expedition useful experience of square-riggers – *Discovery* was among the last traditional three-masted ships built in Britain – and found the testimonials from shipmates were also very encouraging. Officers at Union Castle reported that he was 'a very good fellow' and his superiors concluded that Shackleton was 'more intelligent than the average officer'.

On 17 February 1901, while still at sea, Shackleton was appointed Third Officer of the National Antarctic Expedition at a salary of £250 a year (less than £15,000/€18,000 today). As Longstaff's nominee, Shackleton was the only officer appointed without a formal interview and the only one who did not undertake a routine medical examination before sailing.

Shackleton's role was to take charge of provisions and to stow the holds, plus a few more minor chores, such as building the ship's library. Before long he also took command of planning the entertainment, including staging plays and musical nights, to help pass the long dark months of Antarctic winter.

Shackleton threw himself into the enterprise with characteristic gusto, arriving at the expedition offices like a gale-force wind. His garrulous personality and limitless drive created an immediate impact. Markham said he was a 'marvel of intelligent energy' and Scott reported that Shackleton was 'always brimful of enthusiasm and good fellowship'. Bernacchi remembered Shackleton as 'full of flashing new ideas', many of them impracticable.

Armitage saw a coltish, almost manic bundle of energy with an overwhelming eagerness to please. At 27, Shackleton was no colt but, as Armitage observed, 'I thought him extremely boyish and almost extravagantly enthusiastic.'

Shackleton, on the brink of the greatest adventure of his life, still resembled the schoolboy truant who wanted to run away to sea.

chapter 5

Fortune Hunting

Not even the thrill of going to sea for the first time could compete with the exhilaration Shackleton felt at joining the expedition. He excelled when fired by the excitement of something novel and fresh. Routine was boring to a man with a limited attention span who was easily distracted once the sheen of newness had worn off. It was the journey which mattered more than the arrival for Shackleton. Hope and anticipation were often more appealing than reality.

The intensity of readying *Discovery* for a two- or three-year journey was precisely the scale of challenge that appealed to Shackleton. He was naturally self-confident and had few, if any, doubts about succeeding in any task he attacked. When combined with his formidable reserves of energy and commitment, Shackleton was soon recognised as one of the expedition's strongest personalities.

No task seemed too great as he mobilised and stowed seemingly endless boxes of stores and assorted equipment. The chore was made even more difficult by the need to restrict the weight of boxes to a maximum of 56 lb (31 kg) for ease of unloading in the Antarctic where formal docking and quay facilities were non-existent.

In between, he travelled to Scotland to assist with *Discovery*'s sea trials off the Scottish coast – the ship was launched on 21 March – and took a brisk course in detonating explosives, a useful contingency against the vessel getting trapped in the ice.

A further diversion from his most pressing assignment with supplies came only a few days before departure when Shackleton was summoned to the Royal Engineers' establishment at Aldershot for trials with manned observation balloons which the expedition would take south. The balloons were recommended by Sir Joseph Hooker, the 84-year-old survivor of Ross and Crozier's expedition who believed they would provide superb long-distance views of the continent's unexplored interior. Hooker, a commanding intellect, could not be ignored and despite more pressing duties, Shackleton and four others spent hours at Aldershot trying to master the technique of operating the hot-air balloons.

With his infectious good humour and lively chatter, Shackleton was a highly visible figure as he moved freely among the officers, scientists and crew, oblivious as ever to rank or status. Shackleton, the most egalitarian of officers, had little time for the formal divisions, preferring to pick his own company than follow the conventions of the day which kept officers and crew strictly apart. He was equally at home at fine dining tables with fellow officers or in pubs with ordinary sailors. James Dell, a young sailor on *Discovery*, said Shackleton was 'both fore and aft' and Clarence Hare, a steward, recalled that he was a 'good mixer'.

For some, however, the relentless jokes, storytelling and habit of attaching nicknames to almost everyone became a little wearisome. Bernacchi found that the stories were 'only true in a poetic sense' and explained: 'His aptitude for satire, for bantering his companions, could be embarrassing and sometimes annoying'.

Those less accustomed to the banter were invariably smitten by Shackleton's breezy charm, particularly the women visitors. On one occasion he spotted two elderly women making a tour of *Discovery*. Shackleton stepped in and took the women on a private inspection of the ship. One of the women, Elizabeth Dawson-Lambton, was mesmerised by the flattery and easy eloquence and asked if there was anything the expedition still needed before sailing. When told that money was needed to buy Hooker's observation balloons, Dawson-Lambton, a wealthy spinster, immediately donated £1,000 (about £57,000/€68,000 today) to the expedition funds. In later years she became one of Shackleton's most reliable sponsors.

Shackleton's easy-going, classless style was in sharp contrast to Scott, a formal man who had been at sea since 13 and who ran *Discovery* along the conventional navy lines which had scarcely changed since the era of Nelson. This caused difficulties on *Discovery* because the Admiralty had refused to staff the ship with an all-Royal Navy crew and Scott was forced to accept men like Shackleton and Armitage from the merchant fleet.

Merchant navy men were accustomed to a less formal routine and the arrangement did not sit easily with either side. Shackleton, despite his unflagging efforts in handling *Discovery*'s provisions and cheerful good humour, was dismissed as 'just a cargo shifter' by Royal Navy seaman Dell.

Antarctic bound. Officers and scientists pictured on board Discovery *in 1901 shortly before departing south. (L–r) Wilson, Shackleton, Armitage, Barne, Koettlitz, Skelton, Scott, Royds, Bernacchi, Ferrar, Hodgson.*

A further compromise was that *Discovery* was registered as a merchant ship flying the blue ensign under special warrant from the Admiralty. It was not a Royal Navy vessel. In effect, Scott was running a merchant ship on Royal Navy lines.

Amidst the whirl of activity before sailing Shackleton somehow found time to complete the formalities of entering the slightly mysterious realm of Freemasonry. On 9 July, only three weeks before *Discovery*'s scheduled departure, he was initiated into the Navy Lodge of Masons.

Entering the arcane, all-male domain of the Freemasons was faintly interesting but carried no great significance for Shackleton. He saw the private guild as little more than an old boy network that could be exploited if the occasion arose. Shackleton was never seriously committed to the Masons, though it was necessary to undergo the craft's customary vetting procedure and peculiar ancient rituals of initiation. But he never attended Navy Lodge again and the 10 years which elapsed between his initial entry and gaining elevation to the next level of Masonry was a record for the time.[1]

Once inside the Freemasons, Shackleton discovered that Scott had also been initiated into the Navy Lodge only three months earlier and Roald Amundsen, whose feats in the ice would eclipse all others, was also a Mason. Joining the Freemasons is by invitation only and Shackleton's membership was proposed by Markham's cousin, Vice-Admiral Sir Albert Hastings Markham, while the initiation ceremony was held jointly with Lieutenant Charles Royds, a fellow officer from *Discovery*.

Amidst everything else, Shackleton was preoccupied by the image of Emily, still tantalisingly beyond reach. In the weeks and months before *Discovery* sailed, the pair met more regularly. The Dormans had moved from the suburbs of Sydenham to Wetherby Gardens, a more central location in a smart area off the Old Brompton Road in London. He was also concerned that other men were in pursuit of her and was anxious to formalise the arrangement by getting engaged.

He appealed directly to Emily to end the uncertainty, writing that it was 'a man's way to want a woman altogether to himself'. In the past he had asked her to love him 'just a little' but now, in the weeks before *Discovery* began the long voyage, he insisted: 'Love me altogether and only me.'[2]

Emily responded favourably, leaving Shackleton convinced after four years of indecision that she would finally agree to marriage. All that remained, he believed, was the approval of Charles Dorman.

Whether Emily, an independent-minded 32-year-old woman, needed the permission of her father to marry is unclear. Nevertheless, Shackleton chose to maintain decent old-fashioned protocol and wrote a formal letter to Dorman asking for his daughter's hand.

Writing a letter, rather than chatting directly with Dorman, a man he knew well, was odd. It was particularly out of character when measured against Shackleton's strongest card, the gift of the gab. Even more telling is that Shackleton delayed writing to Dorman until 3 August. By this time, *Discovery* had slipped out of London, rounded the Kent coast and was anchored at Stokes Bay near Portsmouth.

Shackleton's timing was intentional and meant Dorman could not reply until *Discovery* was far out to sea. A fear of rejection hung in the air and for once the normally self-confident Shackleton was unsure of himself.

Shackleton opened his heart to Dorman. He explained that the sole reason for joining the expedition was: 'to get on ... so that when I come back or later when I have made money I might with your permission marry Emily if she still cares for me as I feel she does now.'

At the back of his mind was money, a constant source of concern for Shackleton throughout his life. The lack of money, or even the prospect of making or inheriting a small fortune, was one of the few issues which ate into his bullish self-assurance. Mixing in the company of wealthy men like Dorman only increased his unease.

Shackleton was honest enough to concede that his poor finances and moderate prospects posed 'considerable difficulties' in providing a future for Emily. But, Browning-like, he was defiantly optimistic. In a bold declaration which he hoped would sway Dorman's opinion, he pledged: 'As for me, my fortune is all to make but I intend making it quickly.'[3]

Emily had gone down to the Thames a few days earlier to watch the expedition depart. Flag-waving crowds were everywhere on 31 July as *Discovery* made her way towards the Kent coast, serenaded by a cacophony of hooters and sirens and cheering. Standing alongside were Helen, Kathleen and Gladys, his younger sisters. In preparation for the moment of departure, Shackleton had taught them semaphore and using borrowed handkerchiefs, signalled 'Goodbye Helen, goodbye Kathleen, goodbye Gladys', in strict order of age.

If his intention was to impress Charles Dorman, Shackleton could hardly have orchestrated a higher-profile send-off. *Discovery* was at the centre of public attention in the summer of 1901. The expedition was carrying far more than an assortment of expectant sailors and scientists to the ice. *Discovery* had become a symbol of national potency and a show of defiance against the emerging powers of America and Germany.

Shackleton relished being centre stage and was in his element when *Discovery* arrived in the Solent to meet the new King. It was Cowes Week, a high point in the social calendar for the rich and ambitious. After 64 years on the throne, Queen Victoria had died earlier in 1901 and Cowes was a welcome opportunity for King Edward VII and Queen Alexandra to enjoy the limelight they had waited so long to attain.

Edward, a short, portly figure nearing his 60s, was an extravagant playboy prince who arrived on the throne with a reputation for fine dining, fat cigars and a string of scarcely concealed marital affairs with the wives of others. Those closest called him Bertie while many lampooned him as Edward the Caresser. American writer Henry James said he was an 'arch vulgarian'. The King, in turn, shared Shackleton's enjoyment of the big occasions. A further unspoken connection was that both men were Masons.

Markham, whose ruthless ambition had created the grand venture, was on hand to witness the royal seal of approval and so was the modest, undemanding Longstaff. Shortly before *Discovery* sailed, with money still short, Longstaff had topped up the expedition's funds with a fresh donation of £5,000 (£285,000/€343,000 today), which meant that almost a third of the expedition's money came from his pocket.

Standing on deck, the King honoured Scott with the Victorian Order, Fourth Class and proudly announced that the expedition would be 'valuable not only to your country but to the whole civilised world'. Shortly afterwards, Queen Alexandra's dog fell overboard and had to be rescued by a gallant seaman.

Early on the morning of 7 August, *Discovery* caught a final glimpse of English shores and steered towards the gusty swells of the Bay of Biscay, a familiar passage to Shackleton after numerous voyages to the Cape. Ahead lay 12,000 miles (19,000 km), down to South Africa and across the Indian Ocean to Australia and New Zealand, where the last of the supplies would be loaded before the ship made the final 2,500-mile (4,000 km) crossing to Antarctica.

Unknown to Shackleton, the news he wanted to hear from Charles Dorman was delivered while the ship was barely halfway across the Bay of Biscay. Writing the day after *Discovery*'s sailing, Dorman gave his full blessing to the marriage. He told Shackleton, '... if and whenever the time comes when you are in the pecuniary position you so long for and that if you and Emmy are still of the same mind my consent to your union will not be wanting ...'

Shackleton remained unaware of Dorman's approval and he would never be able to thank him. By the time the post caught up with *Discovery* months later in New Zealand, Charles Dorman was dead.

chapter 6

A Hunger

Discovery, to quote one voyager, was a 'sluggish sailer'. The ship lacked speed, devoured copious amounts of coal, steered poorly and rolled wildly. Scott said the ship 'tossed about like a cork' in the choppy waters. More important, *Discovery* leaked badly and Lieutenant Royds, the executive officer who had supervised the sea trials, reported 'one or two great mistakes' in the building of the vessel. As the holds filled with water, Royds blamed 'downright carelessness' and 'want of supervision' for the difficulties.

A three-masted barque, the 1,600-ton *Discovery* cost the expedition £51,000 (almost £3 million/€3.6 million today), more than half the entire budget. In many ways, the ship was a monument to Markham's ambition.

Shackleton, with his long sailing experience, shared the general unease. *Discovery*, he found, was poorly rigged with 'too much sail aft and not enough forward'. The masts were considered too short and the yards too long. It would, Shackleton predicted, be a 'serious mater' in the stormier southerly waters.

The early days at sea, full of excitement and expectation, gave Shackleton the opportunity to acquaint himself with his new colleagues and develop new friendships. One relationship made in the first days of the expedition proved deeper and longer lasting than any he ever made and, but for a toxic combination of ambition and tragedy, the other might also have proved long-lasting.

It was by chance that Shackleton was first introduced to Hugh Robert Mill, a former librarian at the Royal Geographical Society and the man who became his closest friend. Mill, a 40-year-old scientist, was drafted in at the last moment to instruct some of the party on collecting meteorological and oceanographic data. Among those in need of training was a somewhat reluctant Shackleton.

Mill, who sailed only as far as Madeira, was asked to drill Shackleton on testing the density and salinity of water, a fairly straightforward task which called for patience and painstaking accuracy with the statistics. Patience and attention to detail were invariably the qualities Shackleton found most difficult to muster and Mill, the meticulous academic who had perfected the essentials of good science, gloomily reported: 'He found the minute accuracy required rather irksome and was long in grasping the importance of writing down one reading of an instrument before making the next.'[1]

While both were quick to recognise that science was not Shackleton's strength, the two men – opposites in many respects – were drawn to each other. In Shackleton, the reserved, bookish Mill saw the gregarious, thrusting adventurer that was beyond him. To Shackleton, Mill was the wise and loyal counsellor he needed.

Mill was a small, highly intelligent, considerate man with an enquiring mind and a fragile body. He suffered from tuberculosis as a child, his eyesight was poor and yet he overcame the physical setbacks to become a much-respected scientist and an authority on the polar regions. Behind the drooping moustache, owlish glasses and studious demeanour, Mill was a dreamer who nursed a forlorn ambition to explore the ice alongside a generation of men he considered polar giants, like Amundsen and Nansen. He knew them all.

It was Markham who blocked his only serious attempt to join an expedition when he opposed Mill joining a minor venture to Spitsbergen in 1898. 'The proper place of a librarian is the library,' Markham decreed. Although Mill never saw the Antarctic continent, he was justly called the 'Finest Antarctican who never went there.'[2]

Despite Shackleton's shortcomings as a scientist, Mill was attracted by his 'inexhaustible good humour' and the hint of romantic adventurism which separated him from most on board. To Mill, Shackleton was a prototype hero drawn from the same cast of Elizabethan adventurers as Drake and Raleigh. Through Shackleton, Mill could vicariously live out his dream as an explorer.

The two men, though markedly different in character, became firm friends, each one relying on the other in significantly different ways. Shackleton's strength, vision and energy were as vital to Mill as Mill's keen understanding, shrewdness and generous spirit were to Shackleton.

Mill, who understood Shackleton better than anyone did and came as near as any individual to being his mentor, saw another side to his character. 'Shackleton was always at his best when in danger, always most prudent and careful when taking the greatest risks,' he wrote. 'The Yorkshire Quaker in his ancestry took command in such emergencies: the dare-devil Irishman had his fling only in hours of ease.'[3]

Shackleton put it more simply, writing to Mill: 'You always believed in me.'

Shackleton's other great friendship, which was not destined to last, involved Edward Wilson, another dedicated scholarly type who was drawn to Shackleton through a shared interest in the poets and spells of lively conversation during long nights at sea. Wilson was also attracted by Shackleton's quick wit and trove of anecdotes and Shackleton, talkative and animated, always liked a good listener. Wilson also had distant Quaker roots.

Wilson, Cambridge-educated and devoutly Christian, was a 29-year-old qualified doctor who joined *Discovery* as junior surgeon, though he was also a keen naturalist and gifted artist. As an abstemious figure of self-denial who lived a bare Ruskin-like existence, Wilson was severe with himself but enormously kind and thoughtful to others. Wilson saw God's hand in everything and was described by a colleague as 'the personification of Christ on earth'.[4]

At times he cut a slightly unworldly figure among the hardened seafarers and adventurers jammed together on *Discovery*. Although known as Ted to his family, Wilson was Bill to his shipmates on *Discovery* and Shackleton, perhaps sensing someone slightly out of place in the rough and tumble of the ship, took him under his wing. 'He has quite taken me in his charge,' Wilson wrote in his diary.

Wilson often ventured onto the bridge at night during Shackleton's watch to pass the hours chatting about poetry. On occasions Shackleton would rouse Wilson in the early hours to witness the type of spectacular sunrise only visible at sea.

Wilson, a patient man who always found time for others, was the most popular member on board and also developed a strong bond with Scott, a more unsure and remote figure who did not make friends easily. 'The Captain and I understand one another better than anyone else on the ship,' he wrote. Even a strong difference of opinion on religion – Scott was agnostic – did not complicate the relationship.

Wilson and Scott became the closest of friends and were destined to die side by side in the Antarctic a decade later. Before then, Wilson would be forced to choose between Shackleton and Scott.

Discovery's sluggishness meant that the heavily laden ship could make little more than 7 or 8 knots on the four-month journey to New Zealand. Even a moderate headwind risked slowing progress to a crawl. To preserve coal, *Discovery* needed to rely on prevailing winds for large portions of the voyage. However, it soon emerged that, despite sea trials, the ship had never been fully tested under sail. The vessel's first real examination would come in the 'roaring forties and fifties' of the Indian Ocean and in crossing the Southern Ocean.

The serious matter foreseen by Shackleton duly materialised during the third week of August with the ship nearing the equator. On a routine inspection of the holds, he was aghast to see water at almost head height in places and boxes of food reduced to a slimy, putrid mess. The stench of rotting produce was so overpowering that a ventilation shaft had to be drilled to improve the air.

Shackleton, demonstrating his liking for a crisis, hurled himself into the task of unloading, cleaning and repacking the stores. All hands, including scientists, were summoned to assist the pumping and disinfecting of the holds, building a new floor to store provisions and to jettison the rotting produce. Scott was relieved at how efficiently his Third Officer, an 'indefatigable worker', tackled the problem.

Discovery, still leaking badly, reached Cape Town in early October. Shackleton was hoping to catch up with his brother Frank who was still serving in the Royal Irish Fusiliers. But *Discovery* was already more than a week behind schedule and Frank Shackleton, who had been wounded in action, had already been sent home.

Scott now dropped plans to call at Melbourne and instead drove straight for New Zealand, taking a more direct southerly route across the Indian Ocean on the fringes of the ice to save time. Tons of supplies and sections of three prefabricated wooden huts loaded on the quayside at Melbourne awaiting Shackleton's attention were hastily rerouted to the New Zealand port of Lyttelton.

Despite the rough seas and troubling cross swells, *Discovery* made surprisingly good progress. At times waves surged to a height of 40 feet (12 m) and the ship lurched over to an angle of 47°. After an occasionally alarming crossing of 46 days, *Discovery* entered Lyttelton late in the evening of 28 November. *Discovery* had passed its sea trial.

Shackleton, in his eagerness to collect the mail from home, went ashore at 2 a.m. to rouse the Lyttelton postmaster from his bed. There, on the other side of the world, Shackleton learned of Charles Dorman's death and that Emily was free to determine her own future. He may have wondered why, without the need for her father's approval, they were now 12,000 miles (19,000 km) apart. But for now the adventure was more pressing.

Shackleton had little time to reflect since *Discovery* arrived with a myriad of urgent problems. The unrelenting leaks were so serious that the ship was taken into dry dock for major repairs and once more Shackleton was ordered to clear the holds. He also found the paperwork was in disarray and space had to be found on the already-crowded ship for the additional 1,000 boxes and huts shipped from Melbourne.

A different problem emerged as the crew, unleashing the pent-up frustration of nearly seven weeks at sea, went ashore and descended into an orgy of drunkenness and fighting. One officer reported 'not a single sober man' on board as officers struggled to cope with the brawling, insubordination and even desertion which soon left Scott short-handed. Several hands were laid off or fled and Scott had to call in casual reinforcements from *Ringarooma*, a navy cruiser moored alongside *Discovery*, to assist with the work.

One notable member of the working parties from *Ringarooma* was Thomas Crean, a tough 24-year-old seaman from County Kerry. Soon afterwards, one of *Discovery*'s ratings struck a petty officer and deserted, leaving Scott with another vacancy. Crean volunteered to take his place and before long the two most conspicuous Irishmen on board struck up a friendship.

Discovery was finally made ready to sail on 21 December. The irritating leaks, though still occurring, had been stemmed to a point where the pumps could cope and the mood in Lyttelton was noisily festive for the send-off. The Bishop of Christchurch blessed the party, the marine band played stirring tunes and enthusiastic crowds, who had been carried to the port by special trains from nearby Christchurch, lined the quays in gleeful celebration.

But tragedy struck when Charles Bonner, a 23-year-old naval rating from London's East End who had been drinking, fell from the top of the mainmast still clutching the wind vane and was killed instantly. The cheering stopped and *Discovery* headed to Port Chalmers, the last port of call, to pick up final stocks of coal and leave the unfortunate Bonner for burial.

Bonner's death cast a pall of gloom over proceedings and delayed departure for another couple of days. It was not until Christmas Eve 1901 that *Discovery*, an awkward-looking vessel, lumbered uneasily into open water, weighed down with supplies and equipment for three years, including 45 petrified sheep taken south to provide fresh meat. The freshly painted black hull and contrasting yellow funnels hinted at a spruce, well-organised enterprise but, as Bernacchi reported, 'every hole and corner' was filled with something or other. At the last moment, an extra 45 tons of coal was loaded on deck because there was no space below. *Discovery*'s freeboard amidships was just 9 feet (2.7 m) as they prepared to enter the violent Southern Ocean and Bernacchi said the Plimsoll line had 'sunk so deep it was forgotten'.

However, *Discovery* was highly fortunate: the weather held and the seas, though occasionally rough, were moderate by the standards of the Southern Ocean. *Discovery* even managed a comparatively smooth passage of only five days through the pack ice, the giant belt of ice encircling the continent of Antarctica. The pack, which extends from around 300 miles to over 1,500 miles (480–2,400 km) in width, is a hazardous labyrinth of constantly moving ice and fluctuating lanes of open water. *Erebus* and *Terror* had taken 46 days to penetrate the pack during one leg of their historic four-year voyage in the 1840s and the *Belgica* expedition became the first to overwinter in the south in 1898 after becoming trapped by the pack.

Discovery followed the route taken by Ross and Crozier 60 years before, almost directly due south from New Zealand before running along the white-capped mountains of South Victoria Land and into the broad expanses of the Ross Sea.

Shackleton, surprisingly, was moved to a rare display of silence by the experience. He offered few thoughts beyond an apologetic 'lack of facility' in explaining his feelings as he crossed the Antarctic Circle for the first time on 3 January 1902.

The bleak volcanic slopes of Cape Adare, where Bernacchi had overwintered during the *Southern Cross* expedition, were spotted on 9 January. A swift trip was made ashore to inspect the party's hut, an untidy relic made from Norwegian spruce which has the distinction of being the first man-made structure in Antarctica. Wilson said the area looked like 'the centre of a rubbish heap' and the party left after depositing a written record of *Discovery*'s visit for any relief ships.

Shackleton climbed into the crow's nest as *Discovery* pushed south along the ice-bound coastline in dazzling clear skies which brought new mountaintops and glaciers onto the horizon with every passing hour. An interesting inlet, which Scott thought might be a suitable place to overwinter, was spotted on 20 January and Shackleton took his first steps on the continent when he joined a small party to inspect the area.

Surrounded by an arc of mountains rising above 5,000 feet (1,500 m), it is a region of granite rock formations and huge boulders, with a striking glacier spewing out into the bay. It was later named Granite Harbour. By chance, Shackleton's arrival on the continent was made in an area rich with dark green moss and orange-coloured lichen and Shackleton's first discovery as a polar explorer was not a new range of mountains or an unseen stretch of sea. Shackleton, it emerged, had found traces of primitive plant life clinging to an uncertain existence in the deepest south.

Scott felt Granite Harbour was too far north for a winter base and pressed further south into the more promising area of McMurdo Sound, a secluded bay marking the junction between the Ross Sea and the Great Ice Barrier. But McMurdo was choked with ice and Scott decided to take *Discovery* further east along the Barrier to explore other opportunities.

The Great Ice Barrier is a stunning geographical phenomenon. Discovered by Ross and Crozier in 1841, it is a vast, flat, floating table of ice about 400 miles (600 km) long, extending to a height of around 200 feet (60 m) in places. More than 90 per cent of the constantly moving Barrier lies beneath the water and is close to the size of France. It is the largest ice shelf in the world. Ross called it a barrier because it prevented his ships sailing further south towards the Pole and the name stuck for over a century. (It is now known as the Ross Ice Shelf.)

Discovery, dwarfed by the immensity of the ice shelf, sailed alongside the Barrier for over a week, establishing a new record 'furthest south' of 78° 30' S and catching the first glimpse of new undiscovered land in the distance which marked the end of the shelf itself. Jutting out into the waters ahead, the distant peninsula was the expedition's first important geographical discovery and named King Edward VII Land after the new monarch.

Shackleton was enthralled by the thrill of seeing sights which no human had ever seen before. It was, he said, a 'unique sort of feeling'.

The expedition's main priority was to find a suitable winter base before the days grew shorter with the onset of autumn. *Discovery* had survived two potentially serious brushes with pack ice during the cruise along the Barrier and Scott was under strict instructions to avoid getting trapped like *Belgica*.

Besides, *Discovery* had ventured into hazardous, uncharted seas without the guiding hand of an experienced ice master. Armitage, the navigator, was the only one on board with any familiarity of sea ice, though his experience was limited. It was a curious oversight to sail without more expertise since Britain possessed a sizeable pool of skilled sailors from the whaling fleets, notably around the port of Dundee where *Discovery* was built. These men had spent years navigating the ice, but they were merchant seamen and Markham, with his unwavering attachment to the Royal Navy, declined to tap into this national resource.

Scott ordered a return to McMurdo Sound, where it was hoped the ice might now have gone out. But instead of beating a hasty retreat before the ice encroached, Scott rashly decided to break off and make a landing at a small inlet to test the observational balloons.

The inlet, which ran about 12 miles (19 km) into the Barrier, offered a rare opportunity to climb onto the ice shelf. The edge of the ice sloped down to the water like a natural slipway and the men, many in high spirits, poured ashore. Some rigged up the balloon equipment and some played football or attempted to ski. Emergency stores were landed in case the ship had to make a quick escape. Armitage took a six-man party inland for the expedition's first trek into the interior but in the rush to get away they forgot to take a second tent and six burly officers and seamen had to spend the night wedged together in a three-man tent. It was a sign of worse to come.

Next day Scott asserted his authority by becoming the first man to ascend into the skies above Antarctica. Perched unsteadily in the fragile-looking basket, he rose to about 600 feet (185 m) and gained the first view southwards across the icy flatlands of the Barrier.

Shackleton, with his boyish enthusiasm for anything new, was the next to go aloft. He carried a camera and took the first photographs of the bleak interior. In brisk winds and tethered by a single length of wire, Shackleton soared to a height of about 650 feet (200 m).

Wilson, unimpressed by the hazardous experiment, said it was an 'exceedingly dangerous amusement in the hands of such inexperienced novices' and Bernacchi concluded that the apparatus was not worth the space it occupied in the ship. Later that day a serious leak was discovered and the balloon never flew again. However, the area was named Balloon Inlet in memory of the short trial in aerial observation.

Discovery narrowly avoided another serious collision with the ice before venturing into McMurdo Sound on 10 February. On inspection, they found a sheltered stretch of water about 30 miles (48 km) wide running into the face of the Barrier at the southern end and flanked on one side by Ross Island and on the other by the towering mountains of Victoria Land. A little way inland on Ross Island, the gently smoking 12,450-foot (3,785 m) beacon of Mount Erebus, the most southerly active volcano, stood imperiously. The South Pole lay untouched almost 900 miles (1,440 km) inland. The bay, which was named after Lieutenant Archibald McMurdo from *Terror*, was the 'most perfect little natural harbour imaginable', according to Wilson.

Shackleton saw something more. He recognised a 'weird and uncanny look' about the scene which, he said, reminded him of a poem by Browning, *Childe Roland to the Dark Tower Came*.

There are numerous interpretations of Browning's complex, gloomy work which deals with a young man's quest for the Dark Tower, a ghostly

Holy Grail of sorts which he finds after wandering through treacherous wastelands packed with real and imagined horrors. Childe Roland's journey ends abruptly when he reaches the tower, but we never learn what he discovers at the end of the long search.

It was much the same for Shackleton, who found the journey was more stimulating than the arrival in the desolate surroundings of McMurdo Sound. Or as Bernacchi suggested, 'Antarctica to him did not exist'. Shackleton, he said, was simply 'hungry for adventure and fame'.[5]

chapter 7

Baptism by Ice

Scott's decision to establish a winter base in the sheltered confines of McMurdo Sound settled once and for all the uncertainty about the expedition's plans. The initial idea was that a small party would be left behind to overwinter and for *Discovery* to return to New Zealand. Some sensed that Scott always intended to overwinter, but it was not until early February, when *Discovery* was steaming back towards McMurdo Sound, that Scott finally revealed his plans.

The secrecy over his intentions was typical of Scott, a naturally guarded and self-doubting character who found it difficult to confide in others. Officers and crew were regularly kept in the dark about plans until the last moment.

Wilson noted that Scott was 'strangely reticent about letting a soul on the ship know what his immediate plans are'. Thomas Hodgson, the biologist, added that none of the party knew what was planned until five minutes beforehand.

But Scott's decision to overwinter *Discovery* at McMurdo Sound was music to the ears of Shackleton. As a junior officer from the merchant service, he suspected he would be sent packing if Scott chose to send the ship back to New Zealand. Shackleton wanted more than a simple voyage.

Much work was needed to establish a proper base and there was a critical need to acclimatise before the onset of the harsher winter conditions when the sun would disappear for four months. No expedition had wintered this far south before and only three of the party – Armitage, Bernacchi and the surgeon, Dr Reginald Koettlitz – had any experience of the ice.

The men from *Discovery*, the experienced trio apart, were spectacularly unprepared for the ordeal. Every task was a troublesome challenge as they struggled to adapt. Early attempts to master skis and handle the dogs summed up the tortuous early experiences. The men floundered,

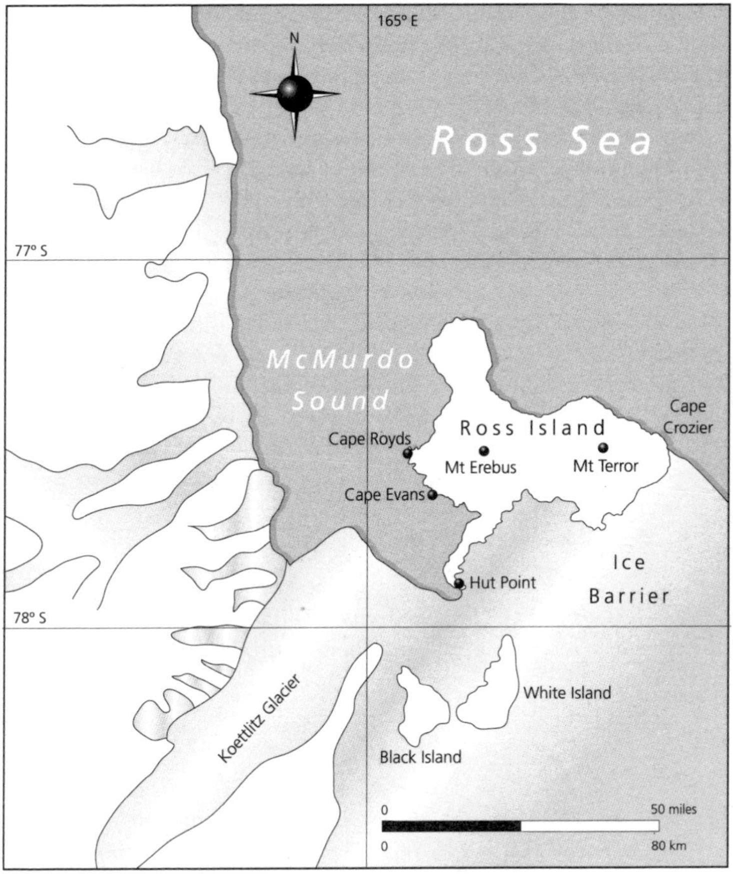

Ross Island in McMurdo Sound. Discovery *was moored near Hut Point in 1902–04 and Shackleton built winter quarters at Cape Royds in 1908. Scott's hut at Cape Evans was a refuge for Shackleton's Ross Sea party in 1915–17.*

repeatedly falling heavily, while the dogs fought viciously with one another in noisy disarray.

Reginald Ford, the chief steward and purser, broke his leg in two places and Scott suffered severe bruising to his knee during the first attempts to cope with skis. Several dogs were killed in the brutal fighting and another simply disappeared. Scott, after only a few days' hapless struggle, came to the conclusion that dogs were of 'little use for men dragging'.

Shackleton's first attempts at skiing were typical. Shackleton, lacking the necessary patience to practise, thrashed around in comical fashion before proudly declaring himself the worst of everyone. 'Must practice the more,' he added half-heartedly.

Nor was it fully realised that *Discovery*'s luckless students were attempting to master the wrong form of skiing. On the gentle slopes of Ross Island, the sorry-looking novices were struggling to learn downhill skiing when the expedition's coming journeys into the interior of Antarctica would demand a sound grasp of cross-country skiing.

In between the unequal battle with skis, the party unloaded countless boxes of supplies and equipment and erected three small huts – a 36-square-foot (3.3 sq. m) building and two small observation huts – on a small headland jutting out into waters of McMurdo Sound. The headland, pointing southwards to the Barrier like a directional finger, was named Hut Point Peninsula. Scott had decided that the party would remain on board *Discovery* throughout their stay, while the hut was used as an emergency store of coal and provisions.

Shackleton soon found the chance to impress with a short journey into the interior. A pair of islands, sticking out from the generally flat Barrier, could be seen to the south and Scott reckoned the view from the highest point would provide vital clues to the travelling surface beyond. Shackleton, untried and ill-equipped, was asked to lead a team of three men to make the observation.

Improbably enough, Shackleton was chosen for the trip on the toss of a coin with another officer, Lieutenant Michael Barne. While the knowledgeable Armitage, Bernacchi and Koettlitz remained on board *Discovery*, Shackleton was joined on the trip by two other novices, Wilson and Hartley Ferrar. Ferrar, a 23-year-old geologist who came from the same Anglo-Irish roots as Shackleton, sailed south only a month after taking his final exams at Cambridge.

The tyros set off to the south on 19 February, hauling an 11-foot (3.3 m) sledge containing three weeks' provisions and a pram, a collapsible dinghy which Scott insisted on taking in case the sea ice broke up. Shackleton said it was a 'weird white world' and at Markham's insistence, the three men flew their own personal pennant or flag on the sledges. Shackleton's flag carried his family motto, the singularly appropriate *Fortitudine Vincimus* ('By endurance we conquer').

Shackleton, just a few days after his 28th birthday, seized the assignment with both hands. It was precisely the sort of challenge which had prompted him to volunteer for *Discovery* in the first place. But while Shackleton was in charge, he was not in control.

Penetrating the interior of Antarctica is among the toughest trials of strength and tenacity facing any human, let alone three beginners on their first venture into the ice. Severe difficulties emerged from the start, with winds blowing hard and temperatures dropping sharply as the men moved inland from the relatively warm coastal area. Wilson calculated that the two islands were only 5 or 10 miles (8–16 km) away and within easy reach. But without many geographical features to provide perspective, distances can be deceptive on the Barrier. The two islands were closer to 20 miles (32 km) from *Discovery*'s anchorage.

Hour after hour, Shackleton, Wilson and Ferrar staggered forward in soft snow. The islands, which once seemed so close, appeared to be getting no nearer and the pace slowed markedly as the men tired from the punishing march. Ferrar estimated they were advancing at the pitiful rate of 6 inches (15 cm) per step. More experienced travellers would have dumped the pram, but it was not apparent to Shackleton, Wilson and Ferrar that they had stepped away from the unstable sea ice onto the firmer footings of the Barrier where the dinghy was unnecessary weight.

Winds increased and a puzzling gloom of white-out descended on the scene. Unable to see very far ahead, they recklessly decided to press on regardless. The men, enduring their first Antarctic squall, pulled almost blindly for 12 hours before stumbling to a halt, not entirely sure where they were and utterly exhausted. Frostbite had nipped them all. Shackleton's ears were badly blistered and one hand had gone ghostly white with the cold.

Erecting the tent in a strong wind, another first, was a tortuously cold and awkward chore for the freezing, worn-out men. 'Hanging on like grim death to the tent pole to prevent the whole bag of tricks going to blazes,' Wilson recalled.

Once inside, they patiently nursed each other's frostbitten ears and fingers back to life. Their socks, soaked with sweat from the hard labour of pulling, were frozen solidly inside their boots. Routine chores took longer to carry out in a depth of cold that none of them had ever experienced before. To add to the woes, the men struggled to cook a hot meal on a primus stove which they had never used previously.

After a few hours' rest, the slog was resumed, with heads bowed in a futile attempt to shield their faces against the biting wind. But they were quickly halted in their tracks by crevasses and decided to make camp, about 2 miles (3 km) from the nearer of the islands. Once again, they grappled with the wind in erecting the tent and eventually managed to snatch some much needed rest. They slept for over eight hours.

By mid-afternoon on 20 February it was decided to leave much of the gear behind and push on to the island with the highest peak, now called White Island. Unaccustomed to climbing even the modest slopes of White Island, the men struggled badly and found that the penetrating wind chilled them to the bone.

From the freezing vantage point of 2,700 feet (820 m), Shackleton, Wilson and Ferrar drank in the marvellous sight of the Barrier extending unbroken southwards as far as the eye could see, the gateway to the Pole itself. It was 'a splendid view of level barrier surface stretching away to the South,' Shackleton reported. To the south-west a chain of mountains, a continuation of the range which began in Victoria Land, could also be detected stretching at least 100 miles (160 km) into the distance. Shackleton verified their position and Wilson made a quick sketch, though he admitted being 'nearly frozen' in doing it.

Invigorated by the thrill of his first geographical discovery, Shackleton decided to return to the ship as quickly as possible. Like an eager schoolboy, Shackleton raced back to *Discovery* in rapid time and engulfed the wardroom with an animated account of the party's findings.

Reginald Skelton, the engineer, said he 'hardly stopped talking until everybody had turned in' and a sardonic Royds noted that Shackleton was 'full of talk as was expected'. Scott reported the men 'bubbling over' with their accounts of the highway to the south.

Shackleton was right to be excited by the trip, although the party was fortunate that the weather, though troublesome, was not far worse. Scott was pleased with the outcome but quietly alarmed how easily Shackleton, Wilson and Ferrar had run into trouble on what should have been a routine round-trip of 40 miles (64 km). He was grateful for their good luck. Others were not so fortunate.

A fortnight after Shackleton's return, a group of 12 men, hauling four sledges and struggling with eight disorderly dogs, set out for Cape Crozier, one of the prearranged 'post' boxes where it was planned to leave a record of *Discovery*'s position for relief ships. Led by Royds, the group laboured badly in appalling conditions and low temperatures, recording over 50° of frost. Travelling far slower than expected, Royds was concerned provisions were getting low and sent nine men back to *Discovery* under the raw Lieutenant Barne.

Barne, the aristocratic 24-year-old son of a wealthy MP, only joined the Cape Crozier party because of the knee injury Scott sustained during ski practice. He had never led men over the ice before. Inexperienced and uncertain, Barne blundered along in atrocious weather with tragic consequences. George Vince, a naval rating who was wearing flat-soled fur boots, lost his footing on a steep icy slope, plunged some 300 feet (90 m) into the sea and was drowned.

The party broke up into confusion and further tragedy was averted only by the timely intervention of Frank Wild, a resourceful naval seaman. Wild saw the chaos unfolding and calmly took control, leading a group of six men back to *Discovery*. Barne and two other seamen staggered on board some hours later, incoherent from the cold and badly frostbitten. Hare, the last member to return, only narrowly survived after getting lost for 48 hours.

Search parties were hurriedly assembled and Shackleton volunteered to take a small boat into the icy waters to look for Vince. After six hours of hopeless searching, he found no trace of the sailor.

Antarctica is an unforgiving place and the early encounters had exposed the party's rawness and painful shortcomings. Scott said losing Vince, the second fatality in three months, was 'one of our blackest days' and grumbled that the men were 'terribly hampered' by their inexperience on the ice. Only a week before the death of Vince, Scott had written in his diary that 'our ignorance is deplorable' and that the 'lack of system was painfully evident'.[1]

Bernacchi, who had seen it all before, was more critical. He saw a shambles unfolding before his eyes.

Born in Belgium to Italian parents, 25-year-old Bernacchi was a methodical, idealistic man with the world-weariness of someone older. The family had emigrated to Tasmania where he was educated at Hutchins School, which Ross and Crozier had helped to establish while en route to Antarctica in the 1840s. After developing an interest in the polar regions, Bernacchi joined Borchgrevink's *Southern Cross* expedition at the age of 22. Although a slight figure at less than 5 feet 6 inches (1.67 m) and weighing only 10 stone (69 kg), Bernacchi emerged from the ordeal of the first overwintering as a dependable, mature and calming influence.

Bernacchi reported that *Discovery*'s men could not put up a tent in a blizzard, cook or dress properly. He wondered whether time wasted playing football on the ice would have been more efficiently used learning how to ski and handle the uncontrollable dogs. As autumn began to descend and the shadows lengthened, Bernacchi wrote: 'Sledging has been a failure. Food, clothing – everything was wrong. There would be much to think about and much to rearrange during the long winter night.'[2]

The burden of leadership sat uneasily on the shoulders of Scott, a complex man who concealed his insecurities behind a curious mixture of charm and ill-temper. He was moody, irascible and reacted badly to any perceived challenges to his authority. The other side of Scott was a powerfully strong, combative and occasionally appealing character with a sharp, enquiring mind and a special interest in science. Although he had no formal training, Scott had effectively assumed command of the expedition's scientific programme and *Discovery*'s pioneering work in areas like geology, glaciology and biology was the basis for many future scientific studies in Antarctica. It is easy to imagine that if Scott had not entered the navy as a 13-year-old cadet he would have forged a career somewhere in the field of science.

Scott's principal guiding influence on *Discovery*, even from the other side of the world, was the overpowering Markham whose fingerprints were evident on almost every aspect of the expedition. It was Markham, with his mindset firmly rooted in the Arctic exploits of Parry and Franklin, who fashioned *Discovery* along much the same lines as the cumbersome naval expeditions of the 1820s, dictating everything from the areas to explore to the emblematic flags carried on the sledges.

During the years while Markham was plotting Britain's assault on the Antarctic and struggling to launch the *Discovery* expedition, Fridtjof Nansen, Otto Sverdrup and Robert Peary were among a new breed of Arctic explorers who successfully modernised polar exploration. The old-fashioned British model of large-scale naval enterprises sent into the ice for two or three years had been replaced by a new style of lightweight expeditions, deploying smaller teams and adopting the survival and more efficient travel techniques of native Inuit. Clothing and diet were modified, and lighter, more manoeuvrable sledges replaced the heavyweight contraptions which had broken the backs and hearts of earlier generations of sailors. Dogs were used more widely to haul hefty loads, easily doubling the range of distances men could travel.

In 1902, as *Discovery* was slowly being embedded in the ice of McMurdo Sound, Sverdrup was completing a prodigious three-year expedition across the Arctic which demonstrated the effectiveness of skis and dogs in the right hands. During an extraordinary series of journeys around the area of Ellesmere Island, the 47-year-old Norwegian charted 100,000 square miles (260,000 sq. km) of new territory, the largest survey ever made on foot in the polar territories. To Sverdrup it was simply impossible to cover such distances without dog teams. 'Without them we would get nowhere,' he declared.[3]

It was a revolution which Markham resolutely ignored. Markham's baleful influence was overwhelming and largely accepted by Scott who, placed in command for the first time in his life and with no prior knowledge of the ice, could not challenge the authority of the man who had put him there.

Markham's extraordinary resistance to skis and dogs flew in the face of all the recent experience and most expert advice of men who had tested their mettle in the extremes. He claimed that skis could be an 'intolerable nuisance' on rough ground and was equally dismissive of dogs which, he claimed, were 'worse than useless' for polar work. Markham instead gloried in the crude muscularity of naval ratings yoked together in harness in the unequal struggle against the elements. He wrote: 'In my mind no journey made with dogs can approach the height of that high conception which is raised when a party of men go forth to face hardships, dangers and difficulties with their own unaided effort. Surely in this case, the conquest is more nobly won.'[4]

Nansen, the most respected explorer of the time, was consulted before *Discovery*'s departure but Markham and Scott were selective in which pieces of advice they took. As a result, *Discovery* was dispatched into the ice reliant almost entirely on the archaic regime of man-hauling sledges. *Discovery* carried more sheep than dogs. Nor had Scott recruited a fully trained dog driver and few on board had come to terms with skis.

Bernacchi, who had seen at first hand the stark contrast between the expert use of sledges being pulled by dogs and the appalling ordeal of man-hauling, later wrote: 'Even in 1902 man-hauling of sledges was an out-dated idea.'[5]

Another failing was that Scott did not make full use of Koettlitz, a man with a solid understanding of the ice. Tall, remote and serious, Koettlitz was a doctor who branched out into the fields of bacteriology, botany and geology. His roots were from faded Prussian nobility, but the family had washed up in England during the mid-19th century. Koettlitz qualified to practise medicine and joined the Jackson–Harmsworth expedition to Franz Josef Land on an impulse in 1894.

Koettlitz, who at 41 was older than most on board, was not a good mixer and his unfashionable socialist beliefs stuck out like a sore thumb among the conservative middle-class officers and scientists in *Discovery*'s wardroom. He loathed the undercurrents of snobbery on board and creeping inefficiency of some colleagues. At the end of the expedition, he wrote to his brother: 'I want very little to do with this class of man again.' The waspish Markham determined that Koettlitz was 'exceedingly short of common sense'. Koettlitz, in contrast, was a highly conscientious character who sensed a lack of professionalism among *Discovery*'s senior ranks. He wrote: 'Nothing can be discussed seriously.'[6]

Koettlitz was among those who saw the flaws in *Discovery*'s planning even before the ship sailed. In a letter to Nansen, he warned that preparations would be 'muddled through *à l'Anglais*' and predicted particular problems with the dogs. 'To think that men can be such fools,' he wrote. 'Such blindness has a tendency to disgust and weary one with the whole business were it not for the hope that one may be able to do some good in the south notwithstanding.'[7]

The gloomy curtain of Antarctic winter, which brought more than 120 days of darkness, descended on 23 April with few of the concerns yet addressed. Instead, the wardroom held a lavish champagne dinner and the mess deck spliced the main brace with traditional naval zest.

Scott ensured that the officers, scientists and crewmen were kept busy during the long winter sojourn and a regular pattern of work and adequate leisure time was quickly established. Scott wisely saw that idleness or apathy could be toxic influences, particularly during the long winter, even if it occasionally irritated the scientific corps and merchant service men. However, Scott could point to the experience of the *Belgica* expedition, which was ravaged by scurvy, 'cabin fever' and madness, including one forlorn sailor who leapt onto the ice announcing that he was walking back to Belgium.

Poetry, naturally enough, was a regular source of discussion for those within earshot of Shackleton and he and Bernacchi went head to head one night in a fierce debate on the respective merits of Tennyson versus Browning. Tennyson won by a single vote.

Ten of *Discovery*'s officers and scientists enjoyed the comparative luxury of a small personal cabin off the wardroom which offered a measure of retreat for those wishing to 'sport his oak', a familiar signal employed in boarding schools and universities to respect the privacy of a man whose door was closed. The scientists Bernacchi and Hodgson lived either side of Shackleton's quarters.

Mealtimes, a focal point of most days, bore the hallmarks of a sedate gentleman's club, with a polished dining table, Doulton china and engraved cutlery and meals served by a steward. The wardroom, however, was noticeably colder than the mess deck, although the aim was to maintain a temperature of between 50° and 60° (10–15 °C) inside the quarters. Ice formed on the walls overnight. In contrast, the more crowded mess deck was cluttered with rows of hammocks slung from the ceiling, a jumble of half-dried clothing and a suffocating mixture of stale body odour and a dingy cloud of tobacco smoke. But with temperatures outside down to as low as -62° (-52 °C), the seamen rejoiced in the fact that they were warmer.

A large canvas awning, which resembled a marquee, was draped over *Discovery* in a reminder of how little had changed since the ships of Parry, Ross and others had overwintered in the Arctic. Electric lighting was initially provided by a windmill, though high winds later damaged the blades and the company fell back on oil lamps and candles to illuminate their quarters.

Discovery's isolation was complete by late March as temperatures dropped to -40° (-40 °C). It would be impossible today to be as isolated as the 47 men were in 1902, far beyond the reach of ships and radio contact. The only other humans on the vast continent were six men under the command of Swede Otto Nordenskjöld. They were camped in a small hut 2,500 miles (4,000 km) away at Snow Hill Island on the Antarctic Peninsula. The green fields of New Zealand were nearer to *Discovery* than Nordenskjöld.

The isolation, at least at first, did not bother Shackleton too much. He was still enthused by the excitement of the groundbreaking White Island journey. He was also anxiously waiting to discover if he was to be included in Scott's plans for the spring sledging season. Like everyone else on board, he would have to wait.

Shackleton decided to divert his pent-up energy and enthusiasm into something new and turned to journalism. After the success of *OHMS* on the *Tintagel Castle,* Shackleton's taste for the written word made him a natural choice to edit the *South Polar Times*, the expedition's house journal which was seen as another diverting pastime for the winter months. A corner for an office was found in *Discovery*'s damp holds and in the dim candlelight Shackleton assumed the role of magazine editor.

The journal, published once a month, was a cross between the rollicking fun of *Boy's Own* and the earnest periodical of a public school. He pulled in articles and drawings on a wide range of subjects from all corners of the ship. Poetry figured heavily and space was found for both serious scientific pieces and lighter-hearted items. Highlights of the journal were Wilson's outstanding illustrations and some finely crafted caricatures from the pen of Barne.

Shackleton contributed a poem under his favoured pseudonym of Nemo, a Kipling-like piece called 'To the Great Barrier.' It was a poem which might easily be interpreted as application to join Scott's spring sledging parties. He wrote:

This year shall your icy fastness resound with the voices of men
Shall we learn that you come from the mountains? Shall we call you a frozen sea?
Shall we sail Northward and leave you, still a Secret for ever to be?

True to style, Shackleton also welcomed contributions from across the ranks. Among those who contributed pieces was seaman Wild. Shackleton saw something appealing in Wild. Perhaps it was his cool head in a crisis or perhaps it was because they had much in common. Both had yearned for the sea as youngsters and Wild's first voyage, like Shackleton in the *Hoghton Tower*, was made in a clipper. In the half-lit confines of *Discovery*'s holds, the men from either side of the ranks became firm friends, a bond that would be unbroken for the remainder of their lives.

The winter months, particularly the time spent editing the *South Polar Times*, also saw Shackleton draw closer to Wilson. He was attracted by Wilson's sound intellect and kindly knack of seeing the best in everyone and every situation. Most of all, he found Wilson a good listener, especially as Shackleton talked repeatedly about his ambition to be part of the drive for the South Pole.

The opportunity to spend even more time together arose when a new meteorological observatory was established on a nearby rise, Crater Hill. Shackleton and Wilson, perhaps seeking an excuse to escape the monotony of the ship, readily agreed to take the weather readings, even if it meant climbing the hill in the bitter cold and pitch darkness. 'Blowing, with heavy drifts and black as Hades', Shackleton reported one night as the temperature sank to -46° (-43 °C).

Shackleton spoke warmly of 'Billy' to anyone who would listen and 'Shackle' had become Wilson's closest confidant. 'Shackleton's conversation is sparkling and witty to a high degree,' he told his wife in a letter. 'He has a wonderful memory and has an amazing treasure of most interesting anecdote. That and his quick wit and keen humour are his strong points at table.'[8]

Taking regular observations on Crater Hill was a perfect release from the dull routine, which inevitably gnawed at morale. Shackleton was easily bored with the weeks of inaction and moaned of 'doing the same thing' day after day. Even Wilson, a man blessed with the patience of a saint, was affected by the ennui and driven to write: 'God knows it is just about as much as I can stand at times and there is absolutely no escape.'

So far, Scott had only disclosed that the centrepiece of expedition was to be a major push south across the Barrier towards the South Pole. While the Pole itself was assumed to be beyond reach, a high southerly latitude of around 85° was thought possible. A target of 85° – about 350 miles from the Pole – would get Scott close to the record northerly latitude of 86° 13" 6' N and would ensure a place in history for the men who attained it (see map on p. 207).

Scott ended months of speculation in mid-June by announcing that two men, himself and Wilson, would make the trek towards the Pole. Initially, Scott had considered taking Barne, who was young, athletic and eager. But the shadow of seaman Vince's death hung over Barne and Scott had also decided that the second man in the southern party should be a doctor.

Wilson was slightly taken aback by the decision. Wilson, at heart, was a scientist and naturalist, not an explorer. He harboured no great ambitions for the tedium of a long sledging journey, preferring instead to concentrate on studying the wildlife, geology and indulging in his artwork. The trek south, as he explained to his wife, would be 'taking me away from my proper sphere of work to monotonous hard work on an icy barrier for three months.' Wilson's weakness was that he would not say no to his friend. Against his better instincts, he agreed to join Scott on the trek south.

However, Wilson did recognise the inherent risk of a two-man team in the wilderness, where the breakdown or injury of one person might be fatal for the other. Quietly and firmly he urged Scott to reconsider and add a third man.

Scott agreed and asked Wilson to name the third person. Wilson modestly told Scott it was not his decision to choose and Scott, seeing through Wilson's polite reserve, replied that he hardly need ask because he knew his choice. 'So then I told him it was Shackleton's ambition to go on the southern journey,' Wilson revealed. 'So it was settled and we three are to go.'[9]

Wilson was not telling the whole story. Behind his air of scholarly detachment, little escaped his keen eye and there was something uncomfortable about Shackleton on the ice. Wilson had spotted a weakness in 'Shackles'. Perhaps it was a physical problem, or perhaps a deeper psychological flaw. Either way, he kept his fears to himself. Remarkably, not even Scott was told.

The only person with whom Wilson shared his concerns was his wife, Oriana, who was on the other side of the world. In a letter home, Wilson wrote: 'I feel I am more equal to it than I feel for Shackleton: for some reason I don't think he is fitted for the job. The Captain is strong and hard as a bull-dog, but Shackleton hasn't the legs the job wants; he is so keen to go, however, that he will carry it through.'[10]

With his medical eye, Wilson had spotted that Shackleton suffered from occasional shortness of breath and bursts of coughing which pointed to possible heart or respiratory problems. Wilson was right to be apprehensive. One night, shortly before the start of the southern journey, Shackleton was kept awake with a prolonged bout of heavy coughing. Wilson was elsewhere at the time and unaware of his friend's condition.

And Shackleton never told Scott.

chapter 8

A Step into the Unknown

A noticeable change had come over Shackleton during the torpid months of Antarctic darkness. Some of the rough edges of boyish animation and irritating impulsiveness had been rubbed off, influenced perhaps by the sober decency of Wilson and promotion to the expedition's southern party, the elite corps.

He seemed to have matured a little. Shackleton, who was aroused by the thrill of the coming adventure, had also begun to find himself. For the first time he felt a sense of belonging, as though he was always meant to be an Antarctic explorer.

The centre of his focus, as ever, was Emily. Armitage noticed that he was 'greatly influenced' by the romance and the prospect of getting married on his return. 'Emily was no doubt mainly responsible, together with the life of open spaces, in raising him from the dreamy, ambitious boy, with no settled ideas, to a man of strong character,' said Armitage.

Emily was clearly at the front of Shackleton's mind as he made final preparations for the journey south. The night before departure Shackleton wrote a letter which was marked to be read only in the event he failed to return.

Showing a faint hint of insecurity about the relationship, he urged Emily to remember that he was her 'true lover'. In his pocket he carried a small photograph of the woman, though six years his senior, whom he called 'Child' and said it was her face that would be 'with me to the last'. In asking her not to grieve if he were lost, he was emphatic and unequivocal in his love: 'I love you truly and purely and as dearly as a woman can be loved. And now my true love goodnight.'[1]

Shackleton, Scott and Wilson posed self-consciously for the formality of a photograph on the morning of 2 November 1902. Standing alongside were 19 undisciplined dogs and five heavily laden sledges carrying 1,700 lb

(750 kg) of supplies, which would sustain them through a planned journey of around 13 weeks.

Shackleton's emotions were a mixture of eager anticipation and slight apprehension, topped off with a longing to get back to the ship to read Emily's letters. 'I do hope the time will go quickly on our journey,' he wrote, 'so before we can realise it, the relief ship will be down here with our letters and little presents from home.'

A support group of 12 men under Barne had set off three days earlier ferrying about 650 lb (300 kg) of extra provisions onto the Barrier and the remainder of *Discovery*'s roll call cheered loudly as the pull south began in dank overcast skies. Among the pennants carried south on the train of sledges was a flag with the touchingly naive message: 'No dogs need apply.'

Bernacchi called them 'three Polar knights', a description which fitted the chivalrous vision of Markham. More prosaically, the stoker Bill Lashly wrote in his diary: 'It is to be hoped they will have a pleasant and successful trip and come back safe.'

Markham would have been pleased had he witnessed his knights depart. The men were strung out in single file, a line of dark shapes on an unending white landscape, trudging manfully forward like a column of crusaders embarking on some noble cause. Even the unpredictable dogs performed reasonably well in the early days and Scott, encouraged by their progress, increased the animals' loads. At times the three caught up and passed Barne's support party, who travelled without skis and stumbled along in soft snow at little more than one mile an hour.

Half the support party returned on 13 November after celebrating a new 'furthest south' of 78° 55' S, a few miles beyond Borchgrevink's record established a few years earlier. Two days later and a little earlier than anticipated, Scott took the critical step of sending the remainder of Barne's team back to *Discovery*. The extra weight which was now placed on their sledges, though they did not fully realise it, inevitably restricted the ultimate length of the journey.

When Barne turned for home on 15 November, Scott, Wilson and Shackleton were alone on the Barrier with around 80 days of food, enough to sustain up to 12 weeks of man-hauling. As far as the eye could see, the land ahead was unremittingly flat, like being at sea, with a chain of mountains plainly visible off to the west. The fond hope was that smooth Barrier plain stretched all the way to the Pole.

The three men made an unlikely team. Shackleton, the determined adventurer eager to make a name for himself, was in sharp relief to the sensitive and insecure Scott, while Wilson, thoughtful, calming and

Southern Party: (l–r) Shackleton, Scott and Wilson in November 1902 before establishing a record 'furthest south'.

exercising a firm moral leadership, was the solid emotional prop on whom they both leant.

Scott, quick-witted and analytical, was accustomed to the unquestioning obedience of naval routine but unaccustomed to leadership. An orthodox character, Scott was at his best following carefully laid plans, but less sure-footed when circumstances demanded improvisation. He concealed his doubts and uncertainties well and rarely, if ever, shared his apprehension with others.

Shackleton, by contrast, was a more self-confident, strong-willed character from the less formal merchant marine. He relished challenges, and improvisation came more naturally to the inventive and spontaneous Shackleton. While his mood could change in an instant, Shackleton could never hide his true feelings. 'His was no poker face,' a colleague once remarked.

Shackleton was also a natural fighter, afraid of nothing and no one. Rank or status mattered little. According to Bernacchi, Shackleton was a buccaneer in some ways but dominating, truculent and challenging in others. 'He could be very unpleasant if he were attacked,' Bernacchi recalled.[2]

Scott, uncertain of himself in an alien world, sensed a rival and Shackleton sensed a weak leader. In the middle sat the reassuring presence of Wilson, a wise counsel untroubled by Shackleton's ambition or the pressure of leadership felt by Scott.

Overlaying the personality differences was the question of both Shackleton and Wilson's health. Only Scott, a physically strong, broad-shouldered figure of great determination, could lay claim to a clean bill of health as the men took their first steps into the wilderness.

Shackleton's condition, as Wilson had spotted, was open to question even before departure. It was noticeable how easily Shackleton had tired after even short journeys onto the ice and there were other signs of potential weakness. Wilson was surprised how Shackleton had lost weight on one straightforward trek to lay supply depots in the spring. Then, only four days after leaving *Discovery* on the march south, Shackleton developed a persistent and annoying cough.

Nor was Wilson entirely free from problems. His first attempt to join *Discovery* had been turned down because he had barely recovered from a debilitating bout of tuberculosis which left him with permanent lung damage. His case was not helped when he arrived for the Naval Board medical examination with an arm in a sling after picking up a serious infection while working on cadavers in a hospital. But Scott liked what he saw in the quietly determined Wilson and insisted on taking the young surgeon. Wilson had gone south, regarding Antarctica as 'kill or cure' for his health.

Scott chose his companions largely on sentiment, picking Wilson because of their friendship and choosing Shackleton largely on Wilson's recommendation. Yet there were other more suitable men available, particularly the experienced Armitage, Bernacchi and Koettlitz. There were also other choices, principally from the mess deck, where there was an assortment of muscular, disciplined and dependable characters. Among the tough, resourceful seamen were Crean, Evans, Lashly, Quartley, Wild and Williamson but Scott appears never to have looked beyond Wilson and Shackleton.

The party's difficulties began to emerge soon after parting company with Barne. Soft snow, caused by relatively high temperatures, combined with the heavily laden sledges to make the going very tough. Wilson reported aching knees and tight hamstrings as the strain of daily marching took its toll. The skis, which might have eased his aches, were packed on the sledge.

It was also apparent that the dogs were struggling from a combination of poor management and growing hunger. Less than a fortnight into the march Scott reported the animals were 'pretty done' and shortly afterwards noticed that the dogs 'seemed to lose all heart'.

The fundamental weakness was that Shackleton, Scott and Wilson had no understanding of dogs and no means of remedy. The dogs were working animals, a concept largely unknown to all three men who came from a society where dogs were pampered as pets and often treated better than children.

The other glaring weakness was the failure to include a fully qualified dog driver in the party. Bernacchi, writing years after the expedition, summed up the serious flaw: 'Possibly the appointment of two or three men to specialise in dog driving would have lessened our transport inefficiency.'[3]

Scott saw the vulnerability too late and had addressed the problem only weeks before the departure of the southern party. His remedy was to order Shackleton to take charge of the animals.

Shackleton was a poor choice as dog trainer. As someone who always needed immediate results, Shackleton lacked the patience needed to train animals and veered from friendly persuasion to vicious use of the whip in the slim hope of getting the best from the animals. He was perplexed when the dogs did not respond.

Training dogs is more art than science, and Shackleton had no feel for the task. It never occurred to him, for example, that working dogs become easily discouraged if their loads are too heavy or why it takes time to mould dogs into efficient working teams. Or that dogs and skis work together in harmony where the average speed of a human gliding over the surface comes close to matching the natural trotting speed of a dog.

A more qualified eye would have recognised the perturbing signs when Shackleton took the dogs onto the ice for a few trial runs in the weeks before heading south. The results were mostly disappointing and summed up by Wilson after one trip when he described two of the underperforming animals as 'sooners' – because they would do anything sooner than pull. Shackleton's frequent complaint was that the dogs 'refused to pull', without ever understanding why.

Bernacchi watched it all unravel in confusion but was in no doubt about the effectiveness of taking sensibly managed dogs. No polar expedition, he declared, should venture onto the ice with fewer than 100 to 200 trained dogs, which he estimated could travel up to 40 to 50 miles (64–80 km) a day, depending on the size of their loads. Generations of man-haulers on average found 10–15 miles (16–24 km) was near the limit or about a fifth of a good day's run with dogs. Mismanagement of dogs, Bernacchi concluded, was a weakness of all British explorers, and added:

'The unreasonable prejudice against them has led to suffering and hunger, heroic deeds and death.'[4]

Frank Debenham, the geologist who served on Scott's last expedition, was another who observed the disappointing struggle between man and beast in the Antarctic and wrote: 'The fact of the matter is that neither Scott nor Shackleton, the two great exponents of man-hauling, understood the management of sledge dogs.'[5]

In fairness, it was not fully appreciated that the dogs on the southern journey were badly underfed. The feed, a Norwegian dried codfish mixed with biscuit, had been soiled during *Discovery*'s voyage south. At a moment when the animals needed the best feed possible, they were eating a mouldy and inadequate mixture which left them hungry and disgruntled.

The animals were also eating the wrong food. At least half the diet of a dog working in a very cold climate should be fat. During the winter the dogs had eaten copious amounts of fatty seal meat but the mixture of codfish and biscuit contained barely any fat. One night a desperately hungry animal broke loose and devoured enough seal meat to feed the men for a week.

Hunger was also starting to afflict the men as well and the pace of the march began to drop. After one arduous day of struggle in soft snow, the party had advanced only 3 miles (5 km) south and drastic measures were needed. Scott decided to split the loads and to relay the sledges, the torment of taking half the weight forward and returning for the other half – thus travelling 3 miles for every mile advanced.

The outcome was dramatic, with the average distance covered halving from 10 to only 5 miles (8 km) a day. A cache of supplies – Depot A – was built to lighten the sledges but the pulling, according to Shackleton, was still 'trying work'.

Shackleton, still troubled by the cough, was a compelling influence whose determination set a formidable example. In Scott's words, Shackleton was 'bent forward with his whole weight on the trace' in a gritty show of strength. 'In spite of his breathless work,' Scott added, 'now and again he would raise and half turn his head in an effort to cheer on the team.'

At night they polished off their modest dinner wishing for more and huddled together for warmth. On occasions they read aloud from Darwin's *On The Origin of Species*, an appropriate choice when the survival of the fittest was so apposite. At times they skipped a midday meal to save food. A laconic Shackleton wrote: 'Read some Darwin for lunch.'

Ahead lay the horizontal plain of the Barrier and to the right on the western horizon an increasingly clear range of mountains, rising well above

10,000 feet (3,000 m), was coming more sharply into focus. Behind the men, the three distinctive landmarks in the vicinity of *Discovery* – Mount Erebus, Mount Terror and Mount Discovery – began to shrink and fade from view. 'Slowly but surely we are finding out the secrets of this wonderful place,' Shackleton wrote.

But the combination of hunger, relaying the sledges and handling the weaker dogs was slowing the march to a crawl. In early December, less than three weeks after separating from Barne, Scott recorded that 'we find difficulty now in gaining even four miles a day'. Hopes of a significant southern latitude were slowly evaporating.

Skis were tried and discarded, Wilson was suffering the aggravating pain of arthritis and some of the weakened dogs could scarcely walk. The hunger intensified. 'Could do good feed,' Shackleton wrote abruptly one night.

The first dog died on 9 December and by 13 December the faltering pace had dropped further. The men, still relaying the sledges, advanced just 2 miles (3 km) south in treacherously soft snow after another draining day of hard labour which pushed them to the limit. 'We cannot go on any more like this ... tired with hauling,' Shackleton scribbled.

Trudging slowly forward without skis, Scott reported that the heel of the advanced foot was never planted beyond the toe of the other. 'We do little more than mark time' he added as they struggled through patches of soft snow. Even the comfort of sharing a few consoling words with each other to break the monotony was impossible since the relentless howl of Antarctic winds drowned most conversations, leaving them alone to contemplate the daily grind.

The loads were eased a little more on 14 December when a second depot – Depot B – was built. Ahead the Barrier remained much the same, but the magnificent line of mountains, some now stretching up to 14,000 feet (4,250 m), was starting to turn directly into their path.

A month's gruelling toil had reduced men and dogs to shambling wrecks and yielded a paltry distance of little more than 100 miles (160 km) south, though the relay work meant they had travelled about three times that distance.

Across the continent, Nordenskjöld had wrapped up a major sledging trip along the Antarctica Peninsula at the same moment Scott, Wilson and Shackleton left *Discovery*. Nordenskjöld's three-man party, taking two sledges and five dogs, covered almost 400 miles (600 km) in just 33 days. The assistance from the dogs was 'immense' according to Nordenskjöld.

Food now haunted Shackleton, Scott and Wilson. It was decided to cut back on rations to prolong the march and in his diary Shackleton devoted a whole page to the theme of 'Desire' which was simply a 'wish list' of sirloin steak, crisp fried bread, jam pastries and porridge.

Breakfast was a mug of chopped bacon and biscuit and lunch restricted to biscuits and hot chocolate. At night they managed a mixture of pemmican, bacon, biscuit and cheese and a protein additive called 'plasmon'. It is likely they were consuming little more than half the 5,000–6,000 calories needed daily for the punishing exertion of man-hauling. In fact, they were burning up the reserves of fat. Scott noted in his diary that the men were passing from 'the hungry to the ravenous'. At night they each dreamed of feasts they would never eat.

By 16 December, after a terrible month of slog, the drudgery of relaying the sledges was ended. A depot of dog food was left and the men began the grim process of slaughtering the weaker animals to feed the strongest. Scott, a sensitive man who went cold at the sight of blood, left the butchery to Wilson and Shackleton. One day a dog dropped dead in the harness.

Pushing on through 81°, each man pulling the equivalent of around 170 lb (75 kg), the party was plodding south at less than a mile an hour. 'Either the surface is extraordinarily bad or we are growing weak,' Scott wrote.

Shackleton's calculation was that, at best, they could continue south only for another three weeks before turning for home. All hope of reaching 85° was long forgotten and by now 82° was probably the limit of their endurance.

A more disturbing problem emerged on 21 December when Wilson, conducting his routine medical checks, found signs of scurvy in Shackleton. Wilson quietly told Scott that Shackleton's gums were inflamed, an early symptom of the disease. But Shackleton was not told. A few days later both Wilson and Scott were showing the same angry gums.

The three men were already well into the second stages of scurvy. The fatigue and aching muscles that troubled them from the earliest days, which they put down to the rigorous demands of man-hauling, were the initial signs of scurvy. The inflamed gums and noticeably more painful joints, already apparent in all three, were symptomatic of the second stage. The onset of the third stage, involving severe pains in the muscles and bones, loosened teeth, spontaneous haemorrhaging and outbreaks of gangrenous ulcers, was a matter of time.

Wilson's discovery was no surprise. Scurvy had been apparent among *Discovery*'s personnel in the weeks before the southern journey began and Scott, Wilson and Shackleton carried early stages of the disease on their first steps onto the Barrier.

Scurvy is caused by a lack of vitamin C, which is found mainly in fresh fruit and vegetables and – in lesser quantities – in fresh meat. Humans are among the few species which cannot store vitamin C and scurvy emerges slowly after about 6–10 weeks without fresh sources of the vitamin. Shackleton, Scott and Wilson had been on the march for seven weeks before Shackleton's gums betrayed the party's first signs of problems.

However, the southern party was not alone in not being able to identify the causes or treat the symptoms. Vitamin C's crucial role in preventing scurvy was not discovered until the early 1930s, although it had cursed travellers from the Ancient Greeks and Egyptians onwards.

The disease took a major grip in the late Middle Ages as sailors began to travel further from land and essential sources of the vitamin. Estimates suggest up to 2 million seamen died from scurvy in the early years of global discovery between 1500 and 1700. Sir Richard Hawkins, the Elizabethan mariner, called it the 'plague of the sea'. A more modern verdict is that scurvy was probably the largest occupational disease in history.

Some blamed poor hygiene and lack of exercise, while others thought it stemmed from contaminated food, especially meat. Prescribing lemon juice and fresh vegetables to sailors as far back as Elizabethan times showed that science was edging closer to a solution, although the navy's later switch to lime juice was less effective because the vitamin C content in limes is lower.

Surprisingly, none of the British naval expeditions to overwinter in the Arctic alongside the Inuit people in the 1820s ever pressed hard enough to discover why the local population, whose diet was largely raw meat, fish and blubber, never suffered from scurvy. There are no fresh vegetables or fruit at high northern latitudes, but the connection between the native diet and the absence of scurvy was never made.

Both Armitage and Koettlitz, helped by their time in the Arctic, saw fresh meat as the likely antidote. Koettlitz, in fact, had repeatedly urged Scott to slaughter seals for fresh meat during *Discovery*'s early days but his pleas fell on deaf ears because of the unpleasant taste. 'He more or less pooh-poohed it,' Koettlitz explained.[6]

Shackleton, too, favoured eating fresh meat, even if he did not fully understand the importance. Shortly after *Discovery*'s arrival at McMurdo Sound, he advised Scott to serve freshly killed seal and ordered the cook to make the seal steaks more appetising for the sceptical crew. Henry Brett, the surly New Zealand cook, objected and in retaliation produced badly overcooked steaks, not realising that overcooking killed off much of the vitamin C.

Discovery's diet since the men first arrived in the south was notably deficient in vitamin C, relying instead on tinned meats, fruit and vegetables. The canning process had robbed the food of its vital vitamin content and as winter gave way to spring, scurvy was slowly beginning to take hold throughout the crew.

Matters came to a head six weeks before the southern party's departure when Armitage returned from a sledging trip with several of his men showing clear signs of the disease. Scott was away at the time, but Armitage knew that men on the Jackson–Harmsworth expedition to Franz Josef Land who had eaten polar bear steaks had somehow escaped scurvy. He ordered Koettlitz to examine every member of the ship's company and was horrified at the grim results. 'I found that practically everybody, officers and men, were tainted with the disease, of course myself included,' Koettlitz wrote.[7]

Armitage, who had been somewhat marginalised by Scott, saw the looming health crisis as a means of imposing his authority on affairs and ordered a radical rethink of the diet. He instructed Brett – 'a wretched specimen of humanity' – to serve seal steaks every day and meals from tinned food to be curtailed. Lime juice was placed on mess tables at meal times. It was a wise move because a vitamin C intake has almost immediate results. Within weeks Bernacchi said that symptoms of the disease had almost disappeared. But it had not been eradicated.

While the southern party took some seal cuts on the march, the meat had been pre-cooked and the level of vitamin C was much reduced. Instead, the core diet was pemmican, a concentrated mix of dried meat and fat. It was boiled and mixed with biscuits and chunks of bacon or slices of seal to create a thick porridge-like substance called 'hoosh'. Pemmican 'hoosh' contained virtually no vitamin C.

By Christmas Day the three men were inching towards 82° and shared a brief moment of respite in the splendid isolation. At breakfast they gorged on seal's liver and bacon and enjoyed the rare indulgence of a hot lunch. They were so invigorated by a full stomach that the daily march extended to 11 miles (17 km), the best for some time. At night, the 'hoosh' was so thick a spoon would stand up in it.

Shackleton rounded off proceedings with a flourish by producing a small plum pudding which he had hidden in a spare sock. 'It was a glorious surprise to them,' he added. For once they went to sleep without discussing food. The relief did not last.

After some debate in the tent, it was decided they would turn for home three days later on 28 December, having crossed 82° S. Shackleton, who had finally been informed about his scurvy, explained: '... I have slight scurvy signs. It will not be safe to go farther.'[8]

chapter 9

A Beeline

The 82° parallel was passed, as anticipated, on 28 December with the men in rapid decline. Fatigue was matched by ever-present hunger, a noticeable loss of weight and the alarmingly clear symptoms of scurvy. Wilson, struck down with a severe attack of snow blindness, was marching blindfolded but remembered that, appropriately, 28 December was Innocents' Day. 'We have almost shot our bolt,' Scott wrote. But they did not turn for home.

Scott decided to press on south, probably because he wanted something more than 82° S to show for the colossal effort. He was determined to make one last push towards the steeply rising chain of mountains to the south and west. Knowing that the end was not far, he named a twin-peaked massif, which soared to over 14,000 feet (4,250 m), after his patron Markham and a small collection of peaks on the distant horizon after the generous Longstaff.

A blizzard struck on 29 December confining the men to the tent. It was a setback which worried Shackleton and Wilson, who both recognised there was no time to spare if they were to get back safely to *Discovery*.

Conditions next day were slightly better, but instead of marching due south, Scott took the group south-west towards the mountains. The scientist lurking in Scott wanted to pick up a few geological specimens, even at the risk to the return march.

However, they were halted in their tracks by insurmountable pressure ridges and crevasses around the chaotic jumble of ice where the Barrier ice collides with the solid mass of mountains. At lunch a sighting placed the men at 82° 15' S. It should have been their 'furthest south' but still Scott was not satisfied.

Taking one last gamble, Scott left Shackleton behind in the tent while he and Wilson ran to the south for one last sighting. In thick, blowy weather, with visibility down to a few yards, the gamble failed. 'We saw nothing,' Wilson reported.

Afraid of getting lost in the white-out, the pair stopped at a spot they calculated to be 82° 17' S, the expedition's 'furthest south'. It was little more than 2 miles (3.5 km) beyond the spot where they left Shackleton. (More recent studies suggest that the 'furthest south' was more likely to have been 82° 11' S.)[1]

Why Shackleton was not permitted to share in the modest advance of 2 miles beyond the last camp is not clear. Although he was clearly weak, there was no evidence that he could not walk or that anyone was needed to 'guard' the isolated little camp. Nor is there any clear evidence that Scott deliberately wanted to exclude Shackleton from sharing the honour of reaching the record southerly latitude. However, it was a clumsy decision and little consolation that a nearby gap between the mountains was named Shackleton Inlet.

The men rose on 31 December and took their last sighting of the land to the south through a misty haze of low-lying cloud. Straining their eyes between breaks in cloud some new mountainous features could be made out as far south as 83°, though the route towards the Pole itself remained unresolved.

The anticlimax was acute. Scott, with his ambitions thwarted, wrote of a 'deep sense of disappointment' at not getting further south. A more dispassionate Wilson celebrated the 300 miles (480 km) of new territory surveyed for the first time, but admitted that 83° was not a good record in the quest for the Pole, which lay undisturbed more than 550 miles (880 km) across the unknown.

Shackleton was more philosophical. It was, he wrote, a 'wonderful place and deserves the trouble it takes to get here'.

Turning north on 31 December 1902 to repeat the hard-won steps was a slog from the start and began with an unfortunate incident for Shackleton. At the end of the first day's march north he knocked over the boiling pot of 'hoosh' and was forced to scrape the contents off the dirty floorcloth of the tent. Hungry men are not choosy and with *Discovery* some 280 miles (450 km) to the north, every mouthful would count.

The first goal was Depot B, the hoard of supplies left 100 miles (160 km) to the north. The men carried about 14 days' food, which demanded travelling at least 7 miles (11 km) a day. Stronger, well-fed men would have found it a comfortable target, but 7 miles a day was now the very best they could hope to advance and the delay in turning left the party with little margin for safety in case of navigational error or blizzards pinning them in the tent for days. The return would be touch-and-go and finding the depot was critical.

Without fully realising the significance, Scott had marked the provision depot with a single black flag planted on a mound of snow in the level field of ice, like an isolated marker buoy at sea. On the flat Barrier surface there were no obvious geographical features for guidance and the group was heavily reliant on picking up the tracks made on the outward march. The solitary flag, said Scott, was a 'very small spot on a very big ocean of snow'.

It was another error of judgement which should have been rectified by consulting Armitage and Koettlitz before setting out. In Franz Josef Land, as a matter of routine, depots were flagged with a multiple collection of markers on bamboo poles planted in a line in either direction away from the cache. The risk of missing the depot in poor weather was greatly reduced but somehow Scott never adopted the idea.

However, the urgency of their position seemed to escape Scott. Soon after starting back, he ordered another detour to pick up geological samples and insisted that the skis be dumped on a sledge, adding more weight to be dragged.

Speed and the need to extend the daily marches were required, but exhaustion meant they were capable of hauling only for six or seven hours a day at little more than a mile an hour. They could expect no help from the wretched dogs, who were now on their last legs. In Wilson's words, the dogs were now 'only a hindrance'.

Just 13 animals remained at the start of the return march and within a week only five were left, trailing forlornly alongside the man-haulers. The sorry mismanagement was complete when some of the doomed dogs, with only a few days to live, were placed on a sledge to be carried as yet more extra weight. Even as the dogs were slaughtered, the party defied all the basic instincts of human survival by not eating the animals. At the back of their mind was the belief the dogs had been poisoned and conventional wisdom was that tainted meat caused scurvy.

Taking advantage of the strong winds, the tent floorcloth was rigged as a makeshift sail. Initially it helped to propel them along, but they were at the mercy of the variable wind direction and they were soon hopelessly lost in the gloomy haze of a white-out. With food short and the depot flag no more than a dot on the dismal landscape, Scott feared they would miss the depot in the overcast conditions. He reported: 'We cannot now be far from our depot, but then we do not exactly know where we are.'[2]

Next day, as Scott was taking a sighting, a break in the misty blur miraculously threw up the welcome sight of a black speck in the distance.

Seconds later the mist descended again, wiping out the sight of the flag. Scott would have missed the depot had he looked up at a different moment.

A few hours later the men walked into the depot and hurriedly devoured a huge steaming pot of 'hoosh'. It was a temporary relief, though, as not even a full stomach could disguise their worsening condition. Shackleton was now coughing up blood.

Shackleton's deterioration was starkly apparent as the march north resumed. His gums were swollen and dark and he was increasingly short of breath. An alarmed Wilson pulled Scott aside and reported that Shackleton was 'decidedly short-winded and coughing constantly'. For the first time, Wilson sensed that 'Shackles' might not pull through.

Wilson's diagnosis galvanised Scott. He decided they must make a beeline for the next depot, 'now that human life is at stake.' Shackleton's version of events was that he was 'not very well'. A few days later, as his condition deteriorated, Shackleton was more realistic and admitted that his coughing had become 'more severe and haemorrhage had started.'

Shackleton, to his utter despair, could not pull, leaving the entire burden of around 525 lb (250 kg) to be hauled by the increasingly weary Scott and Wilson. At best, all he could manage was to boil a pot of pemmican at night. It was around 150 miles (240 km) to *Discovery*.

Shackleton trundled alongside the sledges one day with the words of Tennyson's *Ulysses* running through his head. Tennyson, with his melancholic genius for giving voice to personal grief, was a fitting choice for the grim struggle. Perhaps the words that most readily came to mind were those with the same rhythmic beat as the daily march itself: 'To strive, to seek, to find and not to yield'.

Shackleton, weak, breathless and hungry, was in deep trouble and Scott's options were fading as he watched the decline. Abandoning Shackleton was out of the question. But so, too, was carrying the added weight of an incapacitated man. The only realistic option, Scott recognised, was the suicidal labour of relaying. 'We could only carry him by doing relay work and I doubt if Wilson and I am up to covering the distance in that fashion,' he wrote in his diary.

In a mood of mounting panic, everything but essentials was dumped, including two sets of skis. The third set, said Wilson, was kept for 'emergencies' and packed on the sledge. Next day the last two dogs were slaughtered and the fresh meat left behind in the snow. Shackleton, who accepted the general view that scurvy was caused by tainted meat, said it would be 'madness' to eat dog flesh.

All three were now plumbing reserves of resolve and spirit. But Shackleton, as the weakest, was also drawing heavily on the strength of his companions. 'Captain Scott and Dr Wilson could not have done more for me than they did,' Shackleton wrote. 'They were bearing the brunt of the work and throughout the difficulties and anxieties of such a time showed ever cheery faces.'

That night a breathless Shackleton barely slept and was engulfed by what Scott called 'violent paroxysms of coughing'. Shackleton, by contrast, reported only being 'on the sick list' or that he had to 'go easy' because of spitting up blood. On 18 January he collapsed after only a few hours on the march and Scott was forced to camp early.

Shackleton was now surviving on willpower alone. He was still keeping up with the target of 7 miles (11 km) a day, a remarkable effort for someone who, in Scott's words, ended each day 'panting, dizzy and exhausted'.

Inwardly, though, the humiliation of being reduced to a passenger was wounding to Shackleton's pride. Scott said he took the breakdown 'much to heart' and noted how his naturally energetic companion found it difficult to take things easy. 'He feels his inactivity very keenly,' Scott wrote.

It needed an unexpected twist to help revive Shackleton. On 21 January, after weeks of slogging through the soft snow, he was given the remaining set of skis, which transformed his movement. It may have saved his life, too. Instead of sinking into the yielding surface, Shackleton was suddenly able to glide along more freely and although he was no expert on skis, it made travelling significantly easier. After watching Shackleton's progress, Wilson admitted that he now regretted dumping the other sets of skis.

Next day, helped by a strong following wind, the group managed a remarkable 10 miles (16 km) and a few days later spirits were lifted by a welcome sight. Through breaks in the mist and clouds they could pick out the faint wisps of smoke rising from Mount Erebus.

By 26 January, nearly four weeks after beginning the retreat, their luck changed when they suddenly ran into tracks made by one of Barne's surveying parties. At one point Barne's six-man group had been little more than 40 miles (64 km) away on the vast Barrier landscape and they missed each other by a matter of days.

The tracks, coupled with the increasingly clear sight of the mountains near McMurdo Sound, instilled fresh hope. Two days later the group walked slowly into Depot A where they plundered the provisions with unrestrained delight. For the first time in nearly two months the threat of hunger had finally disappeared.

But the extra food could not prevent Shackleton from collapsing. He was unable to move from the tent on 29 January and relieved for once to hear the howling blizzard which kept them pinned down for the day. 'There is no doubt Shackleton is extremely ill,' Scott wrote. Wilson said he was 'utterly knocked up' and 'quite unfit' to travel.

Shackleton was now on the brink and recalled years later hearing Wilson whisper to Scott that he would not survive the night. Shackleton was roused by the suggestion and woke next day in defiant mood. After being helped into his ski bindings, Shackleton drove himself forward like a man possessed, as if determined to prove Scott and Wilson wrong. Shackleton's sheer bloody-minded determination was astonishing.

Although the ship was near, Wilson still feared Shackleton would not survive a relapse. In an act of great kindness, the exhausted Scott and Wilson persuaded Shackleton to sit on the sledge and be carried along for a few hours while he recovered a little strength. With a strong following wind, Shackleton's sole task was to provide the 'brake' to prevent the sledge hurtling off their path.

While the indignity of being carried was humiliating, Shackleton had come to terms with the shame because, above all, he was a survivor. Getting back to *Discovery* alive was all that mattered.

At night Shackleton coughed up more blood while all three, now close to the limit of their endurance, summoned one final effort to make the last dozen or so miles to the ship. Scott's ankles were very swollen, Wilson was limping badly and Shackleton was gasping for every breath. 'We are as near spent as three persons can well be,' Scott wrote in his diary.

The morning of 3 February broke in brilliant sunshine and the rock-hard surface made the going a little easier. After a few hours two dark specks were seen in the distance. At first it was thought they were penguins. Slowly the shapes materialised into the familiar figures of Bernacchi and Skelton, who had come out to meet them.

The sight of a bedraggled, frostbitten Shackleton, Scott and Wilson was a shock. Bernacchi said the long beards and hair, dirt and bloodshot eyes made them almost unrecognisable. 'They appeared to be very worn and tired and Shackleton seemed very ill indeed,' he added. Skelton described Shackleton as looking 'very weak & seedy'.

In 93 days of struggle, Shackleton, Scott and Wilson had covered a total of 960 miles (1,540 km), including the many miles relaying the sledges. Around 300 miles (480 km) of new territory had been surveyed to 83° S and the three men had penetrated further south than anyone before. The trail to the Pole, though not fully established, was opened for the first time.

A boisterous welcome of warm handshakes, raucous cheering and cheerful singing greeted the men as they stepped unsteadily onto *Discovery*. The ship was garishly decorated with flags and the crew climbed onto the rigging in traditional naval salute.

It was too much for Shackleton. He limped home some way behind Scott and Wilson, helped by Koettlitz and Royds. 'I turned in at once when I got on board, not being up to the mark after having a bath – that was the first for ninety four days,' he wrote. 'It is very nice to be back again; but it was a good time,' he reported.[3]

Shackleton made a valiant attempt to join the celebrations. He took his place at the wardroom table for a fine celebratory three-course dinner of soup, mutton and plum pudding, the first proper meal in three months. He did not have the strength to finish the first course.

chapter 10

Rejection

Nothing suffered on the three-month ordeal on the Barrier prepared Shackleton for the blow that awaited him on his return to the ship. Within two weeks of returning to *Discovery*, Scott ordered Shackleton to leave the Antarctic, expelled from the expedition like a feeble invalid. Even the shame of being carried on the sledge for a few miles paled into insignificance beside eviction.

Shackleton was profoundly shocked at the decision. In Bernacchi's words, Shackleton was 'deeply disappointed and would give anything to remain'. But Wilson, who had seen Shackleton's plight close up, sided with Scott. 'It is certainly wise for him to go home,' he wrote.

The southern party returned to find that *Discovery* was still locked firmly in miles of solid ice and a relief ship, the three-masted barque *Morning*, had arrived in McMurdo Sound. *Morning*'s task was to provide fresh supplies, deliver mail from home and deposit a scattering of new faces to replace a handful of men heading back after a single season.

Scott asked for volunteers to sail home on *Morning*, hoping to weed out the slackers and those he felt were not up to the task. To his relief, the majority of volunteers were men from the merchant service, who found the isolation and Scott's naval regime tiresome, without fully appreciating the wisdom of maintaining firm discipline and routine as a sensible precaution against boredom and inactivity.

Scott turned next to Shackleton, who was apparently making a good recovery from the southern journey. Koettlitz, as senior doctor, was formally asked to examine Shackleton. Scott, perhaps sensing a potential dispute in the offing, went to the unusual lengths of putting the request in writing.

After his experience on the Barrier, Scott had set new medical parameters for his executive officers which left Koettlitz with little room for manoeuvre. An officer, Scott insisted, should 'enjoy such health that [he] can at any moment be called upon to undergo hardships & exposure'. Scott's message was explicit: 'I do not think the health of an executive officer should be open to any doubt,' he said.

Koettlitz's diagnosis was mixed. Shackleton, Koettlitz decided, had 'practically recovered' from the effects of scurvy, helped by a regular diet of fresh seal meat. But, critically, he concluded: '... I cannot say that he [Shackleton] would be fit to undergo hardships and exposure in this climate.'[1] The problem with the breathing and coughing, said Koettlitz, was 'a sort of asthma'.

Wilson would later write that Shackleton's illness stemmed from a combination of poor weather and scurvy. The attacks of 'dyspnoea [shortness of breath], cough and blood spitting' were induced by the approach of a southerly blizzard,' he wrote in the *British Medical Journal*. Wilson also said that Shackleton's 'superabundant energy and untiring zeal for work' were partly responsible for the breakdown. 'He never, unless actually ordered to do so, would consent to save himself,' Wilson wrote, 'and this, however admirable in itself, is a bad trait in a scurvy patient.'[2]

Although Scott's new rules were an important insurance against further breakdowns, the same standard did not apply throughout the wardroom. Wilson, most notably, remained bedridden for a month with rheumatic pains and a niggling leg injury after returning from the Barrier. But he was not ordered home on *Morning*.

Shackleton, in his eagerness to join the southern party, had played into Scott's hands by concealing his coughing fits in the weeks before departure. What began as a minor irritation at night soon developed into a full-blown crisis which left Shackleton a passenger and potentially put the lives of all three men in danger.

Scott, rightly, sensed that Shackleton had deceived him. But so, too, had Wilson, a doctor who failed to reveal his suspicions about Shackleton's condition in the months before the men took on the Barrier. However, Scott never knew about Wilson's doubts.

Not that Shackleton was ever willing to discuss his health or allow himself to be examined. Had he been examined before leaving England, it is possible the 'sort of asthma' diagnosed by Koettlitz might have been detected and Shackleton, in all probability, would never have been allowed to join *Discovery*.

The reasons for Shackleton's aversion to doctors are unclear, except that they appear to have gone beyond the usual anxieties about medical examinations. Those with an aversion to doctors are often reacting to a personal trauma in early life or perhaps a distressing illness in a close relative. In Shackleton's case, it may be that his mother's mystery ailment, which confined her to the bedroom for over 30 years, was a contributory factor. Shackleton was at the formative age of 13 when his mother fell ill.

Bubbling beneath the surface was the uneasy relationship between Shackleton and Scott which had threatened to unravel at difficult moments on the return march. Scott could be a coldly unsympathetic character and referred to Shackleton in his southern journey diary as a 'lame duck' or 'our invalid' at a time when his companion's condition and the safe return of all three men demanded a more compassionate tone. Wilson, as unofficial mediator, once took Scott aside to deliver a few 'home truths' about the simmering tension between the two.

But Scott always insisted that it was purely on health grounds that Shackleton was sent home. He explained: 'It is with great reluctance that I order his return and trust that it will be made evident that I do so solely on account of his health and that his future prospects may not suffer.' Scott also separated Shackleton from the other 'crocks' he was sending back on *Morning* and added: '[Shackleton] is a very good fellow and only fails from the constitutional point of view.'[3]

Two other episodes have been cited to support claims of a deeper fracture in the relationship between Shackleton and Scott. However, the source was Armitage who, by the time he put pen to paper, had become an embittered and unreliable witness. He did not publish his version until more than 20 years after the event when Shackleton, Scott and Wilson were all dead.

According to Armitage, the first eruption occurred on the Barrier when Scott suddenly shouted in the direction of Shackleton and Wilson: 'Come here, you bloody fools.' Wilson calmly asked if Scott was referring to him and was told no. 'Then it must have been me,' said Shackleton. 'Right, you are the worst bloody fool of the lot and every time that you dare speak to me like that you will get it back.'

Armitage also stirred the controversy further by claiming to have challenged Scott's decision to remove Shackleton on health grounds. Scott, according to Armitage, replied: 'If he does not go back sick, he will go back in disgrace.'[4] According to Armitage, the decision encouraged Shackleton to return to the ice in an attempt to prove himself. Shackleton, said Armitage, intended to go south again 'to prove that he was a better man than Scott'.

However, Armitage was an unhappy and often unpopular figure who had clashed with Scott and never quite found his niche on the expedition.

Shackleton on board Morning *in 1903 after being invalided home from the Antarctic.*

Coming from the merchant service, he described himself as an 'interloper' in the strict Royal Navy environment imposed by Scott. Scott, in turn, was equally unhappy with Armitage and wanted to send him back on *Morning* with Shackleton. 'I absolutely refused and thus quite unconsciously spoilt Sir Clement Markham's dream – another Great Royal Naval Polar Expedition,' Armitage wrote many years later.

Although Shackleton was generally a popular character on *Discovery*, some were quietly relieved at his departure. The breezy exuberance and wisecracking, which some interpreted as shallowness, had worn thin at times.

Skelton, the engineer, grumbled about his 'gassing' and 'eye serving' and Ford admitted that Shackleton was not as highly regarded as Scott, Wilson and others in the wardroom. 'This I think was due to a certain lack of consistency in his character,' he explained. 'You did not know where you were with him as certainly as with the others.' According to Ford, Shackleton's early charm had become, in part, 'pose and showmanship'.[5]

It was an inconsistency captured by Hugh Mill who was fascinated by the contradictions in Shackleton's character which produced such different reactions in people. Mill found that Shackleton was capable of inducing 'dislike without making an enemy' and added: 'If Shackleton had lived in the sixteenth century he might have been knighted on the quarter-deck of a ship and in the greater swing of chances in those spacious days he might equally as well have been beheaded in the Tower.'[6]

Shackleton struggled to come to terms with the ignominy of being sent home. Having gone south with high expectations of making a name for himself, his pride was wounded and his reputation badly damaged. In a clumsily desperate attempt to avoid the inevitable he asked Ford to exchange places on the trip home. Ford's various duties, which included routine matters like keeping accounts and records, were clearly far less taxing than the more vigorous role of sledging and Shackleton hoped to stay at McMurdo Sound in a minor capacity to avoid the embarrassment of a berth on *Morning*. But Ford, a 23-year-old Londoner, was among the thousands of eager young men who had volunteered for *Discovery* and was not prepared to sacrifice his position for Shackleton. Ford went on to become the expedition's oldest surviving member.

The funereal pace of Shackleton's walk across the solid ice to *Morning* on 1 March suited the sombre mood of the occasion. The seamen, who liked his unconventional, informal style, scaled the rigging to give Shackleton an affecting and raucous send-off. 'I cannot write much about it, but it touched me more than I can say when the men came on deck and gave me 3 parting cheers,' he wrote.

Ferrar and Barne, who accompanied him on the long walk, noticed that even after a month's rest and good feeding, Shackleton was still 'shaky' on his feet. He stopped regularly to catch his breath. 'I went slowly,' Shackleton wrote, 'for I had only been twice out of the ship since I came back from the southern journey.'

Snow was falling and wind bit deeply into the spectators watching from the shore as *Morning* eased gently away from McMurdo Sound on 2 March 1903. Shackleton watched his companions slowly fade into the distance and broke down and cried.[7]

'Ah me it was a sad parting,' he wrote in his diary. 'I turned in and read for a bit but thoughts would go back to those I left on the floe.'

In London, Emily was unaware of events and still expecting Shackleton to be away for another year. Instead, she received a telegram from Shackleton in New Zealand which said: 'Broken down in chest returning southern sledge journey suffering scurvy and overstrain dont worry nearly well coming home'.[8]

chapter 11

Two Characters

The call of the Antarctic, like the mythological Sirens luring sailors to their doom, was never far from Shackleton's senses as he returned to England in June 1903. He was warmly embraced by a relieved Emily and the family, but his thoughts were already turning to how he might find his way back to the ice.

Shackleton, rested, fit and tanned after the long sea journey back to England, looked far from the forlorn figure invalided out of the Antarctic a few months earlier. At Sydenham he was greeted by a proud father, a tearful mother and a procession of high-spirited sisters all thrilled to see their favourite brother. 'The road was dotted with Shackleton sisters of all ages and sizes at various intervals,' Kathleen remembered. He kissed them all, one by one.

Emily was now prepared for marriage to her returning hero. After the death of her father, she was now a woman of independent means and in the rare position of earning more money than her future husband. The trust, which Charles Dorman left in his will, was worth £700 a year (nearly £40,000/€48,000 a year in today's terms) or nearly three times the £250 salary which Shackleton earned on *Discovery*.

How Shackleton planned to provide for his wife was a mystery. The sea remained the obvious choice and a return to a Union Castle liner was always a possibility if nothing else materialised. However, Shackleton had moved on and, with his natural instinct to look ahead rather than backwards, he searched for new opportunities.

Initially he hoped to return to the sea in a different guise. His plan was to sidestep the normal procedures and join the Royal Navy through a side entrance. Before leaving on *Discovery*, Markham had arranged for Shackleton to join the Royal Navy Reserve. What Shackleton now proposed was to transfer his rank into the Royal Navy proper with the assistance of Markham.

Markham turned to Lady Constance Barne, wife of an MP and mother of Michael Barne from *Discovery*, in the hope that she would use her circle of prominent friends to promote Shackleton's case for entry to the navy. It happened that Lady Barne knew Sir Evan MacGregor, the long-serving Permanent Secretary and most influential civil servant at the Admiralty. MacGregor had occupied the post for 23 years and was a man capable of pulling strings.

Lady Barne told MacGregor that Shackleton was a 'first rate man'. But MacGregor recognised the handiwork of Markham and stuck to procedure. The pair had crossed swords during the years of intrigue over *Discovery* and MacGregor was still hostile. Markham, he informed Lady Barne, was a 'pachydermous gentleman' and he rejected the appeal. Shackleton resigned from the Navy Reserve itself a year later.

Shackleton began to examine other possibilities, always mindful of a return to Antarctica. Even before arriving in England, Markham had written asking for his assistance in fitting out the relief expedition to help release *Discovery* from the ice of McMurdo Sound.

Markham, now 73 years old and under intense pressure over his handling of the expedition's affairs, was looking for all the support he could muster. The expedition had run out of money and he had badly misjudged the political mood when asking the Treasury to finance the second relief expedition to bring Scott home. Amid garish newspaper headlines claiming mismanagement and an extravagant waste of public funds, the cost to taxpayers of £45,000 (around £2.5 million/€3 million today) rankled with some.

Temperatures in London rose sharply as the increasingly belligerent Markham first sought £6,000, then £10,000 and eventually £12,000 of public money to liberate *Discovery*. The Treasury and the Admiralty, by now tired of Markham's bluster, took affairs into their own hands and assumed full command of the rescue.

Arthur Balfour, the Prime Minister, told the House of Commons that the government's confidence in the RGS and Royal Society had been 'rudely shaken' by the affair and that, in effect, ministers no longer trusted the figures given by the two societies. Markham's histrionics had played into the hands of his many enemies in Whitehall. Mill said Markham would have saved himself a 'world of trouble' if he been subtler in dealing with the government.

With *Morning* already in New Zealand being made ready to sail south again, the Admiralty moved quickly to ensure the operation was wrapped up as efficiently as possible by sending a second vessel to assist with the evacuation. *Terra Nova*, a sturdy Dundee whaler, was purchased to accompany the *Morning* and Shackleton was asked to serve as Chief Officer.

However tempting it was to turn the tables and sail to Scott's rescue, Shackleton resisted the Admiralty's offer. Perhaps it was Emily, who was unhappy that the voyage would disrupt their plans to marry in the spring of 1904, who influenced him. Or perhaps Shackleton was merely repaying his loyalty to the increasingly isolated figure of Markham. Shackleton was indebted to Markham and basked in the old man's praise. In one testimonial, Markham said Shackleton was 'admirably fitted for the leader of a Polar expedition' and possessed 'rare gifts of head and heart.'

In his loyalty to Markham, Shackleton also snubbed a personal appeal from Admiral Sir William Wharton, the Royal Navy's Hydrographer, to provide first-hand advice about *Discovery*'s predicament. But as a conciliatory gesture he agreed to travel to Dundee to assist with the outfitting of *Terra Nova*.

In the event, *Terra Nova* sailed in late August under the command of Captain Henry McKay, a hard-nosed veteran of 25 years in the whaling fleet and among the most experienced ice masters in the country. McKay was precisely the type of seasoned professional that Professor Gregory had in mind years earlier during the planning for *Discovery*. Markham had scuppered Gregory's proposal in favour of Scott's large naval-led operation and the irony was that McKay was now sailing to relieve Scott.

Another curiosity was that, with Markham in semi-disgrace and Scott stuck in the ice, Shackleton had emerged as official quasi-spokesman for the *Discovery* expedition. He was asked to deliver public lectures and write articles for magazines and soon found that he had stolen a little of Scott's thunder.

Shackleton slipped easily into the role as the public face of the expedition. He was a decent writer and lecturing was second nature. Audiences responded positively to his rich brogue and casual style of bringing the wonders of Antarctica to life. Few men had ever spoken in public about the continent and, with his knack of telling a good story, Shackleton soon found he was able to hold an audience.

Shackleton was also called upon to help tackle a gathering Antarctic crisis involving Nordenskjöld whose party was marooned after a relief ship – *Antarctic* – was crushed by the ice of the Weddell Sea and sank. The sinking left 20 crewmen stranded on a drifting floe and Nordenskjöld's party of six scattered across two sites on the Antarctic Peninsula.

As international rescue operations were hurriedly set in motion, Shackleton was asked to assist Lieutenant Commander Julian Irizar, the

Argentine naval attaché in London who had been placed in charge of the gunboat *Uruguay*, which was sent to snatch Nordenskjöld and the marooned sailors off the ice. *Uruguay,* in the skilled hands of Irizar, penetrated the same waters which had crushed *Antarctic* and successfully lifted all hands off the ice before returning in triumph to Buenos Aires. Shackleton's advice to Irizar is not recorded, but the inescapable lesson was that taking ships into the Weddell Sea was highly risky.

Although tasks like refitting *Terra Nova* and advising Irizar kept Shackleton occupied for a time, he was no nearer to finding a niche that would fulfil his twin ambition of making both money and a name for himself. Ideas came and went, but nothing tangible emerged.

Shackleton was slowly changing. At home, he was a restless, unfulfilled character with an uncertain flow of income and drifting towards the milestone of a 30th birthday with only a hazy vision of the future. The only certainty was the forthcoming marriage to Emily.

In contrast, the figure which Shackleton cut on the ice was noticeably different. On *Discovery* he was self-assured, assertive and determined, if sometimes a little too cocky for the more conservative types at McMurdo Sound. Not even the shame of being invalided out of the Antarctic had dented his confidence or self-belief. Shackleton on the ice was a different person from the man at home. He was comfortable in the wilds and it is no surprise that his attention was being drawn towards the place where he was at ease with himself. Or, as Emily later remarked: 'One must not chain down an eagle in a barnyard.'

In October he sensed an opportunity when he wrote offering help to Captain Joseph-Elzéar Bernier, a larger-than-life Canadian mariner who was putting together a bold plan to reach the North Pole in 1904. Bernier's scheme was a repeat of Nansen's daring journey in *Fram* a decade earlier which involved allowing his ship to become trapped in the ice and to drift across the Arctic Ocean in the currents before launching a dash for the Pole from a high latitude.

Shackleton saw the chance to assist and told Bernier that his experience on *Discovery* '... enables me perhaps to be of use'. The venture never quite materialised and Bernier did not try for the Pole in 1904. But his subsequent series of surveying voyages to the northern regions were a vital episode in asserting Canadian authority over vast tracts of Arctic territory.

As the Bernier initiative fizzled out, Shackleton looked for something else and took the plunge into the colourful and challenging world of journalism. In the autumn of 1903, Shackleton was appointed subeditor at the *Royal Magazine*, a monthly literary publication in Sir Arthur Pearson's stable of papers which included the popular *Daily Express*. It was his first full-time job on shore.

Journalism, like many other ventures, had been on Shackleton's mind for some time. The moderate success of *OHMS* and the enjoyment of editing the *South Polar Times* had whetted his appetite for the written word. Armitage recalled from conversations on *Discovery* that Shackleton had 'leanings' towards journalism. Writing to Mill years after, Armitage even suggested that he might have made a 'great journalist'.

The *Royal Magazine* was barely five years old when Shackleton persuaded the editor, Percy Everett, to give him a job. It was a nice, unchallenging semi-literary journal produced from comfortable offices in London's Covent Garden and aimed at a sober middle-class readership seeking carefully polished light entertainment.

However, Everett soon realised that Shackleton, for all his talent with words, was not cut out for the noble craft of journalism. 'His knowledge of the technical side of bringing out a magazine was nil,' he freely reported. But Everett, like so many others, was mesmerised by Shackleton's engaging personality, where an easy charm, warm-hearted friendliness and knack of spinning a good yarn somehow compensated for a lack of journalistic skill.

'He was the most friendly "hail-fellow-well-met" man I have ever come across,' said Everett. 'I am convinced that if he had gone to a stock-broker, a butcher, a carpenter, or a theatrical manager and asked for a job, he would have got it,' he explained. 'There was something about him that compelled confidence.'[1]

Shackleton was hardly prime material for the role of subeditor on a magazine. Subeditors are the worker bees of journalism and Shackleton, as Everett soon discovered, was no worker bee. 'Subs' are largely desk-bound and anonymous members of a journal's staff, routinely checking raw copy for grammar, spelling and facts, fitting together the jigsaw of columns, photographs and advertisements and writing thought-provoking headlines to entice readers. By tradition, 'Subs' are frustrated scribblers who rarely get the chance to write their own articles and are condemned to handle the work of better-known journalists, never receiving a byline of their own.

Shackleton was too much of a maverick for a desk job and more ideally suited to the job of roving or war correspondent. He appeared to be cut from the same cloth as another colourful Irishman, William Howard Russell of *The Times*, who became the first modern war correspondent in the Crimea and was described as a 'vulgar low Irishman [who] sings a good song, drinks anyone's brandy and water and smokes as many cigars as a Jolly Good Fellow.'

A flamboyant Russell-like existence was never possible on the *Royal Magazine* and Shackleton quickly became bored with the desk-bound routine nature of the job. At first he buckled down to standard back-room duties, but it was clearly not enough and he bristled with ideas, some original, some unconvincing and some impractical. But he was always stimulating. At times, work on the editorial floor came to a standstill as Everett and his staff sat in a circle listening intently to Shackleton pouring out tales of the ice. 'And no man told a story better,' Everett declared. 'He made us see the things he spoke of and held us all spell-bound.'

The honeymoon at the *Royal Magazine* lasted less than three months. 'Office work,' Everett recalled, 'was out of his line altogether.'

In November, Shackleton was invited to travel north to speak about *Discovery* at meetings of the Royal Scottish Geographical Society (RSGS) in Aberdeen and Dundee. Shackleton, with his new-found ability to captivate an audience, was very well received and created a strong impression. He also discovered that the post of Secretary to the RSGS had fallen vacant.

Although effectively another desk job, Shackleton was fired up by the challenge of the RSGS. It paid much the same as the *Royal Magazine* and necessitated moving to Edinburgh. But the role carried a lot more prestige than the magazine and Shackleton saw it as a stepping stone.

'I should think that I would do all right here [*Royal Magazine*], but the other job [RSGS] has the best position I think,' he told Emily on 2 December. Two days later he formally applied for the post.

The RSGS had established a fine reputation as an accomplished centre of geography in Scotland with a strong academic core in education, research and science. The prime mover in the creation of the RSGS 20 years before was John George Bartholomew, the distinguished cartographer and grandson of the founder of the well-known Bartholomew map-making company in Scotland. It was Bartholomew, called the 'Prince of Cartography', who in 1890 had first placed the name 'Antarctica' on maps.

Bartholomew wanted a fresh face at the Society and was keen on Shackleton who, he thought, would stir things up. He saw Shackleton as the sort of outsider who could revitalise an institution that had changed little over the years. He warmed to Shackleton's imposing presence, driving energy and was impressed by the glowing testimonials from influential people in London. These included Markham and Vice-Admiral Pelham Aldrich, the Admiralty grandee and veteran of the *Challenger* expedition.

Another important sponsor was Hugh Mill, a Scot and RSGS member with a solid background in geography and a paternalistic interest in the future of Shackleton. Mill shared Bartholomew's belief that Shackleton was the man to enliven Edinburgh.

Mill had become a key figure in Shackleton's life at this time. The pair chatted regularly over lunch in fashionable London clubs and Mill had become Shackleton's main confidant, offering wise words of encouragement and sound advice. He sensed that Shackleton was destined for great things and when he sounded out Shackleton, Mill detected that the restlessness and eagerness to make a mark had reached fever pitch. He, too, saw the RSGS as a stepping stone for his friend.

Mill took up Shackleton's cause with renewed zeal and even threatened to resign from the RSGS if they did not give him the job. He went further, exaggerating Shackleton's ability as a scientist. Mill, who had reported Shackleton sadly lacking on *Discovery*, told the RSGS that he was a 'painstaking scientific worker.'

Mill's embellishment was never exposed and in January 1904, Shackleton was appointed Secretary at the RSGS on a salary of around £200 a year (about £11,000/€13,000 today). On 10 January, a day before his official appointment, Shackleton delivered one of the Society's Christmas lectures and found that the audience 'quite fell in with all the jokes'. It was, he admitted, 'better than going to sea'.

Shackleton arrived like a hurricane into the sombre, sleepy atmosphere of the RSGS. 'Grave and ceremonial' Mill called the Society's two rooms on the ground floor of the imposing neo-Gothic red sandstone edifice of the National Portrait Gallery in Edinburgh's Queen Street. It was, Mill said, 'impossible to represent the RSGS Council in 1904 as smart and up to date'.

Society members, mostly dressed in traditional black coats, were astonished to see Shackleton stride into the offices wearing a light tweed suit and smoking a cigarette. Jokes were soon flying around a building more accustomed to the quiet hum of hushed reverential tones. 'There is a certain lack of humour,' Shackleton reported back to Mill. Ralph Richardson, who held the title of Honorary Secretary at the RSGS for 39 years, was typical of the Edinburgh elite who made up the society's membership. He was, said Mill, a man of 'slow humour'.

The RSGS in 1904 was functioning on much same the lines and with much the same membership as when it was founded by Bartholomew and Agnes Bruce, the eldest daughter of Dr David Livingstone. With his customary boundless energy, Shackleton set about the tasks of modernisation, increasing the membership, generating new sources of advertising revenue for the Society's *Scottish Geographical Journal* and stretching the horizons beyond the familiar territory of Africa where it was embedded. He amazed members by installing a telephone and buying a typewriter, and gleefully told Mill: 'You would have laughed had you seen their faces when the jangle of the telephone disturbed them.'

Shackleton revelled in the novelty of the role and the unfamiliar surroundings of Edinburgh. While things remained fresh, he was fully occupied and fully motivated. He became so involved that he asked Emily if they could postpone their honeymoon so that he could remain in Edinburgh. 'I think we would be happier in our own little home than out there,' he suggested.

He seemed capable only of looking ahead at the next adventure. On *Discovery*, Ford recalled how before travelling home on *Morning*, he collected a list of personal items from colleagues remaining at McMurdo Sound which he promised to send back on the next relief ship. 'As far as I know, not one of these commissions were executed,' Ford said. It is unlikely that he even remembered the list. Shackleton had a curious ability to both charm and hurt people without ever fully appreciating it. Both came easily to him because he lived for the moment and lacked the guile to conceal his true feelings. In the words of one associate, he had the 'artlessness of a child'.

In preparation for his marriage, Shackleton found a home at 14 South Learmonth Gardens in the western suburbs of Edinburgh. He called it a 'little house' but in truth it was a substantial terraced property of three floors and a basement, easily capable of accommodating the newly-weds and two servants. It looked across the fields to the distinctive spires of Fettes College and beyond to the broad stretches of the Firth of Forth.

For the moment, Shackleton was passionately in love, eager to immerse himself in the marriage. 'My whole heart and life is crying out for the loved one whom I shall see ...' he wrote a few days before the ceremony. On another occasion he mocked his characteristic shortage of money with the playful promise: '... my love is so strong that it will redeem the poverty of the rest of me.'

Emily, for all her outward independence, was a willing partner to Shackleton's whims and fancies. While never totally subservient, she readily placed her husband's peace of mind and keenness to get ahead before her own feelings. Another consideration was the nature of the relationship. Emily was strongly maternal and it appeared at times as though a mother-and-son bond existed between the two. In a letter to Mill, she admitted: 'He will always be a boy you know.'

She accepted her passive role with grace, partly because it was the convention of the time and partly because she, more than anyone, fully understood the futility of attempting to 'chain an eagle in a barnyard'. The honeymoon was duly shelved.

After seven years of fluctuating courtship, Ernest Shackleton married Emily Dorman in London on Saturday 9 April 1904 in the solemn setting of Christ Church, Westminster. Best man was Cyril Longhurst, secretary of the *Discovery* expedition, perhaps because Markham was indisposed. As the marriage vow was formally pronounced, he whispered an ironic pledge into Emily's ear: 'With all my worldly goods I thee endow'.[2]

Only a few days earlier, *Discovery* had come in from the cold by steaming into the New Zealand port of Lyttelton following the successful relief by *Morning* and *Terra Nova*. Dynamite had been used to release the ship from the ice of McMurdo Sound and Scott was saved the humiliation of having to abandon *Discovery*.

Shackleton was back at work in Edinburgh within two days of the wedding, driving the RSGS forward with familiar fervour and discovering that the Society opened the doors to more fashionable and influential circles. He found himself rubbing shoulders with Edinburgh society and an array of politicians, industrialists and academics. Among those he met were former prime minister and statesman Lord Rosebery and William Beardmore, one of Scotland's most powerful businessmen. In the words of Mill, his new-found acquaintances were people who 'held the keys to many locks'.

Shackleton, perhaps for the first time in his life, was truly content, having made the remarkable transition from junior officer on a passenger steamer to explorer and finally marrying the woman he loved. Marriage, he found, was everything he hoped for and the RSGS provided the exciting new challenge his restive temperament demanded.

The most significant event of the summer came in late July 1904 when Shackleton was at the centre of activities to welcome William Speirs Bruce back from a two-year spell on an RSGS-sponsored expedition to the Antarctic. Bruce's achievements were impressive and Shackleton saw the expedition as a model for his own ambitions.

Bruce was an intense, committed biologist with an equally serious devotion to the cause of Scottish nationalism. Short, dark and heavily bearded, Bruce was a fiery 37-year-old who cared little for self-promotion or the establishment in London. A close friend said he was 'as prickly as the Scottish thistle itself'. Where some men sought new territories or crossed oceans for personal glory and rich rewards, Bruce went to the ice for the cause of science. Reaching the Poles, he declared, was an 'athletic feat on the same level as an Olympic race or gymnastic performance'. He did not regard pole-hunting as 'serious scientific' work.

As a qualified naturalist and experienced traveller, Bruce had offered his services to the *Discovery* expedition. During the 1890s he had travelled on five separate voyages to the ice – including spells with Armitage and Koettlitz on the Jackson–Harmsworth expedition and on *Balaena* to the Antarctic – and was an ideal candidate for *Discovery*. He could also ski. But Markham was indifferent, perhaps because he was not a Royal Navy man. Bruce, irritated by the slight, launched his own private expedition in *Scotia* and pointedly named his enterprise the Scottish National Antarctic Expedition.

Scotia's two years in the Weddell Sea and along the Antarctic Peninsula proved highly productive. The Saltire flew proudly as Bruce discovered many miles of new coastline, conducted scientific studies, logged a remarkable 1,100 species and established a weather station on the small, remote Laurie Island in the South Orkney Islands. It was the Antarctic's first permanent scientific base and is still in operation more than a century later. But under the influence of Markham, none of the party ever received the prestigious Polar Medal from the RGS.

To Shackleton, Bruce had brought back far more than weighty scientific reports and an assortment of rocks and other specimens: he had demonstrated that it was possible for an individual to mount a small but effective expedition which could operate outside official channels and still deliver valuable results.

The most persuasive factor was that Bruce raised the money for the venture entirely from private sponsors. The funds for *Scotia*, Shackleton noted, came from prominent Scottish industrialists and philanthropists, precisely the sort of men he now met on routine RSGS business and the social circuit around Edinburgh.

Bruce's chief patrons were James and Andrew Coats, whose family created the thriving Coats cotton threads and textile business at Paisley. The wealthy Coats brothers had known Bruce for some years and readily donated £30,000 (over £1.7 million/€2 million today) to the expedition while others, mostly Scots, topped up the expedition funds to £36,000. Equally significant to Shackleton was that Bruce's undertaking cost less than a third of the *Discovery* expedition.

It was no surprise when Shackleton began to get increasingly restless in the months after Bruce's return from the ice. The enthusiasm of his early weeks at the RSGS had already begun to wane and his mind was elsewhere, partly dwelling on vague thoughts of finding a new expedition.

Money was an issue. The RSGS earnings were respectable but unexciting and Shackleton was also interested in exploring ways of following Bruce by unlocking the wealth of private benefactors.

The one reassuring factor was Emily. Marriage was enjoyable and the delayed honeymoon finally took place in the summer when the couple ventured to the Highlands to play golf at Dornoch. At the famously scenic course overlooking Dornoch Firth, they quickly discovered that golf is a game for patient souls and Emily soon emerged as the better player. A little later they also discovered that Emily was pregnant with their first child.

Duty called Shackleton to London in September to welcome Scott and his old *Discovery* pals back to Britain. It was 18 months since the uneasy parting in McMurdo Sound, though Shackleton held no grudges. During his absence, Shackleton had visited Scott's mother on several occasions. The past was the past and he now invited Scott to Scotland to address the RSGS.

Most reservations about *Discovery*'s cost and management were quietly forgotten in the following weeks, with Scott promoted to captain. Shackleton was among those to receive a medal from the RGS – he received the RGS Silver Medal – and Scott went to Balmoral to meet the King. In private, Scott was also contemplating a return to the Antarctic.

Shackleton remained a restless, indecisive figure who was uneasy about his work but unsure what to do next. His mood fluctuated and he told Scott that all ambitions of going back to the ice had been abandoned. 'I am married and settled down,' he told his old commander. 'I had thought of going on another expedition sometime but have given up the idea now as there seems to be no money about. It would only break up my life if I could stand it which Wilson says I could not.'[3]

How much weight Shackleton's declaration carried is hard to tell. At around the time of writing to Scott, Shackleton had quietly drawn up an outline plan for a new expedition. He circulated the four-page prospectus among a few potential investors but no one was prepared to put up any money.

Around this time some strange impulse persuaded Shackleton to try his hand at politics. On a flying visit to London in October, he was approached by the Liberal Unionist Party. Someone had witnessed his popular appeal in Edinburgh and natural ability to hold an audience, and Shackleton was flattered. After meeting Sir John Boraston, the influential party agent, he agreed to stand as an MP for the seat of Dundee at the next general election.

Shackleton was not the first to believe that an appealing persona and dazzling oratorical skills might easily be transferred to the political stage. His hubris was that he believed charisma alone would unlock the doors to Parliament. But Shackleton, showing little political judgement from the start, had blundered into a doomed cause and a doomed party careering towards one of biggest disasters in electoral history.

The Liberal Unionist Party was a breakaway splinter group from the traditional Liberal Party whose main policy platform was an implacable opposition to Home Rule for Ireland. Liberal Unionists – and close allies in the Conservative Party – believed that Home Rule was a dangerous first step along the road to breaking up the union of the United Kingdom. Many were also members of the landowning Ascendancy whose estates would be vulnerable under Home Rule.

As a minority party in a coalition with the Conservatives, the Liberal Unionists had kept the parties in power for a decade. But a sharper political mind than Shackleton's would have seen that the mood in the country was changing and Liberal Unionists, sucked into the maw of the Conservatives, lacked any clear identity. It was a problem joyously highlighted by Oscar Wilde in *The Importance of Being Earnest.* In an exchange between the redoubtable Lady Bracknell and an anxious Jack Worthing, Wilde wrote:

> *Lady Bracknell:* *(Sternly)* What are your politics?
> *Jack Worthing:* Well, I am afraid I really have none. I am a Liberal Unionist.
> *Lady Bracknell:* Oh, they count as Tories. They dine with us.

Complications over Shackleton's candidature arose from the start. The Party's committee in Dundee let slip that Shackleton had been adopted as their candidate before it was ratified by the ruling General Committee. In addition, he was mistakenly called 'Lieutenant Shackleton' or a 'Noted Naval Officer'. In fact, Shackleton had resigned from the Royal Naval Reserve months earlier and held no rank. For the moment Shackleton was happy to play along with the fiction.

Nor had Shackleton explained his decision to his employers at the RSGS. He naively believed he could stand as an MP while continuing to run the Society and struggled to understand why some members felt uneasy about the possible conflict of interests. Despite Shackleton's new broom, the RSGS remained an unashamedly conventional institution which cherished its independence from political influences. So far, the membership had only tolerated the change in style ushered in by Shackleton. It did not mean it was universally popular.

Others at the RSGS, like Bartholomew, were prepared to tolerate the maverick in Shackleton in return for a modernised Society. He instinctively knew that Shackleton was no ordinary pen pusher or committee man. 'I certainly do not sit in the office if there is nothing to do,' Shackleton wrote. To Bartholomew this was perfectly acceptable. As he explained:

'He [Shackleton] cannot settle to sedentary work but is splendid at bustling around.'

However, the most sensitive intervention came from Mill, his closest ally, who understood the inner workings of the RSGS. Mill felt Shackleton was putting his personal interests before the Society's and was not convinced he was serious about a career in Parliament. Mill also recognised that the controversy played into the hands of those opposed to Shackleton's reforms. On a personal note, Mill was an old-fashioned Liberal.

Shackleton tried to paint the picture of a committed political animal and claimed to have chosen to stand as an MP after 'careful thought and a conviction that what I uphold is right'. Mill was not persuaded. To Mill, Shackleton's attempt to be an MP was little more than 'a fine adventure and a tremendous lark'.

Mill was right. Shackleton saw the House of Commons as another quick route to the top. Shackleton could also point to other distinguished men without a political background who embraced the Liberal Unionist cause. Sir Arthur Conan Doyle made two unsuccessful attempts to become an MP and Henry Morton Stanley, Africa's most accomplished explorer, won a seat for the Liberal Unionists in 1895 without even bothering to canvass. Political work, said Stanley, involved 'lying, backbiting and wordy abuse'. Shackleton, in sympathy with Morton's haughty disdain, told Mill: 'I want to get on in any line I take up.'

Matters came to a head in January 1905 when the Liberal Unionists formally approved Shackleton as their candidate for the Dundee seat. Soon after, Shackleton tendered his resignation from the RSGS, though it would take fully six months for his departure to be settled.

Although Shackleton was now adopted as official candidate, he soon discovered that the Conservative–Liberal Unionist coalition was in no hurry to call an election. After 10 years in power, the party was deeply unpopular and suffering from major divisions over contentious issues like higher food prices because of tariff reforms. Prime Minister Balfour was also aware that the political landscape was changing with the growing working-class vote coalescing under the fast-emerging Labour Party. In the circumstances, Balfour intended to delay calling an election for as long as possible.

While his political ambitions were placed on hold, Shackleton became a father for the first time. Emily gave birth to a son, on 2 February, who was named Raymond. According to Shackleton, the child was blessed with 'great fists for fighting'.

The extra responsibility encouraged Shackleton to explore new opportunities in the commercial world in an attempt to secure his future.

Three generations. A rare photograph of Shackleton, taken around 1906, with his father Henry and his first child, Raymond. Courtesy: Athy Heritage Museum

He had taken his first steps into business in 1904 when, unknown to the RSGS, he joined a firm called the Tabard Cigarette and Tobacco Company. It was run through a tobacconist shop in New Burlington Street, off Piccadilly in London. His partner was Forbes Lugard Smith, a modest cigarette maker and shop owner. Smith was a fellow Freemason who, seeing the chance to exploit Shackleton's profile in Scotland, saw the potential of opening a branch at Lynedock Place in Edinburgh.

Shackleton, by now a heavy smoker, was mildly interested in the project at the outset and there was vague talk of floating the company on the stock market. But he never summoned his full energy to the venture and it remained a peripheral interest for a few years. The ambition of a stock-market flotation never materialised.

A possible re-entry to journalism was considered when Shackleton ran into Neils Grøn, a flamboyant Danish entrepreneur who was even more nakedly ambitious than Shackleton himself. The principal difference was that Grøn was more focused.

Grøn's latest venture was *Potentia*, an embryonic global press agency through which he promised to publish the unembellished 'truth' about great issues of the day to an expectant world. It all sounded too good to be true and it was.

A gullible Shackleton swallowed Grøn's sales patter and invested £500 (£29,000/€35,000 today) that he could barely afford in the venture. 'I feel it is going to be the great thing of the future,' he reassured Emily. He also persuaded others to invest small amounts, but *Potentia* never existed outside of Grøn's fertile imagination and the venture soon disappeared.

Shackleton was fascinated by the idea of becoming a successful businessman, but he lacked the entrepreneurial vision to find the right proposition or suitable partners. He was also afflicted by chronic impatience which meant he sought instant returns from any new venture and was baffled when the money failed to come rolling in.

He was, however, endlessly persuasive. Among those attracted to Shackleton's dreamy notions was Dr Charles Sarolea, the Belgian Consul in Edinburgh and first Professor of French at Edinburgh University. Sarolea was engaged to Julia Dorman, Emily's elder sister, who was now in her mid-40s and 10 years older than Sarolea. He sensed that Shackleton was neither happy nor fully appreciated in Edinburgh and needed new goals. To Sarolea, Shackleton was a 'lion in a cage' and full of 'inexhaustible animal spirits'.

Sarolea was an eloquent Europhile, a suave and well-connected academic with a fondness for self-publicity and the byzantine intrigue of international affairs. He wrote extensively and claimed to have knowledge of 20 languages. *Potentia*, with its hint of influence, appealed to Sarolea and he was content to introduce Shackleton to his circle of friends which included King Leopold of Belgium.

Shackleton by now was looking far beyond the horizons of *Potentia*. Watching Sarolea glide effortlessly through the social circuit encouraged him to begin sounding out more potential backers to fund a new expedition along the same lines as Bruce.

One tantalising prospect was to learn that Michael Barne, his old *Discovery* colleague, was putting together a plan to visit Graham Land on the Antarctic Peninsula, the same area which had repelled Nordenskjöld. Shackleton discussed the idea with Barne and Markham, but the Admiralty and RGS were not interested and the venture failed to get off the ground.

The most promising person in Shackleton's widening network of contacts was William Beardmore, one of the most commanding figures on the business stage in Scotland. The pair met at RSGS functions and Shackleton quickly recognised that the wealthy Beardmore might be useful, perhaps doing for him what the Coats brothers had done for Bruce. He stayed at Beardmore's palatial home outside Glasgow and sensed that somewhere in his sprawling empire there might be an opening for a man of ambition.

Beardmore was an industrial colossus, whose steel-making and ship-building operations dominated Glasgow and the surrounding area on the Clyde. He owned the largest steel mills in Scotland, ran the giant Parkhead works in the east of Glasgow and could boast the most modern shipyard on Clydeside. At its peak, Beardmore's engineering powerhouse employed 40,000 men. He specialised in producing armour-plating for battleships and had recently won valuable Admiralty contracts to build submarines. By 1903, Beardmore had also seen the potential of the motor car and taken control of the troubled Arrol-Johnston business.

The multimillionaire, who was approaching his 50s, enjoyed the trappings of wealth. He lived in grand style in the 200-year-old Tullichewan Castle in the Vale of Leven to the west of Glasgow and owned the handsome Flitchy House near Loch Ness which came with 3,000 acres of sporting estate. Beardmore, with an impressive moustache and a liking for cigars, married Eliza Tullis, who was 15 years younger, in 1902 and enjoyed the company of adventurers like Shackleton and Scott. Both were guests at Tullichewan Castle.

Beardmore had not risen from shop-floor apprentice to captain of industry purely by chance and hesitated over Shackleton, whom he regarded as engaging enough but without any of the obvious qualifications for the rough and tumble of rolling steel plate or building battleships. However, his wife persuaded Beardmore to give Shackleton a job if he was unsuccessful at the Dundee election.

Mrs Beardmore, born Eliza Small Tullis, was a quietly determined woman. She preferred to be called Elspeth, the Scottish form of Elizabeth. Elspeth was the daughter of David Tullis, one of Glasgow's 'leather barons' who ran the thriving St Anne's Leather Works in Bridgeton, turning out industrial belting to drive the machinery of Scottish factories. William Beardmore sat on the board of the Tullis family business.

At 34, Elspeth Beardmore was the same age as Shackleton. While Beardmore's millions gave Elspeth respectability and a castle to live in, Shackleton undoubtedly provided the excitement in her ordered life. After his visit to Tullichewan Castle, Scott described Elspeth as 'young & nice looking & I think has social ambitions.' To Shackleton, she was also a good listener and the pair drifted closer.

To complicate matters, Shackleton took Beardmore's hint of a job as a firm promise and felt that, regardless of the election outcome, his future was secure. Shackleton told Emily there were 'four things I can go into' without ever specifying what he expected. Beardmore, he reported, was prepared to pay him £300 a year (about £17,500/€21,000 in today's terms) and suggested he would 'raise me another £300' if the job went well.

While waiting for Balfour to call an election, Shackleton received a copy of Scott's book, *The Voyage of the 'Discovery',* which reached the shelves in October and became an instant success. The book, he told Scott, was 'beautifully got up and splendidly written'. Nevertheless, it made difficult reading for Shackleton, throwing the spotlight once again on his breakdown during the southern journey and the humiliation of being sent home. Scott, with casual indifference, wrote of 'our invalid' on the return march and rekindled the story that Shackleton was a passenger who had to be carried on the sledge. He also sensed that Scott blamed Shackleton's ill health for the party's failure to penetrate further south when, in fact, all three were suffering from scurvy.

Shackleton did not have long to brood on the matter because shortly before Christmas Balfour resigned, forcing an election. Voting at the time was spread over a number of weeks and Dundee was scheduled to go the polls on 16 January 1906, which gave Shackleton barely three weeks to transform himself into an electable MP.

The breakneck pace of the canvassing suited Shackleton more than most prospective MPs. With all his customary energy, he plunged into the task, running from one meeting hall to another to deliver fiery speech after fiery speech. On one day alone, he spoke to over 2,000 people at five separate meetings. In the space of three hectic weeks on the campaign trail, Shackleton crammed in 55 political meetings or what he called 'straightforward talk and straightforward answers'.

The local *Dundee Courier* reported that his 'breezy personality and attractive manner' won many admirers. Shackleton thrived on handling the boisterous crowds or dealing with the robust heckling. His willingness to exchange banter from the floor with his quick wit only enlivened proceedings and he reported that one particularly rowdy session was 'heckling right up to 10pm'.

Heckling was a form of blood sport in elections at the time and a candidate's reputation often hinged on how well they handled the baying crowds. Conan Doyle, who failed to win a seat at the same election, wrote afterwards: 'It is a vile business this electioneering, though no doubt it is chastening in its effects. They say mud baths are healthy and I can compare it to nothing else. This applies particularly, I think, to Scotland, where the art of heckling has been carried to extremes.'[4]

Despite his florid rhetoric and lively stage manner, Shackleton's chances of winning the election were not good. Personal appeal carried only so much weight and Shackleton, never a natural politician, was never fully at ease with the wider political issues of the day. He tried to occupy the safe ground by demanding closer trade links within the colonies and played the traditional anti-foreigner card, arguing that it was a 'menace to the country' to employ non-nationals on British-registered ships. One British sailor, he insisted, was worth three foreigners. When asked if he would give votes to women, Shackleton avoided the sensitive issue with a quip: 'Hush! My wife is present.'

A more perceptive political antenna would also have detected the major change in the politics of Dundee. Dundee, Scotland's third largest city, was traditionally a Liberal stronghold. But the huge growth of the jute industry during the 19th century brought a population explosion and a seismic change in the demographics of the area. The population, which had been about 45,000 in 1841, had soared to around 165,000 by 1900 and the majority of voters now came from the poorly paid millworkers who lived in squalid, overcrowded conditions and were ready to embrace the more radical policies of the fast emerging Labour Party.

Shackleton's other miscalculation was attempting to oppose Irish Home Rule in a city where some 10 per cent of the population were Irish immigrants who had fled to Scotland in search of work. The teeming disease-afflicted slum at Lochee was known as 'Little Tipperary' and suffered the highest infant mortality rate in Scotland.

Despite the odds, Shackleton remained true to his Anglo-Irish roots and fought hard to support the Liberal Unionist's key issue. When challenged to justify subsidies given to Irish landlords, he responded by saying: 'I wish I were an Irish landlord.' On another occasion he simply declared: 'I am an Irishman and I consider myself a true patriot when I say that Ireland should not have Home Rule.' One night a heckler claimed that 95 per cent of Irish people supported Home Rule and demanded to know if Shackleton would throw his weight behind the cause. Shackleton responded: 'I'm an Irishman myself and I would never give them anything that is not good for them.'[5]

Curiously, Shackleton's stance contradicted his father who strongly supported Home Rule and passed on his convictions to his other children. While studying at Trinity College, Henry Shackleton was nicknamed 'Parnell' after the distinctive and similarly bearded Irish nationalist, Charles Stewart Parnell.

Unsurprisingly, the election brought a landslide defeat for the coalition of Balfour's Conservatives and the Liberal Unionists. The traditional Liberal Party was swept to power, winning 400 seats, while Labour gained its first significant foothold in Parliament. Even Balfour lost his seat, the only occasion a sitting Prime Minister has been defeated in his own constituency.

Shackleton also crashed to defeat. He came fourth of the five candidates, picking up 3,865 votes, or 13 per cent of the poll which was creditable in the context of the landslides elsewhere. Only the Conservative candidate fared worse.[6]

Fortunately, Shackleton never regarded politics too seriously and saw the possibility of a Parliamentary seat as little more than a shortcut to the top. It was much the same way he treated Freemasonry and he did not dwell for long on the heavy defeat.

In a cheery assessment of his brief political career, Shackleton concluded: 'I got all the applause and the other fellows got all the votes.'[7]

chapter 12

Finding a Niche

Shackleton was still unemployed and living off his wife's earnings in February 1906 as he marked his 32nd birthday. The RSGS and politics were echoes of the past he rarely considered and the focus once again was to find a new opportunity to make money. In spite of short bursts of promise, the prize was always beyond his grasp.

Typical of his experience was an opportunity to make a quick killing from the dying embers of the bloody war between Russia and Japan. The Russo-Japanese War was the first great international conflict of the 20th century and heralded casualties on a scale which came to define wars in the later years of the century. At least 200,000 combatants and civilians died in just 18 months of bitter fighting and the seeds of the revolution that was to engulf Russia a decade later were sown in the disastrous campaign.

After the humiliating defeat, Russia faced the major problem of getting thousands of soldiers and sailors home from the fighting in Southern Manchuria and the seas around Korea and Japan. Bringing forces home overland was impossible and, in desperation, the Russians began chartering a fleet of merchant ships to evacuate the troops.

Shackleton entered proceedings when a consortium of opportunist businessmen was put together in London with the aim of supplying ships to Russia for the mass evacuation. Shackleton was to be the public face of the new venture and his partners were Thomas Garlick, an accountant with links to Frank Shackleton and George Petrides, the younger brother of Nicetas Petrides, an old school friend from Dulwich.

It was a scheme cobbled together with the optimistic hope of evacuating 40,000 Russians from the port of Vladivostok and Shackleton was counting the money even before the contract was signed. 'There is a chance of our little steamboat company doing a big deal in a few days,' he wrote to Emily. Each officer, he explained, was worth £40 and the lower ranks some £12 a

A pensive Shackleton contemplating his next venture. COURTESY: ATHY HERITAGE MUSEUM

head. 'It would mean £10,000 to me, but I cannot go into details now,' he told her. 'It is awfully exciting.'[1]

By mid-February the deal had collapsed. The talks with the Russians, it emerged, were simply a ruse to drive down the price for a separate deal between the Russians and a major German-American shipping line which had already sewn up the bulk of the contract to bring troops back to the Baltic ports.

Shackleton, with the irrepressible capacity of putting defeat behind him, turned next to William Beardmore with a gentle reminder of the promised job. Helped perhaps by Elspeth Beardmore's recommendation, a small niche was soon found in a corner of Beardmore's widespread operations at Parkhead Works, Glasgow.

Shackleton was barely through the door at Parkhead before visions of prosperity and a new place in the social order seemed to flood his vision. Self-doubt was not a failing, even if Parkhead was his first experience of the inner workings of big business. 'I may become a director before long,' he assured Emily soon after arriving. 'If I had say ten thousand pounds in the business it would pay from 10% to 14% and then the directorship is at least worth one thousand a year so we ought to do well.'

His role was a good deal less than a directorship. Initially Shackleton was appointed secretary of a small committee set up to assess the design of a new gas turbine engine, effectively a glorified minute-taker or clerk.

Shackleton was spectacularly unsuited to both secretarial duties and evaluating the machinery. He quickly found himself isolated among a phalanx of Beardmore's top engineers whose committee chairman was Archibald Barr, the brilliant Scottish scientist and inventor of the pioneering rangefinder for weapons. At the end of meetings Shackleton took his notes along the corridor to be checked by A.B. MacDuff, Beardmore's personal secretary. It was MacDuff who later 'filled in the bare patches' of the minutes.

Shackleton's other job was as a roving commissioner in a quasi-ambassadorial role for the company, entertaining Beardmore's important clients at Parkhead or in more salubrious offices in central London. It was an early form of public relations which played up to Shackleton's strengths as an engaging and natural communicator. To keep a close eye on his new ambassador, Beardmore installed Shackleton in an office directly opposite his own.

MacDuff, who loyally served the Beardmore family for 56 years, remembered Shackleton as a likeable, charming character who created a good impression throughout the building but was largely ineffective in the day-to-day affairs. Without a proper job, Shackleton wandered around the corridors for a chat with colleagues. 'Even if I was in the thick of things, I'd give them up to do what he wanted, I'd such a liking for the fellow,' MacDuff said. It was like the storytelling interludes at the *Royal Magazine* all over again.

Shackleton remained on the periphery and was never allowed to stray into the serious commercial affairs of Beardmore's business. MacDuff, with his pivotal position at the heart of Beardmore's empire, explained: 'I can see him as a fine fellow, but it wasn't in any way a really important job in connection with the business.'[2]

MacDuff also noticed a strange paradox in Shackleton's casual attitude to money. At Parkhead, for example, Shackleton rarely bothered to pick up his wages. 'He left the salary with us and forgot all about it for five months,' a slightly bewildered MacDuff explained. In a fiercely competitive profit-driven commercial environment, Shackleton's indifference stood out like a sore thumb.

It did not take long for Shackleton to discover there was no goldmine at the Parkhead Works. He plugged away for a while, commuting from Edinburgh to Glasgow at 7 a.m. each morning in a suit and crisply ironed shirt like thousands of workers who packed into the trains. But he needed instant results and something far more than glad-handing businessmen. The old familiar restlessness began to take a grip.

He was also spending more time away from home. On frequent trips to London he began to see a Miss Havemeyer, an American who lived not far from the Dorman family home in Kensington. In Edinburgh he was also seeing more of Elspeth Beardmore. 'You are always so cheerful,' he wrote to her, 'and make me feel so much better after I have seen you.'

Shackleton's increasing restiveness coincided with the news that Emily was pregnant again. From Shackleton's perspective, the news was badly timed. Although he proudly celebrated the prospect of a second child, Emily's pregnancy emerged at the same time as he had decided to mount a new expedition to the ice. In his mind's eye he held a vision of reaching the South Pole itself. But he did not tell Emily about the undertaking. In Mill's words, he kept the information from Emily 'in order not to add to his wife's anxieties'.

By contrast, he freely discussed his ambitions with others. Each day at Parkhead, MacDuff had seen his restlessness and asked if he was thinking of leaving Beardmore. Shackleton replied: 'Yes, I want to go on a further expedition soon. This time, I want to command it myself.'

Another who knew all about his plans was Elspeth Beardmore. She was now a supportive, sympathetic ear and someone who might hold the key to her husband's money. 'Elspeth ... you have always been such a real friend and confidant to me that it is to you alone I can talk,' he wrote to her. 'You looked so beautiful the other night.'

Shackleton had other worries in the family. Emily, now 38 years old, found pregnancy difficult and was occasionally highly strung. Raymond, barely 18 months old, was poorly and Dr Shackleton, who was approaching his 60s, had money problems. Deafness had forced him to stop treating heart patients and Shackleton had to scrape together a few pounds to make up for his father's lost income.

Equally unsettling was historic news from the Arctic. At the end of October Roald Amundsen's ship *Gjoa* arrived in San Francisco after completing the first navigation of the North-West Passage, a feat that had eluded sailors for over 300 years. Weeks later the American Robert Peary landed in New York to claim – perhaps fraudulently – a new record 'furthest north' of 87° 06' or just 200 miles (320 km) from the North Pole itself.

With the North Pole seemingly within reach, Shackleton sensed that others would turn their attention to the south. 'The lure of the [ice],' Peary once said, 'It is a strange and powerful thing.' It was something which rang true with Shackleton.

Towards the end of 1906, as Emily entered the final days of her pregnancy unaware of her husband's plans, Shackleton stepped up his efforts to raise money for an expedition. Two days before Christmas, Emily gave birth to a daughter, Cecily Jane Swinford. A 'splendid little girl', he told Mill. In the same letter he also wrote: 'What I would now give to be out there again and this time really on the way to the Pole.'

Emily, still recovering from the birth, adopted an air of resignation a few weeks later when he finally summoned the courage to reveal plans for a new expedition. Going to the Antarctic, she now accepted, was his way of providing for the family.

Shackleton, more than any of his contemporaries, saw exploration as means of making his fortune. Equally, exploring was his means of proving his worth to Emily. He promised to return rich and never have to go away again. 'I shall come back with honour and with money and never part from you again,' he assured her.[3] In Mill's words, she offered 'no discouragement'.

Emily recognised that Shackleton's ambitions went far beyond simply making money. Exploration and adventure defined her husband and *Discovery* had only whetted his appetite. She, too, understood that Shackleton on shore was a different character from the man on the ice. Above all, Emily wanted her husband to be happy. 'She was never the woman who wanted to raise a finger to make it difficult for him to go,' Cecily recalled in later life. Or, as Emily herself wrote, Shackleton's spirit was 'whipped on by the wanderfire'.

Money remained the biggest immediate problem. Encouraged by the success of Bruce's undertaking, Shackleton once more broadened his search for capital. He looked to the City markets for backers, explored the potential of writing a book and examined ways of selling the exclusive rights of the expedition's story to the highest bidder among Fleet Street's newspaper barons. The lecture circuit, a lucrative by-product, was primed for his triumphant return.

The prospectus, which he had drawn up a year earlier, was dusted off and placed in front of potential sponsors. Among the first to come forward was Elizabeth Dawson-Lambton, the elderly spinster who had first met Shackleton on the deck of *Discovery*. Dawson-Lambton's cheque for £1,000 had paid for *Discovery*'s observation balloons and she readily agreed to donate another £1,000 to Shackleton's new venture.

A few others followed, including Emily's elder brother, Herbert Dorman, a cousin from Ireland called William Bell and Gerald Lysaght, the steel manufacturer first encountered on a liner bound for South Africa.

Raising money, however, proved far more difficult than he expected. There was no single large-scale benefactor like Longstaff. Shackleton, slightly bewildered by the reluctance of sponsors, could never fathom why others were not ablaze with his burning enthusiasm. He told Mill that a 'black mark' had been placed against the names of more than 70 people who had rejected his appeal for support.

One potentially fertile area was the City of London's financial community where he knew rich pickings could be made for the right man with the right proposition. Entrepreneurial risk-taking runs through the veins of City investors and Shackleton hoped that his venture would appeal to those with the same speculative spirit as the merchants who financed the Elizabethan explorers or the buccaneering swagger of an empire builder like Cecil Rhodes.

His brother Frank Shackleton put him in touch with Douglas Spens Steuart, a mining engineer and partner in the City consultants of Poore, Pettit & Steuart. He operated a company called Celtic Investment Trust, a prospecting venture set up to exploit potential mineral riches in regions as far apart as Cornwall and Siberia.

Steuart was soon impressed with Shackleton's talkative enthusiasm and warmed to suggestions that valuable gems and minerals might lie beneath the Antarctic ice sheet, waiting for the right entrepreneur to seize the opportunity. However, Steuart's support did not go far beyond vocal backing and he was not prepared to sink his own money into Shackleton's expedition. He limited his support to the donation of 10,000 shares in Celtic Investments, a 'paper' company with no real assets. The shares had no value.

Beardmore remained the most likely source of money. It is also likely that he half-suspected Shackleton would come calling sooner or later. Shortly after arriving at Parkhead, Shackleton had faithfully promised Beardmore that his ambition of returning to the Antarctic was a thing of the past. But Beardmore recognised Shackleton's driving ambition and took the promise with a pinch of salt.

Now, with Elspeth Beardmore on hand to offer a few well-chosen words of advice, Shackleton measured the mood at Parkhead before making his crucial pitch. 'I at last took my courage in both hands and asked him straight out,' he said. 'He came up splendidly.'

Beardmore was no Llewellyn Longstaff and was not prepared to plough money into a venture without seeking something in return. He weighed up Shackleton's scheme in a cold, calculating manner like any other business proposition and soon sniffed out the essence of the proposal. He doubtless saw through the flimsy promise of Celtic Investments or other vague pledges of money.

Beardmore was sympathetic but keen to limit his liability. After some thought, he agreed to guarantee a £7,000 loan with the Clydesdale Bank. In return, Shackleton agreed that the 'first profits' of the expedition would cover the guarantee.

Shackleton estimated that the expedition, including a ship, supplies and personnel, would cost no more than £17,000 when a more realistic assessment was three or four times that amount. But when combined with the few personal donations already made by friends and the optimistic hopes of a bonanza from Celtic Investments, Shackleton believed that Beardmore's guarantee was enough to get things under way.

Beardmore may have had an entirely separate motive for supporting Shackleton. There were suspicions that Shackleton was secretly having an affair with Elspeth. Shackleton and Elspeth were very close, meeting regularly and exchanging personal letters which indicate something beyond friendship. The question of whether they were intimately close remains unclear.

On the other hand, encouraging Shackleton to lead an expedition to the Antarctic for two years had the benefit of removing the suspicion at a stroke.

chapter 13

Looking South

There was a hint of theatrical audition on 11 February 1907 as Shackleton went to the Royal Geographical Society in London to unveil his plans to reach the South Pole. Unfortunately, Shackleton did not have the stage to himself.

The main attractions at the RGS that night were Fridtjof Nansen and Roald Amundsen, the most accomplished explorers of the age. The two Norwegians represented polar exploration's new age and presented a cold-eyed professionalism which, in many ways, was the opposite of the RGS's gentlemanly institution.

Nansen, tall, imposing and unmistakably Viking in appearance, was Norway's ambassador in London and, though in his mid-40s and apparently retired from the ice, quietly nursed an ambition of making an incredible comeback and being first to stand at the South Pole. He stood alongside Amundsen, grimly focused and inscrutable, who was in London to recount his saga of the North-West Passage. Amundsen, behind a sphinx-like demeanour, was also plotting his next venture, to seize the North Pole from under the nose of Peary.

Shackleton also had to share the occasion with Henryk Arctowski, a 45-year-old Polish-born scientist who came to London with the bare bones of a Belgian plan to reach the South Pole using motorised sledges. Like Shackleton, Arctowski was struggling to raise money or impress enough people that he was capable of making history. But Arctowski was no idle threat, having survived the ordeal of *Belgica*, the first overwintering in the Antarctic. Among his companions on *Belgica* was Amundsen.

To Shackleton, Arctowski probably appeared a more real danger than the enigmatic Norwegians, who were a closed book and offered few outward signs of their intentions. All Shackleton spotted was a little restiveness in Nansen. The role of diplomat rested uneasily on the shoulders of the pioneer who had made the first crossing of Greenland while in his mid-20s and once held the record for 'furthest north'. Nansen had unfinished business on his mind. 'Perhaps he may want to be off to the ice again,' Shackleton mused.

There was also talk of Barne, still struggling to put his expedition together, while most knew that Bruce was hoping to make a return to Antarctic waters. Some mentioned Dr Jean-Baptiste Charcot, the Frenchman who returned from the Antarctic Peninsula in 1905 and was now building a polar ship with the impressively defiant name, *Pourquoi Pas?*

As a matter of routine, men like Shackleton and Arctowski trod the well-beaten path to the RGS offices in search of backing for their ventures. It had been the case with generations of explorers since the founding of the RGS in 1830. With the imprimatur of the RGS, they secured a significant semi-official status which added a gloss to their enterprise and invariably made it easier to attract sponsors. As Barne could testify, the task was far more difficult without RGS support.

In his customary broad-brush style, Shackleton laid out his plan with stunning simplicity and precious little detail. Reaching the South Pole and locating the South Magnetic Pole were the principal targets, he disclosed. There was also talk of a strong scientific programme, although the precise nature of the work was unclear beyond a plan to observe the Emperor penguin colony on Ross Island and to take magnetic and meteorological recordings. Unlike *Discovery*, the expedition ship would not overwinter in the ice and instead would be despatched to trace the continental coastline. At this stage, Shackleton planned a landing party of between nine and 12 men to be stationed in a purpose-built hut near the old *Discovery* quarters in McMurdo Sound.

To stiffen the sinews of prospective sponsors, Shackleton tried to cloak his expedition in the flag of imperial endeavour. 'I am representing 400 million British subjects,' he said.

Shackleton, as ever, was a man in a hurry and looking for a rapid response from the RGS. He hoped that with the Society's backing, the King would provide the royal seal of approval to the venture and open the floodgates of sponsorship.

In the hurly-burly of a busy day at the RGS, he went straight to the top, seeking out John Scott Keltie, the Society's Secretary, and Sir George Goldie, who had succeeded Markham as President. At the same time, he targeted other influential RGS members in the hopes of drumming up support. 'I will try and get a few big fish [life members] into my net and try others,' he wrote to Mill. 'Am hoping that by the end of this week I will have all the money guaranteed and shall announce it before the 12th. I think the end is in sight.'

Shackleton played heavily on the inherent British fear of foreign powers. Nothing concentrated the mind more than the dread of being forestalled by another nation. Despite waning power and influence in global affairs, Edwardian Britain still viewed the world through the prism of ruling by divine right. Or when reality told them otherwise, they simply belittled the exploits of others. Markham, in a statement of astounding pomposity about the age of Antarctic exploration, once declared: 'Foreigners never get much beyond the Antarctic Circle.'

Shackleton was not so sure and decided there was no time to waste. He aimed to sail from England in the summer of 1907, striking out for the Pole in 1908 before others could mount a rival expedition. Arctowski, for example, was not ready to sail for well over a year and unlikely to start his trek south until late 1909 at the earliest. In Shackleton's mind, he would be back in England celebrating before Arctowski took his first steps towards the Pole.

To his complete surprise, however, Shackleton was met with indifference by the RGS hierarchy. Keltie and Goldie were sympathetic to his aims but non-committal about giving official support. Was it because they were unimpressed by Shackleton's flowery talk of having raised £30,000 or was there another explanation?

Keltie, a hard-working Scot in his mid-60s with a closely trimmed beard, tightly drawn lips and piercing eyes, was not a man to be underestimated. After studying to enter the Church, he made the unexpected change of direction into journalism before joining the RGS in the 1880s. After serving as librarian for 10 years, Keltie moved to the heart of the institution as Secretary and held the post into his late 70s.

In trying to unpick the finer points of Shackleton's plans, Keltie found only 'many mysterious questions and hints' which left much unresolved. 'He is very confident of success,' Keltie wrote in a private letter to Scott, 'but I am doubtful about it myself and it is just possible he may have to return within 18 months after he set out without doing much.'

What Keltie pointedly did not tell Shackleton was that the RGS was already primed to support Scott when he returned to the south. Keltie and Goldie, in fact, had known about Scott's intentions months before Shackleton even turned up at the RGS with his own plan. Barne was already acting as Scott's agent. When Shackleton showed Keltie a press statement about his plans, which mentioned some possible RGS support, Keltie deleted the reference to the Society.

Shackleton, unaware of the RGS's duplicity, was puzzled but defiant on the journey back to Edinburgh. As the train sped north, the enormity of the task ahead began to crystallise in his mind. What he did not fully appreciate was that where *Discovery* had enjoyed full backing – the King, government, RGS, Royal Society, Admiralty and Longstaff's money – Shackleton effectively stood alone.

Shackleton had given himself the ambitious target of launching the expedition in a mere six months. He had only a blurred outline of arrangements, there was no ship or equipment and not a single member of the party had been recruited. Beyond Beardmore's modest loan guarantee, there was little money. All he possessed was the grandiose name, the British Antarctic Expedition.

Turning to personnel, Shackleton sought to recruit men from among old colleagues on *Discovery* and the first choice was Wilson, his trusted confidant and companion on the 'furthest south' journey. Shackleton regarded Wilson as his best friend and freely circulated his name as an experienced explorer in trying to raise funds. Wilson, doctor, naturalist and proven traveller, was offered the post as the expedition's second in command. 'I want the job done and you are the best man in the world for it,' Shackleton said. 'If I am not fit enough to do the Southern journey there could be no one better than you,' he added in reference to his breakdown on the southern journey.

Shackleton was shocked when Wilson replied only two days later, turning down his offer. Wilson had taken an important job investigating the causes of an epidemic wiping out thousands of grouse on the Scottish moors. Wilson, committed more to science than exploration, was not prepared to abandon his work. 'I am in honour bound to carry this grouse work through,' he declared.

Shackleton, in a desperate attempt to persuade Wilson to change his mind, reworked the old chestnut about foreigners and appealed to his national pride. 'It is the country before the grouse,' he wrote. But Wilson was unmoved and urged Shackleton: '... don't waste more money in long telegrams.'

While he continued to pursue Wilson, Shackleton also approached other old *Discovery* colleagues, including Armitage, Hodgson and Skelton, who for different reasons all said no. He asked Barne to lead the small subsidiary party hoping to determine the exact location of the South Magnetic Pole. Barne also declined.

A more Machiavellian mind than Shackleton's would have read the danger signals. But the dark arts of subterfuge and plotting did not come easily to Shackleton, a man who could be curiously naive and artless. Shackleton possessed a touching innocence, which meant he usually saw the best in people and found it difficult to conceal his mood or intentions. He was an open book. As a friend said: 'He was direct and simple as a child.'[1]

The puzzle of the RGS's coolness began to make more sense after Shackleton approached George Mulock, the man who had replaced him at McMurdo Sound in 1903. Mulock, a 25-year-old naval lieutenant, came highly regarded and was a strong candidate for Shackleton's team because of his mapping skills. But Mulock casually let the cat out of the bag by revealing that he had already volunteered to join Scott. A few days later Barne confirmed that he, too, was planning to sail with Scott 'in about 2 years time'.

Shackleton, in Keltie's words, was 'very much astonished' by the first public declaration that Scott was returning south. The ambivalence of the RGS now became a little clearer.

Keltie reinforced the message shortly after when he told Scott that he 'need not have any doubt' whom the RGS would support if both he and Shackleton launched separate expeditions. 'I do not believe the Society will lend him [Shackleton] any financial support at all,' Keltie wrote. 'I do not think the [RGS] Council will do anything whatever that will involve any responsibility towards the expedition.'[2]

Scott, who first read about Shackleton's plans in newspapers, responded to the news by going on the attack. He wrote two sharply worded letters bristling with indignation and self-righteousness and claimed that Shackleton was 'cutting across my plans'. Scott also insisted that Shackleton should not establish his winter quarters at McMurdo Sound.

'I think anyone who has had anything to do with exploration will regard it [McMurdo Sound] as mine,' Scott wrote. 'It must be clear to you now that you have placed yourself in the way of my life's work. If you go to McMurdo Sound you go to winter quarters which are clearly mine.'[3]

Scott's claim of proprietary rights to McMurdo Sound was plainly absurd. But in the strict moral code of the time, it was a demand taken very seriously by Shackleton.

Scott's demands, of course, were impossible to enforce. The Antarctic land mass of 5.4 million square miles – it is larger than Europe – was not controlled by any single nation. Barely 100 souls had set foot on the continent by 1907 and territorial claims were not clear. On the same basis as Scott decreed, Borchgrevink, who had skirted McMurdo Sound two years before *Discovery* anchored there, might have claimed priority in the region. Mill, with a dash of scholarly rationale, cut through Scott's bluster to observe that all territories were 'absolutely open and free to anyone who has the courage, perseverance and good luck to reach it'.[4]

Shackleton, however, had drawn Scott into the open for the first time and exposed two sensitive issues. Firstly, Scott was a long way from raising the necessary funds and secondly, the navy had not been told he intended to seek another two years' leave. Scott was also struggling to provide for his elderly mother and dependant sisters and Shackleton's expedition threatened his own ideas of making money from bagging the Pole.

Scott was even more belligerent in private, accusing Shackleton of going behind his back and rushing to put together his expedition before Scott had time to assemble his own undertaking. 'Shackleton owes everything to me,' he told Keltie. 'I hold it could not have been playing the game for anyone to propose his expedition to McMurdo Sound until he had ascertained that I had given up the idea of going again.' Rising to new heights of virtuous anger, Scott complained that Shackleton might 'ruin the cause of true exploration' and added: 'It is a question of how far the Society should condone an act of disloyalty.'[5]

Scott's demands were nonetheless embarrassing to Shackleton who had raised money from men like Beardmore in the belief that he would operate from McMurdo Sound. Withdrawal from familiar territory for the uncertainty of establishing quarters in an unknown spot only added to the risks and threatened the loss of vital funding.

A clearer-thinking, less personally ambitious commander might have considered combining the two expeditions, with Scott perhaps offering Shackleton the position as his deputy. But the soaring ambitions and the differing personalities of the two men made the concept unworkable.

Besides, Scott did not trust Shackleton. '... I personally never expect much in this sort of work from a man who isn't straight,' he told Keltie. 'Shackleton is the least experienced of our travellers and he was never very thorough in anything – one has but to consider his subsequent history to see that he has stuck to nothing & you know better than I the continual schemes which he has fathered.'[6]

Keltie, too, had reservations about Shackleton. 'He looks strong enough, but it is clear I think that he is not absolutely sound and Heaven knows what may happen if he starts on his journey Pole-wards,' he told Scott.[7]

Shackleton was under intense pressure as Scott's position hardened. He suffered four sleepless nights, torn between his own ambitions and the moral dilemma of doing the right thing. Nor did he want the affair to become public in case it deterred potential backers. At times he pondered switching his base to the largely unexplored Weddell Sea side of the continent. At another moment he considered abandoning the south altogether and making a dash for the North Pole.

In search of mediation, Shackleton turned to the reassuring figure of his friend Wilson. Wilson, sounding board, peacemaker and moral guardian, would know best. He was to be bitterly disappointed.

Wilson was unequivocal in supporting Scott and upholding the right to keep Shackleton out of McMurdo Sound. It was Scott, he argued, who had a 'prior claim' to the region. '… I think you ought to offer to retire from McMurdo Sound as a base,' Wilson said in a bluntly worded note to Shackleton. 'I do wholly agree with the right lying with Scott to use that base before anyone else.'

Switching winter quarters to an unknown region, as Wilson knew, would seriously reduce Shackleton's chances of getting to the Pole. But Wilson's unambiguous stance left Shackleton with little room for manoeuvre.

Wilson felt Shackleton had made a mistake by not telling Scott about his plans in advance, which conveniently overlooked the fact that Scott had not bothered to let Shackleton into his own secret. Wilson went further by warning that all Shackleton's achievements, including the Pole itself, would be devalued if the expedition camped at McMurdo Sound. 'One's motives are always mixed,' he said, 'but I think that the tarnished honour of getting the Pole even as things have turned out will be worth infinitely less than the honour of dealing generously with Scott.'[8]

Almost inevitably, Markham could not resist stirring things up and Shackleton found cracks had emerged in a second supposedly strong friendship. Markham first offered Shackleton all possible assistance towards the expedition and a week later wrote to Scott accusing Shackleton of duplicity. 'He [Shackleton] has behaved shamefully,' Markham told Scott. 'It grieves me more than I can say that an expedition [*Discovery*] which worked with such harmony throughout should have had a black sheep.'

Through a mixture of Scott's ruthless ambition and Keltie's secrecy, Shackleton found himself portrayed as the villain of the piece. Yet he remained surprisingly composed and measured. To Scott, he promised to give 'earnest consideration' to his argument and in early March he travelled to Wilson's home in Cheltenham in search of a compromise.

Wilson, with his cast-iron principles and calm authority, had exercised an important influence over Shackleton since their earliest days on *Discovery*. Shackleton had total respect for Wilson. If anyone could square the circle it was Wilson. But as they sipped tea and explored the options it was soon evident that Wilson had no intention of withdrawing his crucial support for Scott.

In the face of Scott's bullying and Wilson's persuasiveness, Shackleton reluctantly withdrew his plan to overwinter at McMurdo Sound. It was a hugely generous climb-down, perhaps too generous. 'I would rather lose the chance of making a record,' he told Barne, 'than do anything that might not be quite right.'

From Cheltenham, Shackleton sent a telegram to Scott, who was serving on *Albemarle* in the Atlantic Fleet. 'Will meet your wishes regarding base,' he cabled. 'Please keep absolutely private at present as certain supporters must be brought round to the new position.'

Shackleton's options were to find a suitable base in King Edward VII Land, the territory at the far eastern reaches of the Ice Barrier he had seen from *Discovery* in 1902 or at Barrier Inlet from where the observation balloons had been flown. But time was running out for a departure in 1907 and Shackleton now faced a major new uncertainty.

Wilson was not finished. Before Shackleton had time to consider a new landing site properly, Wilson wrote demanding that Scott should first approve the area where Shackleton intended to overwinter. 'Don't on any account make up your new plans until you know definitely from Scott what limits he puts to his rights,' Wilson declared.

Shackleton was furious, realising for the first time perhaps that the friendship with Wilson was built on shifting sands. It meant Scott could effectively determine where Shackleton should establish his base. 'I do not agree with you, Billy, about holding up my plans until I know what Scott considers his rights,' he responded. 'There is no doubt in my mind that his rights end at the base he asked for, or within reasonable distance of that base. I consider I have reached my limit and I go no further.'[9]

In Shackleton's words, abandoning McMurdo Sound to Scott was 'bad enough' and he was not prepared to abandon King Edward VII Land, too. 'I will not consider that he has any right to King Edward the Seventh's Land,' he told Wilson. 'There are limits as to what one may give way in and I consider I have reached mine.'

For all the arguments, the fate of both expeditions still rested on finding enough money. The state of Shackleton's finances was more illusory than real and Scott, though in the earlier stages of planning, was no better placed. 'I don't believe he really has his money yet,' Shackleton told Elspeth Beardmore.

Shackleton and Scott met face to face in May and despite some uncomfortable moments, drew up an agreement which appeared to suit both sides. It was helpful to clear the air and Shackleton told Elspeth: 'Now we have everything squared away and all is settled.'

Shackleton made all the concessions, promising to establish winter quarters at King Edward VII Land or Barrier Inlet and not to stray west of the 170° meridian. It was a one-sided arrangement which effectively barred Shackleton from operating within the known territories of Victoria Land or McMurdo Sound and drove him inexorably towards mostly uncharted areas of the continent.

Although the arrangement was unappealing, Shackleton was clear that the British Antarctic Expedition would 'rigidly adhere' to the agreement and would not intrude on Scott's supposed domain in McMurdo Sound. The flaw in the agreement was that it was impossible for Scott – or anyone – to enforce and it relied entirely on Shackleton keeping his word.

chapter 14

Dreams and Realities

Shackleton's expedition was an enterprise built largely on credit and airy promises. It was stitched together in a hurry with a combination of a few small personal donations of money, a series of loans and guarantees and a flurry of pledges to settle outstanding debts from the proceeds of future book sales, newspaper articles and public lectures after the expedition's triumphant return. It was also an enterprise with no contingency for failure.

The budgets were also a movable feast. Having initially calculated a figure of around £17,000, Shackleton saw the potential expenses spiral dramatically and the ultimate cost disappear into a fog of uncertainty. By late June, less than eight weeks before he was due to sail, Shackleton put costs at between £24,000 and £27,000 (around £1.5 million/€1.8 million today). However, Shackleton was reluctant to open his arrangements to scrutiny and was anxious for privacy. 'Of course I do not want this sum of money mentioned as it is quite a private affair,' he told Keltie.

In early May, with the expedition's finances hanging by a thread, he wrote a wildly optimistic letter to Elspeth Beardmore, claiming: 'I have had offers mounting up to £60,000 for books and lectures if I reach the South Pole and I really think Elspeth that I am going to manage it this time.'

Shackleton's calculations, vague in the first place, were thrown into further disorder by the decision to withdraw from McMurdo Sound. Having to establish a base camp on King Edward VII Land or elsewhere was likely to be more costly, especially if a larger ship was needed to penetrate unknown waters away from McMurdo. But even that was unclear.

Shackleton was still hopeful that the RGS, despite the earlier rebuff, would provide some measure of support, or at least encourage others. In an attempt to remove all doubts, he blithely claimed to have arranged 'sufficient funds and a well thought out plan' to mount the expedition. But in the same breath he asked for an additional loan of £1,000 which, he said, would enable him to 'extend my operations'. The RGS rejected his appeal and a sceptical Keltie asked: 'Perhaps you would not object to state precisely what funds you have at your disposal?'

The reality was that Shackleton's only major source of money was the £7,000 guarantee from Beardmore, plus a few comparatively small sums donated by benefactors like Miss Dawson-Lambton which in total came nowhere near to meeting the full cost of the venture. He also found that the bonanza from Celtic Investments, if it ever existed, had not come good. The expedition was threatening to do the same.

Shackleton's difficulties were illustrated by the frustrating attempts to buy a suitable ship. Adrien de Gerlache, the former commander of *Belgica,* helpfully located an ideal polar vessel. The two-year-old 600-ton ship, named *Bjorn,* offered robust engines, vast holds for stores and equipment and abundant space for up to 50 men. Unfortunately, *Bjorn*'s cost – some £11,000 – was far beyond Shackleton's means and his credit did not extend that far.

Shackleton turned instead to a cheaper option, a small, foul-smelling old Arctic sealer called *Nimrod.* Even Shackleton's legendary optimism was tested by his first examination of the vessel. 'She was much dilapidated and smelt strongly of seal-oil,' he reported.

Built in Dundee in 1866, the careworn sealer had been at sea for almost half a century and was in need of a major overhaul before tackling the Southern Ocean. The masts were in need of urgent repair, sails were inadequate and holds were filthy, cramped and choked with the penetrating stench of fetid seal waste. Top speed was little more than 6 knots and *Nimrod,* at just 136 feet (41 m) in length, looked horribly small for the rigours of the roughest waters on earth. At £5,000, *Nimrod* at least fitted the budget.

While *Nimrod* was a compromise, the deal to purchase the ship was an important signal that the expedition was finally under way. At one point, Shackleton even considered changing the ship's name to *Endurance* in reference to the family motto, *Fortitudine Vincimus* ('By endurance we conquer'). Nimrod is a name which some associate with the Biblical king who rebelled against God while others claim Nimrod was among the early founders of the ancient craft of Freemasonry. In the event, he kept the name *Nimrod*, perhaps because he felt some affinity with both the rebel and the mason.

Nimrod arrived in London in mid-June for extensive modification and refitting at the specialist Thames-side shipyard of R. & H. Green at Blackwall. New masts and sails were fitted, the grubby holds and living quarters were cleaned and reshaped and the ship was converted from a schooner to a barquentine. A new engine was fitted, though it did little to improve the vessel's speed. Almost inevitably, the bill for the work proved far larger than expected.

With only weeks to go before he was due to sail, Shackleton faced a renewed cash crisis. He needed a fresh injection of around £8,000 or the embarrassing possibility of delaying things for a year which would open the door for Scott and Arctowski. Yet Shackleton kept his nerve and, with a mix of sheer brass neck and engaging charm, somehow managed to find a potential new source of funding.

His target was the Earl of Iveagh, a wealthy aristocrat and someone he did not know. Out of the blue, Iveagh was asked to guarantee a new bank loan. Edward Cecil Guinness, the 1st Earl of Iveagh, was the highly successful head of the Guinness brewing dynasty and reputedly the richest man in Ireland. He was an acclaimed philanthropist, who was said to have donated £1 million (close to £60 million/€72 million in today's terms) of his large personal fortune to good causes like slum clearance and housing for the needy in both London and Dublin. Iveagh, as Shackleton recognised, was another Anglo-Irishman. He was also a Freemason.

Iveagh was impressed with Shackleton's brio and agreed to guarantee a loan of £2,000 if other sponsors could be found to raise the total to £8,000. In a frantic round of meetings and arm-twisting, Shackleton worked tirelessly through his network of friends and contacts and somehow managed to find the money.

The frenetic last-minute rush to raise support typified the scramble to put the expedition together in half the time others needed. Early on, Shackleton had left Edinburgh and taken a small office at 9 Regent Street in London to coordinate the complex task of recruiting suitable men, preparing the ship and arranging the multitude of supplies in time for sailing by early August. The office was so small that all typing jobs had to be farmed out because there was no space for a secretary.

While there was none of the committee wrangling which plagued *Discovery*'s preparations, the hefty burden of organising the expedition fell squarely onto the shoulders of Shackleton. He was helped by business manager Alfred Reid, but it was Shackleton who bore the brunt of the work.

From Regent Street, Shackleton sent directives and orders to procure supplies and equipment from sources as far apart as New Zealand and Manchuria and from Norway to Australia. He spent three weeks in Norway examining sledges, clothing and other winter gear.

At times he worked from 6 a.m. to nightfall and though Emily also moved the family to London – a modest house in Bayswater was rented – Shackleton was rarely at home. 'There are 1000 and 1 things I do and the time seems all too short to do them in,' he wrote to Elspeth Beardmore.[1]

In London he consulted Nansen, who was quietly brooding in the Norwegian government offices not far from Regent Street. Norway had gained independence from Sweden two years earlier and Nansen, among the best-known Norwegians alive, had willingly agreed to serve his new country's needs as ambassador in the most important capital in the world. However, the mass of geographical and scientific papers scattered across his broad office desk was a strong indication of Nansen's real priorities. Much of the legation's work was left to others as the father of modern exploration entertained visitors and sifted through maps and data with liked-minded souls such as Shackleton.

If Nansen saw Shackleton's bubbling enthusiasm and boundless energy as a threat to his own ambitions of the South Pole he kept the secret to himself. But, at 46 years of age, there was no denying Nansen's hunger. 'I only long to break these chains,' he confided to his diary shortly before meeting Shackleton. 'I cannot be tamed!'[2]

For all his dreams, Nansen remained a generous, unselfish spirit. He was happy to assist Shackleton's work, even if it meant thwarting his own ambitions. To Nansen, the wider geopolitical and commercial interests of nations were always less important than the feats of the individual. 'It is the man that matters,' he said.

Shackleton's planning and preparation, as Nansen soon discovered, were a mixture of bold innovation and unhappy reliance on the tried and tested procedures which had failed so badly on *Discovery* and other enterprises. At times Shackleton made daring advances in techniques and equipment, while at other moments he seemed as mired in a bygone age as Markham and his disciples.

One notable innovation was the introduction of multi-purpose packing cases made from thin, lightweight and weatherproof layers of composite board called Venesta, which could be reused as partitions and furniture in the expedition hut. The standardised cases, made in uniform dimensions of 30 inches by 15 inches (76 x 38 cm), were easy to pack and significantly lighter than conventional boxes. It was said that using Venesta cases saved more than 4 tons (4,064 kg) in weight.

He also bought sledges from Norway built to Nansen's specifications, ordered a dozen one-man fur sleeping bags and sent to Lapland for the specialist hard-wearing fur boots called finnesko which were made from reindeer skin with the hair on the outside. The hut, in contrast to the cumbersome contraption taken on *Discovery*, was broken down into prefabricated sections that were simple to store on the ship and easy to assemble. No furniture was taken, the expedition relying instead on recycling empty Venesta packing cases.

Shackleton's experience on *Discovery* had taught him the importance of a good and varied diet for medical and psychological reasons. Well-fed men performed better than the malnourished and after the problems with scurvy on the 'furthest south' journey with Scott and Wilson, he proposed that the men should eat more fresh meat and fish, though pemmican 'hoosh' would remain a core of the diet while on the march.

Another feature was a complete printing press on which he planned to produce a magazine during the winter. *Discovery*'s *South Polar Times* – edited by Shackleton in the first year – was a simple typed paper document, illustrated with drawings. Shackleton intended to go a significant step further by writing, editing and printing a bound volume and to use discarded Venesta cases and sealskins as the book's cover.

But Shackleton's most audacious and eye-catching move was to take a motor car to the ice. It was a specially adapted Arrol-Johnston made at Beardmore's Paisley works, and the first motorised vehicle on the continent.

Beardmore was enough of a visionary to see Arrol-Johnston as the foundation for a future Scottish motor industry. Arrol-Johnston's co-founder was Sir William Arrol, the engineer who built London's Tower Bridge and the Forth Bridge in Scotland. Beardmore saw himself in the same entrepreneurial mould as Arrol and regarded Shackleton's expedition as a source of good publicity for his new venture into motor vehicles.

Shackleton's car was the novelty which captured the public's imagination and sparked just the cloudburst of publicity which Beardmore intended. A lurid cartoon in a popular newspaper of the day depicted a devilish-looking Jack Frost sitting on top of a long pole overlooking the ice and proclaiming: 'Well, I've beaten dogs and ships, and balloons, and now they think they'll master me with petrol! Humph! We shall see!'

Autocar magazine quoted Shackleton as claiming that the vehicle could travel 150 miles (240 km) in 24 hours and added the highly optimistic suggestion: '... he thinks there would be a fair chance of sprinting to the Pole.'

With a 12–15 horsepower engine, the Arrol-Johnston was capable of speeding along at 16 mph (25 km/h) on conventional roads and the twin petrol tanks carried enough fuel for 300 miles (480 km). Although the seating was open to the elements, hot air from the exhaust was channelled under the chassis to warm the driver's feet.

While both Scott and Arctowski were also examining the possibilities of motorised transport, Shackleton was first. However, motor vehicles were still in their infancy in 1907 and notoriously unreliable.

Shackleton was happy to subscribe to Beardmore's public relations exercise, but privately he doubted whether the vehicle would run effectively on soft snow. He had not bothered to test the Arrol-Johnston's capabilities in cold-weather conditions and explained to Skelton: 'I am not depending on the car as the main mode of traction.' Shackleton, though interested in new ideas, intended to rely almost entirely on better-known means of transport.

Transport was Shackleton's Achilles heel, just as it had been the weak spot on the southern journey with Scott and Wilson. It was as though he had learned nothing from his year in the south.

The centrepiece of Shackleton's travel arrangements for the Pole was a combination of conventional man-hauling and the unconventional use of horses to drag sledges. In a genuflection towards the feats of Nansen and Sverdrup, he proposed taking a few dogs. But they were assigned a minor supporting role.

Horses, like the Arrol-Johnston, were another Antarctic first and Shackleton's conversion to horses was remarkable, particularly after the southern journey. After his experience, Shackleton had initially come around to believing that dogs held the key to more efficient travel. Shortly after returning from *Discovery*, he wrote: 'We only had twenty three dogs when we started. I wish we had had about sixty or seventy, for then we would have reached the Pole.'[3]

He changed his mind a little later, claiming that poorly managed dogs had prevented the men getting further south. 'Dogs had not proved satisfactory on the Barrier surface,' he wrote.[4] In the event, Shackleton took more horses south than either dogs or sets of skis. It was a daring gamble. But it was a gamble that failed.

The roots of Shackleton's error of judgement can be traced back to seemingly casual discussions with Armitage on *Discovery*. Armitage became an enthusiastic convert to horses during his time in Franz Josef Land with Frederick Jackson on the Jackson–Harmsworth expedition in the mid-1890s. In much the same way that Markham passed on his faith in the noble slog of man-hauling sledges to Scott, Armitage accepted Jackson's belief in horses and somehow instilled the same conviction in Shackleton.

Frederick Jackson was a bluff and persuasive character from the coterie of mildly eccentric gentlemen-explorers who characterised the Victorian age. He was more big-game hunter than pioneer. A man brought up riding with hounds across open English fields, he gloried in the kill and once, dressed only in his pyjamas, chased a polar bear across the ice before shooting the animal.

Jackson took a few hardy Russian ponies to Franz Josef Land to prove his theory that the animals were suited to the ice. But while he accepted the positives – notably the extra loads a horse carried – he was unwilling to accept the negatives like the self-defeating burden of the animals being forced to carry huge quantities of their own feed. Jackson saw how easily his animals crashed through the ice or snow bridges without fully appreciating that the weight-bearing hoof of a horse is four to five times greater than a dog's paw. Or that, while three of his four horses died, the dogs survived.

Jackson swept aside all the apparent weaknesses to pronounce the animals 'an unqualified success'. Ponies, he argued, could be used to 'very great advantage' in the ice and Shackleton, with no knowledge or experience of managing horses, was carried along with the same enthusiasm. Cossack cavalry units had successfully used Manchurian ponies during the Russo-Japanese War and Shackleton optimistically believed an animal could haul 1,200 lb (540 kg) for 20 to 30 miles (up to 48 km) a day. The biggest risk, he felt, was the sea journey from Asia to the Antarctic.

Through the London branch of the Hong Kong and Shanghai Bank, Shackleton ordered 15 Manchurian ponies and a local veterinary surgeon in Shanghai was sent to Tientsin (Tianjin) in China to purchase the animals. The ponies, each standing around 14 hands (56 inches or 147 cm), were slightly smaller than the accepted measure of a horse (14.2 hands) and had peculiarly short legs and necks and powerfully built bodies. The animals were also highly temperamental and, at 12 to 17 years old, were quite elderly.

Nansen, knowledgeable and perceptive, was dismayed at Shackleton's choice. He was, said Nansen, 'bound to experience disappointments with things he had never tried properly.' It was a sentiment likely to be shared by Amundsen, who famously said: 'Victory awaits him who has everything in order – luck we call it.'

Nansen had put his finger on Shackleton's inherent weakness. A child could lead a pony. It needed no training or experience. Dogs and skis were the most efficient means of travel, but Shackleton did not have the patience or aptitude to master either skill. Nor did he consider recruiting an expert dog driver. Shackleton wanted instant results. He opted for the easy way out.

The most bizarre and unpredictable decisions centred on Shackleton's choice of men. Given the shortage of time, Shackleton was forced to make hurried and often impulsive recruitments.

In choosing his men, Shackleton remained hopeful that a few of his old *Discovery* colleagues would join up. According to Koettlitz's version of events, Shackleton had initially considered him as joint leader of the expedition but the partnership soon dissolved, leaving Koettlitz angry and disappointed. 'Shackleton had originally planned his expedition in conjunction with me and we had almost decided to go as leaders jointly,' he later explained in a letter to Nansen. 'But then the plans hung fire. I could not wait. Shackleton, when I was out of sight, forgot me, so that, when the wherewithal in money was forthcoming, he decided to go alone and ignored my existence and has done so ever since, though he did not forget my plans.'[5]

Another who did not travel south was William Colbeck, the man Shackleton wanted to captain *Nimrod*. Colbeck did not want to leave his position with the Wilson shipping line and instead recommended Lieutenant Rupert England. *Nimrod*'s First Officer was John King Davis, a tall, flame-haired 23-year-old making the first of his seven voyages to the Antarctic and who, like others, joined on something of an impulse.

The shore party was made up from fellow travellers, adventurous men like himself who wanted something more than routine. Many were rootless and 10 of the final landing party of 15 men were unmarried.

After the conflicts on *Discovery*, Shackleton was determined that *Nimrod* would be a largely classless operation. 'The temperament of the various members of the expedition is one of the most serious and important factors in such a case as ours,' he wrote. 'I feel that the success of our work depends as much on the general attitude of the members to each other as on the work they individually have to do.'[6]

Fitness was a key factor, even if Shackleton was reluctant to discuss his own health. '[They] must be free from any heart troubles,' he wrote. Emily managed to persuade him to see a doctor before departure but, according to one report, 'he examined the specialist instead of the specialist examining him.'

Second in command was Jameson Boyd Adams, a plain-speaking 27-year-old lieutenant in the Royal Naval Reserve, who had first met Shackleton in 1905 while he and Emily were taking a holiday in Scotland. Adams was another to be spellbound by Shackleton's ambition and enthusiasm. On the spur of the moment, he asked: 'If you go again will you take me with you?' Two years later Adams was on the verge of promotion to the Royal Navy proper when Shackleton suddenly invited him to join the shore party as his deputy. Adams promptly abandoned his naval career for the gamble of going south with Shackleton.

Another eager volunteer was Dr Eric Marshall, a strongly built athlete from the public school ranks who intended entering the Church before changing his mind and qualifying as a doctor. Marshall, a robust 28-year-old rugby player and rower, had met Shackleton socially and was another who, attracted by the prospect of adventure, leapt at the chance to join *Nimrod*.

Shackleton found only two men from *Discovery* prepared to join the expedition. One was Frank Wild, the able seaman with whom he had struck an unlikely friendship in the south. Wild was a short, quiet man in his early 30s who was probably better educated than most ABs and disillusioned with the navy. He was serving at the shore establishment in Sheerness and tried to purchase his release from the navy in his eagerness to join *Nimrod*. The navy refused to release him but, to Wild's surprise, agreed to second him to the expedition.

Another old *Discovery* hand was Ernest Joyce, a stoutly built and much experienced naval petty officer. Joyce, 32, was another rootless wanderer and fond of self-promotion. According to one story, Shackleton had spotted Joyce from his office window sitting on the top deck of a London bus. On the spur of the moment, Joyce agreed to buy his release from the navy and join the expedition. A further intriguing tale, which remains unproven, is that Shackleton promised to reimburse the cost of Joyce's release and reserve a place in the South Pole party. Neither happened, but the story bore all the hallmarks of Joyce.

Bernard Day, a trained mechanic, was hired largely to handle the Arrol-Johnston. Day, a tall, thin, fresh-faced young man who worked for Beardmore, was a few weeks short of his 23rd birthday as *Nimrod* sailed and described as a 'cynic and philosopher'. William Roberts, by contrast, was in his mid-30s and earning a living as a chef when he was appointed expedition cook. It was said that Roberts, a rough-edged character with few social graces, 'never liked anybody'.

Far more popular was George Marston, a jovial broad-shouldered character with the features of a cherub and the deft hands of an accomplished artist. His circle of artistic friends included Shackleton's sisters Helen and Kathleen, who were instrumental in getting Marston to apply for the role as the expedition's artist and photographer. Marston, an art teacher in his mid-20s known as 'Putty', was a good-humoured character who liked practical jokes and was described as having the 'frame and face of a prize-fighter and the disposition of a fallen angel'.

Picking the right calibre of scientist was important, though Shackleton's interest in science was modest. However, he recognised that science held the key to the expedition's credibility and fund-raising prospects.

'My great object in this expedition is to make it of definite value to science,' he said before *Nimrod* sailed. On another occasion, however, he advised another polar voyager: 'Don't saddle yourself with too much scientific work. You must decide whether you want to be a scientist or a successful leader of expeditions, it is not possible to do both.'

Instinctively Shackleton preferred a straightforward dash to the Pole without the extra baggage of a scientific agenda. But he also wanted recognition where it mattered and he turned to knowledgeable men like Sir John Murray and Bruce to help with selection. It was Bruce, who always put science before discovery, who recommended the experienced and much-respected Scottish biologist James Murray. Murray was a dependable, composed man of 42 who fulfilled Shackleton's criteria. Another Scot to join *Nimrod* was Dr Alistair Forbes Mackay, a big, robust and intense man of 29 who had served with Baden-Powell's police force during the Boer War and later worked as a naval surgeon.

A more impulsive decision was to recruit Raymond Priestley, a quiet young student from Tewkesbury in Gloucestershire who was studying geology at University College, Bristol. Shackleton came to the College to interview a potential geologist for the expedition. Bert Priestley, his elder brother, heard that the man turned down the job and casually asked Priestley: 'How would you like to go to the Antarctic, Ray?' Priestley looked up and said: 'I'd go anywhere to get out of this damned place.' Soon after, Priestley received a telegram from Shackleton inviting him for an interview.[7]

The subsequent interview was pure Shackleton. Although many trained geologists were available, Shackleton evidently liked the look of the unqualified Priestley who was 21 and only halfway through his studies. In a peculiar exchange, Shackleton asked if Priestley could sing and then enquired if he would know gold if he saw it. 'He must have asked me other questions but I remember those because they were bizarre,' Priestley recalled. A few weeks later, Priestley received a telegram from Shackleton demanding to know why he was not in London collecting his equipment for the journey. 'I could never understand why Shackleton took me,' a bewildered Priestley later admitted.

Although unorthodox, the episode was among the earliest examples of Shackleton's great instinct for picking his men and seeing the potential in people. Priestley, in fact, would become a distinguished geologist, receive a knighthood and serve as chairman of the British Association for the Advancement of Science and President of the RGS.

The selection of Sir Philip Lee Brocklehurst, another raw recruit, as assistant geologist was equally odd. But Brocklehurst, who was just 20, brought the two qualities which were always so elusive to Shackleton: money and an entrée to the upper echelons of society.

Brocklehurst was a wealthy Old Etonian baronet from the manorial Swythamley Hall in Staffordshire. The pair had met through a mutual friend, Miss Havemeyer, the American woman Shackleton had been seeing in London. Brocklehurst, tall, hearty and sporting, was enthralled by the aura of adventure which surrounded Shackleton. He also noted that Shackleton was 'one for the ladies and extravagant with taxis'. Captivated by the prospect of striding to the South Pole, Brocklehurst promptly volunteered to join the expedition.

Shackleton scented money and the cachet of circulating at the tables of high society. In announcing Brocklehurst's appointment, he joyfully wrote to Elspeth Beardmore: 'One is a Baronet! but he is a really good chap.'

Shackleton was introduced to Lady Annie Lee Brocklehurst, Brocklehurst's widowed mother. Refined, wealthy and impeccably well connected, Lady Brocklehurst was another sophisticated widow in her 50s who found Shackleton's style appealing and she agreed to guarantee a loan of £2,000 (almost £120,000/€145,000 today). In opening the right doors for Shackleton, Brocklehurst also became the first person to purchase his place on an Antarctic expedition.

Lady Brocklehurst, it appears, was also influential in persuading a few well-heeled acquaintances – nobles and millionaires – to provide some extra guarantees in support of the £2,000 promised by Lord Iveagh. She also held the key to Shackleton's aim of reaching the King.

The veneer of respectability offered by royal patronage was an obvious target for Shackleton and he discovered that Lady Brocklehurst's cousin was Major-General John Fielden Brocklehurst, a distinguished soldier and equerry to Queen Alexandra. Fielden was a man likely to have the ear of the King. Using the Brocklehurst name, Shackleton wrote to Lord Knollys, the King's private secretary, asking for the monarch's support.

Buckingham Palace declined but offered Shackleton the next best thing. The King, the Palace explained, would come on board if *Nimrod* attended the annual Cowes Week regatta before leaving for the south. This was a notable achievement for an unofficial expedition and it gave Shackleton the same royal send-off as *Discovery* in 1901.

Nimrod left East India Docks on 30 July 1907, sailing down the Thames and pausing long enough at Eastbourne for the expedition to pay its respects to Elizabeth Dawson-Lambton, Shackleton's faithful supporter who was given the honour of inspecting the ship before the King.

On 4 August the small ship picked a path through a cavalcade of around 200 assorted ships, scattered for miles in the packed waters of the Solent for the grand spectacle of Cowes Week. It was as much a celebration of British naval supremacy as a social gathering. Improbably enough, the modest, elderly *Nimrod* was stationed alongside the mighty *Dreadnought*, pride of the world's greatest navy and the most advanced battleship of the day.

King Edward was piped aboard for a brief ceremony. First he pinned the medal of the Royal Victorian Order on Shackleton, the same honour given to Scott six years before. Shackleton was then given the rare honour of a unique personal gift from Queen Alexandra.

Queen Alexandra, the forgiving wife of the grey-bearded roué, had maintained a dignified distance from official matters in over 40 years of marriage, a life at times left to opening bazaars or performing respectable charitable work while waiting patiently for her husband to ascend to the throne. She had quietly fought the stifling domination of Queen Victoria's court and stoically tolerated her philandering husband's string of high-profile affairs in the interests of a stable monarchy.

However, the Danish-born Alexandra – Alix to her family – was a gracefully attractive figure of Edwardian elegance still capable in her early 60s of turning a man's head. Mark Twain was among those fascinated by Alexandra's striking good looks. 'I think it is no exaggeration to say that the Queen looks as young and beautiful as she did thirty-five years ago,' Twain remarked to the *New York Times*.

Something about Shackleton stirred the soul of Alexandra, too. His engaging manner and breezy informality was a change from the customary deference and subservience of court. Like Elspeth Beardmore, she was attracted by the hint of excitement which surrounded him.

Alexandra was something of a free spirit in the suffocating atmosphere of court and survived the humiliation of the King's indulgences by managing to pursue her own private interests. She was an enthusiastic horsewoman and keen photographer whose pictures were published and went on public display. Among the photographs she took for her new book was an image of *Nimrod* chugging slowly amidst the phalanx of grey battleships and colourful yachts packed into the Solent on 4 August 1907. Later that year, the same photograph of *Nimrod* featured on her set of personal Christmas cards sent to friends and associates.

In an unusual break from protocol, Alexandra gave Shackleton a Union flag to plant at the South Pole. 'May this Union Jack which I entrust to your keeping lead you safely to the South Pole,' she wrote in a note attached to the flag. 'This is the first time it has been done,' a plainly delighted Shackleton reported.

Cowes was a welcome pause in the helter-skelter of getting the expedition away in time, but the shortage of money, as ever, continued to cast a long shadow over his affairs. Not that Shackleton allowed his impoverishment to dim his confidence. Future book sales and the fees from public lectures, he believed, would come to the rescue. He even managed to convince himself that the various loan guarantees would ultimately be turned into outright gifts because rich men like Beardmore and Iveagh would never ask for their money back.

'I have already made arrangements with Heinemann to publish the book on my return and it means £10,000 if we are successful,' he told Emily. 'And that is quite apart from all newspaper news which we hope to fix up. It will leave me all the lectures, etc., free and the book can pay off guarantees if the people really want them but I am of the opinion they will not ask for them if we are successful. I think it will be worth £30,000 in lectures alone.'[8]

Shackleton was also counting on further support from so far unidentified investors in Australia and New Zealand, where *Nimrod* was scheduled to travel before entering the Southern Ocean. 'I am feeling very confident we will get all the money that is needed in Australia,' he wrote.

Many of those owed money took a more realistic view of the chaos and pressed for payment before Shackleton disappeared over the horizon. In an attempt to finalise things and find more backers, Shackleton remained behind when the ship finally left England on 7 August. William Bell, his Irish cousin, suddenly came up with the promise of £4,000 which potentially raised the kitty to some £20,000 (around £1.2 million/€1.5 million in today's terms). A friend of the Brocklehursts, Campbell Mackellar, also provided some backing, but Shackleton was still in dire need of help.

Faced with a trail of unpaid bills, Shackleton went back to his original benefactor, Beardmore. He successfully borrowed another £1,000 as a short-term loan to smooth over an immediate cash-flow crisis and promised to repay the money in a matter of weeks. How he planned to repay the loan was unclear. Nor was it clear what Shackleton planned to do with the money. Had Beardmore known the truth, he would never have handed the money over.

The money, which was desperately needed by the expedition, instead ended up in the hands of Shackleton's young brother Frank who was deeply embroiled in one of the great scandals of the Edwardian era.

In July 1907, while Shackleton was in the final stages of preparation, it was discovered that someone had stolen the Irish Crown Jewels from a safe in Dublin Castle shortly before King Edward was due to arrive on a royal visit to Ireland. The jewels and other insignia, officially the regalia of the Order of St Patrick, were hugely symbolic as icons of the Protestant Ascendancy and worth at least £40,000. Frank Shackleton, who was closely associated with key figures in the conspiracy, was immediately identified as a possible suspect.

It was discovered that no doors or locks were forced during the burglary and the safe had been opened with a key. The safe happened to be in the office of Sir Arthur Vicars, the Ulster King of Arms, whose immediate staff included Frank Shackleton, one of the Heralds at Dublin Castle. Investigation into the robbery sparked intense speculation about an 'inside job' at Dublin Castle, lurid tales of wild parties among a coterie of homosexuals on the staff and a cover-up extending to the offices of King Edward himself.

Frank Shackleton, who had a history of poor business dealings, was known to be in serious financial difficulties. He was also involved in a separate controversy over unpaid bills and fraudulent trading on the stock market. He was also a homosexual and associated with the Duke of Argyll, the King's brother-in-law, who had a dubious reputation for indulging in orgies with obliging guardsmen. Engaging in homosexual acts was a criminal offence at the time and the King, fearing the scandal would engulf the Palace, later issued a royal directive that Vicars and the Heralds should be dismissed and a lid placed on the murky affair. Frank Shackleton was never arrested but Vicars left a note in his will – he was shot dead by the IRA in 1921 – naming Frank as the culprit. The jewels have never been recovered and the crime remains unsolved to this day.

Shackleton rightly feared that he would get drawn into the scandal with disastrous consequences for the expedition if his backers took fright and withdrew their support. But he was reluctant to leave his younger brother out on a limb. In the hopes of avoiding public embarrassment over unpaid debts, he gave Beardmore's £1,000 to Frank Shackleton to settle a few of his most pressing bills.

'Frank has caused me a lot of worry and expense,' Shackleton told Elspeth Beardmore. 'But now he is out of his trouble and will pay me back the money he owes.' Beardmore's short-term loan was still unpaid when Shackleton finally left for the ice.

chapter 15

Broken Promise

It is difficult to imagine a less convincing and uncoordinated enterprise in the summer of 1907 than the British Antarctic Expedition as the day of departure for the south grew near. Men, horses, dogs and equipment were scattered across the high seas in a variety of ships slowly converging on a rendezvous in New Zealand. Creditors everywhere were pressing for payment.

Aside from the urgent affairs of the expedition, Shackleton was also struggling with the personal issues of leaving Emily for up to two years and the unsettling matter of the outstanding loan to Beardmore. In the background was the alarming prospect of getting dragged into his brother's murky affairs. 'I am going through a very heavy rough time as I have so much to do,' he wrote to Elspeth Beardmore.

Shackleton remained behind in England for over two months after *Nimrod*'s official send-off at Cowes. He scrambled around to plug gaps in the arrangements, placate creditors and to find new sources of finance. At the end of October he finally crossed the Channel, took a train through France and picked up a steamer going through the Suez Canal. He reached Melbourne in early December.

The long journey, freed from the immediacy of his financial problems, gave Shackleton ample time to nurse his anxieties. To Emily, he wrote that the parting was the 'worst aching heart moment in my life'. He said that were he forced to turn back just 10 miles from the Pole, it would 'not mean so much sadness' as when they separated. He would not, he emphasised 'run any risk' for the sake of getting to the Pole. But he reassured her that if successful in his quest there would be 'ample money' in future.

Shackleton was also convinced that *Nimrod* would be his sole opportunity in life to make his fortune and carve out a respectable position in society. 'I can really and truly promise darling that when I come back again I will never go away from you,' he wrote. It was the same promise he made before sailing on *Discovery*.

A different measure of guilt gripped Shackleton when he wrote to Elspeth, anxious to make peace over her husband's loan. 'You cannot think much of me whilst I have not paid back to Will [Beardmore] all the money he so generously lent me,' he said. 'But things have been very bad for me. I wish I could see you and have a long talk and tell you all the news.'

Shackleton was torn between Emily and Elspeth, yet needed both. While Emily provided the comfortable home and domestic peace and stability he could never muster, it was Elspeth who seemed to understand him best and who offered the sort of encouragement he craved.

Emily's unquestioning and loving support was as essential as the oxygen he breathed. 'You are a thousand times too good for me,' he told her. Emily, however, was a passive force. The rough and tumble and life-and-death struggle of exploration were unfamiliar territory to the cultured, mild-mannered Edwardian woman nearing her 40s who yearned for the comfortable orthodoxy of home and motherhood. While she did not stand in the way of her husband's ambitions or complain too loudly about his wayward behaviour, she did not actively encourage Shackleton onto each new quest. Emily had come to terms with wanting a conventional husband but loving an unconventional adventurer.

Elspeth, by contrast, was a more positive champion, eagerly encouraging Shackleton to fulfil the dreams he laid out before her at their private meetings. 'God knows for never a day passes that I do not think of you,' he wrote shortly before leaving London. 'My words were ever poor and feeble to express all that I felt and all I thought about you dear girl,' he said. 'Only know and understand this that the greatest factor in the world and in the work I am trying to do is the thought of what you think ... [I] want and want so much for you to be proud of me.'[1] In Shackleton's words, Elspeth gave him 'more courage and greater desire'.[2]

Shackleton's fondest hope was that he would never have to choose between the two women. However, he gave a clue to his thinking by promising to carry a small photograph of Elspeth Beardmore in his kit on the forthcoming trek south. 'Your picture will be the one that will reach the Pole if the gods are kind and I reach it,' he told her. 'I cannot express all I feel.'[3]

Travelling to Australia was a period of transition for Shackleton. It was the phase when he slowly evolved from the restless, unfulfilled character and into the self-assured, ebullient adventurer. Away from the unsettling pressures of home life, Shackleton could now be himself.

He arrived in Australia to discover that his financial difficulties had chased him to the other side of the world. The loan from William Bell in Ireland, on which he was relying, had failed to materialise because of unrelated banking problems elsewhere. Shackleton, resourceful as ever, turned to new faces.

The most promising acquaintance was Tannant William Edgeworth David, a notable Australian geologist. David, now closing on 50, had built a formidable reputation as a field geologist in Australia – he discovered the vast Hunter Valley coalfields of New South Wales – and lecturer at the University of Sydney. Though born in Wales, David had been in Australia for 25 years and was now a household name.

With an eye on David's influence in Australia, Shackleton had initially offered him an opportunity to join *Nimrod* for the voyage south to King Edward VII Land in return for advising the novices Priestley and Brocklehurst. David liked the idea and became even more enthusiastic after meeting Shackleton.

The pair met in Melbourne where Shackleton was delivering a public lecture and David was much impressed with his breeziness and the easy way he captivated the audience of 4,000 packed into the theatre. Shackleton responded to the warmth of the Australians with typical generosity and donated the proceeds of the lecture to local charities. It was a remarkable gesture considering the expedition's precarious finances. But, as a colleague noted, Shackleton's heart was always bigger than his pockets.

Australia, in turn, responded with similar generosity. At David's request, the government agreed to provide a grant of £5,000 (around £300,000/€360,000 today), which effectively ended Shackleton's immediate worries. It also provided a stark contrast to the lacklustre backing from Britain.

Shackleton's knack of judging people worked well in the case of David. Strong in both character and determination, David was a national symbol for Australia, still a young, emergent country which was slowly piecing together its own national identity. Federal government had arrived in Australia only six years earlier and David was among those who recognised that exploration was a natural way of creating a broader national profile. He was also the perfect man to pioneer the trail.

David seized on the prospect of going south with Shackleton, emphasising in particular the importance of scientific research and the boost to national pride. After his achievement in unearthing the New South Wales coal deposits, David was also enthusiastic about finding mineral reserves. It was a theme which echoed with Shackleton's own belief that out there somewhere was a pot of gold waiting to be found. Assisting Shackleton, David argued, would gain prestige for nations who supported the expedition and he believed there was 'a very fair chance of the South Pole being reached'. With little hesitation, the Australian government duly approved the grant.

Buoyed by the support, Shackleton seized the opportunity to expand the expedition and incorporate a sizeable Australian contingent to the operation. The men chosen were David, Douglas Mawson and Bertram Armytage.

Mawson, a strongly built, 25-year-old former student of David's, was lecturing in geology at the University of Adelaide. He came to Australia as a child and was keen to obtain first-hand knowledge of a continental ice cap. Mawson, tall, humourless and highly motivated, was appointed as official physicist even though he was not, in fact, a physicist. The Australian-born Armytage was recruited to help manage the ponies. At 38, he was older than most of the party but his track record – Cambridge-educated and a distinguished record in the Boer War – was impressive.

Shackleton next hurried to New Zealand to meet *Nimrod* and began drawing together the expedition's many loose ends. One last-minute decision was to move Aeneas Mackintosh, one of *Nimrod*'s officers and the son of a colonial planter, to the landing party and replace him with Arthur Harbord.

New Zealand, if anything, was even more enthusiastic about the expedition than Australia and Shackleton was eager to exploit his popularity. His closest contacts were Joseph Kinsey and Leonard Tripp who began to sound out influential local businessman and politicians for support.

Kinsey, Shackleton's agent in New Zealand, was an avuncular English-born shipping representative who had acted for *Discovery* and managed to secure the free use of facilities at Lyttelton Harbour. *Nimrod*'s crew were given rail passes for the local area.

Tripp was a well-appointed lawyer in his mid-40s who had also met Shackleton on *Discovery* and now took him to the higher echelons of New Zealand society. It was Tripp who introduced Shackleton to Prime Minster Sir Joseph Ward, in the hope of securing a government grant.

'I've interviewed fifty millionaires and not one would give me a penny,' Shackleton told one newspaper. 'I hope your New Zealand government ... will give a lead.' Shackleton was a journalist's dream, providing lively quotes and flamboyant stories and in return the newspapers responded by urging the government to donate money to the expedition. 'Will New Zealand Help?' one headline demanded. A few days later the Cabinet approved a grant of £1,000 to the expedition.

Crowds 50,000-strong packed the compact little port of Lyttelton on New Year's Day, 1908 to watch *Nimrod* depart for the south. A flotilla of ships gathered to provide an informal guard of honour as *Nimrod* edged along the harbour's narrow corridor towards open water. Brass bands played stirring tunes like 'Auld Lang Syne' and the crews of three Royal Navy warships assembled to deliver three rousing cheers.

The enthusiasm of New Zealanders was both welcome and extremely fortunate for Shackleton. Shortly before sailing into the Southern Ocean, it became apparent that *Nimrod* was too small for the task of carrying nearly 40 men, tons of supplies and equipment and assorted animals to King Edward VII Land. Every corner of the ship was packed tight and there was a critical shortage of space in the bunkers to store coal for the 5,000-mile (8,000 km) round trip. *Nimrod*, a poor sailer, could not rely on favourable winds and without the vital ballast provided by tons of coal, the vessel was also at serious risk of being swamped by the heavy seas.

Entering the Southern Ocean with an unseaworthy vessel was impossible and Shackleton's hasty piece of improvisation was to arrange for *Nimrod* to be towed to the edge of the ice by a much larger steamer. Shackleton took his bold idea to the Union Steamship of Dunedin which agreed to charter the 1,000-ton tramp steamer, *Koonya*. Sir James Mills, the company's chairman and a prominent local businessman, agreed to fund half the cost and New Zealand government, to Shackleton's great relief, agreed to pay the remaining half.

The wisdom of towing *Nimrod* to the ice was apparent as soon as the ship left the sanctuary of Lyttelton Harbour. Heavily overloaded, the vessel struggled towards the rendezvous with *Koonya,* with a freeboard of little more than 3 feet (1 m). The Plimsoll line had long disappeared beneath the waves.

The lifeline to *Koonya* was initially about 400 yards (365 m) of 4-inch (10 cm) steel cable shackled onto *Nimrod*'s two chain cables which were attached to either side of her bow. Although the chains acted as a form of shock absorber, it was soon evident that the added weight of around 9 tons (over 9,000 kg) dragged the nose of the ship down into the choppy waters. *Nimrod*, said Shackleton, moved through the seas 'like a reluctant child being dragged to school'.

Conditions on *Nimrod* were appalling and made significantly worse when the ship ran into foul weather within hours of leaving Lyttelton. The storm lasted unbroken for 10 days and *Nimrod* at times rolled over to an angle of 50° in ferocious hurricane-force winds. Some estimated the waves at nearly 100 feet (30 m). At one point, *Koonya*'s skipper, Captain Frederick

Pryce Evans, was asked to pour oil on the seas to calm the turbulence, though it made little difference. 'I have never seen such large seas in the whole of my seagoing career,' Second Officer Harbord recalled. 'What a seasick crowd of passengers I had,' Captain England noted.

The tenacity of Captain Evans on *Koonya* was remarkable. Dr Eric Marshall said that 'Not more than one skipper in 100' would have clung onto *Nimrod* in the mountainous seas. On *Nimrod* Shackleton said *Koonya* was 'just a funnel and a mast lurching through the spray.'

Every inch of space was filled with either boxes of equipment, bags of coal and stalls for the suffering ponies. On the spur of the moment, Shackleton had added to the shocking congestion by suddenly giving a berth to George Buckley, a local New Zealand farmer and keen yachtsman from Ashburton near Christchurch. Buckley gave £500 to the expedition in return for a round trip to the ice and, in another last-minute decision, Shackleton agreed. Buckley dashed to his club barely two hours before *Nimrod* sailed, gave power of attorney to a friend, picked up a few personal items and hurried back to the ship just minutes before departure. He was dressed only in a lightweight summer suit for the coldest seas on earth.

Most of the expedition's landing party were packed into a claustrophobic compartment without proper ventilation measuring just 15 x 8 feet (4.5 m x 2.4 m) and conditions for the crew were no better. Men wore the same wet clothes for two weeks and, with most constantly sick, the stench of vomit was almost overpowering.

Priestley said the compartment, nicknamed 'Oyster Alley,' was not fit for 10 dogs. 'It was more like Hell than anything I have ever imagined before,' he said. For some it was more comfortable to sleep on deck, despite the tumult. Three times a day the little wardroom, just 12 feet long by 9 feet wide (3.6 m x 2.7m), somehow accommodated mealtimes for 22 people. On the eighth day, heavy seas washed into the galley, dousing the stoves and briefly denying the men the basic comfort of hot food.

The scarcity of space meant that five of the 15 ponies were left behind at Lyttelton and one animal had to be shot after falling during the journey. At the height of the storm one of the nine dogs drowned while another produced a litter of six pups.

The first icebergs were spotted on 14 January as *Nimrod* neared the outer fringes of the Ross Sea. Next morning, as they approached the Antarctic Circle, pack ice came into view and *Koonya* prepared to cut the umbilical cord which had carried the ships through more than 1,500 miles (2,400 km).

Shortly before the ships separated, Buckley was rowed across the choppy waters to *Koonya* and a line was rigged to transfer the dripping carcasses of some newly slaughtered sheep which were carried to the ice as a gift from New Zealand. But a heavy swell prevented the transfer of more coal and supplies.

One person who did not transfer to *Koonya* was David, who had decided to spend a year in the south with the expedition as head of scientific staff. Whether or not he always intended to join the expedition proper is unclear, but in any event David did not reveal his intentions until he was far out of reach and he asked Buckley to deliver a note to Sydney University requesting a 12-month leave of absence.

The appointment was a huge boost to Shackleton who at a stroke had transformed the expedition's scientific programme from imprecision to solid and respected endeavour. The geology, as Priestley recognised, would be 'vastly more valuable' in the accomplished hands of David. Equally important was that David's presence allowed Shackleton to delegate the expedition's scientific responsibilities and concentrate solely on getting to the Pole. 'Scientific work,' Mawson later recalled, 'could be undertaken only if it did not interfere with the main object, namely that of achieving the Pole.'

However, the appointment was another unexpected cost to the expedition's already uncertain finances. Shackleton was so keen to secure David's services that he paid a handsome salary of £600 a year (around £35,000/€42,000 today) and guaranteed David's wife another £600 if the landing party was unable to return to New Zealand in 1909. 'I think it is cheap to get such a man,' he told Emily.

The line to *Koonya* was severed at lunchtime on 15 January, leaving *Nimrod* alone on the edge of the pack ice. It needed six hours of hard work in rough seas for the ship's windlass to reel in the full 840 feet (256 m) of cable which had held the ships together for two weeks.

Initially, *Nimrod* enjoyed decent weather as the vessel approached the ice pack's impressive formation of icebergs, some several miles in length, which stretched as far as the eye could see in all directions. A calm stillness fell on the area as the ship entered the icy labyrinth, slowly threading a path along the narrow lanes of dark open water running between the floating mountains of ice.

Shackleton was extremely fortunate for the most challenging part of the voyage. Winds remained light and, after only a few hours of slow steaming, Shackleton climbed into the crow's nest to find miles of open water directly ahead. No ship had ever made a swifter journey through the pack. Shortly afterwards, winds rose sharply, temperatures dropped below freezing point and a heavy snow began to fall.

Nimrod *cruising in Antarctic waters, 1908.*

Thrilled at escaping the pack, Shackleton now changed his mind about seeking winter quarters on King Edward VII Land. The new destination was Balloon Inlet, the opening on the Barrier from where he and Scott had made their perilous ascents in the observational balloon six years earlier. Although no one had ever established winter quarters on the Barrier, the inlet was reckoned to be about 100 miles (160 km) nearer the Pole and worth the risk.

A wave of optimism swept over the party, with some cheerfully expecting to make a rapid landing and have enough spare time to undertake at least two major forays into the ice to lay supply depots before winter descended. David wanted to lead a team eastwards towards the unexplored King Edward VII Land, while Shackleton wanted to place provisions at least 200 miles (320 km) to the south. It all depended on how quickly the inlet could be found.

Nimrod turned east, running alongside the imposing perpendicular face of the Barrier. At one point the ship entered a small bay where hundreds of whales suddenly emerged, blowing and cavorting in what Shackleton described as a 'veritable playground' for the noblest of sea creatures. It was named the Bay of Whales.

Shackleton was invigorated by his return to the ice. Months of strain over preparation, fund-raising and organisation evaporated in what he described as the 'indescribable freshness' of the Antarctic landscape. It was a feeling that permeated his soul and was, he said, 'responsible for that longing to go again which assails each returned explorer from polar regions'.

The ship pressed ahead without seeing a glimpse of Balloon Inlet. It soon became apparent that calving of ice from the Barrier had changed its shape since the visit of *Discovery*. At the place where Balloon Inlet was marked on charts the face of the Barrier was unrecognisable. Sightings confirmed that *Nimrod* stood further south than where *Discovery* had moored in 1902. The area, reshaped by the immense forces of nature, had merged into the larger Bay of Whales and the proposed landing site no longer existed.

Nimrod could not afford to linger. Little more than four weeks remained to unload supplies and erect a hut before the ship would be forced to leave on 1 March and the area was threatened by menacing ice formations. In haste, Captain England turned the ship and hurried away with barely 50 yards (45 m) of navigable water to spare.

Opinions on board were mixed, with some urging Shackleton to make another attempt to navigate the ice in an attempt to land somewhere in King Edward VII Land. Others raised the possibility of abandoning the area altogether and turning west to the safer waters of McMurdo Sound, despite the promise to Scott.

Shackleton, appalled at the potential catastrophe had winter quarters been established on the unstable Barrier ice, resolved to look for a site on terra firma. He retreated into a private huddle with England, who was increasingly concerned about *Nimrod*'s limited coal capacity.

Both Shackleton and England were under intense strain. Shackleton felt that England, a conventional mariner, was too cautious and England sensed Shackleton was too reckless. On the way south, Shackleton had told Emily that England was a 'splendid man [and a] good sailor.' He was less sure now as the pressure built.

Tension between ship's captain and expedition leader was a common difficulty. While Shackleton was the uncontested leader of the expedition, the laws of the sea determined that the captain was ultimately responsible for the safety of the vessel. Both men were feeling their way over new ground. Shackleton was leading an expedition for the first time and England, only 29 years old, had never captained a ship before.

For a brief spell, England took *Nimrod* east again, hoping for one last chance to find a route through the ice to land on the coast of King Edward VII Land. Less than 24 hours later, *Nimrod* ran into an impenetrable wall of ice. 'It must be part of my life that I go on striving for things that are out of reach,' Shackleton wrote. 'The prospect of reaching King Edward VII Land seemed to grow more remote every ensuing hour.'

With precious time running out, the known area around McMurdo Sound was the only realistic alternative as winter quarters. It is not entirely clear who decided to make the contentious switch, though England's growing anxiety over coal was undoubtedly an important factor. But in all probability it was the more decisive Shackleton who made the final choice.

By early evening of 25 January, *Nimrod* turned for the entrance into McMurdo Sound. In England's words, another hour would have 'seen us embayed'.

Shackleton was in turmoil over the change of direction and Harbord reported that everyone was 'sick at heart and utterly disappointed'. Shackleton, fully aware that his reputation would be savaged when news reached Britain, could only write: 'My heart was heavy within me.' But there is little doubt that the decision was correct in the circumstances.

'I have been through a sort of Hell,' Shackleton told his wife. Each mile sailed alongside the Barrier towards McMurdo Sound, he told Emily, was 'a horror' and added: 'My conscience is clear but my heart is sore. But I have one comfort that I did my best.'[4]

In contrast, Eric Marshall said he would never forgive Shackleton's 'double cross' of Scott and would go to his grave insisting that Shackleton never had any intention of overwintering in King Edward VII Land. In his diary written at the time, Marshall declared that Shackleton 'hasn't got the guts of a louse ... he has made no attempt to reach King Edward VII Land.' Four decades later in 1952 he wrote unequivocally: 'I have always been quite convinced that Shackleton never intended to land anywhere but at Scott's base.'[5]

What Marshall did not appreciate was it was the decision of a born survivor. Shackleton had no interest in unnecessary sacrifice. Going to McMurdo Sound was purely practical and he was prepared to suffer the pain of a broken promise to keep his expedition alive.

chapter 16

Ice and Men

Hut Point, the small peninsula jutting into McMurdo Sound close to where *Discovery* had wintered, was the target. The secluded spit at the southerly reaches of the inlet, where the land mass of Ross Island meets the Barrier ice shelf, was familiar territory for Shackleton, an important consideration as he plotted the trek to the Pole.

The inlet of McMurdo Sound is about 30 miles (48 km) long and 20 miles (32 km) wide in places but the same seas which *Discovery* had navigated with apparent ease only a few years earlier, were now blocked by an insurmountable wall of ice some 16 miles (24 km) deep. *Nimrod*'s attempts to ram the ice were fruitless.

The lateness of the season and the immense task of unloading tons of supplies and equipment before *Nimrod* sailed added to the pressure. So, too, did the sorry condition of the ponies. After a month at sea the animals were in a pitiable state and one was shot, reducing the expedition's vital mode of transport to just eight.

Worse followed on 31 January when Mackintosh, the late addition to the landing party, suffered a serious injury while unloading the ship. A crate hook slipped and smashed into his eye, damaging it beyond repair. Marshall and Mackay, the doctors, laid Mackintosh on the cabin floor and removed his right eye under the flickering light of a single oil lamp.

Another setback came when Shackleton pressed the motor vehicle into action to help with the task of getting supplies ashore. However, the arrival of the first car on the continent was a sadly disappointing event.

Nursed by the patient tinkering of Day, the Arrol-Johnston travelled only a few feet and spluttered to a halt, pulsating violently. Day, hunched over the vehicle, managed to coax the engine back to life again but as soon as the wheels began to turn, the car sank deep into the soft slushy surface and came to a standstill. Although the vehicle eventually managed a few minor trips, it was clear that it could operate only on solid ice. Shackleton was correct in not planning his polar journey around the experimental Arrol-Johnston.

On 3 February, with ice still blocking the way south, *Nimrod* steamed slowly along the west coast of Ross Island looking for an alternative landing site. At Cape Royds, a volcanic headland about 20 miles (32 km) north of Hut Point, they found a small natural harbour near the tip of the promontory which appeared to offer a suitable haven.

Venturing a few hundred yards ashore, Shackleton came across an area of flat, bare rock littered with volcanic debris which was an ideal place to build winter quarters. A nearby hill offered natural shelter against the strong prevailing south-easterly winds and a source of fresh water was provided by a small lake. Across the ice-choked waters of McMurdo Sound to the west were the dazzling peaks and glaciers of the Royal Society Range rising over 13,000 feet (4,000 m) in places and to the east, wisps of smoke drifted lazily from the Ross Island's most prominent feature, the towering volcano of Mount Erebus. On the southern horizon lay the great Ice Barrier, the route to the Pole.

What should have been a routine exercise in unloading supplies and equipment soon descended into chaos. A strong squall blew, forcing England to retreat away from the coastline. It was the start of two weeks of frustrating delays as England, desperate to avoid getting trapped or being dashed against the rocks, dodged in and out of the area, depositing loads at irregular intervals before beating a hasty retreat to safer waters.

England was a naturally guarded man who refused to take any risks with his ship and his wariness intensified as *Nimrod,* noticeably lighter as stores were shipped ashore, grew more unsteady in the rough seas. At times, he took *Nimrod* 10 miles (16 km) out to sea to avoid the buffeting while those on shore watched with frustration.

The work onshore was intolerably hard. Without a natural harbour, stores were unceremoniously dumped on the ice and men were forced to drag heavy sledges across dangerously unstable sea ice in appalling weather. Rest was fleeting. Others were digging out the foundations for the hut in rock-hard ground and freezing conditions.

The strain inevitably caused a growing rift between Shackleton and England. Where Shackleton was desperate to get some 180 tons of supplies ashore as fast as possible, England seemed to grow even more cautious as conditions worsened. While Shackleton was accustomed to overcoming obstacles through sheer force of personality, England refused to take 'foolish risks' with *Nimrod.*

Shackleton, initially at least, was sympathetic and supportive towards England. *Nimrod*, after all, was his lifeline to the outside world. He once reprimanded Marshall for criticising the captain. England, too, had personal reasons for his caution. Shortly before leaving New Zealand, he had become engaged to be married.

But Shackleton's patience, thin at the best of times, disappeared as the urgency of the situation began to grow. It was also apparent that the frustrated landing party was on the verge of mutiny, demanding that Shackleton take a firmer grip and order England to be more adventurous. Wild declared that England had 'lost his nerve' and was 'off his rocker' while Mackintosh said he was 'pigheaded & obstinate'.

The episode with England was the first real test of Shackleton's leadership. It was an important moment since the expedition risked descending into anarchy without the confidence of his men. Tackling England now became as much about enforcing Shackleton's status as commander as about unloading supplies.

England, who came from a small village outside York, had done little to foster friendships on the trip and remained aloof from most on board. He became even more isolated as the crisis developed. 'I am growing more & more alone in myself,' he wrote to his fiancée. He rarely spoke to anyone except Shackleton, David and Chief Engineer, Harry Dunlop. 'Most of the landing party have come to the conclusion that the strain was too much for him,' Dunlop said. 'His nerves were in a bad state.'

The turning point came when Shackleton's frustration finally boiled over during a dramatic moment on the bridge. Seas were calm and Shackleton demanded that *Nimrod* be brought close in to resume unloading. England refused. Shackleton, maddened by England's reticence, thrust his hand onto the telegraph to signal 'Full Steam Ahead'. England responded by putting his hand over Shackleton's and forcibly altering the signal to 'Full Speed Astern'.

Soon afterwards, a violent storm carried *Nimrod* – with Shackleton still on board – almost 50 miles (80 km) out to sea and brought new delays. Those on shore were gripped by a fear that England had cut and run, leaving the cold, poorly equipped men critically short of coal and supplies for the winter. It was misplaced pessimism, but Shackleton now grasped the critical urgency of the situation.

In a half-hearted attempt to wrest control, he first looked for the easy way out by asking England to resign on the grounds of ill health. England refused, despite admitting that the burden of responsibility was causing him increasing anxiety. There were occasions, England confessed, when he 'broke down and shook' under the strain. Others saw the pressure only too easily. Davis, the First Officer, reported that England was 'tired and ill' and Dunlop was of the view that England was 'totally unfitted' to be in charge of *Nimrod*.

Sacking England was now the last option. Shackleton, according to Dunlop, was in an 'awful state of mind' as he contemplated relieving England of command. His mood was complicated by a series of extravagant earlier promises made to England which offered little incentive to step down.

The private pledges made by Shackleton included a generous offer of £450 a year for four years and a 10 per cent share in any profits the expedition might make from peripheral activities like book sales and public lectures. 'If I make £30,000 clear,' Shackleton gaily promised, 'you will have £3,000; if £40,000, you will have £4,000; if £50,000, you will have £5,000.' A sum of £5,000 in today's terms would be worth close to £300,000/€360,000.[1]

But Shackleton was left with no choice and he ordered England to be dismissed as soon as *Nimrod* returned to New Zealand. 'I cannot have England down again,' he told Emily. 'He is ill and has lost his nerve.'[2]

It was a straightforward decision, but Shackleton conveniently decided not to inform England of his sacking. Perhaps he was concerned about his mental condition or perhaps he wanted to avoid a time-wasting dispute at a moment when it was critically important to unload *Nimrod*. In later conversations with Emily, Shackleton had instructed Dunlop to 'put [England] in irons if necessary'.

The last stocks of coal were ferried ashore on 22 February, bringing the total to around 18 tons, which was scarcely enough for one winter. Shackleton had wanted 30 tons but time was short. Some wondered how much coal had been squandered by England's reluctance to bring *Nimrod* in to shore.

At 10 p.m. in the evening, *Nimrod*'s bow was pointed north and the ship slipped away from McMurdo Sound, leaving the winter party of 15 men to finish the hut and safeguard the assorted supplies and equipment strewn across the windy cape. Even the departure had an air of haste about it, with little time for farewells. Some pieces of equipment were never taken off the ship. Few of the landing party bothered to say goodbye to England.

Among the letters *Nimrod* carried north was a confidential note to the agent Joseph Kinsey sacking England. In the letter Shackleton declared that *Nimrod* should be brought back to Cape Royds in 1909 by Mackintosh – if he had recovered from the loss of his eye – or by Captain Evans from *Koonya*.

England subsequently learned of his fate on reaching New Zealand. He was deeply upset and strenuously refuted suggestions that his health had broken down in McMurdo Sound. 'I am perfectly sound both in body and mind and my resignation has been forced upon me,' he told Kinsey. He married his fiancée shortly after landing, but either through loyalty to Shackleton or embarrassment at his own dismissal, England always refused to speak publicly about the controversy.

The row inevitably reached the newspapers almost as soon as *Nimrod* docked at Lyttelton on 8 March. 'There are reports of serious dissension between Captain England and Lieutenant Shackleton,' one account proclaimed. With Shackleton thousands of miles away and England rejecting all attempts to discuss matters, the press eagerly filled the void with garish reports of fights, arguments and general discord. 'Struggle on the Bridge,' one headline yelled.

Shackleton's reputation in Australia and New Zealand, which had been flying high before *Nimrod* sailed, was undoubtedly damaged by the episode and exacerbated because he was not on hand to defend his actions. Worse followed when it emerged that, contrary to plans, *Nimrod* had failed to carry out a series of magnetic and oceanographic tasks for the authorities in Australia and New Zealand.

The work was something of a quid pro quo for the money given by the Australians and New Zealanders. It left Shackleton vulnerable to charges of breaking a promise and even to one of obtaining money under false pretences. *The Lyttelton Times* questioned Shackleton's right to 'calmly appropriate' the £6,000 of funding from the nations.

The row was not the only storm to have broken around Shackleton. At home creditors were still clamouring to be paid while Beardmore had gone from friend to enemy over the unpaid loan of £1,000. Beardmore viewed the loan as strictly business and was especially concerned to discover that the money had ended up in the unsavoury hands of Frank Shackleton. In retaliation he simply washed his hands of Shackleton.

News that Shackleton was camped at Cape Royds broke like a bombshell in London. Scott, furious at the broken promise, led the outcry of indignation. He branded Shackleton a 'professed liar' and sought comfort from establishment friends like Markham and Keltie. 'I cannot have any further dealings with Shackleton,' Scott told Keltie.

Anger aside, Scott also feared that Shackleton might, after all, beat him to the Pole. McMurdo Sound was something of a prized possession to anyone contemplating a bid for the Pole. It was mapped and familiar. The same could not be said of King Edward VII Land or Balloon Inlet, where

Shackleton was supposed to have gone. The advantage in the race to the Pole now favoured Shackleton.

The prospect of losing out to Shackleton was mortifying to Scott and that at some point he might be called upon to applaud his success in public. 'It is very awkward in many ways,' he told Bernacchi. 'I shall find it impossible not to doubt any result he claims – I am sure he is prepared to lie rather than admit failure and I take it he will lie artistically.'[3]

Keltie, however, was astute enough to see that the RGS would be placed in a very awkward position if Shackleton somehow managed to defy all odds and return in triumph with the Pole in the bag. Keltie, as the saying went, worked both sides of the street.

He offered sympathy to Scott, suggesting that Shackleton had 'deliberately disregarded' his promises. 'Personally, I am quite with you,' he wrote in soothing terms to Scott. But Keltie took a different tone with Emily Shackleton, offering his understanding of her husband's painful dilemma at selecting acceptable winter quarters in the face of very difficult conditions. 'Under the circumstances as described by him it was difficult to see that he could have done otherwise than he did,' Keltie told her.

It was a stance shared by the wily Markham, who was also quietly laying the ground for the possibility of Shackleton reaching the Pole. Markham had invested nearly 20 years of his life encouraging the British to reach the Pole first and he was determined to share in the glory when it happened. 'I am responsible for having started all this Antarctic business,' he wrote.

Markham, another working both sides of the street, offered a comforting and placatory tone to Emily regarding her husband's choice of McMurdo Sound. There were, Markham insisted, 'two sides to the story' and suggested that '... nothing more should be heard about it'. He did not mean it.

chapter 17

Making Ready

Shackleton signed off from civilisation for at least a year in cursory fashion, writing two short, hurriedly crafted notes to Emily. Grabbing a few moments amid the frantic activity between the ship and Cape Royds, the final letters were a mixture of gentle reassurance, unwavering optimism and an understandable hint of melancholia.

'Goodbye Darling Wife, God keep you and our children,' he wrote on 18 February. 'I think we will get to the Pole. I cannot write more, my whole heart is with you. Your husband Ernest. I am fit and well.'[1]

Four days later, shortly before *Nimrod* sailed north, he scribbled his last note. 'Heaven knows I have been through enough worry and anxiety since I left,' he said. 'I am longing for the time I can clasp you again to my arms darling and hold our dear children in my arms again. Now my wife for the last time for a year goodbye.' The letter ended with '*Prospice*', the word from Browning whose defiant significance was a secret code to each other.[2]

As the plumes of smoke from *Nimrod* disappeared over the horizon on 22 February 1908, the 15 men watching apprehensively from Cape Royds were probably the most isolated humans on the planet. They were the only living souls on the entire continent.

The enormous task of stockpiling and preparing for oncoming winter meant there was no time for reflection in the busy days after the ship sailed. The hut and stables for the ponies remained half-finished and the area was a jumble of coal dumps and packing cases, many covered in layers of ice and snow. Picks and crowbars were needed to unearth some equipment. Some disappeared altogether.

To Shackleton's intense disappointment, the delay unloading supplies from *Nimrod* was a serious blow to his plans to lay valuable supply depots on the Barrier in readiness for the spring drive to the Pole. But the sea ice, which had initially blocked the path to Hut Point, had now drifted away,

Shackleton at Cape Royds on Ross Island, Antarctica, 1908.

making travel to the south almost impossible until the waters froze again in deeper winter. The delay also robbed the untried men of getting useful experience of the ice.

By early March, with the hut, pony stables and stock building largely complete, David offered Shackleton an intriguing suggestion. Eager to test himself in the Antarctic landscape, David proposed sending a party to scale the unclimbed peak of Mount Erebus.

Despite the obvious risks and dangers to men without proper climbing equipment or mountaineering skills, the idea appealed to Shackleton. Erebus was within comparatively easy reach of Cape Royds. If all else failed, scaling Mount Erebus might be regarded as a decent accomplishment.

After hurried preparations, a summit party of David, Mawson and Mackay set off three days later to climb the active 12,448-foot (3,794 m) volcano. Supported by Adams, Marshall and Brocklehurst, they left hauling a sledge with about 560 lb (250 kg) of supplies for six days. Adams, a career mariner who knew nothing about mountaineering, was notionally in charge.

To equipped and experienced men, it was a straightforward climb up gentle slopes of a mountain whose distinctive cone shape had been fashioned by countless years of lava discharges. But the party was neither prepared nor practised.

The sledge was dropped in the early stages of the climb and much of their equipment, such as sleeping bags, a primus stove and food, was slung over their backs in makeshift rucksacks each weighing around 40 lb (18 kg). Tent poles were ditched because they were too cumbersome and some climbed without the aid of crampons. The procession, said David, was 'more bizarre than beautiful'.

From the hut, Shackleton watched through a telescope in the early stages of the climb as the six small dark shapes, silhouetted against the white slopes, edged slowly upwards. What he did not see was that Brocklehurst, struggling with altitude sickness and frostbite, had to be left behind a few thousand feet from the summit. Or that Adams, having gained a taste for climbing, wanted to share in the triumph and decided to press on to the top with David, Mawson, Mackay and Marshall.

After nearly five days of exhausting work, the summit of Mount Erebus was reached on 10 March. At the top they met a choking stench of sulphur and peered into a hissing, steam-filled conical crater half a mile wide, echoing to the belching innards of the volcano. Adams, David, Mackay, Marshall and Mawson were the first to ascend a mountain in the Antarctic.

The descent, by contrast with the laboured climb, was a haphazard clamber down the mountain in less than 48 hours, picking up Brocklehurst on the way. In the rush, the men slithered down snowy slopes, half scrambling, half tumbling. Drained but exhilarated, they staggered into the hut at Cape Royds and celebrated their triumph with a glass of champagne.

The champagne, said Shackleton 'tasted like nectar'. He would not be returning home empty-handed.

However, the edge was taken off the celebrations by disturbing news about the deteriorating condition of eight ponies. One animal died after eating the volcanic sand around the hut and three more died soon after. As winter approached, Shackleton was left with only four of the original 15 animals selected. Six animals were seen as the minimum for the Pole.

The loss of the ponies' pulling power was a serious blow and the condition of some of his men also gave rise to concern. Only weeks after landing, Shackleton was now forced to rethink his plans for the southern journey.

Initially he planned to match six men – Adams, Brocklehurst, Joyce, Marshall, Wild and himself – with six fit ponies for the march. It was a sound blend of experience and youth, muscle and versatility, and the expertise of a doctor for emergencies. Elsewhere, David, Mawson and Mackay, who had appeared to work well together on Erebus, were already scheduled for the long trip to locate the South Magnetic Pole, while

Nimrod party (standing l–r): Joyce, Day, Wild, Adams, Brocklehurst, Shackleton, Marshall, David, Armytage, Marston; (sitting l–r) Priestley, Murray, Roberts. Missing are Mackay and Mawson.

Priestley and Armytage were due to make a trek to the western mountains for geological research.

However, Brocklehurst's injuries on Erebus proved much worse than anticipated. His toes had turned black from frostbite and gangrene began to set in the weeks after his return. Marshall decided to amputate. In April, with Mackay as anaesthetist, Marshall removed Brocklehurst's big toe and placed the blackened digit in a vial of spirits. Brocklehurst, who had celebrated his 21st birthday on the slopes of Erebus, subsequently took longer than expected to recover and was excluded from the Pole team.

A further issue arose when Marshall examined the men and decided that Joyce was also unfit for the journey. According to Marshall, Joyce showed symptoms of liver trouble through excessive drinking and was showing faint signs of heart problems. Joyce had also shown signs of being susceptible to the cold. On *Discovery* he needed a brilliant piece of improvisation from his tent-mates who placed his frozen foot on their bare stomachs to revive the circulation and avoid amputation. The same thing occurred at Cape Royds during a short sledging trip with Shackleton.

With the loss of ponies and two of the six-man team, Shackleton pruned the party to four: Adams, Marshall, Wild and himself. Physically it appeared a powerful and well-balanced body of men.

But another weakness was exposed when Marshall persuaded a reluctant Shackleton to undergo a routine examination. 'Pulm[onary] systolic murmur still present,' Marshall concluded after listening to Shackleton's heart.

Although Marshall was not a heart specialist, the diagnosis was an unmistakable warning that Shackleton might not be fit enough for the strenuous southern journey. Marshall had been concerned for some time that Shackleton's health was fragile. As far as Marshall was concerned, Shackleton had pointedly avoided joining the ascent of Mount Erebus because he feared the effects of high altitude on his heart and lungs. Writing almost 50 years later in 1956, he declared that Shackleton had not ventured up Erebus 'for he knew he could not have stood the altitude, 13,500 ft, and would have proved his incompetence before the southern journey'.[3]

But Shackleton, demonstrating the power of personality over reason, somehow persuaded Marshall to ignore the medical evidence and pass him fit for the march. Perhaps Shackleton once again dismissed his health problems as 'asthma' or perhaps Marshall, for all the surly belligerence of his personal diary, was unable to stand up to Shackleton. Or was it simply that Shackleton overruled the doctor?

Whatever the reason, the decision haunted Marshall for decades afterwards. Writing half a century later, he concluded that Shackleton was 'Never fit to carry out any of his programmes'.

Shackleton nonetheless recognised that he had compromised Marshall's position as expedition doctor. Shortly before the start of the journey south, Shackleton gave Marshall a formal letter exonerating him from any blame or responsibility for any health problems which might arise on the march and declaring that if he failed to return, his executors would defend Marshall's medical judgement.

'I have accepted all your medical opinions and acted accordingly,' Shackleton wrote. Although this was evidently untrue, Shackleton insisted that Marshall's responsibility ended when he submitted the medical report. In fact, Shackleton was being selective. Joyce, for example, was removed from the southern party on the strength of Marshall's diagnosis. In Shackleton's case Marshall's 'medical opinions' were simply interpreted differently or ignored.

It is possible that Marshall's discomfort at being overruled helped stoke his vitriolic criticisms and lifelong contempt for Shackleton. Less than a month after landing, he reported that the pair were 'polite but distant' and later lambasted Shackleton as: 'Vacillating, erratic & a liar, easily scared, moody & surly, a boaster.'[4] Marshall was among those who were not swept along by Shackleton's garrulous charm and showmanship. In later life, he would write that Shackleton was 'an attractive crook' and 'an outstanding plausible rogue'.[5]

Marshall was an unsettling character, strongly opinionated and filled with bullish public school arrogance. Well-educated at Monkton Combe public school and Emmanuel College, Cambridge, he was an accomplished rugby player and rower who considered taking holy orders before qualifying as a doctor at London's St Bartholomew's Hospital. Intellectually and physically he felt superior to most, yet beneath the surface there lurked a disquieting suggestion of being unfulfilled. He invariably saw the worst in everyone.

Set against the bitterness and grumbles, Marshall was nonetheless a key member of the team and brought a crucial range of skills and athleticism to the expedition. His medical opinions carried much weight and his assessment of Joyce and Brocklehurst had almost certainly eliminated the potentially catastrophic effects of two men breaking down on the southern journey. The Barrier, as Shackleton knew only too well, was no place for a passenger. Marshall had also taken a surveying course to become the expedition's main cartographer and his readings on the march would be crucial.

An equally important contribution concerned Marshall's perceptive study of the killer disease, scurvy. Knowledge of scurvy had advanced very little in the years since *Discovery* and it would be two decades more before medical science finally identified a lack of vitamin C in humans as the principal cause. By 1908, the cause of scurvy was still commonly blamed on tainted food and poor hygiene.

Marshall had concluded that fresh food was the best antidote to scurvy. It was a view shared by Shackleton, but Marshall took things further by suggesting that the overwintering party should build up resistance to the disease by eating regular amounts of freshly slaughtered and undercooked seal or penguin meat in the months before leaving Cape Royds.

Although humans are unable to store vitamin C for long periods, Marshall was on the right track. Whereas Scott, Wilson and Shackleton were in the early stages of scurvy when they embarked on the southern journey, Marshall's intervention was important. While fresh meat contains only small amounts of vitamin C, it was enough to make a difference. Shackleton, Adams, Marshall and Wild would depart for the south in a far better condition than the *Discovery* party in 1902.

Marshall was not the only difficult character at Cape Royds. It was a hut vibrating to the sharply different and contrasting personalities of 15 men. Shackleton's choice was to manage them with a light touch. He took an interest in everything, his knack of making each man feel as important as the next was uncanny and there was always time for a private chat with individuals, making sure not to favour one above the rest. Shackleton, said one, was 'very tactful and genial' in dealing with individuals who varied from aristocrats like Brocklehurst to itinerant seaman like Joyce, to strong-minded academics like David and Mawson and to the morose Mackay and light-hearted Marston.

The small, rectangular hut, measuring just 33 feet by 19 feet (roughly 10m x 6m) and without windows, was designed with eight separate two-man cubicles to afford a measure of privacy during the long periods of Antarctic darkness. Most tellingly, there was no separation of wardroom and mess deck. Spare blankets could be hung in a cubicle if, in Shackleton's words, an occupant wished to 'sport their oak'. Shackleton enjoyed the minor luxury of his own cubicle but his 'door' was always open and formality and adherence to rank was kept to a minimum. Before long he was simply addressed as The Boss.

The contrast with Scott's strict regime on *Discovery* was stark, although the firmer disciplinary code of a Royal Navy establishment was notably better at keeping a lid on the tensions between men during the long, dark months of winter confinement. But where Scott ruled by the authority of his executive power, Shackleton's strength of leadership stemmed from his remarkable intuition in handling people and a natural authority which, in the main, was accepted by the assortment of personalities jammed together in the small hut. Buckley, the last-minute passenger on *Nimrod*'s journey south, spoke of the 'magnetic influence' of Shackleton's style of leadership.

Tensions arising from the contrasting characters and personal health problems were inevitable, particularly when the sun disappeared in April and ushered in four months of darkness. Armytage became depressed and withdrawn and the serious-minded Mawson occasionally struggled to rub along with the energetic and talkative David. Mackay, a fiery-tempered man, reacted badly when Marston dressed up as a woman and paraded theatrically through the hut making 'advances' at all and sundry. Later Mackay threatened to throttle Roberts over some minor disagreement and Shackleton, according to Marshall's lurid account of the fracas, threatened to shoot Mackay. Wild liked to drink and Murray suffered debilitating bouts of diarrhoea which prompted one wag to label his cubicle the 'taproom'.

Marshall, the outsider, remained brusque and indignant throughout. Much of his venom was reserved for Shackleton. He wrote in his diary that Shackleton was a 'consummate liar & a practised hypocrite' and someone 'incapable of a decent action or thought'.

Keeping the men as busy as possible had worked well under Scott on *Discovery* and Shackleton followed suit. The difference was that little distinction was made in the status between the men and everyone mucked in with routine duties like washing up, shovelling coal, feeding the animals or acting as nightwatchman.

Shackleton set the example. He would venture into the darkness to help scientists dig trenches or collect rock specimens, assist Day in nursing the Arrol-Johnston to life and find time to exercise the ponies. For two months he surrendered his private quarters to the slowly recuperating Brocklehurst. At night healthy debate around the dinner table was encouraged and he often joined the nightwatchman in the early hours for a quiet smoke and a chat.

Shackleton could always be relied upon to break up the long nights by reciting poetry at length. Although poetry was often the emotional anchor for Shackleton, his love of the written word also reflected his egalitarian nature. His tastes were wide and varied, extending from the philosophical Browning to the realism of Robert Service to the classics of Shakespeare and Milton and the popular storytelling of Kipling. But, as though confirming he was both 'fore and aft', Shackleton was equally comfortable with a lusty sea shanty or a bawdy music hall ditty. 'He was a sociable man and liked company,' said Priestley, 'and was always the life and soul of any group in which he happened to be.'

The most notable diversion during the gloomy winter was the printing press, which had the benefit of eating up time and creating a new interest for the men. On the long voyage south, Murray and Mackay produced a handwritten publication called *Antarctic Petrel*, which Shackleton later encouraged them to incorporate into their own expedition book, *Antarctic Days*. But Shackleton wanted to go much further by producing the first book to be printed in Antarctica.

The press was provided by Sir Joseph Causton & Sons, the well-known City publishing firm. Richard Causton, head of the business, was an MP, the government Paymaster General and a member of the Privy Council who moved in the same circles as the Brocklehursts and was also linked to The Skinners' livery company where the Dormans had close ties.

After an approach by Shackleton, Causton saw the public relations potential in one of his printing presses operating in Antarctica and agreed to provide a hand press. He also threw in the ink, paper and type and gave a crash course in typesetting, compositing and printing to Wild and Joyce. The pair, who had been seamen since their youth, spent a few weeks cramming in the basics of a printing industry apprenticeship which in normal circumstances could stretch over seven years of indenture.

In the event, Wild and Joyce produced around 100 copies of a bound 120-page book entitled *Aurora Australis.* Marston provided the impressive artwork and Day miraculously produced the covers from a few discarded Venesta provision cases. Among the 10 articles were two contributions by Shackleton signed under his pseudonym, Nemo.

By August, with the emerging twilight heralding a return of the sun, Shackleton's focus turned to the spring journey and to preparing the men for the coming rigours of man-hauling. The plan was to transfer several tons of supplies across the solid sea ice of McMurdo Sound to the old *Discovery* premises at Hut Point and provide every member with a taste of sledging. To Shackleton, a 'good baptism of frost' was essential.

In the murky half-light of 12 August, Shackleton, David and Armytage – leaders of the expedition's three principal sledging journeys – made the first trip, accompanied by Quan, one of the four remaining ponies. But Quan was sent back after only one hour because temperatures had sunk 40° below freezing and Shackleton dared not risk losing another pony.

The 20-mile (32 km) journey across the frozen waters took almost 36 hours and all three were worn out by the unaccustomed hard work. The surroundings were eerily familiar to Shackleton. He went a short distance onto the Barrier to test the surface, reviving old memories and galvanising his ambition. 'The fascination of the unknown was strong upon me,' he wrote, 'and I longed to be away towards the south on the journey that I hoped would lay bare the mysteries of the place of the pole.'

The sun reappeared above the horizon a week later as Shackleton returned to Cape Royds, determined to press ahead with more ambitious plans to dump a substantial supply depot well over 100 miles (160 km) onto the Barrier. Without the delays in unloading *Nimrod*, this would have been accomplished during the previous autumn.

The six-man party – Shackleton, Adams, Marshall, Wild, Marston and Joyce – set off on 22 September, each pulling the equivalent of 170 lb (77 kg). They were accompanied for eight miles (12 km) by the stuttering Arrol-Johnston. However, the vehicle ground to halt as they encountered the first soft, yielding surfaces. The dogs and ponies, either undervalued or thought too fragile for the Barrier surface, were left behind.

The harshness of spring weather on the Barrier was a shock and the men struggled badly in the face of strong winds and penetrating cold as temperatures sank to -59° (-50 °C). Joyce suffered another bruising encounter with frostbite. But a dump of oil and pony fodder – Depot A – was laid at 79° 36' S and marked by a single black flag on a bamboo rod.

The party returned to Cape Royds on 13 October with the food bags empty, having taken 21 days to make a round-trip of nearly 320 miles (510 km) – including relaying – in very severe weather. 'We were a most ravenous and weary party on our arrival,' Wild wrote. But the most telling statistic was that conditions prevented them from travelling on one in every three days. A repeat of the conditions on the southern march, forcing them into the tent for days on end, would see them eating into rations meant for the later stages of the trek.

Even the depot-laying journey had shown that the issue of weight would be paramount on the journey south. With only four ponies and the great burden of the march resting on the brutality of man-hauling, another supply depot beyond 79° 36' S would have offered vital insurance for the return leg of the journey to Cape Royds. The simple equation was that the southern party could travel only as far as the amount of food they could haul, though the price of the delays during the landing was that only one major depot could be laid.

Huge sacrifices would have to be made to reach the Pole. 'It was evident that we would be unable to take with us towards the Pole as much food as I would have liked,' Shackleton wrote before departure.

Another monumental man-hauling trek was already under way even before Shackleton's depot-laying party returned to Cape Royds. David, Mawson and Mackay had left the hut in early October in search of the South Magnetic Pole. Taking over 700 lb (320 kg), they headed north-west across McMurdo Sound towards the mountains and the unexplored interior of Victoria Land to a point where the compass needle would stand vertically. David, the leader, would reach his 51st birthday somewhere in vast unknown expanses and they would man-haul every step of the way on a round trip of at least 1,000 miles (1,600 km).

Yet the demanding task facing the South Magnetic Pole party appeared almost moderate compared with the immense scale of the undertaking confronting Shackleton on the eve of the push to the South Pole.

chapter 18

South

'I pray that we may be successful for my Heart has been so much in this,' Shackleton wrote on 29 October 1908 as the party took their first steps towards the Pole.

As the crow flies, the Pole was estimated to lie approximately 860 miles (1,375 km) to the south but only the first 300 miles (480 km) of the journey was proven ground. Everything after that was unknown. Did the tabletop-smooth contours of the Barrier run all the way to the Pole or was there a chain of mountains blocking their path? Or was the Pole, like the North Pole, at the centre of a vast ocean of unstable, constantly moving sea ice?

For a round trip of 1,720 miles (2,750 km), Shackleton had taken provisions for just 91 days, which set the daunting target of needing to travel at an average of at least 19 miles (30 km) a day before the food ran out. This was almost twice as fast as Shackleton managed on his last trip across the Barrier with Scott and Wilson. The southern party on *Discovery* had taken 93 days to march 960 miles (1,540 km) – including much time spent relaying sledges – at an average of little more than 10 miles (16 km) a day.

The early signs were encouraging. Clouds had disappeared and the sun was bouncing off the glistening white landscape as the procession of men, animals and machinery got under way. 'A glorious day for our start,' a confident Shackleton recorded.

The motor car began proceedings, dragging a sledge for a few miles in a notional contribution to the long haul before soft ice and clinging snow brought a predictable end to the vehicle's work. The four remaining ponies – Chinaman, Grisi, Quan and Socks – came next, led by their handlers and each pulling a heavily laden sledge. Armytage, Brocklehurst, Joyce, Marston and Priestley came in support, leaving only Murray and Roberts behind at the hut. The dogs, with no role to play, watched in bemusement.

Shackleton's last thoughts were for Emily. 'My own darling Sweeteyes and Wife', he had written in a letter meant to be read only in the event of his death. 'Think kindly of me.'

Shackleton was under no illusions about the risks involved. Between the genuine outpouring of affection and longing for Emily and the children, the letter carried the underlying message that the possibility of reaching the Pole justified the pain. It was all worth it, he seemed to be saying. 'Remember ... your husband will have died in one of the few great things left to be done,' he told her.

Another woman had crossed his mind the night before the march began. While sitting at dinner, sunlight had momentarily broken through a ventilator and circled the portrait of Queen Alexandra hanging in his quarters. The Queen, it appeared, had left her mark on Shackleton. 'It seemed an omen of good luck for only on this day and at that particular time could this have happened,' he wrote in his diary. 'Today we started to strive & plant her flag on the last spot on the world that counts as worth striving for though ungilded by aught but adventure.'

It was his sense of adventure and optimism which permeated the mood at Cape Royds and radiated a belief among the entire ensemble that triumph was within reach. Buoyed by Shackleton's confidence, the cavalcade south began with a spring in its step. Brocklehurst recalled: 'Shackleton was so enthusiastic and so confident in his own ability that he didn't leave very much for us to think other than success.'

The optimism lasted barely an hour. Socks, the grey, went lame and, shortly after, Quan, the largest of the ponies, kicked Adams and cut his leg to the bone. A few inches higher and Adams would have been forced out of the march with a smashed knee cap, reducing the team to three.

A few days of rest was taken at Hut Point for the benefit of Adams and Socks and it was not until the morning of 3 November that the southern party finally stepped onto the Barrier. Brocklehurst captured the moment with his camera as the line of men and ponies trudged off in single file with pennants and Queen Alexandra's Union Jack fluttering to attention in the brisk wind. Almost immediately the party ran into soft snow and Shackleton's transport arrangements suddenly looked questionable.

The animals floundered badly, either breaking through the crusts of soft snow and sinking up to their bellies or slipping and sliding on the hard-packed ice. Like wading through water, it needed great effort to take each step in soft snow and the distressed animals quickly tired. Even when they encountered rock-hard ice, they appeared horribly out of place. The ponies, which were not shod, were unable to find their footing on the glassy ice and at times it was necessary to cut steps for the pitiful animals to move forward.

Nor did the animals' suffering end with the day's march. At night they shivered outside and in their anguish some were off their feed. They were badly affected by the cold because ponies sweat profusely when working hard, dispersing heat from all parts of their bodies. Conditions on the Barrier were notably colder and the ponies were losing body heat at an alarming rate. Dogs, by comparison, are better suited to the cold since their fur offers a natural protection and they sweat only through their paws and by panting.

However, the supremely optimistic Shackleton looked no further than the impressive weight which the ponies were capable of pulling. Each animal could drag over 600 lb (270 kg) and the awful suffering was regarded, more or less, as acceptable for the greater cause. Yet the ponies were consuming 40 lb (18 kg) of feed a day and this had to be pulled along with everything else.

The men, plodding along without skis, were little better equipped than the unhappy ponies and sank up to their ankles in the soft snow. The surface, said Shackleton just two days out, was 'very bad' for both men and ponies. 'Killing work,' Marshall reported. It was as though Shackleton had somehow forgotten that skis had virtually saved his life the last time he ventured onto the Barrier.

Man-hauling, which had taken Shackleton to the brink in 1903, was still the preferred choice when the evidence – and advice from Nansen – demanded a combination of skis and dogs. (The pressure of a man on ski is about ½ lb per square inch compared with 2¼ lb for a man on foot.) Instead, another winter had passed in McMurdo Sound without anyone bothering to master skis or dogs. As the southern journey began, the skis were stacked in the hut at Cape Royds and dogs, pampered as pets throughout the winter, were redundant spare parts.

After the initial spells of dreadful labour, the party was already behind schedule. Shackleton's response was to cut their rations only days into the march. After discussions with Marshall, he concluded that with 'careful management' the 91 days of food could be stretched out for 110 days. Spinning out the rations also had the effect of cutting the daily average from around 19 miles to 16 miles (25 km) a day. 'If we have not done the job in that time it is God's will,' Shackleton added.[1]

The supporting party turned back on 7 November, with Shackleton ordering Joyce to place an additional load of supplies near Minna Bluff, a short way onto the Barrier and about halfway between Cape Royds and Depot A. Shackleton initially saw the extra cache as a little insurance for the return march. But after cutting back on the rations so soon into the march, Joyce's new depot would now be vital in getting the southern party home in one piece.

The returning party broke the stillness of the occasion with three lusty cheers of encouragement as the two groups separated. It was a battle cry to Shackleton, who was now where he wanted to be. All that mattered was the land ahead and how he coped with the coming challenge. It was as though all his life had been a prelude to this moment.

Appalling weather descended next day and they were marooned in their tents for 48 hours, falling even further behind schedule. The long and frustrating hours of inactivity were passed reading, chatting and making sure not to plunder too much of the precious food supplies. Shackleton was buried in Shakespeare's comedies, starting with the amusing tale of reluctant lovers, *Much Ado About Nothing*. Adams carried Arthur Young's *Travels in France* and Marshall took George Borrow's *The Bible in Spain.* Wild's choice was Dickens' *Sketches by Boz.*

The delay also gave Shackleton further time to weigh up his team. Psychologically he wanted to assert his authority, though his leadership was invariably exercised subtly. Where traditionalists exercised authority with an iron rod, Shackleton instinctively chose to earn respect and support through example; where other commanders kept a gulf between themselves and their men, Shackleton was eager to discuss key decisions openly. Loyalty, he decided, had to be earned.

Shackleton had seen at first-hand how petty irritations and personal tensions between men could cause friction. He realised that the safety and well-being of the marchers might come down to how well they worked with each other. Shackleton instinctively felt prevention was better than cure and to avoid resentments building up or cliques developing he decided to rotate the occupants of the two-man tents on a weekly basis. Cooking duties, too, would be shared.

It was a regime which from the start met with only modest acceptance. Adams and Wild were respectful but still non-committal about Shackleton while Marshall simmered discontentedly and saw the leader as a lightning rod for all his petty grievances.

The soft surface remained the major impediment when the march was resumed on 9 November. It was now mixed with a chaotic jumble of crevasses and sastrugi, the frozen wave-like ridges of ice which made the going additionally tough. In one instant, Chinaman crashed through a weak spot in the ice and almost disappeared into a bottomless cavern with a sledge carrying all the cooking gear, half the oil supply and boxes of biscuits.

By chance, it was the last crevasse in the immediate area and Shackleton, falling back on Browning, paraphrased a line from 'Prospice' for his diary: 'When things seem the worst they turn to the best ...'

Firmer ice conditions made travel a little easier and daily distances rose to between 15 and 17 miles (24–27 km) by the middle of the month. Thanks to Marshall's careful navigation, Depot A, approximately 140 miles (225 km) from Cape Royds, was reached on 15 November.

Despite the hard going and flagging ponies, the party was cheered by the creditable daily marches. Shackleton's optimism, for once, appeared well founded and Wild even allowed himself a moment of black humour as he surveyed the possibilities. On 21 November, he wrote: 'I am beginning to think we shall get to the Pole alright but am doubtful about getting back again.'[2]

On the same day, the feeble Chinaman was shot. Shackleton, like Scott, disliked the sight of blood and both Adams and Marshall refused to shoot the animal. It was left to the hard-nosed Wild to pull the trigger, though Marshall, with a surgeon's skill, dutifully sliced up the animal for fresh meat. Depot B, containing about 80 lb (36 kg) of fresh meat and some oil and biscuits, was left at the spot.

The track took the men further to the east than the southern journey in 1902 because Shackleton wanted to steer clear of the broken and hazardous region where the constantly moving ice of the Barrier runs into the immovable mountain range. However, this meant fewer natural landmarks as a guide, leaving the returning party entirely dependent on locating the isolated supply depots on the vacant landscape.

Marking the depots was a shade more accomplished than on the last southern journey, but still far from effective. All supply caches were marked by a mound of snow with a black flag on a bamboo pole. In addition, Shackleton built separate mounds of snow, some 6–7 feet high (up to 2 m), as a further guide, though they were trusting to luck that the stacks would not be eroded by the sun and wind. Locating the depots in hazy conditions would be as difficult as it was in 1903.

Towering new mountains came into view to the south-west as they pushed through the 81st parallel and the sight of Mount Longstaff and Mount Markham, last seen six years earlier, were a reassuring reminder of their progress. Directly to the west was Shackleton Inlet, the gap in the mountains near to Scott's 'furthest south' of 82° 17' S. From now on, everything they saw would be new to the eye. 'There is an impression of limitless solitude about it all,' Shackleton wrote.

Shackleton, Adams, Marshall and Wild at the start of the southern journey in November 1908.

Shackleton was understandably thrilled on 26 November when they camped beyond Scott's record. 'A day to remember,' he said as they pitched tents at a latitude of 82° 18½' S. 'Not bad going,' Marshall added. 'In excellent spirits.'

For Shackleton, the painful memories of *Discovery*, particularly the indignity of being invalided home, could finally be set aside. He had eclipsed Scott. Besides, Scott had taken 59 days to reach this spot, while Shackleton had needed only 29 days and his party was undoubtedly fitter than Scott's in 1902. 'It falls to the lot of few men to view land not previously seen by human eyes,' he wrote in triumph.

The excitement of standing further south than anyone before could not alter the reality that the men were not travelling fast enough. Already it was clear that, regardless of the good progress, they would not get back to Cape Royds in time to catch *Nimrod*. Even if they reached the Pole, the reward would be another winter in the Antarctic. 'May miss ship and have to winter another year,' a philosophical Marshall wrote.

In a flurry of instructions written before driving south, Shackleton had placed Murray in charge of affairs at Cape Royds. Murray was also told that he should assume overall control of the expedition if both Shackleton and Adams failed to return. This gave Murray, the Scots biologist, unexpected seniority over David, who appeared the more likely candidate for command. However, David was presumed to be deep in the wilderness of Victoria Land in search of the South Magnetic Pole and Murray was insurance against David running into trouble.

This was all a surprise to the modest, unassuming Murray, a self-taught scientist in his mid-40s who had given up a career in the arts – he studied sculpture – to research marine life forms and now found himself in charge of an Antarctic expedition. If Shackleton failed to return, he would be thrust into dealing with the venture's tangled finances and assortment of creditors, arranging passages home for the survivors and even writing a book on the experience. Shackleton had pointedly not given the task to the prickly Marshall. Whether Murray was physically capable of taking control was another matter. He had suffered from rheumatism and inflamed eyes and considered himself a 'wreck of humanity' even before setting out for the Antarctic.

Shackleton's instructions to Murray were explicit. *Nimrod* should ideally leave McMurdo Sound by 1 March 1909, although the final date for departure depended on prevailing ice conditions and was ultimately at the discretion of Murray and the ship's master, presumed to be Mackintosh or Evans. The last possible date for sailing was 10 March. 'If we have not returned by then something very serious must have happened,' Shackleton said.

Before leaving, coal and food supplies to keep seven men for a year were to be unloaded at Cape Royds and three volunteers were asked to remain behind to await the return of the southern party. If three volunteers could not be found, Murray was given the unenviable task of ordering three men to remain behind for another year.[3]

Out on the Barrier the biggest issue was the gnawing hunger. After a month of travel, the burden of dragging the weighty sledges had passed from animals to the man-haulers and significantly larger appetites came with the heavier workload. Grisi was shot on 28 November and Quan, Shackleton's pony, was put out of his misery on 1 December. The four men were now pulling around 600 lb (275 kg) and Socks, the last remaining pony, another 600 lb.

Appetites, Shackleton noticed, had increased 'at an alarming rate'. In fact, the men were probably consuming around 3,000 calories a day when the hard labour demanded something closer to 6,000 a day. Some relief came if they chewed hunks of raw meat on the march. But as Shackleton readily admitted: 'We are very hungry these days and we know that we are likely to be for another three months.'

Relief of a different sort came from the intoxicating sight of a rapidly changing landscape. The formidable chain of mountains, which ran to the right alongside their southward path, had turned inwards and now blocked the route directly ahead. The surface, billiard-table flat for over 300 miles (480 km), had also developed wide undulations like ocean waves frozen in time. Some were a mile wide and each furrow was filled with soft snow, making the going even more demanding.

Mountains changed everything for Shackleton. The hope had been that the flat Barrier surface led all the way to the Pole. He had not expected to be climbing mountains. 'It seems there is going to be a change in some gigantic way in keeping with the vastness of the whole place,' he wrote.

The party had run into the highly disturbed area where the Barrier collides with the spectacular Transantarctic Mountains and throws up huge pressure ridges of broken ice formations and crevasses. The chain of mountains, which stretches for around 2,200 miles (3,500 km) from Cape Adare in Victoria Land to the Weddell Sea on the other side of the continent, rises above 14,000 feet (4,250 m) in places and forms a magnificent boundary between East and West Antarctica. Among the longest on earth, the Transantarctic Mountain range is up to 180 miles (300 km) wide and acts as an enormous natural dam holding back the vast mass of the East Antarctic ice sheet.

Finding a gap between the mountains was now essential. In search of a route they spotted a large glacier spewing out onto the Barrier which, more or less, ran due south between two lines of mountains. Marshall, prophetically, said it appeared to be the 'Golden Gateway' to the south.

It was promising but first Shackleton needed a clearer view of the route ahead. At the mouth of the glacier was a small rocky formation, rising some 3,000 feet (1,000 m). Getting to the foot of the mountain was more taxing than the climb itself. It took six hours to travel barely 7 miles (10 km) across a field of cavernous crevasses, some 80 feet (24 m) wide and hundreds of feet deep. Roped up and moving cautiously over the hard blue ice, they travelled light with only a few biscuits and sticks of chocolate for lunch. The doleful figure of Socks was left in charge of the camp.

It was a comparatively easy climb up the dome-shaped mountain, requiring only two hours to clamber up the fragmented scree and reddish-coloured granite boulders. From the summit their eyes fell on a giant glacier, a causeway reaching out some 60 miles (100 km) to the farthest horizon. 'There burst upon our vision an open road to the south,' Shackleton wrote. Beyond the horizon lay a plateau and the Pole itself.

The glacier, in fact, was Shackleton's greatest discovery. Although he was unaware of the fact, the glacier is around 25 miles (40 km) wide and extends for around 125 miles (190 km) like a mighty frozen waterway running between two lines of mountains before rising sharply towards the Polar Plateau. 'Must be the largest in the world,' an excited Wild noted.

Shackleton was lucky. The 'Golden Gateway' was one of the very few passes in the area where men on foot could negotiate a safe path between the mountains. 'The Almighty has indeed been good to us,' Marshall wrote.

With a suitable sense of occasion, the mountain at the glacier entrance was named Mount Hope. Initially the colossal river of ice was called the Great Glacier. Only later did Shackleton change the name to the Beardmore Glacier. Both seemed appropriate, one recognising the sense of anticipation at the task ahead and the other the generosity of the expedition's most important sponsor. But were there other explanations for the names?

While returning from *Discovery* in 1903 Shackleton had met an attractive young Scotswoman called Hope Paterson. Some form of relationship is thought to have developed. The couple remained in close touch for some years afterwards and Shackleton later sent her a parcel containing a small rock in a silver casing. On the casing was inscribed '83° 33' S Long 170° E', the map coordinates for Mount Hope.

There may be another puzzle involving the Beardmore Glacier, apparently named after the industrialist and benefactor, William Beardmore. Shackleton once told Elspeth Beardmore that he wanted to name one of the newly discovered mountains in her honour and the glacier for her husband. In the event, the glacier was simply named the Beardmore, but no mountains ever carried the Beardmore name and it remains unclear which of the couple was being commemorated.

For the moment, Shackleton was content to luxuriate in the triumph of beating Scott's record and discovering the likely route to the Pole. It was almost seven years since he made his first tentative journey on the ice, the short run to White Island with Wilson and Ferrar in 1902. It was a journey which galvanised his ambitions and now brought him to the foot of the mighty glacier.

Something new gripped him now. Standing on the brink of the glacier, Shackleton had discovered the sheer exhilaration of discovery. All that mattered in the world was beneath his feet and spread out before him. As Shackleton once put it: 'You can't think what it's like to walk over places where no one has been before.'[4]

chapter 19

Penniless

A world away, the shambolic edifice of the expedition's finances had fallen apart. During the northern hemisphere summer of 1908, shortly before the sun reappeared at Cape Royds, the British Antarctic Expedition was effectively bust and looking for an urgent injection of new money.

Shackleton had departed from England leaving the bulk of the expedition's muddled affairs in the hands of a slightly bemused Herbert Dorman, Emily's brother. It was a sensible choice since Dorman, who was a partner in his father's old firm of Kingsford, Dorman, was someone to be trusted with both the expedition and Emily's welfare.

However, Dorman was a traditional London solicitor, accustomed to the humdrum pace of handling divorces, chasing debtors through the courts or representing minor criminals. Nothing could be more unfamiliar to Dorman than the muddled affairs of the expedition. In Shackleton's absence, Dorman now found himself responsible for sorting out the expedition's chaotic mess, refitting a ship on the other side of the world and ensuring that Shackleton's party was safely lifted off the remote headland at Cape Royds.

'It is a great anxiety to me,' Dorman wrote to Emily in mid-June. 'I want something like £7,000 & Heaven knows where it is to come from.' In today's terms this was at least £400,000/€480,000 and as a worried Dorman explained: 'These worries added to my own business are more than I ever bargained for.'[1]

Dorman had also stumbled into the festering dispute with Beardmore, not realising that Shackleton had failed to repay the loan. He was surprised when Beardmore pointedly turned down Dorman's appeal to pump more money into the expedition. In slightly bemused fashion, he explained to Emily that Beardmore 'seems vexed with E'. Had he pressed further, Dorman would have discovered that Beardmore was also unhappy that

Shackleton had not bothered to write a letter of apology. In fact, the only Beardmore that Shackleton had contacted was his wife, Elspeth.

In desperation, Herbert Dorman briefly considered passing responsibility for the expedition relief to Frank Shackleton. But Frank, who was still mired in the scandal of the Irish Crown Jewels theft, was hardly a man to be relied upon in a crisis and Dorman quickly recognised he would get no meaningful help from that quarter. 'I can't rely on FS for anything until I get it,' he reported a few weeks later.

With his options narrowing, Dorman instead proposed the two-pronged initiative of raising money from the government and launching a direct public appeal for funds through the columns of popular newspapers. 'I shall have no alternative,' he told Emily, 'but to appeal to the government or the Press.'

Dorman's personal link to government was Richard Causton, the Paymaster General and printing industry millionaire whose presses at Cape Royds were then churning out copies of *Aurora Australis*. It was a long shot but Causton readily agreed to pass Dorman's appeal for emergency funding to David Lloyd George, the Chancellor of the Exchequer. Lloyd George, the early 20th-century's great political powerhouse and social reformer, was in the early months of his momentous seven-year term as Chancellor and was laying the foundations of the modern welfare state in Britain. But the reformist government's largesse did not extend to rescuing Antarctic explorers and Dorman's request was turned down.

Dorman was deflated by the rejection and admitted: 'There is no use in disguising the fact that the general public do not take much interest in polar explorations so as to put their hands in their pockets except under the magnetic influence of a silver tongued enthusiast like Ernest.'[2]

The gravity of the crisis only deepened as Dorman and friends pored over the figures and watched as potential backers edged further away from the venture. In particular, the costs of refitting *Nimrod*, paying wages and restocking the ship appeared to have spiralled. The ship, according to Captain England in New Zealand, was 'badly strained and requiring a deal of work' after docking at Lyttelton.

The prospects of finding money were bleak. The long-anticipated £4,000 from Steuart's Celtic Investment Trust, which Shackleton still fondly hoped to see, had simply failed to appear. In searching for new sources of money, approaches were made to Thomas Garlick, another business associate of Frank Shackleton. Garlick, an accountant, was chairman of the small shipping company which recruited Shackleton to bring Russian troops home from the Russo-Japanese War. Garlick offered a vague promise of giving £1,000 to the relief fund but this was dependent on Frank Shackleton pulling off a speculative business deal and the money, naturally enough, never materialised.

The one flicker of hope came from the loyal Elizabeth Dawson-Lambton, *Nimrod*'s first donor. The old lady's faith in Shackleton was untarnished by events and she quietly provided another £1,000 (almost £60,000/€72,000 today).

It was far from sufficient and Dorman had other fears. It was now apparent that, with the expedition's finances in disarray, Shackleton was not in a position to provide for Emily and the children. There was little difference between Shackleton's personal affairs and the expedition's and Emily was vulnerable. She had no other income apart from her father's bequest. Dorman's solution was to insist that Emily keep hold of Dawson-Lambton's £1,000 to meet her own bills while Shackleton was away.

In November, as Shackleton was taking his first steps onto the Barrier, Dorman did the simple arithmetic and judged that at least £3,500–£4,000 was needed. In New Zealand, Kinsey urgently required an estimated £2,500 to make *Nimrod* ready and at least £1,300 was wanted in London to settle pressing debts. 'There is only £500 to meet it and apparently no prospect of getting the remaining £3,000 to £3,500 except the possibility of getting £1,000 from FS [Frank Shackleton] next month,' a disconsolate Dorman wrote. 'The matter is very urgent.'[3]

Dorman turned next to the *Daily Mail*, hoping to prick the conscience of readers with an appeal for £4,000–£5,000 to get Shackleton home. Dorman's instinct was correct because the newspaper, with a circulation of more than 1 million a day, had a lively interest in spectacular exclusives and extracting Shackleton from Cape Royds had the hallmarks of a classic *Daily Mail* scoop. Only two years earlier, the paper had offered £1,000 to the first person to fly across the English Channel. But Thomas Marlowe, the *Mail*'s redoubtable editor, felt there was not enough public interest in Shackleton's escapades. Marlowe, as Dorman explained, did not believe the appeal would produce 'the desired result' and it was not carried.

Dorman was now at his wits' end and through Causton tried to reopen lines of communication with Lloyd George. It did not work. 'I am rather sick at this stingy government,' a frustrated Dorman said.

The only remaining option was for the Dorman and Shackleton families to raise the money among their own circle. 'The ship must go even if we have to provide the money ourselves,' he declared. The Shackleton family, notably the impecunious Frank Shackleton, was in no position to assist. But the Dormans responded magnificently. Emily's brothers and sisters agreed to give money from their own savings with Daisy Dorman, Emily's younger sister, alone offering £500.

Modestly wealthy from their late father's estate, Dorman admitted that the family 'can fortunately afford it and shall not really miss it'. While the generosity was impressive, he remained highly concerned that Emily was badly exposed by the crisis. 'I can't agree to your idea that the money which I am finding is to come out of your share of the "estate"', he wrote. 'If E succeeds it should be repaid.'

The finances, in truth, were significantly worse than even Dorman or Kinsey realised. In the Antarctic, out of touch with the day-to-day reality of managing the enterprise, Shackleton had dug the expedition even deeper into the quagmire by making a series of generous promises with money he did not possess or was never likely to generate on his return.

Large sums, for example, were pledged to both England and David before *Nimrod* even departed Cape Royds. England's bonus alone had been promised up to £5,000 (nearly £300,000/€360,000 today) and although England was later dismissed, the full contractual liability of wages and bonuses to *Nimrod*'s former captain remained unclear.

At the same time, Shackleton continued to hand out promises of money in all directions from his non-existent purse. Adams and Marshall had their salaries raised from £200 to £300 a year and both were also promised bonuses of up to £3,000 a head if funds permitted. They were also offered payments of £1,000 a year for carrying out public lectures in the event that Shackleton did not return from the south and Marshall, in addition, was also promised many thousands of pounds from future sales of the expedition's cinematographic films.

Joyce was given a pay rise of just £1 a year, but was promised a bonus of £1,000 and the 'best endeavours' of Herbert Dorman and William Beardmore to find him a suitable job on returning to England. It is unlikely that Dorman or Beardmore were aware of Shackleton's pledge to Joyce.

A separate and private arrangement had also been made with Mawson over the possibility of locating sources of valuable gems or minerals which, in theory, could be worth untold thousands. Shackleton had left imprecise instructions for Mawson to search the valleys across McMurdo Sound or 'any other spot' for mineral deposits or precious stones. It was permission to hunt for treasure. However, there was never enough time for the hunt and the search was not made.

Shackleton's haphazard relationship with money was a never-ending source of bewilderment to those around him. Money seemed to run through his hands like water and he clung to the illusion that his financial problems would be solved at a stroke by finding a spectacular money-spinning bonanza.

In New Zealand, meantime, Kinsey had somehow worked a minor miracle with the small sums scraped together from Dorman in London and a few more promissory notes to suppliers. Despite the controversies over England and the failed oceanographic work, Shackleton had retained a measure of popular support in New Zealand and Kinsey was the ideal man to tap into it.

Kinsey, a cultured shipping executive in his late 50s, was something of a father figure to British polar explorers in New Zealand after assisting both *Discovery* and *Nimrod*. Though born in England, Kinsey had settled in New Zealand nearly 30 years earlier and fully understood the relationship between the mother country and its most distant colony. Kinsey also recognised that Shackleton's dash and unpretentious style appealed to the frontier spirit among New Zealand's pioneering communities. One local newspaper praised Shackleton for being in the 'full flush of vigorous manhood'.

Working his impeccable local contacts, Kinsey found a shipyard prepared to refit *Nimrod*. He also persuaded Sir James Mills of the Union Steam Ship Company to loan the services of Captain Evans, the former commander of *Koonya*, to take *Nimrod* back to Cape Royds.

Nimrod, seemingly without a care in the world, sailed from Lyttelton on 1 December 1908, the day Shackleton pushed beyond the 83° S mark. A small band of well-wishers gathered on the quayside to wave farewell, oblivious to how near the relief had been to collapse.

At home, Dorman had reconciled himself with the enduring chaos and strain of his responsibilities. 'I am getting quite used to these financial anxieties about the expedition,' he wrote to Emily. 'I suppose Ernest must now be thinking of turning back. I often wonder how far he has got.'[4]

chapter 20

Gateway

The climb up the enormous Beardmore Glacier began in almost balmy weather. It was so warm and bright that the men stripped to their shirts and were scorched by the sun reflecting vividly off the glassy surface. Shackleton, Adams and Marshall pulled one load of around 600 lb (275 kg) and the unshod Socks, led by Wild, slipped and slithered along with another 600 lb.

The path to the south was an appalling jumble of crevasses, fragile-looking snow bridges and an endless series of undulating pressure ridges caused by the mighty glacial forces squeezing down the wide mountain pass. Alongside one perpendicular cliff they camped beside an area of freshly fallen debris, ranging from rocks the size of a walnut to 40-ton granite boulders. Gazing up at the 2,000-foot (600 m) cliff face, Shackleton wrote: 'One feels that at any moment some great piece of rock may come hurtling down. Providence will look over us tonight, for we can do nothing more.'[1]

Shackleton was badly affected by a painful bout of snow blindness and, with one eye blocked off from the penetrating light, he trod gingerly through miles of yawning crevasses and hard ice without ever being able to see clearly ahead. Yet he was utterly determined to set an example to the others, eager to lead from the front.

Wild, sharing his longest sledging journey with The Boss, was already starting to appreciate his indomitable spirit and sheer grit. On one occasion he observed that the agony of snow blindness was giving Shackleton a 'fearfully trying time' but added that 'he would not give in'.

Travelling conditions deteriorated badly the following day as the party entered a maze of partially hidden crevasses and slippery, hard, blue ice, forcing them to relay the sledges over impossibly difficult ground. Shackleton, still blind in one eye, said 'every step was a venture'. Socks

Beardmore Glacier. The vast gateway to the Pole discovered by Shackleton in 1908 is among the largest glaciers in the world, extending for 125 miles and rising to around 10,000 feet (3,000 m).

had to be left behind for a while and retrieved later after the sledges had been man-handled across the treacherous surface. The strain on nerves and muscles was intense and Wild ended the gruelling day by concluding: 'I would rather walk 40 miles than do it again.'

Another depot was laid, the fourth, which meant seven weeks' food had now been stored along the route home. The road ahead, an optimistic Marshall noted, was 'open to the south' and would improve once the crevasses had been cleared. However, the optimism soon faded as the surface turned to soft, slushy snow and men sank up to their knees with every punishing step. Crossing crevasses by way of frail ice bridges was as much an act of faith as sound judgement.

To avoid the worst of the pressure ridges, Shackleton steered the party towards the centre of the glacier, away from the more awkward broken ground near the mountains. But there was little relief from the daily grind. At times they camped with crevasses barely 5 yards (4½ m) away on each side and other less visible chasms partially obscured by coverings of snow. Every step carried the threat of falling into oblivion.

Wild stepped into the void on 7 December. Leading Socks at the rear of the procession, Wild suddenly felt the ground drop from beneath his feet and fell with a jolt. An anguished cry for help alerted the others who turned to see Wild and the sledge half-jammed across an abyss. His harness had held firm. There was no sign of the unfortunate Socks.

Socks, who probably weighed around 800 lb (360 kg), had crashed through a snow bridge and disappeared into a deep, black, bottomless hole. His weight, luckily for the men, had snapped the trace to the sledge, leaving behind the precious cargo of food and two of the four sleeping bags. Somehow the sledge had stuck across the yawning gap which had swallowed Socks. 'Had it been lost we should certainly all have died,' Wild admitted.

Losing Socks was a double blow. Although it robbed the party of essential pulling power, the biggest loss was that it deprived the men of vital fresh meat. Marshall reckoned cuts from Socks would have sustained the four men for at least two weeks. Instead, they were left with the remnants of the animal's feed to supplement their own provisions, some 40 lb (18 kg) of maize and 31 lb (14 kg) of 'Majuee' rations, a compressed high-energy concoction of meat, carrots, milk, sugar and raisins. It was a poor substitute for fresh meat.

Without Socks, the men now had to drag around 1,000 lb (450 kg) on the two sledges. Although yoked to the energy-sapping routine of relaying, the men continued to make good progress. On 11 December the party camped at over 3,700 feet (1,200 m), some 390 miles (620 km) from the Pole. 'Difficulties are just things to overcome after all,' a resolutely optimistic Shackleton wrote.

Each day demanded huge physical effort and each man watched the others for signs of slack traces. Minor niggles were often magnified beyond all reason and it was difficult to cajole or urge each other along since the persistent winds drowned out all conversation. Each man pulled in silence, brooding alone.

Wild was particularly unhappy, claiming that Adams and Marshall did not pull their weight. Wild always believed that Joyce and Marston should have joined the southern party instead of Adams and Marshall, who he dismissed as 'two grub scoffing beggars'. To Wild, Marshall was a 'big hulking lazy hog' while Adams, he decided, always did his best but it was a 'very poor best'. Only Shackleton was spared Wild's biting criticism. Shackleton, he said, 'works away like ten devils'.

Marshall, with his mocking disdain for almost everything, directed most of his criticism at Shackleton. When Shackleton was struck down by snow blindness, Marshall dismissed the agony as 'moaning' and claimed it was his own fault. Even as cook, said Marshall, Shackleton was 'useless'. After one heavy day, he lashed out by writing, 'Following Shackleton to the Pole is like following an old woman. Always panicking.'

Shackleton kept his reservations about Marshall largely to himself. His diary entries were factual or descriptive of everything except his personal opinions of his companions. Yet Marshall was difficult to handle because he was always less susceptible to Shackleton's breezy personality. In a letter to Emily, he reported that Marshall was 'a bit young in mind [and] inclined to resent discipline'.

By 16 December, the group had climbed around 100 miles (160 km) up the glacier and risen to 6,000 feet (1,825 m), overlooked on either side by the towering mountain ranges. The party was close to 85° S and some 350 miles (550 km) from the Pole, with perhaps five weeks' food and a fond hope that the relentlessly uphill terrain would soon flatten out.

Ascending the glacier, Shackleton began naming newly discovered landmarks after family, friends and supporters. He named Mount Dorman and the Swinford Glacier after members of Emily's family and two impressive glaciers were named after Mill and Keltie. Adams, Marshall and Wild were also honoured with mountains in their names.

Another intriguingly named feature was Mount Donaldson, a 12,900-foot (3,930 m) peak on the eastern side of the Beardmore Glacier opposite Mount Dorman. On the journey from England to New Zealand in 1907, Shackleton had met a woman called Isobel 'Belle' Donaldson. The full extent of the relationship remains unclear, but a week before *Nimrod* left New Zealand for Cape Royds, Shackleton wrote an affectionate four-page letter to Donaldson which he signed: 'Your Polar Man'. The couple would remain in contact for many years and Mount Donaldson stands to this day as a reminder of the relationship.

Nearing the top of the glacier, Shackleton decided to gamble everything by leaving another cache of supplies – Depot E – and dashing south with lightly laden sledges. Four days' food, a little oil and some surplus gear were stashed and Shackleton wrote: 'We have burnt our boats now'. Marshall, with a rare splash of optimism, commented: 'On plateau, should do this in three weeks travelling light.'

Next day Wild made a startling discovery. After climbing a nearby slope to survey the terrain ahead, he returned with a few stone samples and reports of dark seams in the rocks up to 8 feet (2.5 m) thick. Wild, in fact, had discovered the first traces of coal in Antarctica which, in time, would lead scientists to establish that the frozen continent once formed part of a huge ancient land mass in a warm, swampy environment. Wild's discovery, said Shackleton with touching understatement, would be 'most interesting' to the scientific world.

Food, rather than science, remained the dominant subject as the steady climb continued. Each man saved two biscuits a day from his allowance and eked out the meagre pemmican 'hoosh' by adding scraps of pony maize, which first had to be dipped in water to make it easier to chew. 'We must march on short food to reach our goal,' Shackleton wrote.

Rising slowly above 8,000 feet (2,400 m), it was noticeably colder and the higher altitude was causing slight breathlessness and severe headaches to the men. The biting wind blew directly into their faces, matting their beards with ringlets of clinging ice. Relaying the sledges across pressure ridges and crevasses inevitably slowed the advance to a crawl. Each day ended with the same exhaustion and ravenous hunger. 'Killing work,' Marshall noted.

After advancing nearly 13 miles (20 km) on Christmas Eve, one of the two sledges was discarded. On Christmas Day, the four men camped just short of the 86th parallel at an elevation of 9,500 feet (2,900 m). The thermometer showed 48° of frost.

Extra pemmican was rustled up for breakfast and the typical lunch of four biscuits and tea was supplemented by a welcome hunk of cheese. To celebrate Christmas, the group enjoyed a sumptuous dinner which included a double helping of pemmican filled out with a few slices of pony meat, extra 'Majuee' rations and a portion of plum pudding donated by a friend of Wild's. A mug of cocoa, cigars and a spoonful of crème de menthe rounded off the feast. For the first time in almost two months the men slept contentedly on a full stomach.

The determination to celebrate the ritual of Christmas in a tiny windswept tent on the most inhospitable plateau on earth was a testament to unquenchable spirit. A gale was blowing outside and the thermometer recorded 52° of frost as they bedded down. 'It is a fine open air life and we are getting south,' Shackleton wrote in his diary.

Wild was more down to earth. 'May my worst enemies never spend their Xmas in such a dreary God forgotten spot as this.'

Inside the tent, the party's position was openly discussed. Shackleton saw no purpose in secrecy for secrecy's sake. Survival depended on the men striving together as a team and this was no time to camouflage the reality. Allowing each man to voice an opinion, which ensured no one felt excluded, was also an important way of strengthening the bonds between the four men.

Shackleton had visibly grown into the role of leader. He was calmer, more measured and his decision-making more considered. Both Adams and Wild, after a cautious beginning, were now unquestionably Shackleton's men. Both now evidently shared Shackleton's belief that the Pole was possible, despite the cold, hunger and exhaustion. Shackleton's infectious optimism had rubbed off. Adams would later claim that Shackleton was the 'greatest leader that ever came on God's earth, bar none'. Wild, too, now recognised that Shackleton was a man to follow.

Even Marshall was coming round to Shackleton's side. The scornful criticism which had laced his diary since arrival at Cape Royds was now tempered with more moderate asides and even understanding. While outwardly he maintained his air of superiority, Marshall recognised something new in Shackleton. The Boss, he realised for the first time, possessed the rare quality of inspiring people. Marshall did not.

Shackleton's leadership was now of critical importance. The party was still 280 miles (450 km) from the Pole, with Depot E some 60 miles (100 km) behind them to the north. It was a round trip of approximately 620 miles (1,000 km) to the Pole and back to the vital provisions with no margin for navigational error or delay because of bad weather or injury. To achieve the impossible, the group had only four weeks' food, including just three weeks of biscuit ration. Unrealistic or not, it meant travelling at an average of over 22 miles (35 km) a day. Not once since first entering the Barrier in November had a single day's march exceeded 22 miles.

Marshall soon discovered another more serious problem. During a short medical check on Christmas Day Marshall found that the body temperatures of all four were 2° below normal. Shackleton's response was to cut rations a little further, stretching the food for seven days to ten and reducing the average advance closer to 15 miles (24 km) a day.

'We will have one biscuit in the morning, three at midday and two at night,' Shackleton wrote. 'It is the only thing to do for we must get to the Pole, come what may,' he added emphatically.

But Shackleton was no martyr. He wanted nothing of noble sacrifice. By any realistic assessment, the Pole was beyond reach unless rations were cut to a suicidal level. More than anything, Shackleton was a survivor. After a moment, he crossed out the words in the second half of the sentence: '... come what may.'

During his long courtship of Emily, Shackleton had written a letter which included some tender lines from the Victorian poet George Meredith. Propped up in his sleeping bag nearly 2 miles above sea level in the freezing wilderness, he scribbled a modified version of the same lines in his diary. The sentiments in Meredith's verse, taken from 'Love in the Valley', chimed perfectly with the hard road ahead:

Hard is our love. Hard to catch and conquer.
Hard, but oh, the glory of the winning were it won

Almost everything but bare essentials was dumped on 26 December, including spare runners for the sledge. To their relief, the lighter load enabled them to achieve 14 miles. But they were still hauling 150 lb (68 kg) a head uphill in the thin air at over 10,000 feet (3,000 m) in temperatures 20° below freezing.

Towards the end of December, after nearly four weeks of back-breaking slog, the surface finally began to flatten out and the mountains, which had formed a majestic guard of honour on the ascent, began to fade from view, leaving them four insignificant silhouettes isolated on a never-ending plain of whiteness.

Shackleton peered into the emptiness and gambled once more. Taking only one tent and using the other's tent-poles as markers at 10-mile (16 km) intervals along the route, he proposed pushing on as rapidly as their waning strength would allow. At some 70 miles (112 km) from the Pole, they would take only the minimum amount of food, leaving the remainder at a small depot for the last frantic sprint southwards. 'I hope with good weather to reach the Pole by January 12,' he wrote. 'Then we will try and rush it to get back to Hut Point by February 28.'

The odds were heavily stacked against them. The four men were in an appalling state, starving, skeletal and struggling to maintain normal body heat in the freezing conditions. After each hour's pull they collapsed on their backs, gasping for oxygen in the rarefied air. They felt the cold badly because the meagre nourishment and subsequent drop in metabolism was affecting circulation.

Aside from a little pemmican 'hoosh', they ate small portions of cheese or chocolate and hoped to fill their aching stomachs with a few biscuits. During the unfulfilling ritual of mealtimes, they often soaked a biscuit in hot tea, hoping it would swell up and create the illusion of being larger. To compound the inadequacy of the diet, the men were also suffering from severe dehydration, drinking only a fraction of the liquid they sorely needed. Without spare fuel, melting snow for a drink was a luxury.

At more than 10,000 feet (3,000 m) above sea level, all four struggled with fits of dizziness and piercing headaches. Humans invariably need time to acclimatise to altitude but time was another luxury the southern party could not afford. Shackleton's headaches were so severe that he was barely able to write up his diary at night. Occasional nosebleeds only increased their discomfort.

The biting headwind and unimaginable wind chill sliced through their flimsy clothing. Moisture from their breath trickled down their chins and froze like a sheet of ice on their bodies. All spare clothing had been dumped to save weight. Even the scissors to trim their beards had been left behind.

Although the party did not measure wind speed, winds of 25 mph make air temperatures of -20° (-29 °C) feel more like -50° (-45 °C) and inflict severe frostbite to any exposed skin. The choice of clothing did not help. Furs, which had served Nansen and Sverdrup so efficiently in the Arctic, were dismissed in favour of a Burberry outer garment, trousers, woollen jumpers and underwear. Only gloves, footwear and sleeping bags were made from fur.

Marshall took individual temperatures again on 29 December and was startled to discover that all four registered 3° below normal. Normal body temperature is 98.4° (37 °C) and hypothermia is typically defined as anything below 95° (35 °C) when humans start to suffer a slowdown in some functions and occasional mental confusion.

The desperate state of the men echoed the plight of the thousands of malnourished, freezing soldiers in Napoleon's Grande Armée who perished on the disastrous retreat from Moscow a century before. Shackleton, Adams, Marshall and Wild were now in much the same position. But Shackleton was not yet prepared to accept a Napoleonic-type retreat. Instead, he urged his companions onwards and through force of personality instilled in them the belief that the impossible was possible. 'It is hard to know what is man's limit,' he wrote.

To Marshall the only option was to increase the portions of 'hoosh' for a few days in the hope of restoring some strength to their depleted frames. But the weather, which had been surprisingly kind all the way up the glacier, suddenly turned nasty. On 30 December they made only 4 miles (6 km) before a blizzard drove them into the tent early. Even on minimal rations, they needed to make at least three to four times the distance. 'I cannot express my feelings,' a frustrated Shackleton wrote. 'It is with Providence to help us.'

New Year's Eve brought a remarkable advance of 12½ miles (19 km) through soft snow and the men camped within sight of the 87th parallel. They had just three weeks' food and two weeks of biscuit to travel 575 miles (920 km) to the Pole and get back to Depot E. 'We can only do our best,' Shackleton said.

On the same day six years earlier, Scott, Wilson and Shackleton had made their turn. Shackleton, having beaten Scott's 'furthest south' by over 300 miles (480 km) and led men onto the Polar Plateau for the first time, was still not ready to make his. 'Please God the weather will be fine during the next 14 days,' he wrote. 'Then all will be well.'

The New Year of 1909 broke with a creditable distance of more than 11 miles (18 km) in almost 11 hours of grinding struggle across a soft, cloying surface which taxed them dreadfully. In other circumstances it might have been a day of celebration. The four now stood at a higher latitude than any human had ever managed, having gone beyond 87° 6' N which Peary claimed to have reached in 1906. It hardly rated a mention in Shackleton's diary. Instead, he recorded: 'Everyone done up and weak from want of food.'

Although the glacier slopes were far behind, the men were still climbing gently upwards and the thin air, combined with a driving wind in their faces, was taking a heavy toll. Marshall, at least, felt it was time to turn back before it was too late. Adams and Wild, though struggling badly, trusted Shackleton's judgement. Outwardly Shackleton remained positive. But privately the stark reality was that the Pole was beyond his grasp.

Shackleton's condition was causing growing alarm to Marshall. Shackleton, anxious to lead from the front, was driving himself to the limit. No one quite knew where he found the determination or endurance. Willpower alone seemed to be the only answer. Even Marshall admired what he called Shackleton's 'inordinate personal ambition' but feared he was pushing himself beyond the limit. Shackleton's ambition, said Marshall, soared 'beyond the physical efforts of which he was capable.'

On 2 January, after a draining battle against strong headwinds, soft snow and a temperature of -14° (-25 °C), they camped at over 11,000 feet (3,350 m). It took 10 hours of punishing slog to travel 10 miles (16 km), even with a lighter sledge. Without skis, they sank up their ankles in the snow and burned energy none could afford to lose. The men were almost paralysed by the cold. Wild admitted that 'flesh and blood would stand no more' by the time a halt was called. 'One pannikin of food with two biscuits and a cup of tea does not warm one up much,' Shackleton wrote at the end of a day of monumental struggle.

It was the moment when Shackleton reluctantly conceded defeat. In his diary that night, he wrote: 'We are not travelling fast enough to make our food spin out and get back to our depot in time.' The Pole, perhaps 10 to 12 days away, was still manageable in favourable weather. But safe return was impossible.

The crucial moment was when to stop and turn for home. Extreme cold, starvation and lack of oxygen blurs the reason in humans and Shackleton's faculties were under immense pressure as he reached his life-or-death decision.

Dying gloriously, like a noble warrior in a Victorian melodrama, was not in Shackleton's make-up. It was the critical moment when the raw survival instincts of a fighter took over from the romantic adventurer. 'I feel that if we go on too far it will be impossible to get back over this surface,' he wrote, 'and then all the results will be lost to the world.'

Without the responsibility of leadership, it is entirely feasible that Shackleton would have pressed on regardless. But what mattered most at this point was the welfare and safety of Adams, Marshall and Wild. 'I must look at the matter sensibly and consider the lives of those who are with me,' he scribbled in his diary. 'Man can only do his best and we have arrayed against us the strongest forces of nature.'

It was impossible to hide the disappointment. The only consolation was that all others would have to follow in his footsteps. It was a minor comfort, however. 'All this is not the Pole,' he conceded.

Next day Shackleton formally accepted that the dream had ended. 'The end is in sight,' he wrote on 4 January. The previous night Marshall found that his medical thermometer, which only recorded down to 94°, did not pick up a temperature on three of the men. In normal circumstances this indicated approaching death.

It was decided to risk making a final depot and running south across the featureless plain with the barest of essentials to establish a record 'furthest south.' The only 'luxury' was Queen Alexandra's Union Jack. 'I would fail to explain my feelings if I tried to write them down, now that the end has come,' a dejected Shackleton wrote on the night of 6 January.

Good weather was vital for the dash south. A small flag stuck on a single bamboo pole was the only marker and the depot would easily disappear from sight in foul weather. The option of building a series of snow cairns to mark the route was simply beyond their physical capacity. Survival depended entirely on picking up the outward tracks of the four men.

To ease the anguish of falling short of 90° S, Shackleton set a new target of marching to within 100 miles of the Pole. By now Shackleton had switched from measuring distance from statute to geographical miles.

The new target was less than 100 geographical miles from the Pole, which is 115 miles (184 km) by the more commonly used measure of statute miles. Dipping under 100 statute miles would have involved the impossible feat of marching an extra 30 miles (48 km) or two of three days of trekking on an empty stomach.

The other issue was how distances were measured. Marshall, the navigator, used a theodolite to take sightings from the sun's position at noon. But when cloud and drift blocked out the sun, they relied on dead reckoning or the distance measured by the sledgemeter, a small wheel attached to rear of the sledge which clocked up the daily mileage. Marshall had managed only four noon sightings in the whole of December, though the conditions were clearer in the first week of January as the climax of the march neared.

The Polar Plateau seemed determined to keep its secrets as the men prepared to make the last struggle south. On 7 January a blizzard, driven by 80–90 mph (up to 145 km/h) winds, pinned them down in the tent. Frustration now added to the catalogue of woes. Eating food they could not spare and trapped at 11,600 feet (3,500 m) by violent winds and over 70° of frost, even the symbolic landmark of 100 miles seemed beyond their grasp. 'It is hard to keep any warmth in our bodies between scanty meals,' Shackleton wrote.

After more than 48 hours of fury, the blizzard finally blew itself out. Rising early on the morning of 9 January, the men stuffed their pockets with a few biscuits and sticks of chocolate and hurried south. Between them they took a camera and a compass, a brass cylinder containing some documents and stamps and Alexandra's flag. The sledge and tent, the solitary landmark as far as the eye could see in all directions, was left behind.

It was a bizarre spectacle, four bitterly cold, emaciated men half running, half walking in pursuit of an invisible geographical spot on an interminable white landscape. Fortunately, the surface was rock hard, making travel a little easier. They stumbled and ran, panting for breath, until 9 a.m. when a halt was finally called. 'We have shot our bolt,' Shackleton wrote.

Alexandra's flag flew stiffly to attention as the men took photographs to salute their achievement. Shackleton, with due ceremony, claimed possession of the upland in the name of King Edward. Through binoculars to the south they could see only the deathly white snow plain stretching to the horizon.

The men, cut to the bone by the raw wind, lingered for only a few minutes. Eating their biscuits and chocolate as they walked, the men scurried back to the tent and collapsed, utterly exhausted. 'Whatever regrets may be, we have done our best,' Shackleton wrote.

The 'best' was 88° 23' S, just 112 statute miles (178 km) from the South Pole. In geographical terms, the gap was 97 miles, a shade within the target set by Shackleton.

'Furthest South'. (L–r) Adams, Wild and Shackleton pause briefly at 88° 23' S, just 97 (geographical) miles (178 km) from the South Pole. 'We have done our best,' said Shackleton.

Since the theodolite had been left behind to save weight, the precise position of the 'furthest south' was open to question and carried the inevitable suspicion of guesswork. Marshall's last proper sighting with the theodolite was taken on 3 January and the final reading on the morning of 9 January was based on dead reckoning.

Had they made up the figure simply to claim latitude within the 100-mile margin? And how was it possible for exhausted and starving men to travel so far on the last dash south? From the final tent to 88° 23' S was a return journey of some 18 miles (28 km) which they achieved in around 11 hours. By any measure it was an extraordinary feat of endurance, though they were not hindered by pulling a sledge.

Whatever the doubts about the precise coordinates, the only certainty was that the solitary witnesses to the southerly latitude reached on the morning of 9 January 1909 were Shackleton, Adams, Marshall and Wild and all four agreed on the ultimate figure of 88° 23' S. History would have to accept their word for it.

Equally important was that Shackleton, despite his occasionally obscuring some detail, was adamant that proper records of the journey should be kept. He wanted no doubts cast on his performance. A few days after starting the return march, Adams was knocked off his feet by the strong winds and his meteorological logbook fell down a gully on the edge of a deep crevasse. Adams and Marshall were immediately despatched to recover the log from the dangerous precipice, with Shackleton declaring: 'No good going home without the records.'

However, one element of mystery has left a tantalising uncertainty about the precise 'furthest south' reading. Many years after the event, Marshall said 'the facts will be disclosed in a sealed statement, before or after my death.' The statement has never been found.[2]

The less important debate about the precise spot reached on the plateau should not obscure the remarkable achievement. Under Shackleton's increasingly sure and inspiring leadership, the men had crossed the Barrier, made the first ascent of the unconquered Transantarctic Mountains onto the Polar Plateau and reached closer to either of the geographic Poles than anyone before. They had pioneered the route to the Pole on half rations.

But, as Shackleton readily conceded, it was not the Pole. In fact, they were probably eight or nine days short of the Pole, a round trip of nearly 2½ weeks. Reflecting on his tormenting near miss, Shackleton later estimated he would have reached 90° S had the party carried an extra 25 lb (11 kg) of biscuits and 30 lb (13 kg) of pemmican.

There were several other key factors, including the early loss of ponies, which left the men with the debilitating burden of man-hauling for close to 1,400 miles (2,200 km). The decision not to gamble on wintering in the Bay of Whales was an understandable but costly decision. Setting out from the Bay of Whales would have cut at least 100 miles (160 km) off the round trip to the Pole – the margin of shortfall on the morning of 9 January.

Yet nothing compared with Shackleton's tragic error of ignoring dogs and skis in favour of ponies and man-hauling the sledges, an oversight which cost him the Pole. The sound advice of Nansen and the bitter experience of *Discovery* were cast aside in favour of an unfamiliar mode of transport. In fact, Shackleton spent 12 times as much on the hapless ponies as he did on a handful of dogs.

Less than three years after Shackleton's 'furthest south', Amundsen was propelled to the Pole by expertly driven dog teams and a team of proficient Norwegian skiers. Amundsen also gambled on building his winter quarters at the Bay of Whales.

Amundsen was among the first to salute Shackleton's outstanding achievement. On the way to the Pole two years later, he stopped his procession at Shackleton's record of 88° 23' S. In his diary, Amundsen wrote: 'Shackleton's exploit is the most brilliant incident in the history of

Antarctic exploration.' Shackleton's name, said Amundsen, would 'always be written in the annals of Antarctic exploration in letters of fire'.[3]

Amundsen, the most successful of all polar explorers, was too analytical to ignore the obvious flaws in Shackleton's arrangements. While he unreservedly admired the determination and endurance, it was beyond his comprehension to undertake a major journey across the ice without dogs and skis. 'A little more experience would have crowned their work with success,' he said. 'All my experience in Polar work has convinced me that dogs were the only practicable draught animals for use in snow and ice.'[4]

Whether the highly ambitious Amundsen also possessed the same courage and strength of character as Shackleton to turn back 112 miles (97 geographic miles) from his goal will never be known. Or whether in the same circumstances Amundsen would have placed the safety of his men above the pursuit of the glory.

Wild was in no doubt that Shackleton forfeited his great moment of triumph by putting the lives of his men first. Wild, better than most, recognised the special type of courage needed to make that sacrifice. In his memoirs, he wrote: 'I am perfectly certain that had Shackleton only himself to consider, he would have gone on and planted the flag at the Pole itself.'[5]

Shackleton was not a man to dwell on the past and was able to deal with the disappointment by looking ahead to the next great task. When Emily enquired about the fateful decision to turn with the prize in sight, Shackleton was casually light-hearted. He famously quipped: 'I thought you'd rather have a live donkey than a dead lion.'

Unusually Shackleton did not reach for the great poets to fully express his feelings. Somewhere in his exceptional memory there were surely a few appropriate words to commemorate the most courageous decision in the history of exploration. Perhaps Browning or Tennyson were appropriate. Or perhaps Shakespeare's *Julius Caesar*:

I shall have glory by this losing day.

chapter 21

'Death on his pale horse ...'

The wind, which had blown relentlessly in their faces for over two months, became an unlikely friend as they began the 750-mile (1,200 km) struggle back to Cape Royds in sub-zero temperatures. The floorcloth of the tent was rigged into a makeshift sail and the wind, driving into their backs, pushed them along at almost breakneck speed, clocking up 21 miles (33 km) on the first day and over 19 miles (30 km) on the next. At times the weary men were forced to break into a run to keep up with the racing sledge.

Speed was critically important. It was a little over 200 miles (320 km) to Depot E at the top of the glacier and the food bag contained only 14 days of short-order provisions. Luckily, the fresh tracks made on the outward march were easily spotted in the first few days. The mountains, the only reliable geographical feature, had not been seen for three weeks and until the peaks reappeared on the horizon their lives depended on finding the old trail. 'It has been a big risk leaving our food on the great white plain with only our sledge tracks to guide us back,' Shackleton admitted.[1]

Shackleton, driving himself to the limit, was probably in the worst condition of the four. Added to the headaches, hunger and exhaustion, he now discovered his feet were badly frostbitten. His heels had cracked open in various places and were suppurating. They were all denied a decent rest by the invasive cold.

On 15 January, with weathering slowly erasing the outward tracks, it was discovered that the sledgemeter had fallen off. 'This is a serious loss to us,' said Shackleton. All distances now had to be estimated, adding another layer of uncertainty. Next day, as the tracks began to fade and doubts grew, the mountains suddenly burst into view to the relief of all.

Although the sail was powering them along at around 20 miles (32 km) a day, the scarcity of food was critical. They were still not travelling fast enough and another biscuit was cut from the daily ration. Marshall wrote:

'Never will I refuse a hungry man a feed and feed the hungry whenever possible.'

On 19 January they managed an astonishing distance of 29 miles (46 km) which brought them down to about 7,500 feet (2,300 m) and within half a day's march of the depot. Remarkably, the weather had held. But at the head of the glacier, they soon ran into an area of slippery, broken ground scored by a myriad of half-concealed crevasses. All suffered from heavy falls and arrived at the depot next day with sore and aching bodies. But at least the bitterly cold plateau and rarefied air were now behind them.

Shackleton, who had pushed himself to the limit for close to three months, was feeling the effects of the struggle. Already weakened, an upset stomach now turned him off his pemmican. On 21 January Shackleton was unable to pull the sledge, walking alongside in a scene painfully reminiscent of the ordeal with Scott and Wilson.

Marshall kept a close watch and was concerned about Shackleton's deteriorating condition. After one brief examination he recorded: 'Pulse on march thin and irregular at about 120.' Wild simply wondered: 'I don't know how Shackleton stands it.'

Marshall, the strongest of the party, had grown in stature in recent weeks and had effectively replaced Adams as deputy leader. He was more understanding and less sullen. The nightly diary entries, which dripped with venom on the way south, had become more temperate and he was less eager to point the finger of blame at the others. As he monitored Shackleton's collapse, Marshall's tone became reassuringly positive. 'We shall have to push on at all costs,' he wrote, 'and carry him on the sled if necessary.'

Descending through the rippled ice and crevasses at the head of the glacier, the pace was somehow maintained, helped by the persistent wind filling out the sail. Shackleton, slowly regaining his strength, was able to guide the sledge through the maze of crevasses. But, halfway down the glacier, the food was virtually exhausted and it was about 40 miles (64 km) to the next depot.

The most arduous day they had experienced came on 26 January. Breakfast amounted to the last scrapings of pemmican and pony maize and the broken, crevassed terrain slowed the descent to a tortuous, laboured crawl. Lunch consisted of a mug of tea and a morsel of chocolate. They resumed the march until 10 p.m., gulped down a mug of hot cocoa and continued for another four hours. After snatching a brief rest, the march was resumed at 9 a.m. on the strength of one mug of cocoa. 'I cannot describe adequately the mental and physical strain of the last 48 hours,' Shackleton wrote in his diary.

The men were now collectively on the verge of collapse, four gaunt frames, starving to death and exhausted. It was well over 400 miles (640 km) to the safety of Cape Royds. Hugh Mill later captured the epic daily struggle in an almost Biblical turn of phrase. It was a race for life, said Mill, 'with Death on his pale horse, the blizzard following close'.

Marshall now chose to assert his authority. He first dispensed 'Forced March' tablets, a cocaine-and-caffeine stimulant which he hoped would carry them to the lower glacier depot. Made by the Burroughs Wellcome drugs company, the tablets carried the singularly appropriate prescription for the men nearing the limit of their stamina: 'Allays hunger and prolongs the power of endurance', the blurb on the bottle read.

Marshall next led the party through a confusing warren of crevasses until they could see the rocky formation a few miles in the distance which stood close to the depot. In the past 24 hours, they had somehow slogged through 16 miles (25 km) of soft snow and precarious crevasses fortified only by the odd mug of cocoa or tea. Adams, who had so far stood up well to the ordeal, collapsed within sight of the depot. Shackleton and Wild were both running on empty.

Marshall, the only man still standing, now bravely volunteered to press on alone and return with a little food. Although the cache was only a mile away, the area was heavily crevassed and treacherous for a man alone. Despite falling three times, Marshall staggered into the depot, picked up some pony meat, cheese, biscuits and pemmican and hurried back to his spent companions. Although ravenous with hunger, Marshall resisted the temptation to help himself to some extra food and his only reward for the conspicuous act of courage was to eat two lumps of sugar before racing back to Shackleton, Adams and Wild.

It had been almost 36 hours since they last ate solid food. Wild rustled up a steaming pot of 'hoosh' and horsemeat, followed by tea and biscuits. 'Good God how we did enjoy it.' To Wild, it was the 'finest meal we had ever tasted'.

The clamber down the glacier ended next day as they regained the Barrier. It was a welcome relief to be on level ground after the torture of the glacier and high winds, bitter cold and thin air of the plateau. 'The old Barrier seems quite a haven of refuge after what we have been through,' Wild wrote.

The outlook suddenly seemed brighter. It was only 50 miles (80 km) to the next depot and they had food for six days. But setbacks were never far away and Wild suddenly developed a worrying bout of dysentery. It was put down as a simple reaction to the horseflesh but the loss of bodily fluids and nutrients was alarming for the already severely dehydrated and undernourished Wild.

Wild's condition deteriorated badly over the next few days as violent diarrhoea drained his already emaciated body. Medicine prescribed by Marshall made him drowsy and at times Wild seemed to be sleepwalking across the ice. His only nourishment was the paltry ration of four biscuits a day. Wild, a small man of around 5 feet 5 inches, had the gaunt, pitifully feeble look of someone on the brink of death.

Shackleton's reaction was an act of humanity almost without parallel. With the minimum of fuss, he gave Wild his sole biscuit set aside for breakfast. Although Wild gamely protested, Shackleton insisted and threatened to bury the biscuit in the snow if he did not eat it. It was an extraordinary act of generosity.

'I do not suppose that anyone else in the world can thoroughly realise how much generosity and sympathy was shown by this,' Wild wrote. 'I DO by GOD I shall never forget it. Thousands of pounds would not have bought that one biscuit.' Shackleton did not mention the incident in his diary. But the incident sealed the bond between Shackleton and Wild.

Diarrhoea soon spread among the other three, yet somehow they managed to stumble on to the next depot on 2 February. Wild, slowly wasting away, had not been able to keep down his pemmican for six days and conceded to his diary: 'If I don't soon get over it, I am afraid I shall have to be left on the Barrier.' Two days later the entire party collapsed and was unable to move. Adams alone had to leave the tent seven times during the night to relieve himself and Marshall said the camp was 'like a battlefield'. Shackleton scrawled in his diary: 'Outlook serious.'

Shackleton tried to raise spirits in the tent one night by asking Wild to sing the hymn, 'Lead, Kindly Light', whose familiar words struck a chord with their distressing predicament. Wild, who had a fine baritone voice, had strength enough for only the first verse:

Lead, Kindly Light, amidst th'encircling gloom,
Lead Thou me on!
The night is dark, and I am far from home,
Lead Thou me on!
Keep Thou my feet ; I do not ask to see
The distant scene; one step enough for me.

At the depot Shackleton replaced the worn sledge with another slightly heavier one left behind on the outward march. It was not the only extra weight being dragged.

On the climb down the glacier, Shackleton had collected an assortment of rock samples which he wanted to take back to England for analysis. While the scientific community would welcome the samples, the notion of weak, starving men carrying an additional burden of rocks bordered on madness. To Shackleton the rocks might be the key to unlocking potentially rich sources of minerals or precious stones. Even at the margins of survival, Shackleton could not resist the temptation to search for treasure.

The party staggered on, battling the combination of cold, hunger, fatigue and diarrhoea and making astonishing distances. Wild, fortunately, had responded to eating a porridge-like mixture of powdered biscuits and oatmeal and was regaining his strength. As their hunger intensified the men were forced to reconsider eating horsemeat again. It would, said Wild, 'either buck us up a bit or kill us'.

On a diet of half a pannikin of meat-laced pemmican and five biscuits they once made 20 miles (32 km) in a day, thanks to a strong following wind. Each man plumbed unknown depths of willpower in the struggle to survive. They had already been out for 14 weeks, covering over 1,200 miles (1,900 km) on half rations, and Cape Royds was still was about 240 miles (385 km) to the north.

The next depot, built around the slaughtered remains of Chinaman, was reached on 13 February with the food almost finished. Chinaman's liver was the showpiece of a minor banquet that night. In the search for every scrap of sustenance, they also scooped up the remnants of congealed blood left behind from the animal's slaughter. According to Wild, the blood made a 'beautiful soup'.

Depot A, about 100 miles (160 km) across the Barrier, was the next goal but, as the fatigue grew, the men found it very difficult to maintain distances. After completing 12 miles (19 km) on 15 February, they celebrated Shackleton's 35th birthday with an extra wallop of 'hoosh'. Shackleton, nursing a fearful headache, was given a thin cigarette made from shreds of tobacco and wrapped in coarse paper. 'It was delicious,' he said.

However, it was long way short of what their bodies badly needed. The thin soup of pemmican, a few slices of meat and some biscuits provided fewer than 2,000 calories a day, roughly a third of the 5,000–6,000 calories needed to sustain them.

Morale was raised on 18 February by the sight of Mount Discovery peering over the northern horizon. Mount Discovery, at nearly 9,000 feet (2,800 m), is the first notable feature to be seen on crossing the Barrier from the south. More importantly, the distinctive volcano lies almost adjacent to Minna Bluff, the area where Joyce had been ordered to place the vital depot.

'Furthest south'. Shackleton marched to within 97 miles of the South Pole in 1909. This was over twice as far as his 'furthest south' journey with Robert Falcon Scott and Edward Wilson in 1902–03.

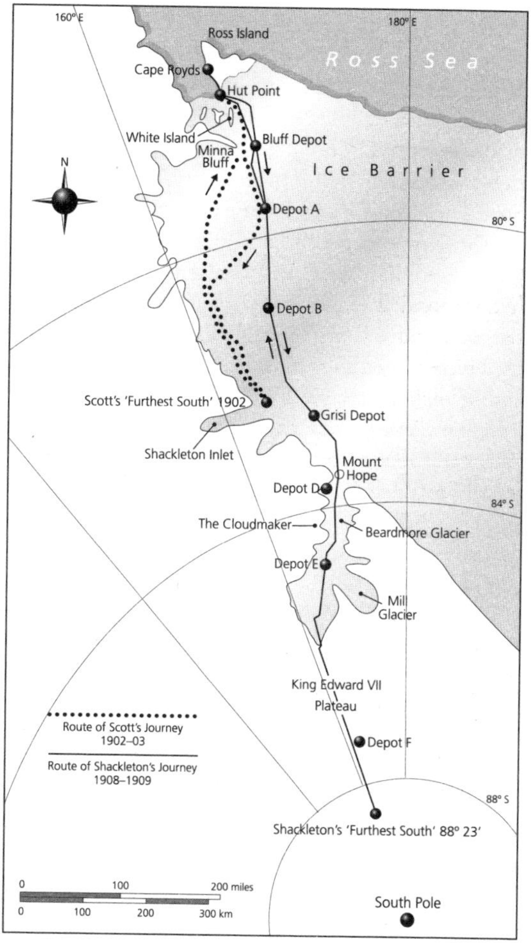

Next day the imperious presence of Mount Erebus, which stands on the same latitude as Cape Royds, came into view.

All now depended on whether their strength would hold out before the food disappeared. 'We are appallingly hungry,' Shackleton recorded.

What followed was a bizarre episode between Shackleton and Wild. Out of the blue Shackleton suddenly asked Wild if he would go south again for another tilt at the Pole. Only a few days earlier, while suffering from severe diarrhoea, Wild had written that the present journey had 'cured me of any desire for more polar exploration'. Now, without hesitation, Wild said yes. Quietly disregarding the shocking reality of their condition, the two men chatted amiably about raising money in Australia for a new expedition. Wild was now a man prepared to follow Shackleton anywhere.

It now took longer to scribble brief diary entries than eat the scanty meals. On 20 February the party shuffled into Depot A, about 140 miles (225 km) from Cape Royds, with the thermometer registering 52° of frost (-29 °C) and the food bag empty. That night they gorged on a full cup of pemmican 'hoosh' and a pudding concoction made from biscuits and jam. After drinking nearly full-strength cocoa for the first time in weeks, the men indulged in the luxury of smoking unlimited cigarettes supplied by Shackleton's Tabard tobacco firm. 'I am sure that the tobacco will make up for the shortage of food,' Shackleton wrote.

The party was invigorated by their full stomachs. But their survival hinged entirely on whether or not Joyce had laid the depot at Minna Bluff, the elongated and hook-shaped promontory about 70 miles (105 km) to the north. They had food for only four days and they prayed that the weather would hold.

Temperatures plunged to -35° (-37 °C) on 21 February as they stumbled forward in swirling snow whipped up by gusty winds. In other circumstances, conditions would have driven men into the safety of the tent. But there was no margin for safety. 'It is neck or nothing now,' Shackleton wrote. 'Our food lies ahead and death stalks us from behind.'

Wild-eyed with cold, hunger and exhaustion, they drove forward at an incredible rate, registering 20 miles (32 km) on two successive days. 'We are so thin that our bones ache as we lie on the hard snow in our sleeping bags,' Shackleton reported.

The relief was palpable on 22 February when they suddenly ran into freshly laid tracks made by men and dogs. The scattered debris of empty tins, cigarette butts and dog excreta was reassuring evidence that Joyce had done his job. 'They must have come from the depot,' Shackleton said.

Camped within a reasonable day's travel to the depot, the men staked everything on reaching the cache in one swift dash north. Virtually all the remaining food was eagerly devoured to fuel them for the run. It was another huge gamble. Shackleton admitted: 'If we do not pick up the depot, there will be absolutely no hope for us.'

Carrying only a few biscuits, the four men plunged forward from 6.45 in the morning until 4 p.m. when Wild's keen eyes spotted a flashing light in the distance. Hurrying forward they found a biscuit tin perched on a pole catching the light of the sun like a cheery eye winking at the weary

Lifeline. With all food gone, the Southern Party staggered into Bluff Depot on 23 February 1909. The night before, Shackleton wrote: 'If we do not pick up the depot, there will be absolutely no hope for us.' (L–r) Adams, Wild, Shackleton.

travellers. 'Good old Joyce,' wrote Wild. As insurance, Joyce had built the depot 10 feet (3 m) high with three flags on top and the reflecting tin.

There was good reason to thank Joyce who had run south with two sledges and eight dogs. Joyce, with a supporting party of Day, Marston and Mackintosh, was the only one at Cape Royds with any faith in the dogs. One stash of provisions was dumped on 25 January as Shackleton was still descending the Beardmore Glacier and Joyce was rested enough to carry another consignment south on 8 February. On the same day, an exhausted and ravenous Shackleton wrote: 'Feel starving for food.' The dogs, in the words of Mackay, had performed some 'wonderful marches'.

At the depot, Shackleton, Adams, Marshall and Wild rejoiced in the rare pleasure of a full stomach. Among the luxuries were freshly boiled mutton, plum puddings and eggs. In addition, there was a note announcing the safe arrival of *Nimrod* under the command of Captain Evans.

But the party was still afflicted by fresh bouts of diarrhoea. Wild succumbed first and soon after leaving the depot, Marshall was virtually paralysed by stomach cramps and unable to move. A blizzard struck soon after and they were confined to the tent for the day.

The delay was hugely frustrating. Shackleton's instructions were that *Nimrod* was due to leave McMurdo Sound on 1 March. It was now 26 February and, with Marshall struggling, it was clear that they might miss the ship.

Astonishingly, the party covered 24 miles (38 km) in 21 hours of forced marching on 27 February, despite Marshall's agonies. 'He never complains,' Shackleton recorded.

But they camped late in the afternoon and Marshall, his dysentery worse than ever, was unable to take another step. Hut Point, the nearest refuge, was a little over 30 miles (48 km) away and the ship was due to sail in 36 hours.

Shackleton moved quickly. Leaving Adams to nurse the stricken Marshall, he struck north with Wild and a sledge carrying a little food and two sleeping bags. Stumbling and staggering forward, the two men marched from 4.30 in the afternoon until 11 a.m. the next morning. They stopped only to eat some food and flash a heliograph in the direction of Observation Hill, the knoll on Hut Point Peninsula beside the old *Discovery* hut. Shackleton had left instructions to keep the hut manned and for signals to be sent from Observation Hill at prearranged times. No flash was returned.

Shackleton and Wild's food was finished by midday and a blizzard was blowing as they approached open water near Cape Armitage at the southern tip of the peninsula. At one stage a party of men could be seen approaching through the haze. The 'men' turned out to be penguins.

Driving forward in the haze, Shackleton encouraged Wild to dig even deeper into his reserves. As they walked along, Shackleton grabbed Wild's arm and said: 'Frank, old man, it's the old dog for the hard road every time.' Shackleton and Wild were both 35 years of age and Adams and Marshall, in their 20s, were lying prostrate on the Barrier.

With the sea ice dangerously unstable, Shackleton abandoned the sledge and sleeping bags. The area was too dangerous to risk a short cut to Hut Point. Instead they opted for the longer route around Castle Rock, the bare ridge which overlooks the peninsula. Castle Rock carried a bad memory for both Shackleton and Wild. It is only accessible through a jumble of hazardous crevasses and slopes and George Vince, the hapless *Discovery* seaman, had plunged to his death from the same slopes in 1902.

In poor visibility, Shackleton and Wild picked their way through the broken ground. At the top of the slope they were greeted by a crushing discovery. There was no sign of *Nimrod* and no trace of activity around the hut. Had the ship and men gone? In Wild's words, they were 'beyond speech' while Shackleton said their minds were 'busy with gloomy possibilities' of being marooned in the Antarctic.

Moments later they entered the deserted hut and found a note from David revealing that the ship would be lying to the north at Glacier Tongue, about halfway between Hut Point and Cape Royds, until 26 February. It was now late in the evening of 28 February. Evans, it seemed, was following the example of Captain England and reluctant to bring *Nimrod* too close to Hut Point.

Sending a signal before *Nimrod* disappeared over the horizon was their first thought. They tried to start a fire by burning a small magnetic observation hut left over from *Discovery* but were unable to get it to light. They scrambled up a nearby slope and tried to attach a flag to the wooden cross erected in memory of Vince. But their hands were so cold they could not tie a knot.

Retreating back to the hut, the men found some biscuits, onions and plum pudding to eat and wrapped themselves in rolls of discarded roofing felt to keep warm. By early morning the warmth had returned to their hands and they were able to set light to the magnetic hut and tie the flag to Vince's cross. Almost immediately *Nimrod* steamed into view. Within two hours the men were on board the ship devouring bacon and fried bread.

To many at Cape Royds and on *Nimrod*, Shackleton and Wild had come back from the dead. It was assumed they had perished on the Barrier.

But Shackleton could not rest with Adams and Marshall still camped on the ice. After less than four hours of recovery, Shackleton led a small party onto the Barrier in search of his men. Wild was too exhausted to travel.

The search group – Mackay, Mawson and seaman Thomas McGillion – reached Adams and Marshall at lunchtime on 2 March. Without much rest, the six men marched for over 24 hours, stopping only to prepare a meal and hot drinks. They reached the ice edge by late evening on 3 March only to find that *Nimrod* had disappeared again. While a weakened Marshall slept, Shackleton fretted and fired a carbide flare to signal the ship to return to Hut Point. By early hours of 4 March, the southern party was together on board *Nimrod*.

Shackleton had been a seemingly indestructible presence in the final stages of the southern journey. In five frantic, nerve-shredding days he had barely rested, travelling close to 100 miles (160km) without adequate rest.

Under Shackleton's astute leadership, the southern party had blazed the trail to the Pole. Shackleton, Adams, Marshall and Wild had marched and man-hauled a total of 1,755 miles (2,800 km) – including relaying the sledges – across largely unknown territory and stretched their rations from an original estimate of 91 to 120 days, giving them effectively another month on the road. They had eaten only one full meal in a 14-week spell

(L–r) Wild, Shackleton, Marshall and Adams on board Nimrod, *4 March 1909, after the harrowing trek of 1,755 miles (2,800 km).*

from mid-November until they staggered into Joyce's Minna Bluff depot on 23 February. Adams alone lost almost two stone (12 kg) in weight. Not a man had been lost.

The crucial moment was Shackleton's finely balanced decision of when to abandon the march and turn for home. In the context of a four-month journey, it was a choice made in a heartbeat. Adams reckoned the four men would not have survived had they marched south for another hour on the morning of 9 January.[2]

chapter 22

Home is the Hero

McMurdo Sound was bracing itself for winter on 4 March 1909 as the bedraggled southern party regrouped on board *Nimrod.* The inlet's waters, open a week before, were slowly filling up with formations of young sea ice and the risk of the ship getting trapped increased with every passing hour.

Hurried arrangements were made to bring personal items and equipment from the hut, though in the rush much was left behind. Among the stuff deliberately abandoned was the generous donation of sufficient provisions to sustain a party of 15 men for a full year.

Winds were freshening to gale force and menacing ice was closing in as *Nimrod* turned away from Cape Royds for the final time. On deck the men mustered for a sentimental rendition of 'Auld Lang Syne' and to deliver three throaty cheers as *Nimrod* dodged the gathering ice to sail north. 'We watched the little hut fade away in the distance with feelings almost of sadness,' Shackleton wrote.

The voyage home gave Shackleton the first opportunity to learn the details of David's historic journey with Mackay and Mawson to make the first fixing of the South Magnetic Pole. Like the southern journey, it had been an outstanding trip, the trio covering a prodigious distance of 1,260 miles (2,000 km) in 122 days, including more than 740 miles (1,190 km) relaying sledges weighing almost half a ton across appallingly difficult terrain.

On 16 January, while Shackleton's party was still struggling across the Plateau heights, David, Mackay and Mawson located the Magnetic Pole at 72° 25' S, 155° 16' E. It was one of the longest feats of man-hauling ever achieved. But, as David admitted, the arduous journey could have been accomplished in half the time with 'an efficient team of dogs' and the knowledge that lugging heavy quantities of food was unnecessary because the area was teeming with wildlife.

A more unhappy revelation was that both the southern party and David's team had come close to missing the ship and spending another year in the Antarctic.

Much of the problem lay with the appointment of Captain Frederick Evans, formerly of *Koonya*, to bring *Nimrod* back to McMurdo Sound. Evans, a commanding, forthright mariner in his early 30s, was ostensibly captain of the ship alone. But the lines of command had become blurred during Shackleton's absence. Kinsey, the agent, was unaware that Murray had been placed in charge at Cape Royds and instead gave Evans the authority to assume command if Shackleton had not returned from the south when the ship anchored in McMurdo Sound. Without hesitation Evans took control from the mild-mannered Murray.

The first priority was the South Magnetic Pole party. Shackleton had left orders that a search should be launched if David's team had not returned by the first day of February. Evans, however, felt the orders were too vague. David could be anywhere in an area of around 200 miles (320 km) of largely unknown coastline and Evans was cautious about expending his precious coal stocks searching for a needle in a haystack.

Evans was on the brink of abandoning the search – leaving the party to make their own way along the coast to Cape Royds – before the three men were eventually picked up on 4 February. They were nearly 200 miles (320 km) from base with the autumn season closing in and facing the likelihood of spending another year in the Antarctic.

Evans was equally forthright over the fate of the southern party and overrode the instructions Shackleton had left with Murray. While Evans was a skilled seaman, he had little knowledge of the ice and was in no position to judge accurately the condition of Shackleton's men on the Barrier. By late February, with the weather worsening, Evans had come to the conclusion that Shackleton's party had perished somewhere out on the Barrier. All that remained, Evans felt, was to 'find the bodies'.

Resigned to catastrophe, Evans now ignored Shackleton's orders that heliograph signals should be sent each day from the top of Observation Hill. Nor did he station men and supplies at Hut Point, as explicitly ordered by Shackleton. In the event, Shackleton managed to reach Hut Point unaided and signal the ship. But it was a close-run thing.

However, Shackleton was curiously equivocal about the episode. It is possible he recognised that the orders left at Cape Royds were genuinely vague and that the hazy chain of command exposed him to charges of poor leadership. As Wild later explained, Shackleton 'forgave those responsible' and never mentioned it again. As a colleague explained: 'As always with him, what had happened had happened. It was in the past and he looked to the future.'

The curiosity is that Shackleton did not always forget a man's lapses. As Bernacchi had noted, there was an occasionally unpleasant side to Shackleton and it showed when he excluded Captain England from the list of men awarded medals for the expedition. 'I do not see that I could recommend England,' he told Leonard Darwin at the RGS, 'it would at once put him on equality with the members of the expedition who were satisfactory and did their work throughout.'[1]

Yet nothing could detract from the comprehensive triumph of the British Antarctic Expedition. Despite a difficult and hurried beginning and haphazard funding throughout, it had been the most successful enterprise ever to visit the continent. And not a life had been lost.

The scientific achievements were outstanding, despite Shackleton's limited personal interest. *Nimrod* contributed much more to the understanding of the continent, helping to lay the foundations for future generations of study into important areas such as biology, geology, glaciology and meteorology. While his involvement was marginal, Shackleton's intuitive ability in choosing the right men was fundamental to the expedition's success. (David, Mawson and Priestley were later knighted for their contributions to science.)

With the sea ice still closing fast, *Nimrod* traced a hazardous course along the coast of Victoria Land on the first leg of the journey to New Zealand, a distance of almost 2,500 miles (4,000 km). Shackleton wanted to round off proceedings by charting the unexplored region to the west of Borchgrevink's old stamping ground at Cape Adare. But on 9 March a wall of pack ice blocked the route and threatened to trap the ship. *Nimrod* briefly came to a standstill before a narrow lead offered a path north and the ship steamed gratefully into open water. It was the afternoon of 10 March, the day Shackleton had determined should be *Nimrod*'s last before leaving the continent.

Less than a fortnight later *Nimrod* dropped anchor at the mouth of Lord's River on Stewart Island off the coast of New Zealand's South Island. After more than a year of bleak ice, glaciers and mountains, the vivid colour and softness of Stewart Island's heavily wooded slopes and sweeping beaches were an invigorating sight. Some dived playfully into the sea, while others climbed trees or made tea on the sand in celebration of the return to civilisation.

Next morning, 23 March, *Nimrod* entered Half Moon Bay where Shackleton went ashore to the small settlement of Oban to send the first of his cables. Using a prearranged code, he sent messages to Charles Dorman in London and to the *Daily Mail*. The newspaper, which turned down Dorman's earlier bid for a public appeal, had paid Shackleton £2,000 (about £120,000/€150,000 today) for the exclusive story.

Shackleton emerged as a full-blown celebrity two days later when *Nimrod* steamed into the port of Lyttelton. The expedition's dramatic story had already echoed around the world and the ship's return was greeted by enthusiastic flag-waving crowds. From London the King sent a personal telegram congratulating Shackleton on the expedition's 'splendid result'.

Shackleton relished the spotlight, eagerly lapping up the applause as he took centre stage in three weeks of hectic celebration. All concerns about unpaid bills, the sacking of Captain England or broken promises were quietly pushed aside in the clamour to applaud the returning heroes. New Zealand's Prime Minister Ward threw a special luncheon, a thanksgiving service was held at the very English-looking Canterbury Cathedral and the Lyttelton Harbour Board generously allowed *Nimrod* free run of its facilities.

In response to the warm welcome, Shackleton delivered a typically florid lecture to an adoring crowd of 3,000 and promptly handed over the proceeds of £300 to the children's ward at Christchurch Hospital and to the Christchurch Technical Institute to help fund a training hostel for young women. 'It seemed as though nothing but happiness could ever enter life again,' he wrote.

Shackleton's life would never be the same again. He was now public property. Praise poured in from all quarters, most notably from the summit of polar exploration. Amundsen told Keltie at the RGS that Shackleton had won a victory 'which can never be surpassed' and added an enormous compliment: 'What Nansen is in the North, Shackleton is in the South.'

Nansen himself wrote to Emily saying the expedition had been 'a complete success in every respect.' Nansen also told RGS President, Leonard Darwin – the son of Charles Darwin – that it was one the 'finest deeds of exploration' and concluded: '[it] reads like a fairy tale and reveals to me a new world.'

The polar establishment at home saw things differently. For public consumption, they could only join in the general applause for Shackleton's achievements. What they said in private was altogether different.

Markham led the counter-attack, questioning the expedition's records and implying that Shackleton has falsified the readings. Markham, now 78 and increasingly deaf, had lost none of his gift for mischief-making and malicious gossiping. 'A scurrilous old man' was how Frank Debenham, the distinguished geologist and co-founder of the Scott Polar Research Institute at Cambridge, once described Markham.

The bitter old man set out his feelings in letters to Keltie and Darwin and in gossipy asides to anyone who would listen. In a note to Keltie, he wrote: 'I do not quite see how it [the record latitude of 88° 23' S] is possible.' A little later Markham told Darwin: 'I cannot accept the latitudes. For 88.20 they must have gone, dragging a sledge and on half rations, at a rate of 14 miles a day in a straight line, up a steep incline 9000 feet above the sea, for 20 days. I do not believe it.'[2]

Markham, a man who had never commanded an expedition to the ice, dismissed Shackleton's enterprise as a failure and claimed that 'faulty management' prevented him reaching the Pole. What gnawed away at Markham was any hint that Shackleton, a merchant seaman, was a better explorer than his protégé, the naval officer Scott. He simply did not believe Shackleton could travel as far or as fast as Scott. 'To reach 88° 20',' he told Keltie, 'Shackleton would have gone at a quite impossible pace.'

Publicly, however, Markham maintained the pretence that Shackleton had performed heroics. He felt no compunction in writing to Emily delivering his 'warmest congratulations' on the expedition. A little later he wrote to Shackleton, offering the 'hearty congratulations of an old friend' and invited the couple to dinner.

Paradoxically, Markham wanted Shackleton to receive the prestigious RGS Patron's Medal. Amundsen, Nansen and Scott had all been honoured with the same recognition and according to Markham, it would be 'a serious mistake' not to award the medal to Shackleton.

The RGS, however, was not moved by Markham's plea. Perhaps the anti-Shackleton feeling ran deeper than even Markham suspected. In the event, the RGS decided that Shackleton's achievement of blazing a trail towards the Pole and reaching a higher latitude than anyone before was not deemed worthy of honour. The Patron's Medal for 1909 was awarded instead to Colonel George Milo Talbot, a 54-year-old Anglo-Irish aristocrat and solider – one of the Talbots of Malahide – for a series of obscure geographic surveys in the imperial outposts of Afghanistan and the Sudan.

Keltie, a shrewder operator than Markham, shared the misgivings but knew the RGS could not ignore Shackleton's achievement. 'I can assure you the appreciation here in the Society and among all interested in geography is all that you could wish,' he told Shackleton. 'You have done more in a few weeks than Peary has been able to do in 12 years,' he added. 'I am personally delighted.'

Yet Keltie was obliged to question the accuracy of Shackleton's readings, evidently hoping to spot some flaw in the expedition's figures. 'I suppose you made pretty sure what latitude you reached,' he asked with scarcely concealed meaning. 'I have no doubt you established your latitude to your complete satisfaction.'[3]

Shackleton was irritated by Keltie's insinuation. Keltie, he told Mill, was 'tumbling over himself' regarding the expedition. 'Even now he asks me if I can be sure of my latitude, as if I had not taken all possible means in my power to ascertain exact positions.'[4]

Although the RGS's unequivocal support for Scott had placed the Society in a difficult position, there was no question of backing down or accepting Shackleton's record with good grace. 'Shackleton owed everything to Captain Scott,' Markham wrote in a private memorandum. 'Without Captain Scott he would never have been heard of,' he claimed. 'To put him on a par with Captain Scott, or his people on a par with the Society's expedition [*Discovery*], would be a serious mistake in my opinion ... indeed an outrage,' Markham wrote.[5] Admiral Lewis Beaumont, Vice-President of the RGS, put it more grandly, explaining that Scott possessed 'superior claims on the Society'.

Scott, according to recycled gossip from Markham, was another who did not believe Shackleton's latitudes. Scott was still bitterly resentful over the issue of McMurdo Sound but, publicly at least, was forced to accept that Shackleton had undoubtedly taken huge strides towards the Pole. 'The private feeling incurred by past incidents,' he told Darwin, 'cannot affect my judgement of his work.'

Scott, in fact, had other motives. Immediately on learning of the 'furthest south', Scott had thrown himself into launching a new expedition. Shackleton's failure to reach the Pole left the quest open for Scott to make his long-anticipated return to the south.

In March, when word of Shackleton's record first emerged, Scott was travelling by train with seaman Tom Crean from *Discovery*. On the platform they saw newspaper headlines proclaiming Shackleton's feats and Scott turned to Crean, announcing: 'I think we'd better have a shot next.' It was the moment, six months before the official announcement, which signalled the start of Scott's last expedition and took him along Shackleton's route up the Beardmore Glacier and across the Polar Plateau to the South Pole.

Shackleton, meantime, had no qualms about submitting his records to the RGS for inspection. The RGS was the guardian of the nation's geographic knowledge and E.A. Reeves, the Society's respected map curator, was the established authority on the subject whose job it was to cast an eye over travellers' records.

Reeves was told that the navigational records of the march south were taken by Marshall using a theodolite and the figures were checked by Shackleton and Adams, both trained in navigation. Using his own methodology, Reeves also assessed the figures and concluded that 'in no case' did the two results differ by more than a minute. The furthest south observation was 'within a few seconds of arc,' he said. To Reeves, there was no doubt about the accuracy of the readings and he declared: 'Taking all the circumstances into consideration, I think Mr Shackleton's latitudes may be accepted as satisfactory.'[6]

It may not have been what the establishment wanted to hear and the discomfort was made worse by Shackleton's sudden popularity. In the space of little more than a year, the obscure doctor's son and merchant naval officer was the name on everyone's lips.

Shackleton's incredible story of hardship and survival on a continent few were ever likely to see touched a nerve and gave Edwardian society a taste of what Cook had brought to the 18th century and Livingstone to the 19th. The King described the expedition as the 'greatest geographical event' of his reign.

Shackleton enjoyed the sudden fame and instinctively knew how to take full advantage of it. Building a public persona came naturally. He knew how to engage with people, either in close proximity or in large numbers at vast meeting halls. 'When Lieutenant Shackleton comes into a room he brings a breeze with him,' a friend said.

Instead of rushing back to England, Shackleton took his time to leave New Zealand and Australia, sweeping through the countryside for several weeks on a well-attended lecture tour. It was a dress rehearsal of what he expected on stepping ashore in England.

The liner *India* brought Shackleton through the Suez Canal where he picked up the mail ship *Isis* for the short hop to Brindisi in the south of Italy to catch a train through to Calais. Skipper of *Isis* was *Discovery* colleague Armitage, who detected something different about Shackleton since they had last met. 'I noticed a great change in him,' Armitage recalled. 'He was no longer so dreamy; he was full of restless, nervous energy and ideas for another journey.'

The prospect of a new expedition was news to Emily. Only a few weeks before Shackleton had written from Sydney telling her how much he loved her and the children and insisted that he would never go on another expedition. 'Never again my beloved will there be such a separation as there

Shackleton's return to London was greeted by crowds packing into Charing Cross Station on 14 June 1909. Shackleton (centre left) stands in the carriage to acknowledge the applause. Emily Shackleton sits opposite.

has been, never again will you and I have this long parting that takes so much out of our lives,' he pledged. At the moment of writing, Shackleton was undoubtedly sincere, as he had been when delivering the same sentiments after returning from *Discovery* and before embarking on his 'furthest south' journey.

The final leg of the trip home gave a telling insight into the way Shackleton's mind was already working as he orchestrated a carefully choreographed piece of publicity management. Along the route home, Shackleton had announced he would arrive by boat train at London's Charing Cross station at 5 p.m. on Monday 14 June. In fact, he arrived at Dover two days earlier to spend a quiet weekend alone with Emily. It was to be their last moment together for a while.

London erupted into a near frenzy of hero worship at the appointed hour when Shackleton emerged from Charing Cross station in the early evening of 14 June. The stage management had worked. Crowds thronged the station concourse and entrance, eagerly hoping to snatch a sight of the conquering hero. The gates to the station were closed to control the multitudes.

Shackleton, like all good showmen, stood up in the open carriage to milk the applause. Sitting beside him, the normally reserved Emily watched, slightly overwhelmed by the clamour and trying to digest the realisation that her husband was now public property. It was a moment when Emily recognised things would never be same again.

Browning, as both Shackleton and Emily knew, had suitable words for the pivotal moments in a person's life. Amidst the cheering, raucous scenes that day the familiar lines from 'Paracelsus' were singularly appropriate:

Are there not, dear Michal,
Two points in the adventure of a diver?
One when, a beggar, he prepares to plunge;
One when, a prince, he rises with his pearl?

Dr Shackleton led the procession of proud family members, including four-year-old Raymond who wore a sailor suit with *Nimrod* emblazoned on his cap. Darwin, the RGS President, led the gaggle of dignitaries which included the Machiavellian figure of Markham, unsure whether to applaud or scowl. Also there was a reluctant Scott, who had been persuaded at the last moment that he was duty-bound to attend the homecoming.

Shackleton was in his element at the centre of proceedings. 'I never saw anyone enjoy success with such gusto,' Mill observed.

Shackleton had anticipated the enthusiastic welcome and wanted nothing but the best. He cabled Keltie from New Zealand with a brash request to 'get the King' and arrange a grand welcoming reception at London's Albert Hall. To Shackleton it was a fitting stage. Just 19 years before, the RGS had packed the Albert Hall with royalty, politicians and dignitaries to welcome Stanley back from Africa. He wanted the same.

The gathering took place on 28 June, though the King was unable to attend. In his place the King sent his son George, the Prince of Wales. This was no snub. As a young man, the King had been largely excluded from public office by a dominating Queen Victoria and he came to the throne with little experience of royal duties. Edward, a far less formal figure, wanted a more sensible transfer of authority and actively groomed Prince George – later King George V – for the throne by giving him an active role in the affairs of state.

Prince George, a small, neat man of 44 who had gone into the navy at the age of 12, listened intently as Shackleton delivered a full account of the expedition in front of 8,000 people packed into the cavernous Albert Hall. Describing himself as a 'brother sailor', the Prince awarded Shackleton a gold medal from the RGS, specially struck for the occasion. Silver replicas were given to most of the *Nimrod* party who attended the event, including Adams, Marshall and Wild.

Behind the scenes, the undercurrents around Shackleton refused to go away. Markham, after hearing that the Prince of Wales would stand in for the King at the Albert Hall, wrote with undisguised glee: 'The King is not coming.'

It was a glee evidently shared by Keltie. A few weeks before the event he delivered instructions to Cuthbert Bayes, the medal makers, which showed that the RGS had not softened its opinion of Shackleton. The RGS, having declined to award Shackleton the Patron's Medal, felt obliged to bestow some sort of honour, particularly with royalty in attendance. It was decided to award him a Special Gold Medal. But it was decreed that the medal should be made smaller than the one given to Scott for *Discovery*. 'We do not propose to make the Medal so large as that which was awarded to Capt. Scott,' Keltie said. However, the RGS later reconsidered the matter and struck Shackleton's medal with the same dimensions as Scott's, though the society's prejudices were abundantly clear. He never received the more prestigious Patron's Medal.

The shabby behaviour was a painful reminder of how spectacularly badly the RGS had misread the public mood. With his broad shoulders, rugged features and striking voice, Shackleton was an assured, articulate character who, to some at least, was the epitome of a heroic Edwardian explorer. Shackleton, said the *Daily Telegraph*, had helped 'breathe new inspiration and resolve into the British stock throughout the world.'

While he luxuriated in the personal spotlight, Shackleton never forgot his men. In this he was an unusual leader. History is generally the preserve of kings and queens, lords and ladies, and admirals and generals. Shackleton saw things differently and wanted to share his moment in history with the men who had made it all possible. 'No fierce limelight of publicity beats down upon them,' he told one meeting. 'But the expedition would never have been a success as it was if it had not been for the loyal co-operation, for the denial of self and for the absolute interest in the objects of the expedition which was shown by the 14 men whom I had the honour to have with me.'

Shackleton was in great demand and hurried through a flurry of speaking engagements, celebratory dinners and public appearances. He was asked to hand out prizes at Dulwich College – 'The nearest I have ever got to a prize,' he said with a smile – and addressed 4,000 people at Leeds Town

Shackleton at his old school, Dulwich College, July 1909. Shackleton was an undistinguished scholar but made a triumphant visit for a prize-giving ceremony after returning from the **Nimrod** *expedition.* COURTESY: GOVERNORS OF DULWICH COLLEGE

Hall in support of the National Life Boat Fund. In 22 hectic days in July he attended 30 separate public events. The month closed with a reward of sorts by witnessing his waxwork effigy unveiled at Madame Tussaud's.

A more meaningful event occurred on 27 July at the Robert Browning Settlement in the slums of Walworth. The Settlement Hall, established on the site where Browning was baptised, was run by Herbert Stead, a noble Edwardian champion of the poor whose tireless campaigning was largely responsible for introducing the old-age pension to Britain's elderly. By coincidence, the first pensions were paid on 1 January 1909, the day Shackleton stood nearer to either geographical pole than anyone before.

Both Shackleton and Stead were familiar with the theme of struggle, albeit from different standpoints. But the occasion had a special meaning for Shackleton. Although he was no radical, Shackleton acknowledged the assembled working men as brothers and gratefully accepted the Settlement's badge as a token of mutual respect. Inscribed on the badge were the words from 'Prospice' which Shackleton had summoned from his memory during the march south: 'Sudden the worst turns the best to the brave.'

The most notable invitation came on 12 July when Shackleton and Emily went to Buckingham Palace at the personal invitation of King Edward and Queen Alexandra. Shackleton was rewarded by being installed as a Commander of the Royal Victorian Order, an honour in the personal gift of the monarch which he had previously given to Scott. A knighthood was next. Whatever was being whispered elsewhere, royal patronage placed him beyond reproach.

Shackleton's fame paid immediate dividends as he was quickly drawn closer to society's inner circle. Less than three months after visiting Buckingham Palace, Shackleton went alone to Balmoral Castle in Scotland to spend a private weekend with Edward and Alexandra and a small coterie of hand-picked guests.

Shackleton dined in style close to the King's elbow and moved freely among the assembled gathering of aristocrats, statesmen and dignitaries. Among the guests was Sir Allen Young, an 89-year-old survivor of the *Fox* expedition which, half a century before, had discovered the fate of Sir John Franklin in the Arctic.

Shackleton delivered his lecture, showed his captivating lantern slides and kept the audience enthralled until 11.30 p.m. Soon afterwards, he was given membership of the exclusive Marlborough Club in London, founded by the hedonistic King as a bolthole for his elite circle of friends. Membership was strictly limited to just 450 people. Shackleton had joined society's upper table in much the same time as it took to cross the Barrier.

In October, shortly after visiting Balmoral, Shackleton went to Scandinavia to give a series of lectures. Places like Christiania, Copenhagen and Stockholm were the capital cities of polar exploration and the Scandinavians, more than anyone, understood the enormity of Shackleton's feats.

Nansen and Amundsen were among the enthusiastic audience in Christiania (renamed Oslo in 1925) who came to pay their respects in boisterous Scandinavian style. Local students, led by Amundsen, conducted Shackleton in a torchlit procession from his hotel to the lecture theatre and afterwards carried him through the streets on their shoulders. Nowhere, Amundsen reminded the crowds, had admiration for Shackleton been greater than in Norway and no assembly was better able to judge his exploits.

Among those to break through the throng for a private word with Shackleton was 21-year-old Tryggve Gran, an accomplished cross-country skier with a wish to explore. Gran talked enthusiastically about the ice with Shackleton and within a year would be travelling south with Scott.

But it was Amundsen, composed and inscrutable, who paid most attention. He hung on Shackleton's every word, gripped by the flowing dialogue and the sheer scale of the human endeavour that carried him to within 97 miles of the South Pole – and then turned back. Would he have done the same?

Amundsen, who had survived the first overwintering in the Antarctic and made the first navigation of the North-West Passage, recognised what Shackleton had accomplished. Nor was he burdened with the snobbery of the British class system. He judged people on merit and in Shackleton he saw something special.

'I shall never forget the look on Amundsen's face while Ernest was speaking,' Emily wrote of the occasion. 'His keen eyes were fixed on him ... the look of man who saw a vision.'

Amundsen had sound reasons for listening so intently. The pace of events in polar exploration had accelerated swiftly in the weeks before Shackleton came to Christiania. Amundsen, who was quietly nursing his own ambitions, suddenly feared that he might get left behind. What he planned was a secret coup.

Amundsen, single-minded and now 37 years old, had long set his sights on beating the Americans to the North Pole. He persuaded Nansen to let him borrow *Fram*, his specialist ice ship, for a mammoth five-year programme of exploration to the Arctic, which would climax in a spectacular dash to the Pole.

But American rivals, Frederick Cook and Robert Peary, had both emerged from the northern ice in the first days of September with separate

Poles apart. (L–r) Roald Amundsen, who reached the South Pole in 1911, Shackleton, holder of the record southerly latitude in 1909, and Robert Peary who claimed to have reached the North Pole in 1909.

claims to have stood at the North Pole. While Amundsen was digesting the news, Scott broke silence in England to announce that he was going to strike out for the South Pole in 1911. In the background, rumours circulated of possible American, German and Japanese expeditions preparing to go south.

Amundsen's response was to switch his objective from the North to the South Pole. As Shackleton recounted florid tales of crossing the Barrier and climbing the Beardmore Glacier, Amundsen sat quietly absorbing every detail, planning his own private raid to forestall all comers.

No detail was too trivial for him as he assessed Shackleton's account and balanced the strengths and weaknesses of the great southern journey. He noted, for example, the folly of not taking dogs or skis. He also noted the long gaps between the food depots and the enormous risk of not marking the vital supply depots more clearly.

Although serious nutritional analysis was beyond Amundsen's capacity, he also knew that Shackleton had come close to starving himself to death on the return march. It was not a risk he was prepared to take.

Yet Amundsen also admired the outstanding leadership and extraordinary depths of endurance needed to get Shackleton to within a few days of the Pole. Shackleton, he recognised, might have reached the Pole with just a few extra pounds of pemmican and biscuits. But, as Amundsen admitted, 'a little patch remained'.

chapter 23

Arise, Sir Ernest

Shackleton's nemesis was money: his adult life was plagued with a mostly fruitless chase to make money through a variety of speculative business ventures or in an often futile chase by his creditors trying to get paid. Money, when available, seemed to disappear in settling old bills or was given away to charity in acts of spontaneous generosity. As Emily explained, he had a fine knack of getting things going, 'but that is not exactly being businesslike'.

Money never stuck to Shackleton. It was impossible to establish exactly how much passed through his hands. Emily once admitted: 'I do not think we could find out all he gave for charity, he did it so often, spontaneously & it was not always recorded.'

The trail of unpaid bills and loan guarantees, left behind when *Nimrod* sailed in 1907, was largely untouched when he returned from the ice. 'Heaven only knows where it is to come from,' Herbert Dorman had cried in desperation as he battled to find £7,000 for the relief operation. Nothing had changed.

The anxiety of creditors was made worse by seeing Shackleton cheerfully mingling with the rich and powerful, a scenario they naturally equated with prosperity. Added to the concern was Shackleton's cavalier attitude to money. At a time when bills were piling up and men's wages were not paid, Shackleton would arouse fury by ordering a taxi and keeping it standing outside his office for much of the day, seemingly oblivious to the paradox.

A typical exercise in money management arose when Shackleton saw a chance to exploit his general popularity by opening a floating Antarctic exhibition on the Thames. It was a resounding success. An estimated 30,000 people flocked on board *Nimrod*, each paying 1s (5p) for a tour of the ship and a chance to see a variety of specimens brought back from the ice. In just two months, the exhibition cleared some £2,000. Shackleton promptly gave the proceeds to local hospitals.

Getting to the bottom of Shackleton's finances was a near impossible task. It is unlikely that accurate records were ever kept and not even Shackleton himself had a clear picture of his circumstances. Spontaneously giving money away or making promises with money he did not possess only added to the muddle and his hard-pressed advisers like Herbert Dorman were invariably left as mystified as everyone else.

Officially the figure given for the total expenses of the expedition was £44,380 14s 9d (about £2.5 million/€3 million today). However, this was only a general outline of estimated costs for major items, like refitting *Nimrod* in New Zealand or paying the shore party's salaries. Whether or not this estimate covered all expenses is not clear. Nor was it fully evident how much was owed in loans and guarantees provided by the likes of Beardmore and the Brocklehursts or to unknown supporters hastily tempted to back the expedition in the frantic days before sailing.[1]

With a mixture of blind faith and wishful thinking, Shackleton pinned his hopes on publishing a book about the expedition and making a major lecture tour. 'There is every prospect of my clearing 30 or 40 thousand pounds,' he wrote confidently to Emily. Within three weeks, the illusory riches had ballooned beyond all recognition as he plucked new figures from the air. 'I think we will make nearly £100,000 all together,' he claimed. In today's terms, £100,000 would be worth close to £6 million.[2]

One debt that Shackleton was particularly eager to repay was the £1,000 guarantee to Beardmore. It weighed on his conscience, partly because of the relationship with Elspeth. Cheered by the self-delusion of riches to come, Shackleton tried to reassure Elspeth by declaring that he was 'financially going to be all right'. In other circumstances a wealthy man like Beardmore might have written off the debt. But Beardmore was furious at the broken promise. Business was business and he wanted his money back as a matter of principle.

The initial signs for Shackleton were mildly promising, having raised £2,000 from the *Daily Mail* for delivering the expedition's exclusive story. Shackleton had conjured up another hopeful scheme to exploit the expedition's popularity which, with a further burst of optimism, he believed could raise at least ten times what the *Mail* contract paid. The source of this imaginary bonanza was the humble postage stamp.

Before going south, Shackleton had somehow persuaded New Zealand's Prime Minister Ward to install him as a postmaster. It was a novelty arrangement permitting Shackleton to operate the continent's first post office. Ward seemed happy to play along and presented Shackleton with an official date cancellation stamp and 240,000 sheets of standard 1d postage stamps. Overprinted on the stamps in dark green ink were the words, 'King Edward VII Land'.

The date cancellation stamp was the key which made the stamps potentially more valuable to collectors. Mail sent from *Discovery* in McMurdo Sound did not carry the cancellation stamp from the Antarctic and was therefore less valuable. 'The stamps alone are worth 10 to 20 thousand pounds,' he merrily told Emily.

Shackleton took the proposition very seriously and to publicise the venture, he carried a few specimen stamps in his pockets on the last dash south. The stamps were ceremoniously buried in a cylinder at his 'furthest south' on the Polar Plateau.

However, collectors were not interested in the scheme and Shackleton's foray into the rarefied world of philately ended before it really began. The specimens remain buried deep in the ice of the Plateau. Ironically, collectors today will pay many hundreds of pounds for an original King Edward VII Land stamp with the distinctive green ink inscription.

It was a lost opportunity in more ways than one. The sheets of 1d New Zealand stamps were proof of sorts that, contrary to the belief of some critics in London, Shackleton always intended to establish his winter quarters in King Edward VII Land or the nearby Bay of Whales and that McMurdo Sound was a last resort. The stamps, carrying the words 'King Edward VII Land', were clearly printed before *Nimrod* left Lyttelton in 1907 and suggest that Shackleton had not intended to overwinter in McMurdo Sound.

After the failure of the stamp-trading venture, Shackleton's next best hope was a book. Agreement was struck with the publishers – Heinemann – and Shackleton began writing his account on the long sea voyage home from New Zealand in the spring of 1909.

Shackleton, despite his literary flair, lacked the commitment and discipline to spend hours at a desk and needed assistance. On the recommendation of Prime Minister Ward, he hired the young New Zealand journalist Edward Saunders as co-writer at a salary of £10 per week (£575/€700 today) plus travelling expenses.

The two men quickly formed a highly productive working relationship. Shackleton liked the company of journalists and in Saunders he found a willing and accomplished collaborator. Words flowed eloquently as Shackleton paced up and down his cabin recounting the story while Saunders sat patiently taking copious notes before turning the rough transcripts into readable prose.

It was an arrangement which worked well for both men. It freed Shackleton from much of the hard labour of writing and played to his natural abilities as a speaker. Dictation came easily to him and he admitted: 'I can talk much better than I can write.' Saunders, on the other hand, was an ambitious young writer who had stumbled into the job of a lifetime. He loved writing and was travelling across the globe at someone else's expense to 'ghost' one of the Edwardian era's most dramatic adventure stories for a man riding the crest of a wave of popularity.

Shackleton said Saunders was 'indispensible' and Saunders reported that the two men 'understood each other thoroughly'. Shackleton subsequently named Mount Saunders, a peak halfway up the Beardmore Glacier, in recognition of his able literary partner.

The book, entitled *The Heart of the Antarctic,* was published in November 1909 and reflected Shackleton's undoubted gift for storytelling and the sound journalistic skills of Saunders. From start to finish, the project took only five months and the book was very well received. One reviewer called it the best book of polar travel ever written and another said the two-volume tome was a 'striking monument' to Shackleton's literary skill. While the skills were largely supplied by Saunders, the curiosity is that he never sought credit for his role and preferred to remain anonymous. The book remains in print to this day.

However, *The Heart of the Antarctic* was never likely to wipe out Shackleton's debts. He needed a stroke of luck and it came in the unlikely setting of the Cowes Week regatta.

It was early August and Shackleton and Emily were invited to the showy social gala for the great and good on the tight waterways of the Solent. Among the other notable visitors was Tsar Nicholas, Queen Alexandra's nephew, who was enjoying one of his final outings on the world stage before the coming war. The Shackletons were guests of Union Castle Line, his old employer, on board the prestigious liner *Armadale Castle.*

Shackleton's fortunes changed dramatically when he bumped into a stout, elderly journalist called Sir Henry Lucy. A stately 66-year-old, Lucy was an institution. He was a pioneer of Parliamentary journalism and immaculately well connected. He was the first great political sketch writer and perhaps the first Parliamentary lobby correspondent whose social status equalled the prominent men he wrote about. As a knight, Lucy was a rarity among the gentleman of the Fourth Estate.

Lucy, like all journalists, enjoyed a good story and listened intently as Shackleton recounted his remarkable tale of the Antarctic. In a separate conversation, Emily had unwittingly let slip to Lady Emily Lucy that Shackleton had returned from the ice with his finances in a shocking state.

Lucy was astonished when his wife passed on the snippet of information. He moved quickly to bring the news to public attention, writing a piece for the *Daily Express* revealing Shackleton's sorry plight at being left to pick up the bill for the expedition. With Lucy's considerable reputation behind the story, the outcry was entirely predictable.

The news filtered through to the corridors of power where, by chance, the country was passing through one of the many political crises of the Edwardian era. The latest emergency was Lloyd George's radical programme of welfare reforms and higher taxes for the wealthy, which were bitterly opposed by Conservatives and the landed gentry. 'A fully-equipped Duke costs as much to keep up as two dreadnoughts,' said Lloyd George, 'but was much less easy to scrap.'

Herbert Asquith, the Prime Minister, was under intense pressure to secure a mandate for the reforming budget by calling a general election and needed a few popular causes to bolster his standing with the electorate. In the search for popularity, Asquith suddenly learned about Shackleton's financial difficulties.

He set the political wheels in motion and quickly arranged a private meeting with Shackleton. It suited both men not to revive the uncomfortable fact that Shackleton had stood as a rival Liberal Unionist candidate against Asquith's government in the 1906 election. Helped by Asquith's strong support, proceedings were wrapped up in a matter of days. Only a few weeks after Lucy's revelation in the newspapers, the government announced that Shackleton would be given a grant of £20,000 (almost £1.2 million/€1.5 million today) to help meet a large slice of the expedition's outstanding expenses.

'Just think, your Boy getting £20,000 from the country,' an ecstatic Shackleton wrote to Emily. 'What oh!!' On the other side of the world, Mount Asquith and Mount Lucy were named in recognition of the politician and journalist who had made it all possible.

Not that Asquith's £20,000 grant had solved all the expedition's problems. In fact, the real state of the expedition's financial affairs was lost somewhere in the fog of haphazard paper records and vague promises kept in Shackleton's head. A combination of grants, book sales and public lectures, he reckoned, would 'make up all the liabilities'.

Beardmore, at last, was paid off, but he never forgave Shackleton and the relationship between the two men was irretrievably broken. Nor was he placated by confirmation that the Great Glacier, Shackleton's most outstanding Antarctic discovery, carried the Beardmore name. Perhaps, after all, he sensed it was named after his wife.

But the world was at Shackleton's feet, despite Beardmore's bitterness. Acclaimed by royalty, politicians and public alike, Shackleton was briefly among the most famous people in Edwardian Britain.

By November, little more than five months after returning to England, Shackleton was knighted in the King's birthday honours list. None of the King's honours, one newspaper suggested, would be more popular with the public than the name Sir Ernest Shackleton.

chapter 24

A Man of Parts

Fame can be fleeting and Shackleton was determined to make the most of his time in the limelight before the public attention was inevitably diverted elsewhere. During a packed final few weeks of the year, Shackleton went to Buckingham Palace to receive his knighthood from the King, *The Heart of the Antarctic* was launched and he embarked on a major lecture tour across two continents.

The packed schedule of speaking engagements was likely to tax even the most robust of men but Shackleton tackled it with much the same determination as he approached the Beardmore Glacier and Polar Plateau. Gerald Christy, the veteran lecture agent, had lined up more than 120 appearances in cities across Europe and America. By some estimates the punishing programme involved travelling up to 200,000 miles (320,000 km) and speaking to a combined audience of 250,000 people. Christy, who numbered Amundsen among his impressive list of public speakers, had never before put together such a demanding timetable for any of his clients.

In November and December alone Shackleton racked up almost 50 appearances throughout Britain, each time delivering his talk with the same flourish and enthusiasm as though it were his first. At Halifax in Yorkshire – just 10 miles (16 km) from the ancestral home of the Shackletons – he was cut off by snow and forced to navigate blocked roads with a makeshift sledge. The blizzards gave a 'homely feeling', he said.

A sentimental journey to Ireland followed in December, where he delivered lectures in Dublin, Cork and Belfast. It was his first formal visit to what he called his 'native land' since leaving 25 years earlier and he was much impressed with the friendliness of the greeting. Ireland had claimed a new hero. Dublin's *Evening Telegraph* had greeted news of the 'furthest south' with the glorious headline: 'South Pole Almost Reached By An Irishman.'

The new year of 1910 saw Shackleton embark on a rapid tour of Europe, taking in Austria, Germany, Hungary, Italy and Russia in just 22 days of hectic travelling by train from one famous city to another. In places like Berlin, Budapest, Vienna and St Petersburg, it was possible to snatch a final glimpse of several European empires soon to be swept away by war and revolution.

In Vienna he watched the glittering parade of archdukes and archduchesses seemingly making a final curtain call for the crumbling 1,000-year-old Habsburg dynasty. In Germany, where Shackleton observed first-hand the rising anti-British sentiment, he came face to face with the stiffly formal court of the bombastic Kaiser Wilhelm II. The warmest welcome came in the frozen splendour of St Petersburg where Tsar Nicholas, the last of the Romanovs, asked for a brief private audience with Shackleton, which overran and eventually lasted two hours. 'He was greatly interested in everything,' Shackleton reported.

Within days of leaving St Petersburg, Shackleton was speaking in Aberdeen at the start of another exhaustive round of appearances in British cities. In the space of seven weeks he spoke at 40 venues as far apart as Hastings in the south and St Andrew's in the north and from Lowestoft in the east to Plymouth in the west. In between he always made time for visits to local charities or hospitals.

Shackleton had honed his natural skills for public speaking. After giving mostly one-off speeches at venues like the Albert Hall or Balmoral, the busy schedule encouraged him to polish his delivery like a touring repertory company actor. Like all good actors, Shackleton rose to the occasion every night because putting on an act was second nature.

He cut a commanding figure, broad shouldered, with a ruggedly masculine square jaw and hair characteristically parted down the centre. Shackleton had mastered the art of soaring rhetoric, speaking freely without notes and engrossing audiences with his easy manner and clear delivery. Mill recalled his 'deep husky voice rising and falling with the movement of his story and sometimes raised to a rafter-shaking roar'. According to Mill, Shackleton's control of audiences was such that he could bring people shaking to the brink of tears one moment and then, with a scarcely perceptible touch, let them fall away in laughter. Christy, the experienced agent, said Shackleton possessed a 'descriptive power without parallel'.

Emily travelled with Shackleton on part of the tour, but returned to Edinburgh as he embarked on the German leg of the schedule. The couple were together again in March, travelling to America on Cunard's luxury liner, *Lusitania*. Amid the opulent melange of *Lusitania*'s famously elaborate interiors – Georgian-style carved mahogany panels to Corinthian columns and neoclassical Louis XVI and Queen Anne decor – Shackleton rested and recharged his batteries before starting another packed and demanding schedule.

Americans liked Shackleton and he received warm applause at a series of packed houses and quickly found himself at society's top table. The down-to-earth informality and ready Irish wit struck a chord in a country less bothered about class distinction and stiff decorum. In England, Shackleton once offered to speak to pupils at the elite Eton College for a modest fee but was rebuffed with the dismissive reply: 'This is five times as much as we pay for a really first class lecturer.'

In America Shackleton was entertained by Britain's distinguished Ambassador, James Bryce, and went to the White House to meet the bulky presence of President William Taft. Robert Peary, still struggling to substantiate his claim of reaching the North Pole, gave Shackleton a Gold Medal at a special gathering of the American Geographical Society in New York.

Shackleton was equally well received when he crossed the border into Canada, where Prime Minister Sir Wilfred Laurier and Governor General Earl Grey led the welcoming tributes. Thomas Shaughnessy, President of the mighty Canadian Pacific Railway, placed his private carriage at Shackleton's disposal for eight days. Shackleton was so impressed by the Canadians that he talked vaguely about raising money for an expedition into the remote Mackenzie River, but it never materialised.

However, the gloss came off the tour as Shackleton travelled away from the more sophisticated audiences along the east coast into the ruggedness of America's frontier states of Iowa, Minnesota, Nebraska and Ohio. This was partly down to poor planning and the failure of his newly appointed US agents – the Lee Keedick Agency on New York's Fifth Avenue – to whip up audiences with a blitz of advance publicity. In one 4,500-seater hall he spoke to a scattering of just 100 souls.

Polar exploration was not fashionable among the settlers in the Midwestern prairie towns and cities. Unlike Britain, America had little tradition of Antarctic exploration. It was 70 years since Charles Wilkes had led the only major US attempt to explore the region and that venture had ended in controversy and recrimination. Since then attention had focused on the Arctic, thanks largely to the efforts of Kane, Hall, Cook and Peary, though by now the dispute over the North Pole discovery had left most Americans thoroughly fed up with *all* explorers.

The strain of touring began to tell and at times Shackleton left Emily behind with friends as he travelled to distant venues alone. Almost inevitably, he became bored with the routine of delivering the same lecture every night and reportedly told friends he was 'sick of it all' as he prepared to address another half-empty hall. In May Shackleton received news from home that King Edward, his most eminent supporter, had died.

Despite the boredom, the reality was that lecturing – and sales of the book – was now his only real source of income. He was also comforted by word that most of the expedition's debts were close to settlement, though some wages from *Nimrod* were still outstanding. Both Brocklehurst and Adams challenged him over the unpaid wages.

This was the essential contradiction in Shackleton's complex character. He expected his men to be loyal, hard-working and committed but never quite grasped that apart from the wealthy baronet Brocklehurst, wages were their only source of earnings. Money meant nothing to Shackleton and he half expected others to feel the same way. 'He didn't know the meaning of the word money except spending it,' a bemused Adams remarked. His generosity 'outran his means', a kindly Mill explained.

The great paradox is that Shackleton always put the safety of his men first. He was cautious by nature and never took unnecessary risks with their lives. As he demonstrated on the Polar Plateau, bringing Adams, Marshall and Wild safely back to the ship was more important than reaching the South Pole. During his lectures Shackleton invariably referred to 'we' or 'us' rather than 'I'. Where possible, he always encouraged veterans of the expedition to stand alongside him on stage to share in the applause. Yet the inconsistencies were vivid. The lives of Shackleton's men were safe in his hands, but not their money.

Part of the reason for Shackleton's lackadaisical attitude to money was an immature belief that, metaphorically at least, he would one day unearth a pot of gold which would solve all his financial difficulties at a stroke. He was a fortune hunter at heart. Most of his business ventures – *Potentia*, Russian troops, Celtic Investments, Antarctic stamps, etc. – were built on the optimistic vision of making a quick killing. Shackleton could even dream of gold nuggets while almost starving to death coming down the Beardmore Glacier.

Shackleton never fully understood the mechanics of business and did not have the patience to allow normal commercial ideas and working practices to develop and mature naturally. He felt that sheer force of personality would carry him through any circumstance, even business. Administration, planning and preparation, the core of sound business practice, bored him to death and he was always baffled when his airy schemes collapsed in the dust. Emily, who tried to be more understanding, said Shackleton was 'too good for trade'.

The only investment which ever appeared to pay dividends was the small Tabard tobacco company, though the profits were slim and never likely to earn the fortune he dreamed of. In 1910 he celebrated winning an order for 20,000 cigarettes but revealed that the profit on the deal was a modest £17 (less than £1,000/€1,200 today).

Another puzzling side to Shackleton's character was reflected in the stark differences between his business partners and the men he selected for expeditions. Where Shackleton possessed an unrivalled knack of picking the right men for the rigours of Antarctica, his selection of commercial collaborators was often woeful. As Mill observed, Shackleton 'had the soul of a poet, not a trader'.

His methods of picking people were unconventional, occasionally bizarre and built more on a man's character than his obvious skills or expertise. Science and seamanship, he said, weighed little against the 'kind of chaps they were'. He picked Priestley for *Nimrod* because he saw potential in the unqualified young geologist and 40 years later Priestley was knighted for his services to science.

Yet his judgement, so often impeccable on the ice, failed badly when it came to business partners. He could spot a loyal, dependable sledging companion among hardened seamen like Wild but could not recognise a fraudster or a shady speculator in a smart suit and tie. Shackleton's judgement at home and on the ice was different.

The latest get-rich-quick scheme emerged during the lecture tour of European cities when he was offered the chance to invest in a gold mine. For Shackleton the treasure hunter, the opportunity was too good to be true.

The prospect arose on a visit to Budapest in January 1910 when Shackleton was invited to address the Hungarian Geographical Society. During informal conversations he picked up stories about rich seams of gold waiting to be mined at Nagybánya, an area where mining dates back to Roman times. (Nagybánya was absorbed into Romania in 1919 and is today called Baia Mare.)

Shackleton leapt at the opportunity with his usual energy and enthusiasm and tried to put together a syndicate of investors to exploit the mine. So confident was Shackleton of pulling off a spectacular deal that he was soon counting the windfall by promising to reinvest his imaginary wealth by diversifying into forestry and timber on the heavily wooded slopes outside the town of Nagybánya. 'There is a good chance of much more,' he confidently predicted in a letter to Emily, 'as the grants are in the hands of the cabinet.'

Shackleton returned to London in search of investors and soon ran into ex-*Nimrod* colleague Mawson. The geologist was in town exploring the possibility of attaching himself to Scott's forthcoming expedition by taking a splinter group of Australian scientists to explore the unknown territory to the west of Cape Adare.

What Shackleton's fertile mind saw was a chance to involve Mawson in a far more elaborate scheme, first to develop a gold mine and then to use the bonanza to finance a new expedition. As a return to the Antarctic had been on his mind for some time, Shackleton's idea, more or less, appealed to Mawson. He was also intrigued by Shackleton's breezy claim that he could lay his hands on the truly remarkable sum of £70,000 (£4 million/€4.8 million today) to fund the operation.

Scott, it turned out, was reluctant to accommodate a separate Australian team on his proposed expedition. In any event, Mawson had taken a notable dislike to Wilson, Scott's sounding board and head of scientific staff. Nor had Mawson raised enough funds to mount his own expedition.

While Shackleton was taking the *Lusitania* across the Atlantic for his American tour, Mawson was despatched to Hungary for a geological survey of the region. He took Mackintosh and John King Davis, two old retainers from *Nimrod*, as assistants.

Anxious not to let the momentum slip, Mawson completed his Hungarian survey and chased Shackleton across the American plains to a hotel in the Midwestern city of Omaha, Nebraska. There he reported that Nagybánya had decent potential but was reluctant to commit himself much further until the venture was placed on a more formal footing. Mawson, circumspect and serious, had seen enough of Shackleton's broad-brush approach to appreciate the importance of formalising things and there were also considerable doubts that the owners of the mining concessions in Hungary were willing to sell.

Together Shackleton and Mawson spent several days discussing plans and eventually drew up an agreement to raise money by floating a speculative company on the stock market. From the proceeds it was also agreed that Shackleton would finally pay Mawson the £400 wages owed from *Nimrod* and expenses incurred in Hungary.

Part of the agreement stated that Shackleton would go to the Antarctic towards the end of 1911 with Mawson as head of the scientific staff. But Shackleton was unsure about the expedition, perhaps because it carried too much scientific commitment or perhaps because Cape Adare did not quite match the gloss of standing at the South Pole. Therefore, an escape clause was written into the agreement allowing for Mawson to take command if for any reason Shackleton was unable to travel south. Although far from explicit, the clause left Mawson with the distinct feeling that 'the chances of [Shackleton] going to the Antarctic had lessened.'

Almost inevitably, the scheme subsequently dissolved into confusion and acrimony. While Mawson waited patiently for Shackleton to commit himself fully, Shackleton took the extraordinary step of taking the plan to the RGS and gave the impression that it was his expedition alone. Mawson was furious. 'In this he was cashing in on my own proposals,' the shocked Mawson wrote.[1]

But Shackleton did not go south in 1911. Instead, Mawson managed to raise money in Australia and New Zealand and went to the Cape Adare region, taking with him Davis, Frank Wild and an enterprising young photographer called Frank Hurley.

Although Shackleton subsequently lent his vocal support for Mawson, the muddled affair was damaging in some quarters. According to Mawson, the Australian Association for the Advancement of Science only agreed to fund his venture – formally known as the Australasian Antarctic Expedition – on condition that 'Shackleton had nothing to do with the undertaking.'[2]

Shackleton, meantime, persevered with the mining project. A syndicate of sorts was formed with Herbert Dorman pressed into acting as solicitor. However, the Hungarian landowners clung to their concessions and Shackleton was once again in the familiar position of struggling to find backers.

Lord Iveagh and the influential newspaper proprietor Lord Northcliffe were among those who declined to buy shares in the Hungarian project. Iveagh, who had helped the *Nimrod* undertaking, was a philanthropist with no interest in mining.

Northcliffe, publisher of the *Daily Mail* and another Anglo-Irishman, had developed a coolness towards Shackleton and was brusquely dismissive of the whole scheme. He listened to Shackleton's sales patter for a few minutes and interrupted by declaring: 'This is an insult to my intelligence.' Northcliffe sensed a crackpot venture and said he would employ an expert, 'not an amateur', had he wanted to invest in a mining company.

As a successful businessman, Northcliffe could also see clear signs that Shackleton's public profile was being exploited by ruthless speculators. Shackleton, he felt, was out of his depth in the cut-throat arena of commerce and he concluded: 'I advise you stick to the things you understand.'[3]

Shackleton went back and forth to Budapest in hopes of securing a deal for the mine, but the windfall remained as elusive as ever and the Nagybánya project followed in the wake of his other stillborn schemes. As Emily admitted, 'I never heard anyone ... say he was good at business.'

Affairs at home were no more comfortable for Shackleton. He was still heavily dependent on Emily's income and yet he was at home less often as he chased his fortune elsewhere. In the middle of 1910, he moved the family from Edinburgh to the sleepy little fishing village of Sheringham on the coast of Norfolk. Sheringham, stuck on England's most easterly coastline, was initially seen as quiet holiday retreat and the house, a neatly furnished property called Mainsail-Haul, was perfectly comfortable for a short stay. However, Shackleton was rarely at Sheringham and Emily, left alone with the children for long periods, grew increasingly isolated.

Shackleton was at London's Waterloo Station in July for the formal business of watching Scott depart for the Antarctic. If there was a tinge of jealously he did not let it show.

The spectre of Shackleton had loomed large over Scott for months and the mistrust between the two men had deepened. Despite Scott's very public preparations, there was always the possibility that Shackleton, knighted, a welcome guest at the royal table and darling of public opinion, might yet forestall him. Only now, waiting for the boat train to depart, could Scott dismiss the prospect with any degree of certainty.

Shackleton's would be an eerie presence throughout the expedition. Scott's plan was to follow Shackleton step by step to the Pole, crossing the Barrier, climbing the Beardmore Glacier and driving across the Plateau in the same tracks Shackleton took in 1908–09. Scott also took Manchurian ponies and a copy of Wild's account of the southern journey for reference. It was Priestley who later described Shackleton as the 'ghostly pace-maker' for Scott.

Scott, reasonably enough, wanted to know Shackleton's intentions. The problem was that Shackleton's plans were a constantly moving feast and what he said and what he did were often different.

During talks with the RGS in February, Shackleton had insisted he was 'particularly anxious' not to clash with Scott's plans. He also promised not to interfere with Scott's fund-raising attempts by launching a simultaneous money-raising exercise for his own expedition. In another breath he was telling Mawson that potentially huge sums of money would be made available for the Cape Adare venture.

Scott's view of Shackleton had not changed since calling him a 'professed liar' in the dispute over McMurdo Sound. Scott accused

Shackleton of introducing a 'terrible vulgarity' to the continent, which hitherto had been 'so clean and wholesome'.[4] At a dinner in London to welcome Shackleton back from the south, Scott had pointedly called for 'an Englishman to reach the South Pole' and gratuitously added: 'All I have to do now is to thank Mr Shackleton for so nobly showing us the way.'

The RGS, which had pointedly backed Scott at the expense of Shackleton, had no doubt that the matter of the South Pole was now in safe hands. It was right, said Keltie, that 'Captain Scott should complete what has begun so well' and insisted Scott would reach the Pole within a year or two.

What Shackleton did not expect was the hardening of attitude by Wilson, once his closest friend and now heading to the Antarctic as de facto deputy to Scott. Wilson, with his unshakeable moral convictions, had turned sharply against Shackleton since *Nimrod*. He refused to accept that establishing winter quarters at McMurdo Sound was Shackleton's only realistic choice. In the black-and-white world of Wilson, a promise was a promise.

'I wish to God before you had done any mortal thing in the whole world rather than break the promise you had made,' Wilson wrote in uncompromising terms. 'You took Scott's job practically out of his hands against his wish & knowing that he was hoping to finish it.'[5]

Before departing for the south, Wilson tried to extract a new pledge from Shackleton which went beyond his condition set in 1907. He now insisted that Shackleton should never be allowed to enter McMurdo Sound again. To Wilson, Scott's right to the region was inviolable and he demanded: 'Play the game.'

Wilson was one of the few men capable of forcing Shackleton into a retreat. Days after a meeting with Wilson, Shackleton wrote to Scott promising not to undertake any further exploration until hearing the outcome of his expedition. 'I may later attempt the circumnavigation of the Antarctic Continent,' he added, 'but my ideas as regards this are indefinite.'

Any emotions felt by Shackleton were concealed as he stood on the platform at Waterloo Station waiting for the train to carry Scott on the first leg of the long voyage south. Watching with scarcely concealed satisfaction were the officers from the RGS, including Keltie. Shackleton generously led a call of 'three cheers for Captain Scott' as the train slowly pulled away in a cloud of smoke. It was the last time they saw each other.

The send-off was a surprisingly low-key affair. Apprehension ahead of the expedition was understandable, but perhaps the portents of other great events were hanging over proceedings. Or perhaps Shackleton felt he was being left behind by it all.

On the eve of departure Scott had spoken to Thomas Marlowe, editor of the *Daily Mail*, about the apparent inevitability of war with Germany. Marlowe's opinion was that Germany would be ready to strike in the summer of 1914 and Scott replied: 'The summer of 1914 will suit me well.'

By chance, a German army officer stood alongside Shackleton as Scott's train pulled away. He was Wilhelm Filchner, a tall, determined and experienced explorer, who was in England to discuss an audacious plan to march across Antarctica from coast to coast.

'See you at the Pole,' Scott had called out to Filchner. This was not entirely far-fetched. Filchner planned to enter the continent on the opposite side to Scott by navigating the Weddell Sea, crossing hundreds of miles of uncharted territory to the South Pole and follow Shackleton's footsteps down the Beardmore Glacier and over the Barrier to McMurdo Sound. Meeting Scott at some point was faintly possible.

If ever there was a moment in his life that Shackleton felt isolated it was now. While Scott and Filchner were heading south, his immediate future revolved around either retelling the well-worn story of the 'furthest south' to dwindling audiences or humbling himself in the uphill search for money to plough into speculative business ventures.

What Shackleton needed was a new adventure and a chance for fulfilment. Within months of Scott's departure, Shackleton wrote to Emily: 'I feel that another expedition unless it crosses the Continent is not much.'[6]

chapter 25

Unrest

'He might have dogs but they are not very reliable,' Shackleton told the *Daily Express.* It was October 1910 and Shackleton was responding to news that Amundsen had abandoned his Arctic plans and was steaming towards the Antarctic to race Scott to the South Pole.

Amundsen's intervention sparked differing emotions in Shackleton. On a simplistic level he was still resolutely clinging to the belief that dogs were a liability on the ice. More probably, the contest developing between Scott and Amundsen was an uncomfortable reminder of his own exclusion from momentous events. Inaction weighed heavily on the shoulders of a restless man.

Shackleton's fear of missing out was made worse by the sudden explosion of interest in the Antarctic. By the autumn of 1910, Scott's *Terra Nova* and Amundsen's *Fram* were heading south, Filchner was preparing his vessel, *Deutschland*, for the Weddell Sea and Mawson was finalising plans to launch the Australasian Antarctic Expedition. From Japan came word that Lieutenant Nobu Shirase, a middle-aged army officer, was taking the small *Kainan Maru* into the Ross Sea with his ambition of striking out for the Pole. Bruce was trying to raise the substantial sum of around £50,000 (almost £3 million/€3.6 million in today's terms) for a second Antarctic expedition which, like Filchner, included plans to cross the continent from coast to coast via the South Pole.

Shackleton's frustration intensified when, instead of joining the others going south, he embarked on the sideshow of another long lecture tour across Europe. In Germany he found that anti-English feeling had grown significantly since his last visit, but the darkening mood did not prevent him lecturing in support of Filchner. 'It is a great strain lecturing in Germany when one does not feel that the people are really with one,' he told Emily.

By now the appeal of the lecture circuit had worn away. It was both tiresome and physically draining and his mind was elsewhere. 'If things [lecturing] do not go better soon I will think very seriously of chucking the whole thing in,' he told Emily from Cologne.

The conflicting forces of domestic responsibilities and the inevitable lure of a new expedition were torturing Shackleton at this time. At times he drew strength from the conventionally solid and loving family environment built around Emily. At other times he simply wished to be elsewhere.

Towards the end of 1910, he told Emily in emphatic terms: 'I am never again going South and I have thought it all out and my place is at home now I can see it quite clearly.' On another occasion, with the Hungarian negotiations bogged down, he sent her a wistful note, declaring: 'I almost wish I had not gone South but stayed at home and lived a quiet life.' How much of this Emily truly believed is open to question. All she knew was that Shackleton was still living beyond his means and hoping for a miracle from the mirage of Nagybánya. 'If Hungary comes off all right, well all our worries are quickly at an end,' he said.

A new anxiety emerged towards the end of the year. Emily, still bottled up in the coastal retreat of Sheringham, discovered she was pregnant.

Emily, now 43 and fearing another difficult labour, was swamped by waves of loneliness as she faced the unhappy prospect of coping with pregnancy at a distance from friends and family. Shackleton, a weekend husband at best, was rarely at home. She begged him to find a house in London where, fleetingly at least, they would spend more time together. In May 1911, with Emily seven months pregnant, Shackleton bowed to her wishes and moved the family to a house at 7 Heathview Gardens in the respectable London suburb of Putney Heath.

Putney Heath was a popular sanctuary for Londoners in search of open spaces and fresh air and a highly desirable home for well-to-do financiers and industrialists needing easy access to London's commercial centre. 'One of the pleasantest of the London suburbs,' a contemporary writer said. Around the corner from Heathview Gardens was the birthplace of Lawrence Oates, the cavalry officer Scott had taken south to handle his horses.

Moving to the genteel suburb was only a temporary solution to Shackleton's restlessness. 'The missus is going to have another baby in July and I must not talk of going away,' he wrote. Shackleton was no longer hiding his real ambition. 'I long for the unbeaten trail again.'[1]

Nor was the family ever fully settled in Putney. Shackleton was smoking heavily and drinking too much. He was 37 when he moved to

Shackleton with Emily and their children, Raymond and Cecily.
COURTESY: ATHY HERITAGE MUSEUM

Putney but looked older. The clean-cut features had given way to slightly puffy cheeks and noticeable bags under the eyes. There were also bouts of illness, including one occasion when he was sent home from a meeting, complaining of severe chest pains. Mawson happened to be in the room at the time and did not accept Shackleton's implausible explanation that it was a touch of 'rheumatism'. Mawson watched Shackleton sweating profusely and struggling with pain and concluded: '... it must have been angina.'

Emily, suffering another troublesome pregnancy, was still unhappy. Moving from Norfolk to London had not cured her isolation and Shackleton, always in a hurry, seemed to be dashing to be anywhere but at home. The couple argued more than ever, though the fault lay squarely at his feet. 'I think I am solely to be blamed,' he admitted to her.

Emily kept her distance from Shackleton's new circle of drinking pals, preferring the more sedate company of family and close friends. While she initially enjoyed the trappings of Shackleton's celebrity, it was never her choice. She always preferred the settled and gentle environment of her upbringing, which was something Shackleton would never deliver.

These were the wilderness years of Shackleton's life. It was a discontented phase marked by increasing restlessness and dark moods, growing estrangement from the family and frustration at not being able to find an outlet for his ambition and energy.

One route definitely closed off was politics. In 1912 the Liberal Unionists once again pressed Shackleton to stand as an MP. Dundee in 1906 had been an interesting diversion, but he did not have the patience for the slow rhythm and essential compromises of political life and he turned down the invitation to stand again.

Emily, best placed to understand the anguish, saw a man ill at ease with himself. Putney, she later recalled, were the 'least happy years' of Shackleton's life. 'They certainly were of mine,' she added.[2]

Friends noticed a change in his behaviour. He became more irritable and was prone to snapping aggressively when under pressure. Christy, the lecture agent, noticed that he 'could be a little hasty'. Others found Shackleton tactless and abrupt and opinions on him were often divided. His personality, Priestley wrote, was so dynamic that he created 'strong prejudices for or against himself' among those he encountered.

In July, shortly before the baby was due, Shackleton left for another business trip to the continent, optimistically hoping to return home before Emily gave birth. At Boulogne he was met by a telegram announcing the birth of a second son, Edward Arthur Alexander.

While Emily settled into the suburban surroundings and poured her energy into the children, Shackleton drifted further from the scene. 'My wife and 3 children are well,' he reported to a friend in early 1912. 'I see little of them though.'

Almost inevitably, he wandered into another affair. Following the awkward business over Beardmore's unpaid loan, the relationship with

Elspeth had more or less withered on the vine. But there were always women in Shackleton's life and the latest was Mrs Rosalind Chetwynd.

Rosa Chetwynd was a young, dark-haired American in her 20s who enjoyed the company of London's rich and famous. She was the daughter of William Secor, a prosperous New York lawyer. In 1902, at the age of 18, Rosa came to England to marry Guy Chetwynd, heir to the Chetwynd baronetcy. They had a son in the same year but were divorced in 1909 after only seven years of marriage on the grounds of the 'desertion of her husband' from the family home. Asked by the judge where her husband was at the time, Rosa said he was 'shooting lions in Africa'.

Short, well built and attractive, Rosa Chetwynd was 10 years younger than Shackleton and wealthy enough to live in the highly fashionable area of London's Park Lane. Her indulgent parents lavished £5,000 a year (almost £300,000/€360,000 in today's terms) on her whims and Rosa dreamed of becoming a celebrated actress on the London stage. Among her circle of friends was Jack Barnato Joel, the mining magnate and one of South Africa's rich and powerful 'Randlords' who, it was said, became so infatuated with Rosa that he gladly paid the rent on her plush Park Lane flat. (After Rosa's sudden death in 1922 at the age of 38, Joel arranged for a specialist ward at London's Middlesex Hospital to be named Rosalind Chetwynd Ward.)

At around this time, Shackleton found himself being dragged into the messy swamp of his brother's dubious affairs. Towards the end of 1911, Frank Shackleton was mired in serious allegations of fraud and faced bankruptcy proceedings over debts estimated at around £85,000. Nor had the intrigue of Ireland's Crown Jewels entirely died down.

These were uncomfortable moments for Shackleton and in the search for either enlightenment or help he turned to the Freemasons. On 2 November 1911, after an absence of 10 years from the craft, he was passed to the second degree of masonry at the Lodge of the Guild of Freemen.

Returning to the mysterious rituals and covenants of the Masons was a sign of Shackleton's desperation. In the decade since his initiation, Shackleton had never once attended a meeting. But, under pressure from a disorderly private life and with no sign of Hungarian gold on the horizon, he was evidently hoping that rekindling his interest in Masonry would unearth a few useful introductions or conjure up a spectacular business proposition.

Nonplussed by the failure to clinch lucrative business deals, Shackleton turned increasingly towards launching a new expedition. In 1912, he told Leonard Tripp: 'I wish I could get another expedition and be away from all business worries. All the troubles of the South are nothing to day after day of business.'

However, the landscape of polar exploration changed dramatically on 7 March when *Fram* docked at Hobart with news that Amundsen's Norwegians had reached the South Pole on 14 December 1911. The remaining 'little patch' had been crossed. But there was still no word of Scott.

News of Amundsen's triumph was carried around the world via an exclusive contract with the London newspaper, the *Daily Chronicle*. By coincidence, Shackleton had brokered the deal and agreed to act as arbitrator between Amundsen and the newspaper proprietors. Under the terms of the deal, Amundsen was paid £2,000 (£120,000/€150,000 today) for his account of the historic journey, the same amount as Shackleton received from the *Daily Mail* for his 'furthest south.'[3]

Tentative news of Scott was received a few weeks later when *Terra Nova* steamed into the New Zealand port of Akaroa. The ship was carrying word that Scott was last seen in early January at 87° 34' S, about 146 geographical miles (168 statute miles or 270 km) from the Pole and was still driving south with a team of five men, unaware that Amundsen had beaten them. In fact, on the day *Terra Nova* dropped anchor in New Zealand, the British polar party – Scott, Wilson, Bowers, Oates and Taff Evans – were already lying dead on the Barrier.

Terra Nova was also carrying the desperately ill Lieutenant Teddy Evans, Scott's deputy and among the last to see him alive. Evans, struck down by scurvy, only narrowly survived the return march to McMurdo Sound, thanks largely to the remarkable courage of Tom Crean who walked alone for 18 hours over the final 35 miles (56 km) to fetch rescue. The harrowing sight of a chronically sick Evans – he described himself as 'a physical wreck' – was the first signal that Scott might be in trouble. But with the expedition cut off by the Antarctic winter, there would be no news of the expedition for another year.

Shackleton, who understood the magnitude of Amundsen's feat better than anyone, was quick to lavish praise. He cabled 'heartiest congratulations' to Amundsen and generously told one newspaper that the Norwegian was 'perhaps the greatest Polar explorer of today'.

What emerged was that Amundsen had taken the audacious gamble of setting up winter quarters at the Bay of Whales on the edge of the Barrier, cutting at least 100 miles (160 km) miles from the round trip to the Pole. Equally audacious was Amundsen's choice of navigating an entirely new route across the Barrier and up the previously undiscovered Axel Heiberg Glacier to the Polar Plateau.

Shackleton did not dwell too long pondering whether things might have gone differently in 1909 had he gambled on the Bay of Whales and pioneered a different route onto the Plateau. (The Axel Heiberg Glacier is one quarter the length of the Beardmore.) It was not in his character to look backwards, ruminating over lost opportunities or misfortune. Emily said he never 'railed' against bad luck. Shackleton summed up his own philosophy by commenting: 'A man must shape himself to a new mark directly the old one goes to ground.'[4]

Amundsen had no such qualms. While docked at Hobart, he had run into John King Davis, who was on business for Mawson's Australian expedition. Davis, tall, angular and as gravely serious as Amundsen himself, went on board *Fram* to pass on Australia's congratulations. Amundsen, according to Davis, told him that Shackleton 'would have reached the South Pole' if the *Nimrod* party had gambled on overwintering at the Bay of Whales.[5]

The warm generosity of Shackleton's praise was not shared throughout Britain. Newspaper accounts were restrained and the polar establishment, irked at being outrun by a foreigner and incensed by Amundsen's subterfuge, fell back on the national characteristic of finding virtue in defeat.

Many people were incensed that Amundsen had broken the unwritten code of conduct by failing to declare his intentions in advance and had not bothered with undertaking a major scientific programme during the expedition. Keltie, a Norwegian diplomat reported, muttered about 'a dirty trick altogether' and Lord Curzon, the new RGS President, said had he 'no intention' of meeting Amundsen if he came to London.

Markham, 81, profoundly deaf and irreversibly spiteful, dismissed Amundsen as an 'interloper' into a domain which he sincerely believed belonged exclusively to Scott. He later resigned from the RGS Council in protest when the RGS hierarchy agreed to meet Amundsen for dinner.

A typical gripe was that Amundsen had 'not played the game', as though crossing 1,600 miles (2,600 km) of unexplored Antarctic ice fields and glaciers was somehow akin to a public school cricket match. Markham was among the first to paint Scott as the plucky loser. He promised that Scott's party would reach the Pole 'dragging their own provisions' and added the jingoistic note: 'This is the true British way.' Although he did not realise it, Markham had begun the process of creating the legend of Scott of the Antarctic.

Shackleton was among the few to examine more closely the reasons why Amundsen's well-managed dog teams and expert skiers had beaten the floundering ponies and laborious man-hauling of Scott to the Pole. In a conversion of Damascene proportions, Shackleton changed his mind about dogs and skis. 'The dogs will keep up the rapid pace of ski runners,' he said, 'and this is naturally faster than the slow-plodding foot movements of the ponies.' Shackleton was 'shaping himself to a new mark'. Next time, he resolved, it would be skis and dogs.

Shackleton had something else in common with Amundsen. Both found themselves as outsiders with Britain's polar authorities. Shackleton was also drawing nearer to Amundsen in becoming a professional explorer. Exploration was Amundsen's only job and now Shackleton, without a traditional means of earning a living, was in much the same position. All he needed was a new mission.

In the spirit of mutual respect, Shackleton willingly shared a platform when the Norwegian travelled to London in late 1912 to speak to the RGS. Although news of Scott's fate had not yet emerged, it was an uncomfortable occasion, particularly when Lord Curzon rose to speak. Curzon, a political grandee with a mastery of the carefully crafted insult, proposed 'three cheers for the dogs'.

Amundsen saw Curzon's remarks as 'thinly veiled' rudeness and would later write in his memoirs: 'Scott was a splendid sportsman as well as a great explorer. I cannot, however, say as much for many of his countrymen. I feel justified in saying that by and large the British are a race of very bad losers.'[6]

Without the possibility of the Pole, Shackleton now turned his mind fully towards the alternative goal of traversing the continent. 'The discovery of the South Pole will not be the end of Antarctic exploration,' he said. 'The next work of importance to be done in the Antarctic is the determination of the whole coastline of the Antarctic continent and then a trans-continental journey from sea to sea crossing the pole.'[7]

First, though, he needed news of Filchner. For that he had to wait until mid-January 1913 when Filchner reached Buenos Aires with news that he had failed in his attempt to cross the continent. The expedition was nonetheless a hugely significant enterprise, having penetrated the treacherous Weddell Sea further than anyone before and traced the coastline from Bruce's Coats Land in the east to the new discoveries of the Prinz Luitpold Coast and Filchner Ice Shelf. At a desolate place on the Antarctic coast named Vahsel Bay, Filchner recognised a possible landing site, though he never established a base there.

Shackleton was in America, supposedly promoting Tabard cigarettes, when word of Filchner's return first emerged. Business was far from his mind, particularly when he shared a platform with Amundsen and Peary. (Peary's claim on the North Pole was now largely accepted.)

Amundsen generously praised the man who had blazed the trail but there was inevitably a hollowness about the occasion for Shackleton. Few wanted to hear about the 'furthest south' when the man who had stood at 90° S was paraded before them.

More than ever Shackleton was now desperate for a new challenge, an opportunity for self-fulfilment. 'Perhaps I will try again to go south,' Shackleton told reporters.

chapter 26

Towering Ambition

Shackleton returned to England in February 1913 to find the nation in mourning. A week before leaving America, *Terra Nova* sailed into a New Zealand port with news that Scott and his four companions had died the previous year on the return march from the Pole.

The outpouring of national grief was matched only by the mourning triggered a year earlier by the sinking of the luxury liner *Titanic* with the loss of over 1,500 lives. *Titanic* sank in the North Atlantic after striking an iceberg and Shackleton, with his experience of the ice, was called to give evidence at the lengthy public enquiry in London. But there would be no public inquiry into the Scott disaster and Shackleton was never called on to offer his insight into the cause of the Antarctic's biggest loss of life.

Yet Scott's death undoubtedly marked Shackleton. Helped by publication of his poignant diaries and the chorus of public sympathy, Scott was quickly adopted as the self-sacrificing and unlucky explorer. Scott's tragic story, which might have been cut from the pages of *The Boy's Own Magazine,* fitted the mould of what the public thought a heroic explorer should be. Moreover, the polar establishment had lost one of its own.

Shackleton, ambitious, garrulous and clearly a man on the make, was regarded differently. He was far too unconventional for the parts of Edwardian society more often concerned with 'character' than ability. As Scott's reputation soared over the following decades, Shackleton was increasingly seen as the maverick outsider and it was no surprise that he drifted to the margins of public awareness.

Scott's death, however, was no deterrent to Shackleton's aspirations. Instead, the tragedy roused him into action with a renewed determination. He began doing the rounds of the homes and offices of his wealthy contacts in search of the next Longstaff or Beardmore prepared to bankroll his ambition of marching across the Antarctic continent from coast to coast.

Shackleton, freed from the irritating diversion of commercial enterprise, was invigorated by the prospect of a new expedition and launched himself into the project with a youthful exuberance. The sheer scale of the endeavour, a journey of close to 1,800 miles (2,800 km) across much uncharted territory, held no fears for a tenacious man with a towering ambition who, after four troubled years, had discovered his next great goal. For a while at least, he shed the troubled look of someone older than his 39 years.

Shackleton's fond hope was that he could attract a single benefactor who would willingly put up the money in return for a share of the rights to the expedition's films, books and newspaper deals, plus the scientific collections. Potential backers were also offered the opportunity to purchase and name the ship that Shackleton, perhaps with tongue in cheek, had tentatively called *Golden Vanitee*.[1] With his loose connections to royalty, he earnestly hoped that King George would provide vocal support and entice others, including the government, to back the venture.

The scale of Shackleton's plan was as daunting as the substantial sums required. The outline scheme – to cross the continent from the Weddell Sea to McMurdo Sound in the Ross Sea – was described as 'the last great polar journey than can be made' and the costs involved were potentially huge. Shackleton was also in hurry and earnestly hoping to leave England in the summer of 1914.

The initial plan was the highly risky one of taking a single ship, depositing six men at Filchner's newly discovered Vahsel Bay on the Weddell Sea side of the continent before circumnavigating the continent to the Ross Sea to pick up the overland party at the end of the crossing. The only insurance in case of delays on the traverse was to leave a small lifeboat at McMurdo Sound capable of reaching the isolated Macquarie Island, halfway between New Zealand and Antarctica. On top of Wireless Hill on Macquarie, Mawson had established a radio link.

It was a plan riddled with obvious flaws. No one knew if Vahsel Bay was a safe landing site and the prospect of a 1,000-mile (1,600 km) open boat journey across the Southern Ocean seemed beyond fantasy in 1914. But the biggest uncertainty was how Shackleton planned to sustain his party on an unsupported march of 1,800 miles (2,800 km).

Sound reasoning took over and the plan was soon modified to include two ships, one vessel going to the Weddell Sea and the other to McMurdo Sound in the Ross Sea. While Shackleton proposed establishing his winter quarters at Vahsel Bay, the McMurdo Sound party would occupy Scott's old base at Cape Evans. From Cape Evans they would lay down a critical lifeline of supply depots across the Barrier to the foot of the Beardmore Glacier to feed the overland party on the final 400 miles (640 km) of the trek.

Shackleton, after his dramatic change of mind about transport, proposed taking around 120 Alaskan or Siberian dogs and was keen to examine the possibility of attaching aero-engines to sledges. Mawson had experimented with mechanical sledges and Shackleton wanted to carry the experiment a big step further. Shackleton spoke enthusiastically about conducting trials in Canada and Siberia and with his usual optimism believed the motorised sledges could haul huge loads of up to 2,000 lb (900 kg) across the ice at a respectable pace of 5 mph.

This was not the only optimistic assumption. According to Shackleton, the transcontinental journey could be covered in just 100 days. Although later amended to 120 days, this demanded an average advance of at least 15 miles (28 km) a day and took no account of delays with weather or the possibility of encountering unknown mountain ranges or open water. From Vahsel Bay to the Pole was close to 900 miles (1,400 km) of totally unknown territory and Shackleton was entirely familiar with the assorted perils of descending the Beardmore Glacier and crossing the Barrier with Antarctic winter closing in.

For reference, Shackleton needed to look no further than Amundsen, who had perfected the model for long-distance ice travel using trained and well-fed dog teams and experienced skiers. Covering much the same distance as Shackleton now proposed, Amundsen and four companions had taken 99 days to reach the Pole and back. Amundsen had eaten heartily on the trek thanks partly to an aggressive programme of depot-laying before the trek began. His party consumed around 5,000 calories a day, almost three times Shackleton's intake on the harrowing return from the 'furthest south' in 1909. While Scott's team died from starvation and exposure, Amundsen returned from the Pole to learn that he had gained weight.

The critical difference between the two expeditions is that Amundsen's team was highly experienced in handling dogs and skis whereas Shackleton was a novice. Among Amundsen's party were Olav Bjaaland, a Norwegian ski champion, and Helmer Hanssen, who had learned his dog-driving skills from the Inuit. Shackleton, at this point, had little understanding of handling dogs and only patchy experience of skis. Nor had he managed to recruit an experienced dog driver.

Effectively doubling the size of the expedition also had a dramatic impact on costs. The cost of a single-ship expedition alone was estimated at around £50,000. But expenses for the larger, more ambitious endeavour of deploying two ships, one on either side of the continent, were likely to be closer to £100,000 (approximately £4.25 million/€5.12 million in today's terms).

With his sweeping generalisations and brisk enthusiasm, Shackleton made it all appear endearingly simple. Yet his coltish zest counted for little in the corridors of power, where there was notable reluctance for another Antarctic journey so soon after the Scott catastrophe. 'Enough life and money has been spent on this sterile quest,' Winston Churchill, the First Lord of the Admiralty, wrote in early January 1914.

Shackleton was undeterred. 'All polar explorers are optimists with vivid imaginations,' he wrote in the preface to Murray and Marston's book of recollections about Cape Royds. It was an ideal summary of his own character and nowhere was this essential optimism needed more than in the painstaking and wearisome quest to attract wealthy supporters. Shackleton was still relying on a combination of easy charm and bold ambition. The quest, said Shackleton, was a simple case of 'nursing millionaires who could put down £100,000 if they cared to.'

Shackleton was anxious to be closer to the centre of London where he could mix more freely with wealthy businessmen or philanthropists and he moved the family from the suburbs of Putney to Kensington. The new home was a sizeable terraced house at 11 Vicarage Gate, not far from Kensington High Street. It was more expensive, but the extra cost was partly offset by spending less on late-night taxis to Putney.

Emily stayed quietly apart from Shackleton's frantic and increasingly distant life, which saw him hurrying from meeting to meeting or running off to a private rendezvous with friends. Calm and graceful, she lived at a totally different pace from Shackleton's whirlwind existence. She was resigned to another year or two on her own. All that remained was the familiar promise that it would be his final expedition. 'Ernest has to go and so the only thing to do is to make it as easy for him as possible,' she said.

Dealing with Emily was more straightforward than the mounting disgrace of Frank Shackleton, whose dishonesty had finally washed up at Shackleton's feet. The timing was a repeat of the Crown Jewels scandal in 1907, which had briefly threatened to overshadow the *Nimrod* expedition.

The law had caught up with Frank Shackleton in early 1913. Frank, now in his late 30s, was tracked down to the former African slave port of Benguela where he was arrested in connection with a suspected fraud involving the misappropriation of £1,000 from an elderly spinster, Mary Josephine Browne. Fortunately, Shackleton was in America when Frank first appeared in a London courtroom and conveniently avoided the backwash of bad publicity.

He was less fortunate a few months later when his brother's sleazy affairs were played out in a public courtroom. It emerged that one of Frank's money trails involved the £1,000 donated to *Nimrod* by Miss Dawson-Lambton and beside him in the dock was Thomas Garlick, Shackleton's partner in the failed scheme to repatriate Russian troops from the Far East a decade earlier. Shackleton somehow escaped any guilt by association but Frank Shackleton was found guilty of fraud and sentenced to 15 months' hard labour.

Shackleton's good fortune continued a few weeks later when the government surprisingly agreed to donate £10,000 to the expedition. The only condition was that Shackleton first had to raise the remaining £90,000 from his own sources.

Although the conditional grant was only half what the government gave Scott in 1910, it was a very good start and signalled a fresh burst of wheeling and dealing. Shackleton opened a new London office at 4 New Burlington Street off Regent Street which, if nothing else, created the useful impression of an enterprise with some substance.

Shackleton set about the task of adding substance with the time-honoured tactic of securing royal patronage. In a confident letter, Shackleton offered to provide the Palace with the 'full plans' of the expedition in return for the King's support. This was somewhat premature given that there were no ships, no personnel and little indication outside Shackleton's imagination that he could put his hands on £90,000 to finance the enterprise.

All Shackleton could realistically claim was an impressive-sounding name for the undertaking. The venture, he told the King, was to be called the Imperial Trans-Antarctic Expedition (ITAE).

Days later, Shackleton went public, revealing his plans in *The Times* on 29 December. 'I can announce that an expedition will start next year with the object of crossing the South Polar continent from sea to sea,' he wrote. (There is an apocryphal story that he placed an advertisement in newspapers which reportedly read: 'Men wanted for Hazardous Journey. Small wages, bitter cold, long months of complete darkness, constant danger, safe return doubtful. Honour and recognition in case of success.' Apocryphal or not, it gives a reasonable summary of polar exploration at the time.)

One intriguing feature of *The Times* report was that Shackleton appeared to have uncovered a mysterious substantial backer. The expedition, he told the newspaper, was only made possible 'through the generosity of a friend'. While he declined to name the enigmatic supporter, he was a little more forthcoming in private correspondence with Buckingham Palace. In his letter to the King a few days earlier, Shackleton named the anonymous benefactor as Alfred Harvey, although it was emphasised that his identity must be kept a secret.

Whether Alfred Harvey ever existed is difficult to establish. Had he been genuine it seems likely that Shackleton would have used him as a lever to persuade others to support the ITAE. However, within a few months Shackleton backtracked over 'Alfred Harvey' and nothing was ever heard of him again. Shackleton told the King that he 'could not continue' with Harvey's financial support because of the 'impossible conditions' he demanded.[2] More likely is that Harvey was a work of fiction.

While Shackleton continued the desperate search for backers in time to get away in 1914, the threat of rival expeditions began to emerge. The much-travelled geologist-geographer Otto Nordenskjöld was planning a major scientific trip to the Antarctic Peninsula and Joseph Foster Stackhouse, an English Quaker, was piecing together a grand scheme to mount a three-year programme to explore King Edward VII Land and the Graham Land peninsula in *Discovery*. But the most serious threat to Shackleton came from the Austrian Dr Felix König.

König, an experienced 33-year-old Alpine mountaineer from Graz, was a member of Filchner's party which had been forced to abandon the first attempt at a transcontinental crossing. König was not discouraged and returned to Austria to begin preparations for a new crossing in 1914–15, starting from Vahsel Bay in the Weddell Sea. Among the skills König brought back from Filchner's expedition was dog handling.

König's plans were far more advanced than Shackleton's and he had already found significant support from the influential Count Johann Wilczek. The 76-year-old Wilczek was a distinguished Austrian nobleman who had backed the Payer-Weyprecht expedition to the Arctic 40 years earlier and was President of Austria's Geographical Society. Both Amundsen and Filchner were also on hand to offer valuable first-hand advice to König.

Around half his funding was in place and König had bought Filchner's *Deutschland*. Originally named *Bjorn*, the Norwegian-built vessel had been Shackleton's preferred choice in 1907 but was too expensive. König changed the name from *Deutschland* to *Osterreich* and intended to sail south at the same time as Shackleton.

Shackleton once more found himself in the uncomfortable position of clashing over proprietorial rights, a dispute which had echoes of the McMurdo Sound affair. König, in a fit of territorial righteousness, claimed Filchner's expedition had established priority over the Weddell Sea's southern coastline and demanded that Shackleton withdraw to another area.

While König accused Shackleton of 'poaching on his preserves' by using Vahsel Bay as winter quarters, Shackleton was in no mood to repeat the mistake of making promises he might be unable to keep. 'I have as much right to use [Vahsel Bay] as Dr König,' he told the RGS. Filchner, knowing both men, tried to mediate. But Shackleton was adamant and told König: 'I cannot alter plans I have long since formulated.'

Although it is likely that Shackleton had been planning his expedition for longer than König, neither could lay claim to being first with the idea of undertaking a coast-to-coast crossing. Bruce, the Scot, first raised the idea of a crossing in 1908. But Bruce had a limited network of support outside Scotland and he struggled to find the estimated costs of £50,000. The scheme failed to get off the ground but Bruce generously stepped aside to allow Shackleton to launch his attempt at the crossing.

Shackleton knew all about the difficulties of raising finance. As the *Dundee Advertiser* put it, he was 'Baffled at the very outset of his enterprise'. Crucially, Shackleton realised he would get little support from official sources like the RGS. 'I cannot look, nor am I going to try, for assistance from the Royal Geographical Society,' Shackleton admitted to Bruce. 'You know as well as I do that they are hide-bound and narrow and that neither you nor I happen to be particular pets of theirs.'[3]

Shackleton nevertheless spent several months discussing his plans with the RGS without ever convincing the Society that it was soundly based. Markham, sniping from the wings, ridiculed the proposal as 'useless and expensive' and claimed the expedition was an absurd piece of self-promotion by a man scarcely fitted for the task. Shackleton, he said, was 'importunate' and possessed a mind 'little adapted for complicated arrangements and exact calculations'.[4]

Markham's venom was not reserved solely for Shackleton. To Markham, Amundsen's South Pole journey was 'men merely sloping along on ski and dogs doing all the work'. Such enterprise, he suggested, was on a 'much lower plane' to the traditional toil of man-hauling, the gruesome labour at the roots of Scott's tragedy.

In contrast, Robert Rudmose Brown, a member of Bruce's *Scotia* party, called Markham an 'old fool and humbug' and claimed his views were 'mainly designed to advertise himself and his beloved Captain Scott and to disparage every one else, especially Amundsen and Shackleton'.[5]

However, the endorsement of the RGS was an important ingredient in attracting the attention of men with money to spend. But the RGS was concerned that Shackleton's plan lacked detail and substance and the risks of the coast-to-coast journey were far too high. It was, said one observer, 'audacious in the extreme'.

The uneasy relationship was apparent when the RGS pressed Shackleton to put flesh on the bare bones of his plans, particularly the scientific programme and overall level of financial support. Shackleton, of course, did not have immediate answers to most specific questions and retreated behind a fog of vague and evasive responses. One RGS committee member recalled the 'impossibility of getting any clear answers' from Shackleton and added: 'He always answered two or three questions together, or one question in two or three difference pieces.' In one revealing and frosty exchange with the RGS committee, Shackleton admitted: 'I am perfectly aware that a lot of people do not take me seriously.'[6]

Shackleton attempted to win over the doubters by promising a full programme of scientific research. For hundreds of years science had gone hand in hand with British geographical discovery and Shackleton was hoping that members would be persuaded by a commitment to study numerous branches like geology, meteorology and magnetic forces. He spoke grandly of despatching scientists to unknown parts of Graham Land and Enderby Land and cannily suggested that a geologist would be taken on the overland crossing.

In a final desperate plea, Shackleton challenged the RGS to provide the funds to mount the largest scientific programme ever sent south. He declared: 'If there is anybody in this hall tonight or in the large audience that will read this tomorrow who is ready to put up ten, twenty, thirty or forty thousand pounds to aid the scientific side of the expedition, I will take as many geologists as they are ready to provide me with.'[7]

The RGS again found themselves in difficulty over the treatment of Shackleton, reluctant to offer full support but aware that he could not be ignored and might even succeed. Knowing that they had underestimated him in the past, the Society compromised by providing a grant of £1,000, which appeared to be enough to claim a decent measure of backing but not enough to smack of profligacy.

Another who thought the scheme too dangerous was Shackleton's old friend, Hugh Mill. This was a wounding blow to Shackleton. Mill, a close ally for over a decade, had loyally supported his friend around many obstacles, but believed the expedition was far too hazardous. When asked to write articles in support of the expedition, Mill refused.

Shackleton, meantime, had found his two ships. The more notable vessel was *Polaris,* a newly launched ship which was moored idly in Norway's

Framnaes shipyard at Sandefjord. It had been built as part of a deal between Adrien de Gerlache and Lars Christensen, the thrusting young owner of a Norwegian whaling fleet, to operate 'luxury' voyages to the Arctic for well-heeled tourists in search of big-game hunting and a taste of adventure. But de Gerlache was unable to raise money for the ship and the deal fell through, leaving Christensen with a redundant *Polaris* on his hands.

De Gerlache, who read about Shackleton's expedition, passed on the information about the availability of *Polaris.* What Shackleton discovered was something of a hybrid, neither a luxury yacht nor an Arctic whaler. But *Polaris*, a three-masted wooden barquentine of 348 tons, was sturdy and a fine example of a master shipbuilder's work. Johan Jakobsen, the builder, was a perfectionist and had built *Belgica* for de Gerlache and Bruce's *Scotia*. His newest creation suited Shackleton's urgent needs to get men and equipment through the Weddell Sea to a landing site at Vahsel Bay.

Christensen was prepared to offload *Polaris* at less than cost. Shackleton, even without the money in the bank, agreed to pay around £11,600 (approximately £650,000/€783,000 today) on condition that he could pay in instalments, giving him valuable breathing space in the search for funds. Soon afterwards, he changed the name from *Polaris* to *Endurance*, following the family motto: 'By endurance we conquer.'

The other ship was *Aurora*, which Shackleton bought from Mawson for £3,200. The Dundee-built *Aurora*, a veteran of 40 years' hunting whales and seals in the ice, was lying idle in Tasmania after returning from the Australasian Antarctic Expedition and Mawson badly needed money to pay his bills. Shackleton sensed a bargain and purchased *Aurora* to take men and supplies through the Ross Sea to McMurdo Sound.

After struggling to find a single donor, Shackleton widened his fund-raising appeal and began auctioning the expedition's exclusive story among the leading newspapers. The *Daily Chronicle* eventually bought the rights and, in search of finance, he sent circulars to hundreds of wealthy individuals asking for the modest subscription of £50 each.

The first big donation came from Frank Dudley Docker, a well-off and well-connected industrialist from Birmingham whose extensive business interests ranged from arms manufacturing to railway wagons and from BSA motorcycles to Daimler cars. DD, as he was known, was among the country's most powerful businessmen and was cut from the same cloth as Beardmore. Unlike Beardmore, DD gave Shackleton £10,000 without strings attached.

The generosity of DD was exceeded only by the unexpected intervention of Sir James Key Caird, a prosperous jute manufacturer from

Dundee. Shackleton may have first met Caird through the Royal Scottish Geographical Society or in 1906 during the election. Out of the blue he sent a hopeful appeal for just £50. The response shocked even the self-assured Shackleton.

Caird, 77 years old and a widower for 25 years, was a notable philanthropist who donated at least £250,000 (nearly £15 million/€18 million in today's terms) of his considerable fortune to good causes in Dundee alone, including a new town hall and a specialist cancer treatment unit at the local hospital. He was a well-travelled and cultured man who was related by marriage to John Ruskin and Sir John Millais and whose friends included the artist James Whistler. By coincidence, Caird shared a lifelong fascination with the same homeopathic medicines as Dr Henry Shackleton.

Caird, a distinguished-looking man with a goatee beard, lived in the rambling castellated splendour of 15th-century Belmont Castle north of Dundee. He had taken little previous interest in polar exploration but something about Shackleton aroused his curiosity. He offered an immediate donation of £10,000 and asked for a meeting to discuss matters further.

Shackleton, he discovered, had been so desperate for money that he made an arrangement with Lord Iveagh and Sir Robert Lucas-Tooth, an Australian brewer and landowner, to surrender rights to future book sales and lectures in return for £10,000 of loan guarantees. It was a very one-sided deal and Caird felt he could do better.

Shackleton was astounded when Caird looked across the room and asked: 'Do you think, Sir Ernest, that those gentleman would release you from that obligation if you were able to tell them that there was a man in Scotland who would find the remaining twenty-four thousand pounds on that condition?'

A few days later Caird wrote to confirm his extraordinary offer: 'The account you gave me of your plan of going to sea is so interesting, I have pleasure in giving you £24,000 without any conditions, in the hope that others may make their gifts for this imperial journey also free of all conditions.'[8]

Caird's contribution – worth close to £1.5 million/€1.8 million in today's terms – was the turning point that Longstaff had been to *Discovery* and Beardmore to *Nimrod*. As Caird's generosity intended, others soon followed, including the endlessly loyal Elizabeth Dawson-Lambton.

The most notable addition to the swelling ranks of sponsors was Janet Stancomb-Wills, the rich adopted daughter of the late tobacco millionaire, Sir William Henry Wills. Stancomb-Wills, a spinster in her early 60s, had inherited half of her father's £1 million estate and divided her time between a fine home at Ramsgate overlooking the English Channel and a sprawling 20-room mansion on the edge of London's Hyde Park. She enjoyed being driven around in a Rolls-Royce but was a generous soul with an interest in women's rights and poured large sums into local amenities in Ramsgate. (Stancomb-Wills later became the first woman to be elected mayor of Ramsgate.)

Stancomb-Wills, sophisticated and imposing, was another older woman who fell for Shackleton's charm. Although demurely attractive in her youth, she had never married. The buccaneering style of Shackleton was disarming and there was something about his direct, engaging manner that was different from the typical fortune hunters beating a path to her door.

'Into my life you flashed, like a meteor out of the dark,' she wrote. 'He was not perfect but intensely human and entirely lovable.'[9]

Shackleton responded to her warmth and the pair became close. Stancomb-Wills, cutting through the blizzard of chatter, understood Shackleton's restless ambition while Shackleton had found someone who was willing to listen. In his longing for attention, Shackleton had always sought the company of good listeners and to the roll call of Mill, Wilson and Elspeth Beardmore he now added the dignified presence of Janet Stancomb-Wills. 'I have hammered through life, made but few friends and it is good to know you,' he told her.

Shackleton accepted her cheque with grace but Stancomb-Wills retained a little of the mystery about the relationship by not disclosing how much money she gave him. It remains a mystery.

Throughout his life it seemed women of a certain age fell quietly under Shackleton's spell. To Elizabeth Dawson-Lambton and Queen Alexandra, he could now include Janet Stancomb-Wills. Partly this was the enduring appeal of the 'lovable rogue' in Shackleton. It was also that his boyish immaturity and lack of guile appealed to the maternal instincts. To some, at least, Shackleton was still a little boy.

With the money, more or less, in place, the pace of events picked up. *Endurance* arrived on the Thames in June and the task of picking men and ordering supplies was also well under way. On the desk was a pile of applications from 5,000 people eager for a taste of adventure that Antarctic exploration promised.

Wild, who had been to the Antarctic with Mawson since returning from *Nimrod*, was in the office in New Burlington Street busily running affairs. Ever since *Nimrod*, Wild had been Shackleton's man and had devoted his life to adventure of one sort or another. In little more than a decade,

Wild had been to the ice three times and served with Scott, Mawson and Shackleton. At the age of 40, when many men contemplated an easier life, Wild eagerly accepted Shackleton's invitation to be his deputy on the Imperial Trans-Antarctic Expedition.

Marston, too, was another recruit after leaving his job as an art teacher. From the naval ranks, Shackleton was also fortunate to recruit Tom Crean, the tough naval petty officer and old *Discovery* hand who had performed with extraordinary bravery with Scott only two years earlier. Crean, 37 years old and a man to be relied upon in a crisis, was appointed second officer on *Endurance*. Shackleton had now recruited three experienced, dependable and unswervingly loyal men as the backbone of his party aiming to cross the continent.

Shackleton's most pressing task was to appoint captains to take *Endurance* and *Aurora* down to the ice. His first choice for *Endurance* was the experienced John King Davis, also just back from the ice with Mawson. Shackleton listed Davis as being in 'command of sea operations' in early versions of the expedition's prospectus, possibly without consulting Davis. However, Davis was unsure about *Endurance*'s capabilities in the ice and worried that Shackleton's eccentric style of recruitment would attract too many adventure seekers and not enough hardened professionals. To Davis, Shackleton was someone who made many promises but delivered on very few. He turned down the task.

Shackleton turned instead to Frank Worsley, a merchant navy officer of 42. Worsley was a light-hearted New Zealander with a broad grin and a lifetime's experience of the sea. He was an accomplished navigator and acting as second officer on a freighter in the summer of 1914 when he landed in London on a spell of leave.

There was a hint of Shackleton in Worsley. Both were broad-shouldered, excitable and unconventional, and had served their apprenticeships on sailing ships. Worsley was just two years older than Shackleton and the men also shared a fondness for a good story. Worsley famously embroidered the background to joining the expedition with a bizarre tale to rival any old sea dog's yarn. 'One night I dreamed that Burlington Street was full of ice blocks and that I was navigating a ship along it,' he said. 'I hurried like mad into my togs and down to Burlington Street I went ... a sign on a door-post caught my eye. It bore the words "Imperial Trans-Antarctic Expedition" and no sooner did I see it than I turned into the building.'[10]

The other key appointment was Aeneas Mackintosh, who had lost an eye on the *Nimrod* expedition. Mackintosh was selected to take command of the Ross Sea landing party based at McMurdo Sound and given the vitally important task of placing a line of provision depots on the Barrier for the overland party. He was not the first choice.

Shackleton wanted Marshall, who had been outstanding on *Nimrod*, to take command of the Ross Sea party. But Marshall, like Davis, had reservations about Shackleton and had little faith in the project. The chances of crossing the continent, he wrote many years later, were 'too remote to be considered seriously' and he turned down Shackleton's offer.[11]

With time running out, Mackintosh was something of a compromise. He was often uncomfortable with responsibility and had little experience of the ice. The most experienced member of the party was Ernest Joyce, veteran of *Nimrod* and *Discovery*, but a tricky character. Mackintosh also had Ernest Wild, younger brother of Frank Wild, among his men. But the majority of the team, like young Irvine Gaze, 21-year-old Richard 'Dick' Richards and the newly ordained Rev. Arnold Spencer-Smith, were complete novices.

The position of *Aurora*'s captain was more difficult to fill and was not decided until weeks after *Endurance* had left British shores. With his limited finances, Shackleton was hoping that the War Office would allow him to second volunteers from the army and navy, particularly to staff the Ross Sea party and *Aurora*. For *Aurora* alone he wanted the Admiralty to release 23 seamen. 'The War Office have put the whole of their help at my disposal,' he optimistically told Keltie in February. 'Any men I want to take from the Army will be reinstated with promotion ... and I think I will soon be in the same position with the Admiralty.'[12]

In truth, the authorities were merely considering Shackleton's request against the background of the growing threat of war with Germany. The sailors, Shackleton assured the Admiralty, would never be out of touch for more than three months and readily available for war purposes if necessary.

Shackleton appealed directly to Churchill, the First Lord of the Admiralty. With a nod towards the history Churchill knew so well, Shackleton reminded him that the 'Senior Service' would be absent from a British polar expedition for the first time in 300 years if the men were not released. Churchill, more than a match for Shackleton's rhetoric, turned down the request.

The coolness of the Admiralty's response stemmed largely from the leftovers of the *Nimrod* expedition. Instruments which Shackleton borrowed had been returned only intermittently and a few bills totalling some £245 (£14,000/€17,000 today) had not been settled. In the event, the debt was written off but the Admiralty exacted firm guarantees before handing over further instruments.

Churchill's only concession was to allow Captain Thomas Orde Lees from the Royal Marines to join the expedition and to permit any Royal Navy seamen who had been with Scott to go south again if they wished. But he was no sea captain. Orde Lees, an eccentric Anglo-Irishman, was a good catch because of his versatility. An experienced officer who knew how to ski, he also had some knowledge of the engines that Shackleton intended for his motorised sledges and was readily posted to *Endurance*.

To skipper *Aurora*, Shackleton selected 26-year-old Joseph Stenhouse, a strapping 6-footer from the merchant fleet with a sorry history of depression and a longing to be an explorer. Stenhouse had failed in an earlier bid to join an Antarctic expedition and when he heard about Shackleton's, he announced: 'I must go with him.' After a perfunctory interview with Shackleton in London, Stenhouse was first accepted, then rejected and finally hired at the third time of asking. 'I am a lucky chap,' he told his father.[13]

Almost inevitably, the scramble to get away was soon disturbed. Mary Browne, the elderly woman defrauded by Frank Shackleton, was trying to recover some of her lost money. With the expedition in the public eye, Browne's solicitors saw the opportunity of recouping the stolen £1,000. Shackleton was targeted and her lawyers managed to bring the case forward to mid-July before *Endurance* sailed. Shackleton, wisely, settled out of court.

On 28 June, a less noticeable incident took place when Gavrilo Princip, a 19-year-old Bosnian Serb, assassinated Archduke Franz Ferdinand, heir to the Austro-Hungarian throne, in the Balkan hotbed of Sarajevo. Over the following weeks, Austria-Hungary declared war on Serbia and Germany supported the Austro-Hungarians. Millions of men across Europe were subsequently mobilised as the opposing alliance of Russia, France and Britain were inexorably drawn into the inferno of blind patriotism, territorial greed and swaggering military recklessness. Princip's attack would lead to the deaths of nearly 20 million people over the next four years.

Meantime, *Endurance* was made ready for sea by early August. South-West India Dock on the Thames was a scene of frantic activity as men arrived, supplies were loaded and quizzical visitors trooped around the ship. On 14 July an assorted collection of 99 large, boisterous dogs, purchased to haul sledges on the overland crossing, arrived by steamer from the Hudson's Bay Company in Canada. Wild said the hefty-looking mongrels were a mixture of 'wolf and almost any kind of big dog' with an average weight of 100 lb (45 kg).

Although Shackleton's conversion to dogs was welcome, the change of tack did not go far enough. He was still short of a skilled and experienced handler. Lieutenant F. Dobbs of the Royal Dublin Fusiliers had originally been selected to take charge of the animals, but he resigned to join his regiment amid the worsening military climate. Shackleton wanted two Icelanders, Jón Björnsson Johnson and Sigurjón Isfeld, but both men were newly married and expectant fathers. One cabled home seeking his wife's permission to go south and found his Antarctic ambitions summarily cut short with the terse reply: 'Come home.'[14]

As a stop-gap Shackleton hurriedly recruited Sir Daniel Gooch, a prosperous middle-aged baronet and grandson of the great Victorian railway engineer of the same name. Gooch, one of the aristocrats strangely drawn into Shackleton's circle, bred greyhounds and dogs for hunting but could offer no experience of the ice. As a generous gesture of support, he agreed to sail as far as South Georgia on an able seaman's small salary.

Failure to find a suitable driver was only one of the problems with the dogs. Shackleton's initial plans called on 120 dogs for the expedition, but only 99 animals reached the Thames alive and of these some 30 were earmarked for Mackintosh's party. Shackleton decided to muddle through by placing the willing Wild in charge of the animals. Wild had only limited experience of dogs but he was resourceful and bright and Shackleton's hope was that he would learn quickly.

It was another of Shackleton's hasty compromises which added another element of uncertainty to the enterprise. The dogs were vital to the overland crossing but Shackleton had left himself with the daunting task of matching Amundsen's South Pole journey with little more than half the animals he wanted and without an experienced handler.[15]

The immediate worries of personnel, stores and dogs were put aside two days later when the Dowager Queen Alexandra, keen as ever to support Shackleton, visited the ship. Her sister, Empress Maria Feodorovna, mother of Russia's doomed Tsar Nicholas II, accompanied Alexandra up the gangplank, followed by a phalanx of admirals with the weighty matter of war on their minds. Emily and the children, with less weighty issues to consider, were quietly subdued.

Alexandra, a trim, elegant 69-year-old dressed head to toe in black, stayed much longer than expected on her tour of *Endurance*'s decks and quarters and insisted that her sister take photographs of the occasion. Shackleton, seemingly more than a ceremonial duty, still fascinated the Dowager Queen.

Queen Alexandra, who took a close interest in Shackleton, touring Endurance *shortly before departure in July 1914. (L–r) Crean, McNish, Rickinson, Shackleton, Queen Alexandra, Princess Maria Feodorovna (Alexandra's sister and mother of Russian Tsar), Emily Shackleton, Frank Wild, Marston, Lord Howe, Princess Victoria and Aeneas Mackintosh.*

Alexandra presented him with a silk replica of her own personal standard and a Union Jack, together with two Bibles, one for the ship and one for his own use. Inside one Bible she wrote a personal inscription: 'May the Lord help you to do your deeds, guide you through all dangers by land and sea. May you see the Works of the Lord and all his wonders in the Deep.'

Alexandra followed up the meeting a few days later with a private telegram to Shackleton which also hinted at something more than affairs of state. 'I am anxious to tell you how much I am thinking of you and the officers ... upon the eve of your departure from England,' she cabled. 'Wish you from my heart all possible success godspeed and a safe return.'

What no one on the Thames realised in mid-July 1914 was that the expedition was perilously close to being abandoned. The issue was Filchner and König.

Filchner, who was trying to smooth things between Shackleton and König over the use of the Weddell Sea, was keen for the two expeditions to cooperate on scientific research. It was hoped that the interests of science and exploration could somehow be kept apart from the rising tension between Britain and Germany.

In the spirit of friendship Filchner invited Shackleton to Berlin for a meeting with König in the last week of July, just days before the two expeditions were due to make separate departures for the south. Shackleton respected Filchner and in other circumstances he would have accepted the invitation. But, in the mad scramble to get under way, Shackleton simply had no time to visit Berlin.

On 28 July, around the time Shackleton was expected in Berlin, Austria-Hungary declared war on Serbia and three days later Germany declared war on Russia, making all-out conflict between the major European powers inevitable.

Had Shackleton visited Filchner he would have been in Berlin at the outbreak of war and interned at the notorious Ruhleben camp, a converted racecourse a few miles outside Berlin. Some 5,000 civilians, mostly odd visitors or seamen stranded in German ports on the outbreak of hostilities, were imprisoned at that camp for the next four years. According to one prisoner's account, 'hundreds of tragedies are being slowly and secretly enacted behind the brick walls and barbed wire fence of Ruhleben'.

It is difficult to believe that *Endurance* would have sailed without Shackleton. Imprisonment might have also left Shackleton unfit for future exploration on release. As one internee suggested, men at Ruhleben were doomed to 'resume the battle of life with crippled constitutions.'[16]

König was less fortunate than Shackleton. His ship *Osterreich*, built in the same Norwegian shipyard as *Endurance*, was moored in the strategic Austro-Hungarian port of Trieste ready to sail on the outbreak of war. Coal had been ordered from South Georgia, Shackleton's proposed destination. It is possible the two rivals might have run into each other shortly before entering the Weddell Sea, a curious echo of the Amundsen/Scott race to the South Pole. But *Osterreich* never left Trieste and König never went south again. König, by cruel irony, enlisted in the army and was captured by the Russians in Austrian Galicia in 1915. He spent the next three years interned in a Siberian prison camp.

All concerns seemed to be cast aside on 1 August as *Endurance* eased into the murky brown waters of the Thames. Germany declared war on Russia on the same day and Britain and France stepped closer to the brink. The mournful sound of a lone Highland piper standing on the quay was a lament for a passing age. Supposedly to salute Shackleton's Irish roots, the piper played 'The Wearing o' the Green'.

By the time *Endurance* moored at Ramsgate on the Kent coast on the evening of 2 August the first military action on the Western Front had taken place. Next day Germany declared war on France, leaving Britain hours away from entering the war. Shackleton went ashore to discover general mobilisation had been ordered and he also learned that four members of the expedition had resigned to join their regiments.

Shackleton, too, was on the brink with the expedition dream starting to collapse in the escalating crisis. Millions of men were on the move across Europe. It hardly mattered that almost everyone believed, in time-honoured fashion before all wars, that the fighting would be over by Christmas.

Shackleton faced a terrible dilemma. *Endurance* would miss the entire 1914–15 season unless the vessel sailed immediately and he knew nothing of König's fate. But the national emergency changed all that.

Shackleton called all hands together, declaring that everyone was free to enlist if they wished. A cable was sent to the Admiralty placing *Endurance*'s personnel and provisions as a single unit at the navy's immediate disposal. 'If not required,' he added, 'I propose continuing voyage forthwith as any delay would prevent expedition getting through the pack ice this year.' In reply the normally loquacious First Sea Lord, Churchill, sent a one-word order: 'Proceed.'

Endurance docked at Eastbourne on 4 August with Shackleton in a fresh turmoil at the war ending his dream. 'My nerves are all on edge,' he told Emily. The huge strain of the past few months had taken its toll. In addition, the couple had rowed a great deal in recent times.

Emily had taken a house for the family at 14 Milnthorpe Road in Eastbourne. She wanted to be away from London. But Shackleton did not linger.

Instead he rushed to London to see the King. Britain had issued an ultimatum to Germany over the neutrality of Belgium and for 20 minutes the minor affairs of a private expedition to Antarctica took precedence over the monumental issue of committing the nation to all-out war. The King, gravely serious at the best of times, took a moment to thank Shackleton for his generous offer of the ship and men. But he insisted that the expedition should go ahead as planned.

'He was perfectly charming,' Shackleton told Emily. The King presented Shackleton with a silk Union Jack and wished him God speed. A few hours later the ultimatum expired and Britain declared war on Germany.

Shackleton hurried to Plymouth to catch up with *Endurance.* While he intended to remain behind to finalise arrangements and replace the men who had left, he wanted to give last instructions to Worsley before the ship sailed to Buenos Aires.

The expedition's affairs, if anything, were bordering on the chaotic. Shipping arrangements were in disarray because the high seas were now a war zone. The first British vessel was sunk on 6 August and Shackleton discovered that promises of free passages for men and provisions were suddenly cancelled and sailing times of steamers across the board were being scrubbed. Assorted equipment from overseas suppliers was piling up in various foreign ports and it was anybody's guess when it might be shipped. But at noon on 8 August, *Endurance* slipped her mooring and steamed south.

Even the departure of *Endurance* did little to ease Shackleton's own discomfort about leaving as the country entered into war. More than once he considered 'chucking the expedition and applying to Kitchener [Secretary of State for War] for a job'.

Shackleton sought guidance from his confidants and sponsors. He first consulted Janet Stancomb-Wills and then hurried north to see whether war had changed the minds of the two other principal backers, Docker and Caird. It had not.

The support of Docker and Caird was vital reassurance and Shackleton now felt he could sail with a clear conscience. 'There are hundreds of thousands of young men who could go to the war and there are not any I think who could do my job,' he told Emily. 'Now I have put myself right with Docker and Caird, I don't care and I feel it is my duty to go.'

There were many old ghosts to haunt Shackleton in his final days in England. Creditors were clamouring for payment, important arrangements were still outstanding and some of the crew, perhaps aware of the problems over pay on *Nimrod*, were pressing for wages to be paid to their families while they were away.

Finally there was the persistent shadow over his health. Shackleton, now 40 years old, was smoking and drinking heavily and sorely tired by the intense workload of the past few months. The spring in his step had gone. 'Perhaps the Antarctic will make me young again,' he wrote earlier to Elspeth Beardmore.

The arguments with Emily before leaving had complicated things and Rosa Chetwynd was still in the background. Shortly before sailing, Chetwynd gave Shackleton a thick woollen jumper with the message: 'Something to keep you warm in Antarctica, dear.'

Yet it was the relationship with Emily which most troubled Shackleton. 'One thing stands out quite clearly that I am to blame for all those uncomfortable months,' he wrote.

Shackleton's final letters to Emily before sailing were full of self-reproach and the mild delusion that, as if by some miracle, he was about to change his ways. 'I think I am solely to be blamed,' he said. 'I know that if you were married to a more domesticated man you would have been much happier.' Clinging to the belief that he would emerge from the ice a different man, he told her: 'I am going to carry through this work and then there will be an end I expect to my wanderings for any length of time in far places.'[17]

Emily could only watch and wait. Although the distance between them had grown since the last expedition, she remained stoically supportive. She had, for the most part, come to terms with the boozing and socialising, even if she was always uncomfortable with it. Perhaps she turned a blind eye to the womanising and wearily ignored the string of botched business ventures. But her loyalty was never in doubt.

Emily undoubtedly loved Shackleton but it was a relationship of unequal compromise. She quietly sacrificed much for so little in return and justified the arrangement to herself with the thought that it was impossible to confine an eagle in a barnyard.

On the eve of departing to the Antarctic, Shackleton had written: 'I am just good as an explorer and nothing else.' That much she knew.

On 25 September, Shackleton sailed to Buenos Aires from Liverpool. 'I love the fight,' he told her, 'and when things are easy I hate it.' Freed from the immediate anxiety of clamouring creditors and the suffocation of domesticity, Shackleton was suddenly in optimistic mood. The spring was back in his step as he surveyed the challenges ahead. 'I feel that I am going to do the job this time,' he reassured her.

He also found a moment to repeat the familiar promise. 'I don't think I will ever go on a long expedition again. I shall be too old.'[18]

chapter 27

Into the Pack

Shackleton sailed into Buenos Aires in mid-October to find a shambles. *Endurance* had developed an annoying leak on the voyage out, the casual port authorities seemed to be in no hurry to fix the problem and some of the expedition's supplies had not turned up. He also found troublemakers among the crew.

Shackleton immediately stamped his authority on affairs, taking command from Worsley and cutting through Argentinian red tape with customary dash to speed up the work on *Endurance*. 'I think he could persuade anyone to do almost anything if only he could talk to them,' the physicist Reginald James wrote.

Shackleton needed to assert his command because Worsley, a frivolous and impetuous character, had no natural leadership ability. Drunkenness was rife among the crew and at Madeira on the voyage south four seamen were thrown in jail – one was flogged – for wrecking a cafe in a boozy brawl. Four unruly seamen, including the cook, were sacked and Charles Green, a chef whose ship was berthed in Buenos Aires at the same time, was appointed expedition cook.

Shackleton had mixed feelings about Worsley. His skills as a deep-water sailor were unquestionable and Worsley had managed to get *Endurance* safely into Buenos Aires despite the severe handicap of sailing with insufficient ballast and a disorderly crew. The question of ballast was not Worsley's fault since *Endurance*'s bunkers could accommodate only 130 tons of coal. This was about half *Discovery*'s capacity and barely a third of *Terra Nova*'s. The gravity of the problem emerged two days from Buenos Aires when the coal ran out and a spare mast and spars were burnt to keep the boilers alight for long enough to make an emergency fuelling stop at Montevideo. Subsequent modification of *Endurance*'s bunkers raised capacity to 160 tons, but this was well below the 200 tons that Shackleton wanted for the testing journey south.[1]

But Shackleton looked beyond Worsley's sailing ability and saw a 'rather curious tactless nature' in his captain. He was also concerned that the remnants of the landing party – those left at Vahsel Bay after the departure of the overland party – risked getting stranded. 'I do not trust Worsley enough to be sure he would get to the station next season to bring out the remainder of the shore party,' Shackleton wrote to Emily.

A more familiar problem was that Shackleton had a cash-flow crisis before leaving Buenos Aires. Expenses in the Argentinian capital were larger than expected and there was not enough money to buy coal for the voyage to South Georgia. Shackleton turned to James Wordie, the expedition's geologist.

Wordie, who came from a prosperous family in Glasgow, agreed to lend Shackleton $25 to avoid the embarrassment of trying to cable London for extra funds when, in all likelihood, there was none available. But it needed the help of the British Consul in Buenos Aires to speed up the clearance. 'It does not amount to very much,' Wordie wrote in his diary, 'but will get him out of a hole without raising trouble in London.'

Drained by months of worry and hard work, Shackleton's old health problems suddenly re-emerged during the days in Buenos Aires. He suffered from what he called 'suppressed influenza', which was not a diagnosis any doctor would have recognised. However, he did not allow himself to be examined by either of the expedition's doctors, James McIlroy and Alexander Macklin.

Endurance left Buenos Aires on 26 October with the warm encouragement of the Argentinians and a reminder of the perils ahead from one of polar exploration's darkest episodes. At a farewell dinner, the party met Colonel David Brainard, who was among the last survivors of the horrific Greely expedition from the 1880s. Brainard, now 60 years old, was one of only six of the 21-man party to the Arctic who survived a gruesome tale of slow starvation, summary executions and even hints of cannibalism.

Endurance, painted a glistening black and heavily laden, sailed down the broad expanses of the River Plate to the sound of cheers and a brass band thumping out 'It's A Long Way To Tipperary'. On deck more than 60 dogs were chained up in a series of kennels built by the ship's carpenter, Henry 'Chips' McNish.

The immediate uncertainty was the condition of the ice in the Weddell Sea. Reports from Filchner and Bruce, although several years old, were the only first-hand accounts available and the charts of the waters were sketchy at best. The most accurate picture of conditions would be found in the personal observations and recent experiences of South Georgia's whaling community.

Shackleton was anticipating bad reports. During his preparations he had come across the intriguing theories of Robert Mossman, the meteorologist on Bruce's *Scotia* expedition, which indicated a poor season and trouble ahead for *Endurance*.[2]

Mossman was a gifted Scottish scientist whose weather station at Laurie Island held the distinction of being the first permanent scientific station in the Antarctic. According to Mossman, there was a clear link between the density of ice in the Weddell Sea and the rainfall in Chile and Argentina some 2,000 miles (3,200 km) to the north. A heavy ice season, Mossman calculated, indicated a subsequent heavy rainfall on the South American grain belt and lighter rains pointed to a more widespread break-up of the ice. With an eye on Mossman's theories, the party reported that rain fell on 11 of the 17 days spent refitting *Endurance* at Buenos Aires. Wordie, who had studied Mossman's work, noted in his diary: '... it looks as if the pack would be very heavy this season.'

Once at sea, the pitch and roll of the ship and familiar banter and songs of the sailors seemed to revitalise Shackleton. He was noticeably different from the tired, stressed figure struggling with the burden of getting away, juggling finances and dealing with pangs of guilt at leaving the family. Where some like Mackintosh and Worsley found command a burden, Shackleton was lifted by the responsibility and was markedly more self-assured.

A different figure once more from the man on shore, Shackleton wrote: 'All the strain is finished and there now comes the actual work itself. The fight will be good.'[3]

He also found a few words likely to chime with the mood at home and deflect any lingering criticism about leaving as the nation entered the war. 'We are leaving now to carry on our white warfare,' he cabled to the *Daily Chronicle*. It was a curious phenomenon that the expedition, expected to be gone for up to two years, was considered by some to be more dangerous than the war itself.

Endurance entered King Edward Cove, South Georgia, on 5 November 1914, the cornerstone of the island's thriving whaling industry and the most remote outpost of the British Empire. In Shackleton's words, South Georgia was the 'gateway to the Antarctic'.

It was a frontier place like nowhere else. The gently curving island, just 110 miles (175 km) in length, sits at the furthest reaches of the South Atlantic and is nearer to Antarctica than to South America. Captain James

Cook claimed the island for Britain in 1775, though nearly a century and half later the interior was a largely uncharted blank space on the map.

The spectacular landscape of mountains and glaciers provided a stark contrast with the odious and overpowering stench of rotting whale flesh and the grimy waste from a decade of blood-soaked plunder. Visitors said it was possible to navigate a path to South Georgia by smell alone. The harbour at Grytviken, one observer noted, was 'red with blood and grease and noxious with the stench of decaying whale carcasses'.

Though under British control, the island could be mistaken as an outpost of Norway. It was inhabited mostly by a motley collection of Norwegian sailors, vagabonds and unfortunates who carved out an existence from the sparse wooden workshops of the seven whaling stations scattered along the sheltered harbours of the island's northern coast. Like Shackleton himself, this was a community living on the edge.

Endurance stayed at the harbour of Grytviken on South Georgia for a month, a peaceful interlude spent restowing provisions and coal, exercising the dogs and prising a few useful supplies from the local storekeepers. Shackleton would have to make do without the cheery assistance of Gooch, whose grand manorial home, Hylands House in Essex, had been requisitioned as a hospital. Gooch wanted to return quickly to supervise arrangements and sole responsibility for the dogs fell into the hands of the untried Wild.

With his usual mixture of blarney and bluff, Shackleton somehow persuaded the locals to give him credit on a few useful supplies, including extra winter clothing, butter and flour. The bills, amounting to over £400, were sent to Ernest Perris, the expedition's agent in London, where they were placed on the pile of other invoices awaiting settlement.

The whalers, a tough, uncompromising bunch, had discouraging news of the Weddell Sea. The pack ice was further north than usual and Mossman's theory seemed to be valid.

Shackleton's plans, fluid at the best of times, needed further revision because of his late arrival at South Georgia. He was well behind schedule and the original plan to land 14 men at Vahsel Bay by late November 1914 was already redundant. Under the first timetable, the traverse would have started immediately and be completed by April 1915. According to Wild, the crossing would be made in 120 days, 'unless some unforeseen obstacle intervened.' But after the delays, it was necessary to fall back on the second option of overwintering the landing party at Vahsel Bay in 1915 and completing the crossing in April 1916.[4]

Shackleton had also changed his plans for *Endurance*. Instead of dropping the landing party at Vahsel Bay and retreating north, the ship would now be moored in the ice like *Discovery*. This raised the severe risk of prolonged entrapment but Shackleton was philosophical. 'What God may arrange I cannot say,' he said.

Hoping that ice conditions in the Weddell Sea might relent, Shackleton stayed a month at South Georgia and even found time to investigate a new business proposition. His target was the thriving whaling industry.

Norwegian whalers and Argentinian financiers, he claimed, were making profits of £500,000 (close to £30 million/€36 million today) a year from the hunting grounds and he wanted to grab a slice of the fortune. It was his second attempt to make money from the local seas, having taken a 21-year lease to harvest fur seals on the Falkland Islands. That deal had fallen through and Shackleton now turned his mind to the riches of whaling. For once, however, his idea was plausible.

To old hands, the repugnant stink of a whaling station was the smell of money. In the 1910–11 season alone, the Compañía Argentina de Pesca operations at Grytviken slaughtered over 1,600 whales and earned more than £80,000 in profits, paying shareholders a handsome dividend of 50 per cent on their investment.[5]

'On a capital of £50,000,' Shackleton wrote, 'one can make for certain 50 to 100 thousand pounds a year net profit.' South Georgia, he explained, was 'a gold mine and only very few people know it.' However, the affairs of *Endurance* were far more pressing and Shackleton's plan to enter the whaling industry never came to fruition.

Shackleton could not wait to get away. The weeks in South Georgia added to his frustration and he would not contemplate risking his reputation by abandoning the voyage for the season. He claimed to be too busy to write farewell letters to his parents and sisters, almost as though they were a reminder of things he was eager to leave behind. 'I have not written to Aberdeen House,' he told Emily. 'I have no inclination to do so and have too much to do here.' In addition, Frank Shackleton had been released from prison and scandal always seemed to follow in his younger brother's footsteps.

To Shackleton there was little appeal in what lay behind, the dread of fund-raising, hurried preparations and even the binding chains of domesticity. He could only look ahead to the invigorating challenges of the future. He was more anxious of home than the ice.

To Emily he could offer only a familiar explanation of the restlessness. 'I have a curious nature and I have tried to analyse without much success,' he said. 'I am hard also and damnably persistent when I want anything: altogether a generally unpleasing character. I want to see the whole family comfortably settled and then coil up my ropes and rest,' he wrote.

Endurance finally sailed out of Grytviken on the dull, overcast morning of 5 December 1914. There were a few farewell cheers and blasts from factory whistles but none of the fanfares that had accompanied *Discovery* or *Nimrod*. 'The clanking of the windlass broke for us the last link with civilisation,' Shackleton wrote. On board were 28 adventurers, seamen, scientists and drifters, and more than 60 dogs. The decks were strewn with extra bags of coal and chunks of fresh whale meat for the dogs, a gift from the islanders, hung from the rigging.

'The long days of preparation were over and the adventure lay ahead,' Shackleton wrote. He marked the occasion by quoting a few lines from *Ship of Fools* – with some modification – by St John Lucas, the English poet and friend of Rupert Brooke:

> *We were the fools who could not rest in the dull earth we left behind.*
> *But burned with passion for the South.*
> *And drank strange frenzy from the wind.*
> *The world where wise men sit at ease,*
> *Fades from my unregretful eyes*
> *And blind across uncharted seas*
> *We stagger on our enterprise*

Across the horizon, British and German battleships were converging in the seas around the Falkland Islands. A month earlier the British navy had suffered its first major defeat in 100 years at the Battle of Coronel off the coast of Chile where almost 1,600 men were killed. At the moment *Endurance* met the first belt of Antarctic pack ice a few days after leaving South Georgia, the navy inflicted painful retribution on the German fleet at the Battle of the Falklands.

'I had not expected to find pack-ice nearly so far north,' Shackleton said as ships drove south. Ahead was at least 1,000 miles (1,600 km) of unpredictable pack. Mossman, with his recent first-hand experience of the region, believed the perilous waters of the Weddell Sea presented a bigger challenge to Shackleton than the uncertainties of making landfall at Vahsel Bay. 'The main difficulty lies in his getting there through perhaps 1,000 miles of pack ice,' he warned.

The early encounters with the maze of ice also raised questions about the performance of *Endurance*. 'This ship is not as strong as the *Nimrod*,'

Shackleton told Emily in a letter. 'I would exchange her for the old *Nimrod* any day now except for comfort.'

The leak had been stopped but he was not impressed at how well the vessel would handle in the rough seas ahead. It was this concern that had persuaded Shackleton to keep the ship wintered at Vahsel Bay. 'I cannot risk her running up and down,' he explained to Emily.

While *Endurance* picked a path through the icy network, the affairs of the Ross Sea party had disintegrated into chaos. Money was short, personnel had not been found and there were doubts about adequacy of supplies and equipment.

Shackleton had despatched Aeneas Mackintosh to Australia with the promise of only £1,000 (about £43,000/€52,000 today) to equip *Aurora* and organise the men for the depot-laying party. This was about half of what he needed. Worse followed when Mackintosh discovered that the money had not arrived and the expedition's expenses were far larger than anticipated. Nor did he have the authority to raise funds on behalf of Shackleton.

Mackintosh had been sent around the world with Shackleton's explicit instructions ringing in his ears: 'You will economise in every way.' He was ordered to acquire coal and supplies 'free as gifts' and rummage through the old expedition huts at Cape Royds and Cape Evans in search of extra clothing and provisions when he reached McMurdo Sound.

Shackleton was trusting to luck that Mackintosh would be able to cobble together supplies and pay men's wages with the familiar bluff, fulsome promises and blizzard of credit notes that he had always used. But with Shackleton beyond reach, Mackintosh was effectively left to his own devices. Exasperated by the mismanagement, Mackintosh cabled London saying, 'money I must have' and added the chilling warning: 'There are lives of men on my hands.'

Mackintosh turned to Professor David, who had maintained close contacts with Shackleton since *Nimrod*. David, a greying distinguished figure and household name in Australia, was impressed with the ambitions of the ITAE and agreed to use his influence.

David helped arrange a mortgage on *Aurora* and met Andrew Fisher, the Prime Minister, in an attempt to raise funds from the government. Somewhat reluctantly, a grant of £500 was provided, though Shackleton's slapdash management astonished the Australians. Alexander Stevens, chief scientist for the Ross Sea party, reported an 'unpleasant feeling' towards the expedition.

With a mixture of arm-twisting and the belated arrival of £700 from London, the expedition somehow fell into place. It was far from ideal,

Endurance *entering the icy waters of the Weddell Sea.*

with last-minute replacements being made to the landing party and ship's crew and an inadequate jumble of hastily purchased provisions. The grossly overladen *Aurora* reflected the chaotic preparations, with boxes of equipment and 18 dogs scattered around the decks and scarcely an inch of spare space. Richards said it was 'difficult to imagine a state of greater confusion' in the days before sailing from Hobart.

The frantic work of getting away came to a standstill when the Governor of Tasmania, Sir William Ellison-Macartney, and his wife Ettie came aboard to inspect the ship. Lady Ettie Macartney was the sister of the late Captain Scott. Without perhaps realising the full irony, she presented Shackleton's vessel with a framed portrait of her dead brother.

On Christmas Eve, as Shackleton was steering *Endurance* through the Weddell Sea pack, *Aurora* finally weighed anchor in Hobart and headed south with a complement of 28 on board, weeks late and sorely under-provisioned. A handful of loafers and passers-by were the few witnesses to the departure. Stenhouse gloomily recorded that 'no one cares a hang about this expedition'.

Amid the muddle, Mackintosh was anxious to get away and begin laying down the vital depots. As far as he knew, Shackleton had already landed on the continent and the overland march was well under way.

Shackleton's original instructions were that the crossing would begin in the 1914–15 season and that depots should be cached as far south as 80°. But after delays on the way south, it was impossible for Shackleton to start the trek until the following season. Unfortunately, Mackintosh sailed without knowing Shackleton's change of plans. According to Shackleton, a cable was meant to inform Mackintosh of the alteration before *Aurora* sailed. Mackintosh never saw the cable and *Aurora* sailed south ready to begin the depot-laying programme immediately.

The journey of *Endurance* into the dangerous Weddell Sea was far more complex and challenging than *Aurora*'s more straightforward route through the better-known waters of the Ross Sea. Shackleton's route was to take *Endurance* down the east side of the Weddell Sea basin, tucking into the coastline of Coats Land, which Bruce had charted a decade before. It was hoped to drive south west in a semicircle along Luitpold Coast and reach Vahsel Bay at 78° S towards the end of January.

Few ships had entered the area in the 90 years since the whaling captain James Weddell made the first penetration of the waters in 1823. Weddell, taking advantage of a mild season, reached the remarkable southerly latitude of 74° 15' S. A century later both Bruce's *Scotia* and Filchner's *Deutschland* only narrowly escaped being crushed.

The Weddell Sea is a treacherous place, a 1 million square-mile warren of packed, mostly impenetrable, ice moving unhurriedly but inexorably in a giant semicircle around a vast continental basin extending from Coats Land in the east to the Antarctic Peninsula in the west. Huge blocks extending for many miles are driven together where the slow-moving ice collides with continental land mass. Joseph Hooker, who sailed around the area with Ross and Crozier in the 1840s, memorably described the Weddell Sea as 'repellent'. On his first sight Shackleton saw a 'gigantic and interminable jigsaw-puzzle' of pack ice.

After skirting through the initial belt of pack, *Endurance* enjoyed a few days of welcome open water. It did not last. Progress was slow, alternating between days of open water and others of dense pack. The ship did not cross the Antarctic Circle until 30 December.

By 10 January 1915 *Endurance* was at 72° S and closing on Bruce's Coats Land, though the 70-foot (21 m) perpendicular ice cliffs to the south were an imposing reminder of how difficult it would be to land in this region. A few days after, the ship passed *Scotia*'s most southerly latitude and entered the uncharted seas between Coats Land and the shore of Luitpold Land. Shackleton named the new territory the Caird Coast after his most generous sponsor.

Shackleton, 1915.

On 15 January a natural bay, formed on one side by a 400-foot (120 m) glacier disgorging into the sea, was sighted. Shackleton called it Glacier Bay and admitted it was 'an excellent landing place' which offered ideal protection from the strong south-westerly gales and an apparently easy slope to climb onto the inland ice. It had echoes of Balloon Inlet in 1902.

This was a critical moment. Glacier Bay appeared to be a more appealing site than Vahsel Bay which, according to Filchner, was a desperately difficult place with the ice wall stretching up to 100 feet (30 m) in places. For all Shackleton knew, the ice face at Vahsel Bay, like Balloon Inlet, might have changed radically since the German expedition. Glacier Bay, at least, was visibly accessible.

Worsley, in particular, urged Shackleton to take advantage and establish winter quarters in the bay while he had the opportunity. But Shackleton was unsure. *Endurance* was at 75° S, some 200 miles (320 km) further north than Vahsel Bay. Adding a further 200 miles to the overland crossing – at least two weeks' travel – was too much. 'I had no intention of landing north of Vahsel Bay,' he wrote. Despite the apparent appeal of Glacier Bay, he ordered *Endurance* to stay on course for Vahsel Bay. With hindsight, it was a decision that Shackleton would come to regret.

Solid pack halted the advance on 17 January and *Endurance*, rocking up and down like a cork, sought shelter in the lee of a massive iceberg. More disturbing was the realisation that strong north-easterly winds were driving *Endurance* south towards the mainland. Unless the winds changed direction, the ship would become trapped between the immense opposing forces of the shifting ice floes and the immovable mass of the Antarctic coastline.

Next day the gale eased and a lane of open water enabled *Endurance* to make 20 miles (32 km) along the glacier front of Luitpold Land. Vahsel Bay was little more than 100 miles (160 km) across the horizon. Below deck boxes of stores were being sorted 'ship' or 'shore' and Wordie persuaded McNish to cut his hair because he expected to be too busy unloading supplies in the coming days.

Ice closed around *Endurance* during the night and in good visibility, the view from the crow's nest on the morning of 19 January was an unbroken field of closely packed ice as far as the eye could see. *Endurance* was firmly beset in 1 million square miles of ice at 76° 34' S, 31° 30' W. The nearest human settlement at South Georgia was 1,500 miles (2,400 km) to the north.

chapter 28

Imprisoned

Time appeared to stand still in the days following *Endurance*'s entrapment. Spells of strong winds and swirling snow alternated with periods of brilliant sunshine while the ship, a single dark object in an ocean of whiteness, was immobilised in the firm embrace of the ice. The north-easterly wind, which was driving the ice against the shore, blew with malevolent intent.

'There are wild remarks being made that we will never get out of our unpleasant position,' Wordie wrote a few days later. 'But I don't think it will be so bad as that.' Orde Lees noted that Shackleton 'least of all exhibits the slightest sign of anxiety' about the position.[1]

Early indications were that the drift was carrying *Endurance* slowly towards the south-west in the general direction of Vahsel Bay. During breaks in the hazy gloom it was possible to catch glimpses of land some 20 miles (32 km) in the distance. Once a lead of open water was sighted and full steam was ordered, but the ice soon closed and the chance of escape disappeared.

On 27 January, with the ice solid in all directions, Shackleton ordered the ship's fires to burn out to save coal. *Endurance*'s slim reserves of coal had been a cause of concern from the start. The coal bunkers were simply too small and the ship was consuming half a ton a day, even while trapped in the ice. At sea Shackleton estimated *Endurance*'s coal consumption at 2 tons a day. As the fires dimmed, stocks were down to just 67 tons, enough for 33 days of normal steaming. Even if the ship were released from the ice, *Endurance* would have no margin of safety for the journey back to South Georgia. But there was no sign of release and Shackleton's hopes of landing this year had gone.

The mood on board swung from high optimism to deep depression as the realisation sank in that landfall was improbable. Thoughts turned

Trapped. Endurance *in the grip of the ice.* COURTESY: STATE LIBRARY, NEW SOUTH WALES

to Filchner's *Deutschland*, which endured eight months of drifting in the Weddell Sea before being freed. Some suggested making the 60-mile (100 km) dash across the ice to spend the winter at Vahsel Bay. But hauling tons of equipment and a prefabricated hut across miles of broken, hummocky ice to an uncertain landing site was hopelessly impractical. Besides, Filchner had made only a sketchy survey of the area and it was impossible to judge whether or not Vahsel Bay was viable.

New open leads of water appeared and a further attempt to break out of the ice was ordered on 14 February. Men slogged for hours with picks and saws in an attempt to cut a path to the open water, but every yard gained soon disappeared as the gaps froze over in the sub-zero temperatures. Next day, with at least 300 yards (275 m) of solid ice still blocking the path ahead, the breakout was abandoned. It was Shackleton's 41st birthday.

Shackleton, having been robbed of the chance to land, accepted that *Endurance* would not be released for months. 'I was beginning to count on the possibility of having to spend a winter in the inhospitable arms of the pack,' he wrote.

On 17 February the slanting rays of the sun warned of approaching winter. On 22 February, the ship edged close to 77° S. It was the most southerly latitude *Endurance* would reach.

'My chief anxiety is the drift,' Shackleton wrote a few days later. 'Where will the vagrant winds and currents carry the ship during the long winter months ahead of us?'

Endurance, at the mercy of the drift, changed course through March and April. After drifting languidly along the shores of Luitpold Land during February, the ship turned north and was carried away from the mainland in a zigzag pattern at a rate of around 1 mile a day.

The comparative serenity and pedestrian pace of affairs on *Endurance* were in sharp contrast to the dramatic chain of events overwhelming the Ross Sea party on the other side of the continent. *Aurora*, snared by ice in the difficult channels of McMurdo Sound, had been torn from her moorings during a violent storm in early May 1915 and carried out to sea, leaving 10 men marooned onshore. Both Shackleton's ships, though separated by 2,500 miles (4,000 km), were now prisoners of the capricious Antarctic pack ice.

Aurora's sudden disappearance had caught the 10 men on shore by complete surprise and left them badly exposed and under-equipped. Only meagre provisions and equipment had been landed before the ship vanished and the only clothing the men possessed was what they stood up in. There was no fresh meat, barely any fuel and they had to ransack Shackleton's old hut at Cape Royds and Scott's camp at Cape Evans for basic supplies. Many of the dogs were already dead and the remaining sledging equipment was minimal.

Mackintosh was in a near impossible position, but steadfastly determined to fulfil his obligations of provisioning Shackleton. He persuaded the others that Shackleton was utterly dependent on the depots and, despite the major difficulties, they agreed to do their best. 'All were agreed,' wrote Richards, 'that the one object that must be attained, no matter what else was sacrificed, was to place food depots for the six men of Shackleton's party.'

The first task of laying depots down to 80° S was managed, though with considerable difficulty. The hope was that this would be adequate if Shackleton came in the first season. If not, the second season depot-laying programme was designed to carry 4,000 lb (1,800 kg) of provisions south across the Barrier to the foot of the Beardmore Glacier on a series of journeys that would total well over 1,500 miles (2,400 km) of sledging with inadequate supplies and makeshift equipment. The final depot was to be placed alongside the appropriately named Mount Hope at the bottom of the Beardmore.

Even more colossal was the demanding schedule that Shackleton had set for Mackintosh. The aim was to travel up to 15 miles (23 km) a day. This was challenging for experienced men, but only Joyce had spent any time on the Barrier and the novices had struggled badly during their first attempts at sledging. Early trial runs, to lay depots out to 80° S soon after *Aurora*'s arrival, proved very strenuous and the group managed only 5 miles (8 km) a day, barely a third of what Shackleton expected.

'Such setbacks & surprises where life and death are mingled so closely I have not experienced before,' an anxious Mackintosh wrote. 'And it's hard to be existing with a sword of Damocles suspended over one as [Shackleton's] life – for the responsibility lies on my shoulders.'[2]

The command of the Ross sea party also rested uneasily on the shoulders of Mackintosh. Though tough and determined, he doubted his own abilities and the obligation to supply Shackleton weighed heavily. 'What on earth am I doing here?' he wrote. Nor did he have the full support of his colleagues, a disparate group of men stranded together in Scott's old hut at Cape Evans. Tensions were especially apparent between Joyce and Mackintosh. Joyce, who considered himself the most senior man at Cape Evans, was difficult to handle and had little confidence in Mackintosh. Joyce even took a leaf out of Shackleton's book by refusing to be examined by the doctor – he had a history of liver problems – before embarking on the lengthy sledging journeys.

Amid the tensions and struggle to make ends meet, the only certainty at Cape Evans was the firm belief that Shackleton was dependent on the depots. One man with a special reason for getting provisions onto the Barrier was Ernest Wild, Frank Wild's younger brother. In his imagination, Ernie Wild might have pictured a chance meeting with his brother somewhere on the icy plains and marching together into McMurdo Sound like triumphant warriors returning home from battle.

On *Endurance*, Shackleton seemed to have none of the doubts and uncertainties that gripped Mackintosh. Command came easily, even if he never quite divulged his true anxieties. Shackleton understood that the best antidote to the expedition's predicament was clear resolve and unshakeable optimism, the two qualities which personified his character. To Worsley, Shackleton was a 'cheery chief, leading his men in a great adventure'.

The 27 men in Shackleton's care were a very loose confederation of unlikely cohabitants ranging from academics, doctors and scientists to polar veterans, hard-boiled sailors and misfit adventurers. It was Shackleton who bound them together. 'Sir Ernest is the real secret of our unanimity,' Orde Lees wrote.

The closest to Shackleton was always Frank Wild, an alert, wiry figure with sharp blue eyes and an intuitive sense of Shackleton's needs. Wild, a few months older than Shackleton, claimed to be related to Captain Cook and was unquestioning in his loyalty and eternally resourceful. He had spent longer in the ice than anyone on board. He was respected by the scholars and seamen alike. Calm, capable and authoritative, Wild was Shackleton's ideal foil, a dependable No. 2 who never aspired to command.

Worsley, generally known as Skipper, provided the essential seafaring expertise Shackleton needed. While Shackleton was occasionally uneasy about Worsley's blithe spirit and hastiness, there was no doubting his acute understanding of the sea. Although his casual attitude grated at times, there was also little doubt that Worsley was loyal.

Loyalty was also crucial in the choice of Tom Crean as second officer. Crean, a big, broad-shouldered Irishman with cheerful grin and an iron will, was as near to being indestructible as any human. After running away from home at 15, Crean joined the navy and volunteered for *Discovery*. Dependable, versatile and good humoured, he was among the first men Scott recruited for *Terra Nova*. Debenham said Crean was 'like something out of Kipling or Masefield'.

Crean was an unassuming character and a highly experienced naval petty officer who let his actions speak for themselves. He was among the last three people to see Scott alive a few days from the Pole in 1912 and was given the Albert Medal – the highest award for gallantry – for saving the life of Lieutenant Teddy Evans on the brutal return march from the Polar Plateau. Having already trekked over 1,500 miles (2,350 km), Crean courageously strode out alone for 18 hours without food or shelter for the final 35 miles (56 km) to fetch help for the dying Evans. Evans survived by a whisker and Crean simply said: 'My long legs did the trick.'

Experience of a different type was provided by Frank Hurley, an energetic Australian photographer with a mop of thick curly hair and a mouth full of profanities. Hurley, 29, was a man of action who had spent a year in the Antarctic with Mawson and earned a swashbuckling reputation as a very capable sledging companion and a pioneering photographer.

Hurley, in fact, was among the finest photojournalists of the 20th century who spent half a century behind the camera lens and in the best traditions of his craft would go anywhere and do anything to capture the right image. A colleague said he was a 'warrior with his camera'. Others found him bombastic and unsympathetic.

Hurley was also part of Shackleton's plan to make money from the expedition. A new company was formed – the Imperial Trans-Antarctic Film Syndicate – to market Hurley's moving footage and still images for sale to newsreels, newspapers and magazines. With Hurley's reputation,

Shackleton saw the enterprise providing the elusive windfall that post-*Nimrod* lectures or New Zealand postage stamps had not generated.

Hurley recognised a fellow traveller in Shackleton and was prepared to snub the advice of Mawson to throw his weight behind the film company. Mawson, still smarting over his dealings with Shackleton, urged Hurley to avoid any business arrangements with Shackleton. Besides the prospect of a successful film venture, Hurley had also been promised a place in the overland party and he ignored Mawson's advice not to join *Endurance*.

With the addition of Hurley, the proposed transcontinental party was to be one of the most experienced sledging teams ever assembled. It comprised Shackleton, Wild, Crean, Marston, Hurley and Macklin. Five of the group were polar veterans and Macklin, though inexperienced, was a strong-looking man whose medical knowledge would be useful in the wilderness.

Alexander Macklin was a 25-year-old qualified doctor with short sight who wanted more from life than the routine of practising medicine. He was working as a surgeon in the Lancashire town of Blackburn when he applied to join the expedition and was recruited after a characteristically bizarre interview with Shackleton in London that involved a few cursory questions and an abrupt: 'All right, I'll take you.'

The other doctor was James McIlroy, a lightly built, restless soul who had practised medicine in distant places like Japan and Egypt without ever managing to set down roots. McIlroy, known as Mick, was an easy-going, roguishly handsome 35-year-old with a small moustache who hailed from Ulster. He first heard about the expedition while drinking in his London club and decided to apply. McIlroy was suffering from an attack of malaria when Shackleton interviewed him for the post as second surgeon but in his eagerness to go south persuaded a doctor friend to pass him medically fit. As it turned out, McIlroy was the only applicant for the job but his Irish roots and cheery brashness nonetheless appealed to Shackleton.

Far less at ease was the small contingent of scientists who frequently found the inactivity and Shackleton's casual indifference to science difficult to accept. According to James, Shackleton had 'very little sympathy with the scientific point of view and had no idea about scientific methods'.

Reginald 'Jimmy' James was a highly intelligent but unworldly character with large round spectacles who was often ill at ease with the rawness of ship life. The 23-year-old son of an umbrella maker, he had buried himself in academic studies for most of his adult life and joined the expedition after a characteristically baffling short interview with Shackleton. 'All that I can clearly remember of it is that I was asked if I had good teeth, if I suffered from varicose veins, and if I could sing,' James recalled. Not once did Shackleton ask about science.

James Mann Wordie, a highly qualified and popular 25-year-old geologist, would emerge as the expedition's head of scientific staff. Wordie, short, precise, dignified and gifted, came from a well-to-do family of Scottish carters and was determined to get first-hand experience of the ice before the age of exploration ended. He came on the personal recommendation of Raymond Priestley and joined the expedition after disregarding the advice of Scott's widow, Lady Kathleen Scott, not to go south with Shackleton.

Robert Clark, a dedicated but dour biologist from Aberdeen, was Wordie's friend and recommended to Shackleton by Bruce. He seemed to prefer the company of his specimens to his shipmates. Clark, in his early 30s, was a man of few words who twice represented Scotland at cricket and was the most accomplished footballer in the party.

Another to join in strange circumstances was Leonard Hussey, the smallest man on the expedition, who came from London and had qualifications in meteorology, psychology and anthropology. Hussey, just 23, was a jolly character who enjoyed playing the banjo. Shackleton looked him up and down, walked around the room and said: 'Yes, I like you. I'll take you.' Shackleton later told Hussey that he was taken 'because he thought I looked funny!'

The seafarers were mostly a combination of merchant seamen and hardened trawler hands. Lionel Greenstreet, the first officer, had considerable experience on sailing ships while Hubert Hudson, the navigator, was the son of a clergyman dutifully making way his way through the ranks.

The burly 35-year-old John Vincent and 22-year-old Ernest Holness were typical of the North Sea trawlermen and merchant seamen working a passage on *Endurance*. William Bakewell, by contrast, was an American who had worked as a ranch hand in Montana before trying his luck at sea. Walter How was an affable Londoner in his late 20s with a deft touch as an artist who had gone to sea at the age of 12. The most popular of all the seamen was Timothy McCarthy, a quick-witted Irish merchant seaman brought up in the narrow waterways of Kinsale on the south coast of Ireland with a natural skill in handling small boats.

The two most experienced hands were 45-year-old Thomas McLeod from Scotland and Alf Cheetham, a chirpy old salt who had run away to sea as a teenager and could boast a unique Antarctic heritage. Cheetham, now 48, was third officer on *Endurance* and after serving as a crewman on *Morning*, *Nimrod* and *Terra Nova* had accumulated more miles through the Antarctic pack than almost anyone alive.

McLeod, a seaman at only 14, seemed to hail from a bygone age of seafaring. He served alongside Cheetham on *Terra Nova* and had a peculiar fondness for the old superstitions of the sea. The oddest crewman was young Perce Blackborow, who had stowed away before the ship left Buenos Aires.

Caught somewhere between the commanders and crew were George Marston, the artist from *Nimrod*, the idiosyncratic Orde Lees and Henry 'Chippy' McNish, the ship's carpenter from Scotland. McNish, one of the oldest on board, was a skilled craftsman from the Clyde with sharp temper and an unerring ability to rub people up the wrong way. McNish, with his working-class socialist ideals, was the antithesis of many of the middle-class officers and scientists. McNish, said Shackleton, was 'the only man I am not certain of'.

By April, *Endurance* had drifted a whole degree of latitude to the north. The course was almost parallel with the drift of *Deutschland* only three years before. At times the two ships were less than 200 miles (320 km) apart, though *Endurance* was on a more westerly track towards the unknown seas alongside the Antarctic Peninsula. 'The devil himself has sealed our fate,' Filchner had written. *Deutschland* was not released until late November and after drifting over 700 miles (1,100 km) finally steamed into South Georgia a few days before Christmas 1912.

A similar outcome would have suited Shackleton, though he was anxious to avoid other disturbing aspects of Filchner's time in the ice. The German party had been ravaged by bitter feuds and Richard Vahsel, the ship's captain, died in midwinter. The enterprise, said one observer, contained the 'worst interpersonal frictions and dissensions' of any Antarctic expedition.[3]

For the moment, Shackleton comforted himself with the prospect of following *Deutschland*'s progress to the north. After re-provisioning in South Georgia, it was possible that *Endurance* could return to the Weddell Sea and embark on the land crossing in early 1916.

However, *Endurance*'s more north-westerly track alongside the peninsula was taking the vessel into totally uncharted waters. If there was land to the west, the possibility existed that *Endurance* would be trapped between the enormous forces of the encroaching ice and the coastline. 'Where will we make a landing now?' Shackleton wrote. 'Time alone will tell. In the meantime we must wait.' Later the same day, the sun dipped below the horizon and disappeared for nearly three months.

Endurance was now a winter station, much the same as the old expedition hut at Cape Royds. The difference was that in 1908 attention was centred almost entirely on reaching the South Pole. Isolated and drifting silently on the vast white ocean in 1915, all that the crew of *Endurance* could do was simply wait and see.

The boilers were emptied and the dogs were moved onto the ice where they were housed in kennels hollowed from the ice and quickly nicknamed 'dogloos'. Stores were placed in the empty coal bunkers and in the space McNish created a series of accommodation cubicles where groups of like-minded souls gravitated toward each other. Shackleton alone kept his personal cabin, though he was never a remote, solitary figure.

Indeed, Shackleton was everywhere, establishing routines, delegating responsibilities and ensuring that cliques did not develop between the widely divergent assembly. He never asked men to do something he would not do himself. It was noticeable how little he slept.

Shackleton's genius was in his sheer force of personality. He wielded his power with a combination of drive and determination, optimism and a clear resolve. He had the knack of making each man feel as though he was as important as the next. In contrast to the impulsive man at home, Shackleton was patient and always ready to listen to ideas from anyone.

There were no favourites. It was reminiscent of the observation made by James Dell on *Discovery* who said Shackleton could be 'both fore and aft'. Or, as Macklin on *Endurance* explained a decade and a half later, Shackleton 'could meet anybody on their own ground'.

Spending time chatting informally with individuals was a vitally important feature of Shackleton's leadership style. It was a radical approach and one unrecognisable to men accustomed to the strict disciplinary codes of the sea or workplace where executive authority was exercised and blind obedience was expected. Although there was discipline on board, it was imposed with a light touch and Shackleton gave the impression that decisions were being taken for the good of the entire company. Most understood the difference between a barked order and a measured command.

All ranks, from sailors to scientists, were asked to scrub the floors, hunt for seals and join in the lusty post-dinner sing-songs. When winter clothing was handed out, Shackleton ensured the crew were supplied first to demonstrate that the seamen were as important as the officers. Although he was expert at nothing in particular, Shackleton conveyed the reassuring impression that he was master of everything.

Brief chats over a mug of cocoa or a long discourse during the lonely hours of night watch gave Shackleton the opportunity to take the measure of his men, weighing up their strengths and weaknesses for the stern challenges ahead. He used these moments to get beneath the skin of his men and to understand how to get the best out of them.

These were valuable moments, giving Shackleton opportunities to stamp his distinctive style on the group and for the men to build trust in his leadership. With a few exceptions, the seafarers, academics and adventurers jammed into *Endurance* soon became Shackleton's men. For many, the trust they developed in Shackleton would be indispensable in facing the ordeal ahead.

Tensions were inevitable. In the claustrophobic quarters below deck, the permutations of friendships and groups were unfathomable. The age gap did not help. While the average age of the 28 men on *Endurance* was 33, this concealed large variations, with Cheetham and McNish twice the age of stowaway Blackborow or the 22-year-old assistant engineer, Alexander Kerr.

Orde Lees seemed to have no particular pals and became the butt of many poor jokes, while there were few points of interest between the rough-hewn seamen and university types. The crew, Hurley noted, were 'not altogether partial' to the scientists like James and Clark. When someone asked if there were two 'c's' in the word 'accompany,' Hussey replied: 'Yes, and one Sergeant Major.'

Food was critical to the equanimity. Mealtimes were kept with rigid punctuality and everyone ate at the same time, even if the crew at first rebelled against eating unpalatable seal meat. Shackleton's instinct told him that men with full stomachs were less likely to grumble and cause trouble, particularly as the boredom and ennui of the Antarctic winter set in.

Shackleton was also wary of the threat of scurvy. Although he knew of no way to eradicate the problem, he insisted on plenty of fresh seal meat in the diet.

Shackleton's keenness to minimise the risk of scurvy had led him to consult a nutritional expert about sledging rations shortly before leaving England. The most authoritative person he could find was Wilfred Beveridge, Professor of Hygiene at the Royal Army Medical College, who had worked on the Plague Commission in India and made special studies of feeding armies on the march. Beveridge, intrigued by the challenge of sustaining the transcontinental party, readily agreed to help.

Beveridge, later to be knighted and made Director of Hygiene at the War Office, recommended an intake of at least 4,000 calories a day for the overland march. He also proposed taking special 'cakes', weighing only 1 lb (0.50 kg), which were a mixture of compressed oatmeal, sugar, beef powder and proteins. These were to be supplemented by nut food, a

½ lb (0.25 kg) concoction of powdered milk, sugar, marmite, tea and salt. Other suggestions made by Beveridge, including carrying penguin eggs on the march and raising the temperature inside the tents to 62° (17 °C) to cultivate mustard and cress, proved impractical.

The dogs were another important matter, particularly as Shackleton held onto the conviction that the expedition would return to Vahsel Bay the following year. In early April he assigned six men – Wild, Crean, Hurley, Macklin, Marston and McIlroy – to look after their teams and arrange training sessions with the animals.

What Shackleton had not bargained for was the loss of so many animals to ill health. Within three months of entrapment, at least 19 of the 69 dogs had died of illness like tapeworms or pneumonia, reducing Shackleton's total for the overland march to around 50 animals. It was also calculated that stocks of seal meat and blubber for the dogs would run out in three or four months, while it was expected that seals and penguins would inevitably disappear from the ice as winter descended.

It was Orde Lees who urged Shackleton to build up stocks of fresh meat while supply was plentiful, sending men onto the ice for a wholesale slaughter of any available wildlife. But Shackleton was reluctant. It was not squeamishness. Shackleton instinctively felt that stockpiling food implied that the entrapment was more permanent than temporary. *Endurance,* for the moment, had ample provisions and Shackleton's gut feeling was that the most precious commodity he could offer his men was the hope of freedom.

On the same day that Shackleton assigned the six dog handlers, another more pertinent event occurred. Wordie, who was on watch during the night, heard rumblings from ice pressure beneath the ice. Luckily, he wrote in his diary, the pressure was 'some little distance' from the ship.

But the groans and strains of the slowly building ice pressure were undeniable and Shackleton could scarcely conceal his concern. Intermittent rumblings continued throughout the winter darkness. Each unusual sound sent him hurrying on deck to check the state of the nearby ice. 'The Boss is naturally very nervous,' Wordie wrote. 'He is not the best of companions for a nightwatch.'

The area around the ship resembled an earthquake in slow motion. In an unhurried but perceptible manner, the currents were forcing massive floes into collisions with each other, causing huge blocks of ice to snap and buckle and lift 20 feet (6 m) out of the sea. It was a scenario played against an eerie cacophony of grinding and crackling sounds from the ice as pressure built beneath their feet. Occasionally a loud thud could be heard as an enormous ice block, weighing several tons, toppled over.

Among the books in the ship's small library was *The Voyage of the Fox* by Sir Leopold McClintock, whose vessel was trapped in the ice of Baffin Bay half a century earlier during the search for clues to the missing Franklin expedition. McClintock described the unnerving noise of mounting ice pressure, '... as if trains of heavy wagons with ungreased axles were slowly labouring along.'[4]

Shackleton's concerns were well placed. *Endurance* was drifting dangerously towards the Antarctic Peninsula, an area today known as the Lassiter and Black coasts of Palmer Land. In Shackleton's words, they were caught in an 'inferno of ice-blocks' between the land and ice, fervently hoping for release before being crushed between two colossal forces.

Essential provisions and supplies were placed on the upper deck in readiness for an emergency escape and space was cleared in case it was necessary to bring the dogs back on board in a hurry. A strong gale from the south blew on 13 July and *Endurance* shuddered under the attack as the pressure of the ice mounted from three sides.

Shackleton had maintained a calm, reassuring composure throughout the months of confinement, rarely seeming to be in a hurry or flustered by events far beyond his control. But the gale of 13 July changed everything. Wild and Worsley were called to Shackleton's cabin for a council of war. Against a background grind of 'ungreased axles' Shackleton revealed the true extent of *Endurance*'s peril, which he had secretly known for months.

'The ship can't live in this, Skipper,' he told Worsley. 'You had better make up your mind that it is only a matter of time.'

Worsley was desolate. Losing a ship is the ultimate ignominy for any captain and Worsley, who sailed by the old-time code of the sea, felt the loss acutely. He also understood that *Endurance* was the most potent symbol of the hope that Shackleton had carefully fostered for months.

But, as Shackleton warned Worsley: 'what the ice gets, the ice keeps.'

chapter 29

Death of a Ship

The pressure came in waves like an incoming tide lapping on a shore. *Endurance* shook and quivered and all around massive blocks of ice spilt from the ocean under the relentless force and piled up in grotesque formations only a few yards from the ship.

The changing landscape around the ship mirrored the seismic shift in the expedition's fortunes. *Endurance* was reasonably safe while the vessel remained trapped in the ice. The real danger would come when the ice began to splinter and break up, unleashing the immense and unpredictable forces of the more rapidly moving pack.

Shackleton was now preparing for the worst while hoping for the best. The dogs were brought on board in case the ice suddenly broke up, but the three lifeboats were made ready for lowering in case it did not.

For three months, *Endurance* rode with the blows, groaning and straining to stay afloat. It was an uneven struggle since *Endurance* was not ideally built for the fight, despite sides of oak, Norwegian fir and greenheart up to 2½ feet (0.8 m) thick and a solid oak keel over 7 feet (2 m) in thickness. The solid oak bow was 4 feet (1.3 m) thick. Shackleton understood that *Endurance*, with a conventional U-shaped hull, was designed for the oceans and not the pack and was particularly vulnerable to being gripped by ice. Nansen's *Fram* was the ideal, a shallow-draught and smooth, rounded vessel built to rise up from the ice. *Fram* had once survived a three-year drift trapped in the Arctic ice, but the chances of *Endurance* doing the same were already remote.

On board men were optimistically taking bets on when the ship might be freed. McIlroy cheerfully plumped for November while the contrarian Orde Lees reckoned on February the following year. Shackleton, with an eye on morale, went for as early as October.

A huge wave of pressure struck on 1 August, lifting the ship bodily out of the water and buckling its beams. Floor linoleum, which Shackleton

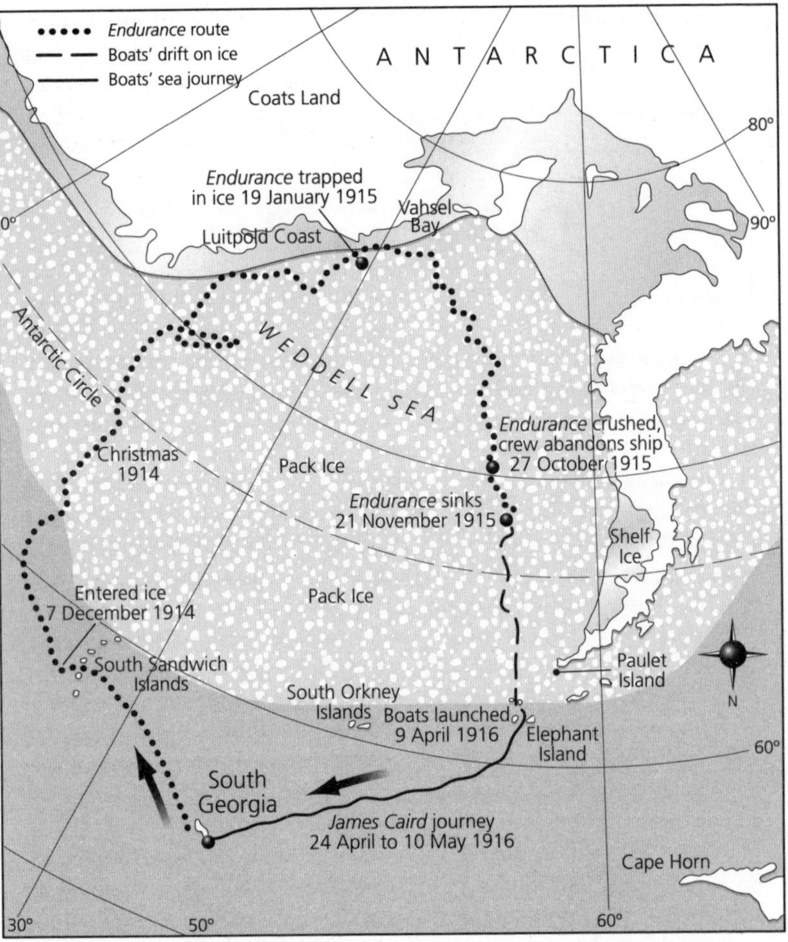

The epic voyage of the **Endurance** *expedition, 1914–16.*

himself had helped to lay only a few months earlier, crinkled up at the edges as the walls warped. A month later, with spring approaching, the ship was again lifted up and beams bulged, iron plates in the engine room buckled and door frames distorted. 'There were times when we thought it was not possible the ship would stand it,' McNish wrote.

The drama of *Endurance*'s battle to survive was conducted against the certainty that the ship was still being carried slowly northwards. By mid-

September the ship had crossed the 69th parallel and had drifted over eight degrees of latitude to the north – over 550 miles (nearly 900 km) – on an irregular path since the 'furthest south' reached in February. Shackleton calculated that the nearest land, the unexplored areas of the peninsula to the west, was perhaps 250 miles (400 km) across broken ice. However, this was uncharted territory and would involve a monumental effort to get there. 'I hoped fervently that we should not have to undertake a march across moving ice fields,' he wrote.[1]

The distant growl of approaching pressure continued in the following weeks, shaking the ship and threatening to snap its beams. By mid-October, *Endurance* was lurching halfway out of the ice at a crazy angle of 30° and losing the battle. Dogs, provision boxes and sledges were scattered across the decks before the pressure eased and the ship settled back into the water. Occasionally open leads appeared as if to taunt the men, but they soon disappeared. Water began to seep into the holds.

On 24 October someone was playing 'The Wearing o' the Green' on the gramophone when a terrific crash struck the ship with the force of an earthquake. On the ice Shackleton surveyed the damage to the ship's sternpost and ordered McNish to build a cofferdam to hold back the tide. Men toiled at the pumps to the defiant sound of sea shanties, though it was another losing battle. *Endurance* was under assault from three sides and Shackleton admitted it was the 'beginning of the end'.

As the pressure intensified and timbers snapped with a sound like rifle shots, Shackleton prepared to abandon ship. On 26 October he ordered the boats, food, equipment and the dogs to be offloaded onto the floe about 100 yards (90 m) from the ship. 'We are the embodiment of helpless futility,' wrote Hurley.

Nearby a parade of eight Emperor penguins ambled alongside and began wailing an eerie funereal dirge over the spectacle. McLeod, the gloomily superstitious veteran of the sea, solemnly warned that the penguins' lament was an omen that no one would ever see home again.

If Shackleton shared McLeod's ominous prognosis he kept his emotions under control, never allowing the mask to slip. In the face of unrelenting pressure, Shackleton was concealing his impulsive tendencies. He needed to set the right tone of composed reassurance, not melodramatics. He also wanted to be seen to be in command.

As the crisis deepened, he stood calmly resolute, quietly delivering a mixture of commands and words of encouragement to the men. 'For most of the time,' Orde Lees said, 'he stood on the upper deck holding onto the rigging smoking a cigarette with a serious but somewhat unconquered

Endurance *broken and crushed.*

air.' It was echoed by Macklin, who recalled how Shackleton watched the unfolding drama and the demolition of his ambitions 'without emotion, melodrama or excitement'.

For the moment, though, Shackleton was forced to admit defeat against the immense forces of nature. 'We were helpless intruders in a strange world,' he wrote in his diary.

In the final attack, *Endurance* reeled under the mounting pressure from all sides, with the stern rising out of the water and the keel snapping and buckling under the strain. 'The floes, with the force of millions of tons of moving ice behind them, were simply annihilating the ship,' Shackleton wrote. 'It was a sickening sensation to feel the decks breaking up under one's feet, the great beams bending and then snapping with a noise like heavy gun-fire.'

All efforts to stem the flood of incoming water were futile. To avoid an explosion when the water reached the boilers, Shackleton ordered the fires to be drawn and steam let down. At around 5 p.m. on the evening of 27 October pumping was stopped and Shackleton gave the order to abandon ship.

Shackleton was last to leave. A gentle southerly breeze was blowing in briskly cold temperatures of -8° (-22 °C) and the blue ensign was hoisted to the faint sound of cheers from the floe. The defiant chorus signalled the end of the maiden voyage of *Endurance* at 69° 5' S, 51° 32' W.

Few people on earth were more isolated than the 28 men assembled on the drifting ice floe. They had travelled over 1,500 miles (2,400 km) on a mazy course through the ice in the nine months since the ship was trapped and it was still hundreds of miles to the nearest outpost of civilisation. The floe, drifting imperceptibly north, was no more than 10 feet (3 m) thick and offered only a fragile hint at security. Clark's last sounding of the ocean depths, taken a month before, reached bottom at 1,876 fathoms or 11,256 feet (3,430 m).

The tiny uninhabited Paulet Island, where Nordenskjöld's rescuers had deposited emergency supplies in 1903, was estimated to be about 400 miles (640 km) to the north-west at the tip of the Antarctic Peninsula. Ironically, it was Shackleton, who had advised Lieutenant Irizar's rescuers, who was partly responsible for placing the cache.

But safely crossing hundreds of miles of badly broken, hummocky ice to the island with 28 men, provisions and three lifeboats was highly improbable. Paulet Island is a small lump of volcanic rock less than a mile (1.5 km) wide and the chances of catching a passing whaler were remote. The seas to the north of Paulet Island, where Shackleton had directed Irizar, were notoriously rough.

So, too, was the hope of a ship coming to the Weddell Sea to rescue the expedition. No one knew the party had been carried into the western reaches of the Weddell and any search for the overdue men was more likely to be around Vahsel Bay. In any event, Shackleton was not expected to emerge from the ice until March 1916. They were on their own.

'It is hard to write what I feel,' Shackleton told his diary as he considered the loss of *Endurance* and his grand adventure. 'To a sailor his ship is more than a floating home and in Endurance I had centred ambitions, hopes and desires.'

chapter 30

Defiance

Sleep was beyond Shackleton the first night on the ice. While others grabbed some fitful rest, he stalked around in the damp chill silently surveying the wreckage of his ambitions and weighing up the options. It was a disturbed interlude for all concerned and three times during the night the men were called to shift the boats and supplies as the floe split apart. 'A terrible night,' wrote James.

At 5 a.m. Shackleton fired up the stove and, with Wild's assistance, went from tent to tent to wake the men with mugs of steaming coffee. No one had slept well. *Endurance* carried only 18 fur sleeping bags so 10 men – they were drawn by lots – had to make do with the discomfort of woollen bags. Yet there was a strange relief at camping on the ice compared with the precarious anxiety of life on board a dying ship.

Shackleton instinctively grasped the need to reassure the men. As the tired, anxious company assembled together on the ice, he stepped forward and announced: 'Ship and stores have gone – so now we'll go home.'[1]

It was a bravura performance designed to stiffen the sinews and instil belief. 'Simple, moving, optimistic and highly effective,' wrote Hussey. 'His simple word, nobly spoken, touched the heart,' wrote Hurley.

Shackleton's personal fears, which he kept at a discreet distance from prying eyes, were another thing. 'I pray God,' he wrote, 'I can manage to get the whole party to civilisation and then this part of the expedition will be over.'

Not that God was likely to be a major part of his plans. After a strong religious upbringing, Shackleton had long ago drifted away from the Church and was no longer a believer, even at moments of great stress. He saw little practical value in organised religion. Or as Mill observed: 'His God was the God of Nature, of the stars, the seas and the open spaces, of the great movements of history and the abysmal depths of personality.'[2]

Colleagues recall how he did not believe in summoning God's help only when things were going badly. 'If he didn't believe in the Lord when things were going well, he wasn't going to call on his protection when they weren't going well,' Hussey once explained.[3]

Yet something about a higher order lurked in the recesses of Shackleton's mind. As the party prepared to embark on their escape from the ice, he tore pages from the Bible, including the personal inscription from Queen Alexandra: 'May the Lord help you to do your deeds, guide you through all dangers by land and sea.'

Paulet Island was the only realistic option of reaching dry land and prior to departure each man was given a new set of clothing and a personal allowance of 2 lb (0.9 kg) they were allowed to carry. Nothing was of value if it impeded their survival and reducing weight was critical. Shackleton rammed home the message with a melodramatic display of his own. He tossed coins and his own gold watch into the snow and also threw away the ship's Bible. McLeod, brooding behind his heavy beard, sensed it was bad luck to throw away a Bible and snatched it from the ice, tucking it inside his jacket for safekeeping. McNish kept some tools and McIlroy and Macklin kept their medical instruments. Hussey was permitted to keep his banjo, despite the weight, because Shackleton felt the men might need a little light relief in the days ahead.

Stores and equipment were loaded onto two boats. Worsley tried to persuade Shackleton to take all three boats, but Shackleton felt the men would move more quickly with only two boats to pull.

The 28 men were split into three distinct groups: trailblazers, man-haulers and handlers for the 49 remaining dogs. Shortly before leaving, the weakest animals, including the pups, were shot, and Mrs Chippy, McNish's pet cat, was also destroyed because of fears the dogs would rip the animal apart when their own food ran out.

Light snow was falling and a misty haze hung over the ice as the procession began on the morning of 30 October. The men were strung out across the ice for about half a mile and Orde Lees ran between the columns on his skis. Orde Lees was the party's most accomplished skier and it was noticeable how easily he raced along. To Orde Lees it was surprising that no one else had been trained to ski properly. But Shackleton, even on his third venture into the ice, had still not come to terms with skis and told Orde Lees: 'I had no idea how quickly it was possible for a man on ski to get about.'

Each boat weighed about one ton and progress was painfully slow. The sledges sank deep into the soft ice and the men found the intense work utterly draining after such a long spell of inactivity. At the end of the day the group had advanced barely a mile, though with the gruelling labour of relaying some had covered up to 6 miles (10 km).

The 400-mile (640 km) slog to Paulet Island was beyond all human endeavour. The group had full rations for only 56 days and after that they would have to rely on hunting seals and penguins. But Shackleton believed that occupying the men was better than waiting idly for the drift to carry the floe to the open waters of the north. In any event, waiting was not Shackleton's style. 'I felt sure that the right thing to do was to attempt a march,' he wrote.

Next day, after hours of exhausting work, the party had advanced less than a mile. 'To sledge to the land dragging the boats will be too big a task,' Wordie scribbled in his diary. Soon after, Shackleton abandoned the march.

A heavier-looking, more stable floe was found nearby and a more permanent camp was established after a further desperate struggle with the loads across appalling surfaces with snow up to 2 feet thick. At times the men sank up to their hips in the soft snow. The floe, which Shackleton called Ocean Camp, was about a mile square and less than 2 miles from the wreckage of *Endurance*.

Frequent trips were made to retrieve items of gear or food from the debris around the ship. Some men cut their way through the tangled lines and masts to risk salvaging possessions below the waterline. Hurley plucked boxes of his precious photographs, taken on heavy glass plates, from the ice and was allowed to keep about 150 of the estimated 550 images. The rejected pictures were smashed to avoid the agony of having any second thoughts.

Wild rescued the ship's wheelhouse, which, with the addition of sails and tarpaulins, was modified to become the party's galley and storehouse. From the roof of the makeshift galley the Union Jack flew proudly in the bracing wind.

The long hours and days spent at Ocean Camp gave Shackleton a fresh opportunity to assess their position with his closest confidants, Wild and Worsley. Also taken into the inner circle was Hurley, whose inventiveness with sparse equipment and a belligerently positive approach to the situation had caught Shackleton's attention. 'Hurley splendid' Shackleton wrote one night.

The worst fears were that the drift would carry the Ocean Camp floe away from the peninsula to the west onto a more north-easterly track towards the wider expanses of the Weddell Sea, opening up the grim possibility of having to spend another winter on the floating ice. The effect on morale, Shackleton understood, would be devastating. Some, like Hurley and Orde Lees, had sensed the danger. Orde Lees, who was acting as quartermaster, began to save quantities of food and odd supplies in case the worst fears were realised.

To counter this threat, one option was to abandon the boats and march due west towards the peninsula with lighter sledges. A small punt would be carried to cross any open leads of water, though this was enormously risky with so many supplies needed for the trek. Once on land, it might be possible to work a passage along the coast towards the area around Wilhelmina Bay where the whalers were known to visit. Either way, survival depended on the unpredictable behaviour of the ice.

Shackleton, however, was not wedded to a single plan. Improvisation came naturally and he was always ready to listen to the advice of others like Wild or Worsley.

The challenge now was boredom. Each day on Ocean Camp was the same and for Shackleton it was summed up with a simple diary entry, which read: 'Waiting Waiting Waiting.' He was forced to stifle his natural hastiness and summon up reserves of patience he barely knew existed. In one diary entry he pronounced: 'Put footstep of courage into stirrup of patience.'

The mood changed on 21 November when *Endurance*, after ten months of unequal struggle, finally succumbed to the ice. Earlier in the day, the bow dipped and the stern rose 20 feet (6 m) out of the water. After a brief respite, the hulk slipped slowly beneath the ice, leaving only a small pool of dark water and bits of floating debris. Seconds later the pool froze over. 'She's gone, boys,' said Shackleton. The isolation was complete.

By a quirk of fate, the loss of *Endurance* seemed to coincide with an acceleration of the drift which carried Ocean Camp through the 68° parallel. In six weeks, they made around 120 miles (190 km) but to the consternation of all, the drift was taking them on an easterly course towards the open waters between the necklace of islands in the South Shetlands and South Orkney chains.

Shackleton might have been cheered by the realisation that *Deutschland* had been released from the ice at 63° 37' S, 36° 34' W on the northern fringes of the Weddell Sea, but this was miles from land in any direction. Away from Filchner's northerly course and with only a couple of small boats at his disposal, Shackleton could not afford to wait for the same deliverance.

Once again, Shackleton considered a dash to Paulet Island or other land in the west. It was an enormous task. From the slowly drifting Ocean Camp to Paulet Island was thought to be about 350 miles (560 km) over unpredictable masses of moving ice. Even if they reached dry land, the party still faced a trek of about 200 miles (320 km) across uncharted territory to reach Wilhelmina Bay.

Preparations for the march were well under way. In the capable hands of McNish, the two largest boats were strengthened and recaulked. All three boats had been named in honour of Shackleton's major sponsors: *James Caird, Dudley Docker* and *Stancomb Wills*. Although Shackleton was unsure whether the party would be able to manage all three vessels, sails were fitted just in case ice conditions were favourable.

Shackleton sensed the need for action. A certain restlessness was evident among some men after two months on the ice and the Ocean Camp floe was disintegrating into a squalid, slushy mess as the drift carried them into the marginally warmer waters above 67° of latitude.

Taking Crean, Hurley and Wild, Shackleton drove west for 7 miles (11 km) with two teams of dogs to reconnoitre the ice. Although they encountered numerous bad stretches, enough flat-looking and passable floes were spotted and Shackleton returned in a more optimistic frame of mind. How much of this optimism was real and how much was for public display is hard to tell. Certainly Shackleton needed to demonstrate that escape was possible but the realistic chances of getting the boats to open water were slim to non-existent.

Shackleton reckoned the men and boats could advance 2–3 miles (3–5 km) a day, which implied a back-breaking slog of up to 6 months just to reach Paulet Island. The other danger was that it would be deepest winter by the end of the march when temperatures were lowest and game scarcest.

Christmas Day celebrations were brought forward to 22 December and stores loaded onto sledges. The two largest boats, *James Caird* and *Dudley Docker*, were made ready. *Stancomb Wills*, the smallest, was left behind. Surplus provisions were abandoned and, before leaving, the men devoured a luxurious assortment of meats, fruits, biscuits and hot drinks in an orgy of self-indulgence. 'A right royal feast,' said Orde Lees.

The stark reality of the toil ahead was soon apparent as the men, dogs, boats and sledges began the long march at around 5 a.m. on the morning of 23 December. The party was divided into groups of trailbreakers pioneering the route ahead, dog handlers and the largest contingent, who were yoked to the cumbersome boats, each weighing around a ton. It was a grotesque struggle with the men strung out for half a mile hacking a way through the broken ice with picks and shovels or relaying the boats inch by inch into the unknown. At times they sank up their knees in soft snow and aside from meal breaks and brief snatches of sleep, the procession continued until 11 p.m. at night.

A few days of gruelling labour followed, though never once did they manage to reach Shackleton's target of 2–3 miles a day. Shackleton went ahead with Hurley on 27 December to plot a course and returned to the hauling parties to discover that McNish was at the centre of a minor mutiny.

McNish, a combustible barrack-room lawyer with a rasping Scots accent, had refused to obey Worsley's orders. To McNish, the exhausting daily labour of hauling the boats was futile and he refused to take another step. He was a man set in his ways, a firm believer in the righteous pillars of socialism and Presbyterianism with a dislike of foul language. McNish, said one shipmate, was 'neither sweet-tempered nor tolerant'.

Trapped in the harness day after day, the cantankerous McNish had nursed a number of grouses apart from what he considered the pointless dragging, including blaming Shackleton for the death of his cat, Mrs Chippy. He was also in pain from persistent piles and upset that Shackleton had rejected his own scheme to rescue the party by building a larger boat. McNish, confident in his carpentry skills, wanted to salvage wood from the wreckage of *Endurance* and build a sloop large enough to hold all 28 men. Though plausible, the plan relied entirely on the drift taking the floe into open water. Shackleton, realising the sloop would be too heavy to pull across the ice, dismissed the idea and left McNish feeling excluded.

Shackleton feared that McNish's disobedience would spread like wildfire throughout the company and needed to quell the rebellion. It was the biggest challenge to his leadership he had ever faced and all hands watched in silence as he squared up to McNish with a bold display of authority.

McNish had tried to justify his refusal by insisting that Ship's Articles – a sailor's terms and conditions – no longer applied after the loss of *Endurance*. To McNish this meant he was no longer obliged to accept orders.

Shackleton grabbed a copy of the Articles and in a calm, measured tone announced to the gathered assembly that he had signed on as ship's master at Buenos Aires and under the terms of agreement all men were subject to the orders of the master. Disobedience to lawful commands, he added, would be 'legally punishable'. He also decreed that the tradition of stopping men's wages with the loss of a ship did not apply in the case of *Endurance*. The men, he said, would be paid until they reached port.

It was a masterful display of authority, part conviction, part expedience and part theatre. In the event, it crushed McNish's revolt before it began and re-established Shackleton as unequivocal leader.

Some accounts say that McNish was taken aside and warned he would be shot if he continued to disobey orders. Whether or not this was an idle threat is impossible to judge. Execution was hardly Shackleton's style, but maintaining discipline and unity of purpose was paramount. In any event, the task of shooting McNish would probably have fallen to Wild.

Shackleton nonetheless was wounded by McNish's disobedience. To Shackleton, it was the worst kind of betrayal. Loyalty to him was a two-way street. He gave it steadfastly and expected the same in return. Anything less than reciprocity was a personal insult, particularly at a moment when he was straining every sinew to keep them all alive. A day after the clash with McNish, Shackleton wrote in his diary: 'I shall never forget him in this time of strain & stress.'

McNish was back in harness next day when the march resumed. Ironically, the procession enjoyed the best day so far, covering 2½ miles (4 km) over a treacherously difficult surface of slushy ice and lumpy ice formations. At times the boats and sledges broke through the ice. But all hopes of continuing the good progress were dashed by the sight of open leads of water, too small to launch the boats but too large to cross. 'The outlook was most unpromising,' Shackleton wrote.

McNish, in some ways, had been right about the futility of the slog. In almost a week of unrelenting hard grind the party had travelled less than 10 miles (16 km) from Ocean Camp and the drift was carrying the floe away from where they started. The arithmetic was simple. At the present rate of advance it would take many months of unimaginable struggle to reach Paulet Island and the food supply was down to 42 days.

Next day the march was abandoned and the party retreated half a mile (0.8 km) to a more stable-looking floe. To the intense disappointment of all hands, Shackleton decided to establish a new permanent base where they stood. All they could do now was wait for the combination of currents and winds to carry the floe north into the warmer waters and hope the ice was loose enough to launch the boats. How long it would take was a matter of conjecture.

The mood on the ice was restless. While the men struggled with the desperately hard work, many abhorred the grinding boredom and longed for at least some activity. Although from different backgrounds, sailors and scientists alike were accustomed to busy lives and the tedium chipped away at everyone. Orde Lees reported a 'distinctly depressing' impact on morale after the march was abandoned.

But Shackleton was adamant. He reasoned that the wounds inflicted on morale were justified to protect the boats for the open sea journey ahead, especially as the boats risked being damaged by the badly broken ice formations.

The new floe, which Wordie estimated at just 7 feet (2 m) thick under a layer of soft snow, was cheerfully described as Patience Camp. Hunting parties were sent out to slaughter seals and penguins and Hurley and Macklin went back to Ocean Camp to retrieve any food or gear left behind.

The hiatus came at the right moment for Shackleton, who was struggling with a combination of fatigue and anxiety and the need to preserve the belief among the men that they would survive the ordeal. 'I am rather tired,' he admitted on 30 December. 'I suppose it is the strain.'

Something of the old problem had surfaced a few weeks earlier when he reported an attack of 'sciatica and a cold'. Wild saw something else, reporting that at times Shackleton was unable to leave his sleeping bag without assistance. It was debilitating enough to prevent him making his regular rounds of the tents, which previously not even blizzards had stopped. On this occasion, he relented long enough to permit the doctors to conduct a quick examination. But he did not allow them to listen to his heart.

Shackleton, in fact, had been under intense strain for months. He was on the go constantly, barking orders or trying to breathe hope into the company without ever showing outwards signs of his fears or anxieties. His self-control was remarkable and it was still apparent to everyone how little he seemed to sleep.

Another feature of his behaviour was patience, not a trait that many at home would have recognised in him. At home Shackleton was characterised by his head-down impulsiveness and often childlike simplicity. On the ice he was guarded and conservative and quietly pleased at the irreverent nickname 'Cautious Jack' given by some on the floe. 'He was proud of his reputation for carefulness,' said Worsley.

Behind his own light-heartedness, Worsley was a sound judge of character and was able to distinguish between the two sides of Shackleton. '[He] was an exceedingly cautious man,' Worsley wrote. 'He was brave, the bravest man I have seen, but he was never foolhardy. When necessary he would undertake the most dangerous things and do so fearlessly; but always he would approach them in a thoughtful manner and perform them in the safest way.'

The major topic of conversation was whether to make another dash across the ice. Shackleton listened carefully but insisted that the mixture of broken ice and soft, slushy surface was too dangerous. Any break-up of the ice would leave them horribly exposed in a no-man's land between the stability of Patience Camp and the unknown territory to the west. Already gaping leads of open water could be seen in the distance and Shackleton was not prepared to take a chance. They would wait to see what the drift brought.

It was a proposition that spelled the end of the road for the dog teams, who were eating precious quantities of food and could not be carried on the boats. Worsley, in fact, still believed it was possible to attempt a fresh crossing of the ice and urged Shackleton to keep the dogs alive. But in mid-January four of the remaining seven dog teams were shot. A few days later Hurley's team recovered a little pemmican, dry milk and cereals from the debris of Ocean Camp and his dogs were also taken aside and put down.

The loss of the dogs, whose companionship was psychologically more important than anyone realised, was keenly felt. Wild, who carried out the grisly task, said it was the worst job he had ever had and added: 'I have known many men I would rather shoot than the worst of the dogs.'

By coincidence, Sir Clements Markham, whose determined resistance to dogs characterised decades of British exploration, passed away two weeks later on 30 January. Markham, 85 years old and apparently still resisting modern advances, set light to his blankets while reading in bed by candlelight and was overcome by smoke. The electric light above his head remained switched off and Mill's assessment of Markham as 'an enthusiast rather than a scholar' seemed painfully apposite.

At Patience Camp, food was the main issue, with many asking why the party had not stockpiled penguin and seal carcasses when supplies were plentiful. Orde Lees, as quartermaster, had repeatedly urged Shackleton to build up stocks and Macklin, normally one of the most loyal to the Boss, said Shackleton had been 'a bit improvident' in not harvesting stocks when the going was good.

Initially, Shackleton had gambled with the idea that hoarding meat would send the wrong signal to the men and suggest that the confinement would be long lasting. Optimism was the key and at this stage Shackleton believed that the survival hinged on the company believing they would survive. When Orde Lees tried to persuade him to change his mind, Shackleton said: 'It will do some of the people good to go hungry – their bloody appetites are too big.'

By late January, game was notably scarce and on 26 January one of the stoves was shut down because of dwindling quantities of blubber. Some of the dogs were eaten, though Wild reported the steaks were the 'nastiest I have tasted and the toughest'. A cup of tea at breakfast was now the only hot drink of the day. 'Our rations are just sufficient to keep us alive,' Shackleton wrote, 'but we all feel that we could eat twice as much as we get.'

The discomfort was increased by intermittent bouts of constipation, a side effect of the meat-only diet. Although they did not realise it, the high-protein diet of seal or penguin steaks was a useful antidote to the predicament. The human body works harder to digest protein and the extra energy generated increases normal body heat, while the small quantity of vitamin C in the fresh meat was a vital ingredient in combating scurvy.

At the outset Shackleton was determined not to dip into the reserve of sledging rations devised by the nutritionist Beveridge. The provisions, he decided, would be needed for the boat journey and whatever lay beyond. But by late January food was so low that he was forced to use the rations to supplement meals.

Another concern was the curious decision to leave *Stancomb Wills*, the third boat, at Ocean Camp. Worsley, in particular, argued forcibly that 28 men would overload the *Caird* and *Docker* in the rough seas ahead and that it was imperative to bring up the *Wills*. His pleas finally got through and on 2 February Shackleton suddenly changed his mind and sent 18 men to recover the boat. It was a desperate struggle over soft ground but Shackleton and Hussey went out to meet the haulers with mugs of steaming tea. 'It was the most acceptable cup of tea imaginable,' wrote Orde Lees.

As Wordie noted, it had taken a long time to persuade Shackleton to change his mind. But this was Shackleton's way: constantly listening, improvising and adapting his plans to suit the changing circumstances. Little was fixed in his mind beyond keeping the men alive.

Next day Crean, Macklin and Worsley embarked on another trip to forage for anything of value left at Ocean Camp and were halted in their tracks by a wide and impassable lead of open water. Had Shackleton waited another 24 hours to retrieve the *Stancomb Wills* it is likely that the flight from Patience Camp would have had to be made with only two boats.

Time on the ice was a life in slow motion. For Shackleton, the mood at Patience Camp was causing concern. The site had quickly degenerated into an uncomfortable, waterlogged mess and everything was wringing wet. To add to the discomfort, the weather was persistently foul and a heavy damp mist blanketed the floe for days on end. The Scots, McNish, McLeod and Wordie, recognised the miserable conditions as typically *dreich* days.

The days passed unhurriedly and hours spent idly passing time only encouraged fanciful speculation and allowed petty irritations to fester. The loud snoring of Orde Lees aggravated his tent-mates and Clark had developed an annoying habit of persistent sniffing. Squabbling was the norm, especially when the dismal weather forced the men to spend time packed together in the tents.

During an argument with Clark one day, Greenstreet knocked over his mug of hot milk. Hot drinks were precious and Greenstreet, a mature level-headed seafarer, was close to tears as he stared at the mess on the floor. Without hesitation, Clark leant across and emptied a little of his hot milk into Greenstreet's mug. Almost immediately Worsley, Macklin, Kerr, Rickinson, Orde Lees and Blackborow each tipped a little of their milk into Greenstreet's mug. Words were not necessary.

Overhanging all else was the fear that the ice beneath their feet might crack at any moment. A man who plunged into the icy water within shouting distance of his colleagues stood a good chance of surviving. Few wandered very far from camp, knowing that a man alone, weighed down by layers of heavy clothing, stood little chance of clambering back onto the floe.

Even the game hunters went out in pairs, although this, too, involved grave risks. One day Crean and Wild spotted a dark shape in the hazy mist half-hidden behind a hummock of ice and Wild drew aim with his Winchester rifle at what he believed was a large seal. As Wild started to squeeze the trigger, the shape stood up and revealed itself to be one of the scientists who was relieving himself behind the mound.

Shackleton was on constant lookout for any hint that the suffering was turning to despair. He prowled around the floe, checking on the men, nursing their gripes and dispensing encouragement. Some simply needed companionship. It was a sixth sense: he instinctively knew what each individual needed and seemed able to judge the right mood for the occasion.

Cutting back on food was the most painful decision Shackleton had to take. Since his time on *Discovery* and *Nimrod*, Shackleton had understood that one of the certainties of living on the margins was that well-fed men were more content and equable than hungry men.

Concerned about possible discontent, Shackleton seemed to spend more time roaming around Patience Camp, chatting with individuals, playing cards and generally making his presence felt. Diversions were vital and he encouraged lusty sing-songs to the accompaniment of Hussey's banjo, though some complained about his very limited repertoire of tunes.

In other moments, Shackleton indulged in his two favourite subjects, reciting poetry at length to anyone who would listen and dreaming aloud about making a fortune from finding buried treasure or clinching a spectacular business deal. Shackleton's enthusiasm was infectious as he talked dreamily of unearthing the lost booty of ancients like King John or Alaric the Goth and getting rich from pearl fishing in the South Seas or opening a tin mine in Paraguay. In Shackleton's words, it all seemed perfectly credible and for a time the bleak reality of their predicament was forgotten by the day-dreaming. But, as James recalled: 'One would realise what a gambler he was.'

The men Shackleton could most easily rely upon during these difficult days were the old polar hands Wild and Crean. Both were hardened by long experience on the ice – seven Antarctic expeditions between them – and were unquestioning in their support of the Boss.

But the true value of Wild and Crean to Shackleton went far beyond simple loyalty and physical endurance. Shackleton's perceptive understanding of men's behaviour showed that volatile temperaments and shifting moods are a liability in moments of great pressure and stress. What Shackleton saw in Wild and Crean was two even-tempered and dependable characters not prone to mood swings or explosive outbursts and with a solid grasp of their own capabilities. Though rough at the edges, Wild and Crean, with their weathered faces and assured manner around the camp, radiated the same belief as Shackleton that, whatever the difficulties, they would survive.

Worsley, too, was a pillar of strength for Shackleton. Without the responsibility of a ship to command, Worsley's frivolity and impulsiveness somehow seemed less intrusive and there was no question about his support for Shackleton's cause. Shackleton also understood that Worsley's skill as seaman and navigator would be badly needed when the boats were finally placed in the water.

Shackleton was less sure about Hurley. For all his abilities and inventiveness as a handyman, he could be prickly and difficult. Hurley, opinionated, brusque and unforgiving, was no natural leader of men and often unsympathetic to those struggling to cope with the physical and mental strain. But Hurley, like Wild and Crean, had the unmistakable appearance of a survivor.

It was the scientists, a generally quiet and introverted bunch, who found the monotony most difficult to overcome. 'The worst thing,' wrote James, 'is having to kill time.' Shorn of intellectual stimulus, they struggled to find ways of occupying themselves and went to extraordinary lengths to improvise useful tasks. Wordie, a qualified geologist without access to the raw material of rocks and mountains, found an ingenious way to practise his skills. With the nearest rocks 2 miles (3 km) beneath the floe on the ocean floor, Wordie gutted penguins and analysed the small stones found in their stomachs. Keeping the blubber stove firing alone demanded

15 penguin carcasses a day and Wordie was able to pick a steady stream of pebbles from the bloody entrails. (Over 800 Adélie or Emperor penguins were killed during the party's time in the Weddell Sea.)[4]

The seamen were also at a loss to fill their days. The officers like Greenstreet and Hudson had little to do without a ship to run and the crew, more accustomed to the hard-working rigours of the sea, were often unsettled by the inactivity and needed Shackleton's careful attention.

Orde Lees, quirky and independent minded, was kept occupied with store-keeping duties but he remained oddly isolated from most of the company. In usual circumstances, Shackleton would have protected Orde Lees from the banter and brought him closer into the fold for the sake of unity. But Shackleton probably accepted the inevitability of some ribaldry and Orde Lees was a useful outlet for the frustration of the men.

Green, the cook, was the most actively engaged and busiest member of the castaways. Engulfed in a cloud of black smoke from the blubber stove, he seemed to ignore the miserable surroundings and turned out a steady stream of hot food and drinks with commendable efficiency. Mealtimes were the highlight of the day and the blackened face of the imperturbable Green peering through the billowing haze was an oddly reassuring sight. When Shackleton asked what he planned to do after returning home, Green replied: 'I'm coming on another expedition with you if I can.'

All the time the assorted collection of castaways was being carried steadily north in parallel with the peninsula by a mixture of currents and a strong southerly wind. By the end of February, Paulet Island was estimated to be around 100 miles (160 km) to the west and a few days later Shackleton thought he had caught a glimpse of Mount Haddington on the distant horizon. Mount Haddington, a 5,350-foot (1,630 m) volcano, is the highest point on James Ross Island at the northern extremity of the Antarctic Peninsula. But the sighting proved inconclusive in the swirling mists and low cloud.

Spirits were lifted in early March when, for the first time in many months, the swell of the sea was felt beneath their feet. With luck, open water could not be far away and Shackleton stepped up watches in case of break-up. The boats were prepared and the men slept fully clothed in readiness for a rapid departure.

On 17 March, the group was brought through the 63rd parallel, the same latitude from which *Deutschland* was freed. Filchner had been released hundreds of miles to the east and far closer to the centre of the Weddell Sea. Shackleton's only comfort was that he was closer to the peninsula in the west. But conditions were appalling with a mixture of storms and low mist making it difficult to stray far from the tents. The floe, originally 1 mile square, had shrunk to barely 200 yards (180 m) across.

Conditions were far clearer on 23 March when Shackleton made a definite sighting of land. 'General rejoicing,' recorded Hurley. It was the first sign of land since *Endurance* had skirted the southern coastline of the Weddell Sea 15 months earlier and Shackleton wrote: 'Please God we will soon get ashore.'

Next day the unmistakable mountaintops of Joinville Island, which lies adjacent to Paulet Island, came into view some 60 miles (100 km) to the west. However, the territory ahead was an impassable stretch of broken ice and numerous open leads. 'It might have been 600 miles for all the chance we had of reaching it by sledging across the broken ice,' Shackleton wrote.

The prospect of reaching land was swept aside as the floe drifted slowly beyond Paulet Island. Shackleton hurriedly changed his plan and attention was turned to Elephant and Clarence Islands, two small dots of mountainous rock jutting from a vast ocean about 100 miles (160 km) to the north. It was not much of a lifeline and even less of a target. But after the nerve-shredding experience of drifting around 2,000 miles (3,200 km) on a disintegrating ice floe, all hands were ready to grasp at any prospect of standing on dry land. Hurley remarked that 'any terra firma that would alleviate our incessant anxiety of drift and insecurity would be welcomed'.

Tensions rose as the men sensed that delivery was at hand. All around the ice was breaking up and wider open leads were appearing, though the jumble of smaller floes created a heaving labyrinth that was impossible for navigation. It was now deep into autumn, temperatures were dropping and blubber was in short supply. Water tins filled with snow were tucked in their shirts at night to provide a drink in the morning and men slept with cans of dog food in their bags. After mixing with hot milk, the soft pasty substance was eagerly swallowed for breakfast. On 30 March the last of the dogs were shot and cut up for Green's pot.

Many leads of open water began to appear as March gave way to April and the slaughter of a huge leopard seal gave a welcome boost to provisions. Dozens of undigested fish found inside the beast's stomach were a welcome alternative to chunks of seal or penguin flesh. With breakout imminent, Shackleton advised the men to eat all they could. It might be some time before they enjoyed a full stomach again.

The far-off peaks of Clarence Island, some 70 miles (105 km) to the north, came into view on 6 April and Shackleton, now growing more restless and anxious by the day, faced the critical decision of finding the right moment to launch the boats. At one point the Patience Camp floe cracked apart in the heavy swells, cutting the boats off from the men. But the lead soon closed again and the vessels were eagerly reclaimed.

Shackleton was now improvising by the moment. The new goal was King George Island, a mountainous outpost of the South Shetlands chain to the west. From there it would be possible to island-hop among the archipelago to the more promising destination of Deception Island.

Deception Island, a small spot about 200 miles (320 km) away on the western fringes of the South Shetlands, is shaped like a horseshoe and boasts one of the safest harbours in Antarctic waters. It was a haven for the whaling fleet and held a known cache of emergency stores for shipwrecked mariners. It was also remotely possible that the last stragglers from the summer whaling season might pass by the island on their way back to South Georgia for the winter. Another tantalising feature was that Deception Island contained a small wooden church built for the whalers. Shackleton believed if they tore down the church, McNish could build a boat capable of sailing to South Georgia.

Open water could be seen in all directions on the morning of 9 April. Shackleton was on tenterhooks, watching the floes rising and falling in the heavy seas, bumping and scraping against each with devastating effect. Once more Patience Camp's floe split, leaving the men, boats and supplies with barely enough room to stand on. The decision of when to leave, in effect, had been taken out of Shackleton's hands.

Dudley Docker and *Stancomb Wills* were the first into the water. *James Caird*, the largest of the boats, was the last to leave and at about 2 p.m. the flotilla shoved off into treacherous seas, the men anxiously searching for any safe channels through the icy jungle.

The capricious floes of Ocean Camp and Patience Camp had given the men a tenuous grip on life in the six months since the abandonment of *Endurance*. But the lumpy ice, violent storms and unknown currents of the Weddell Sea threatened a new series of dangers. And there could be no turning back.

'I confess,' Shackleton wrote, 'that the burden of responsibility sat heavily on my shoulders.'

chapter 31

Into the Boats

Shackleton stood upright in the stern of the *James Caird* like a Viking chieftain sailing into battle as the improbable little armada pulled away from the floe. It was a powerful image, offering a reassuring focal point for the struggle ahead. There could be no doubt who was in command.

The pack ice, as though being shuffled by an unseen hand, was in perpetual motion as the heavily overloaded boats picked a path through the jigsaw of floes, anxious to avoid collisions but welcoming the protection the larger bergs provided against the battering winds. It was already deep into autumn, meaning darkness for almost 17 hours a day. In a fresh change of course, the new goal was either Clarence or Elephant Island, now about 60 miles (100 km) to the north. Everything depended on the wind direction.

The first threat came soon after leaving the floe when a combination of rough seas and gyrating bergs almost smashed the three vessels. Shackleton, pointing the way, survived his first challenge and led the path through the maze.

Progress was surprisingly good and the boats were only halted by darkness descending at around 5 p.m. The boats were unloaded and hauled onto a sizeable floe for the night, while the men, eager for rest, ate a hot meal and turned in, well satisfied.

But Shackleton could not rest, perhaps because things were going too well. Something about their position made him uneasy and at around 11 p.m. he left the tent to check conditions with the nightwatchman. As he walked along, the ice suddenly parted, opening a crack 4 feet (1.2 m) wide beneath one tent. Amid the frantic scramble and shouts of men, he saw a figure in a sleeping bag struggling in the water. Shackleton instantly bent down to grab the bag and hauled the man onto the floe. Seconds later the ice closed together with a resounding thud.

The lucky man was Ernie Holness, the Hull trawlerman. Holness did not have a change of clothes and would freeze to death in the low temperatures and raw winds. Shackleton ordered men to take turns marching the sailor up and down the ice throughout the night to prevent his wet clothes freezing like a suit of armour. Shackleton's inspired piece of improvisation was enough to save the life of Holness, though the sailor still complained that his tobacco had got wet.

The night's drama did not end with rescuing Holness. A small group, including Shackleton, were cut off from the main floe when the ice opened. Under Shackleton's supervision, the men leapt onto the larger floe. Shackleton waited until all hands were together again but then discovered that the floes had again drifted apart. For a brief moment, it looked as though he would be carried off into the darkness. But Wild quickly launched the *Wills* with half a dozen rowers and brought him to safety. 'For a moment, I felt that my piece of rocking floe was the loneliest place in the world,' Shackleton said.[1]

Shackleton's response to his own narrow escape was to reassure his men. Camping on the floe, he decided, was too risky and directed the tents to be taken down. As the men huddled together in the dark anxiously waiting for dawn, Shackleton ordered the blubber stove to be fired up and a round of steaming hot milk served.

Little things, as Shackleton instinctively understood, made a big difference to those struggling with isolation, fear and the cold. It was a similar care for detail that he showed when selecting the crew for the three boats, making sure to mix the experienced with the inexperienced.

Frank Worsley, a natural small-boat man, was given command of nine men and boxes of equipment squashed into the *Dudley Docker*, a heavy, oak-built cutter of just over 21 feet (6.6 m). He also took Greenstreet and the veterans Cheetham and McLeod, plus Orde Lees and Marston.

Hubert Hudson, the navigating officer, was initially given control of the *Stancomb Wills*, the smallest of the vessels, which carried eight men and assorted gear. For support he was given Crean, How and Bakewell, the stowaway Blackborow and the reliable doctor, McIlroy. But Hudson had struggled badly during months of confinement at Ocean Camp and Patience Camp and was also afflicted by a combination of frostbite and a painful boil on his backside. Within a short time, command of the *Wills* passed into the capable hands of Tom Crean.

The 11 men on board *James Caird* under Shackleton's command included robust seafarers like Wild, McNish, Vincent and McCarthy and the men Shackleton was less sure about: Clark, Wordie, Hussey and James. Also in the *Caird* was Hurley, a man Shackleton perhaps felt should be kept within arm's reach.

Loads were lightened next morning by dumping surplus equipment and tins of dried vegetables. After two hours' hard graft, under heavy bombardment from strong easterly winds, the boats emerged close to the edge of the pack. Raising the gunwales of the *Caird* and *Docker* had provided extra freeboard against the incoming seas but, by a cruel twist, it made rowing much more difficult.

The major consolation was that for the first time in 18 months, the men could feast their eyes on stretches of open water ahead and abandon the back-breaking rowing in favour of sails. The relief was short-lived. Moving into open water, free from the shelter of the ice, the vessels were more exposed to the swells. Seas rose and waves crashed over the sides as the heavily laden craft moved sluggishly along in the lumpy waters. Spray froze, covering both men and boats with a ghostly white coating of ice. Men hacked off chunks of accumulating ice and considered dumping more food to lift the boats higher in the water to avoid the threat of capsize.

The first encounter with open seas confirmed all the worst fears about the ability of the boats to cope with the Southern Ocean. The *Caird*, with two masts for a mizzensail and a small jib in the bow, was the best equipped. But the *Docker*, with a single lugsail, and the *Wills*, with a small mainsail and jib, were poorly endowed for the task. From the start, the *Caird* pulled ahead of the others and often had to wait for them to catch up.

Shackleton, fearing a panic, ordered a hasty retreat back into the shelter of the pack. He knew the men, without sleep for 36 hours, were desperate for rest and, against his better instincts, the boats were hauled up onto an old floe. But winds rose sharply during the night and after a fitful rest they were roused to find themselves surrounded by dangerous ice in all directions.

It was impossible to get back into the water in the turbulent seas and their floe was breaking up under the bombardment of constant collisions with other larger bergs. All they could do was wait and hope that the floe survived. Shackleton climbed to the highest point on the floe to observe the scene and the boats were made ready for a quick getaway.

By late afternoon a freak current shifted the floes and produced a large open lead. Shackleton ordered the boats back into the water without delay. In the commotion to get away both Shackleton and Wild almost plunged into the water when a chunk of floe gave way under their feet. Shackleton resolved never to make camp on the ice again.

The men rowed for dear life, straining every muscle to escape the encircling chunks of ice. As darkness fell Shackleton guided the boats to the lee of a larger iceberg. But after the near disaster the previous night, the men were forced to sleep in the boats.

The sight of open water to the south-west persuaded Shackleton to change direction, abandoning the push for Clarence or Elephant Island and instead turning back to King George Island. Beyond King George was the more hopeful objective of Deception Island, about 80 miles (130 km) to the south-west. Worried about the worsening condition of the men, Shackleton was anxious to make landfall as quickly as possible.

A fresh anxiety emerged when a school of killer whales surfaced around the boats. Some sensed the chorus of short, sharp hissing sounds from the beasts was a prelude to being tipped into the water. At 6 tons, a typical 25-foot long (7.5m) killer whale outweighed any of the boats and the men passed an anxious few hours in the company of the fearsome predators, often known as the wolves of the sea because they hunt in packs.

Shackleton was feeling the strain, though he did not let it show. No one could recall when he had last slept properly. When the boats tied up and the men clambered onto a floe for a hot drink, it was noticeable that Shackleton, Worsley and Crean remained on board, ever watchful for encroaching ice or menacing whales.

Shackleton's two preoccupations were the deteriorating condition of the men and the possibility the powerful currents would carry the flotilla away from the direction of Deception Island and sweep them northwards through the 80-mile (120 km) gap between Clarence and Elephant islands and King George Island. Once past the South Shetlands, the boats would be conveyed into the vast open expanses of the South Atlantic. 'I do not think I had ever quite so keenly felt the anxiety which belongs to leadership,' he said.

Among the boats, *Stancomb Wills* caused Shackleton the most concern. Despite the best efforts of Crean, the *Wills* struggled to keep up with the *Caird* and *Docker* and there were times when Shackleton doubted the little vessel would survive. Alone of the three boats, the gunwales of the *Wills* had not been raised and the small craft was dangerously overloaded with men and equipment. Men were often up to their knees in bitterly cold water and the only consolation was that, without raised gunwales, the *Wills* was a little easier to row.

The sudden appearance of the sun early on 12 April gave Worsley the chance to use the sextant to establish their position. The reading, as Worsley briefly recorded, was 'a terrible disappt'.

Despite three days of intense struggle and anxiety, the currents driving out of the Bransfield Strait were far stronger than expected and pushing the boats in the opposite direction to Deception Island. Worsley's reading placed the boats approximately 120 miles (190 km) east of King George Island and still about 60 miles (100 km) south of Clarence or Elephant Islands. They were no nearer land than when they started.

Shackleton did not allow the disappointment to show and with the wind foul for Elephant Island to the north, instead ordered a new course to be set for Hope Bay at the very apex of the Antarctic Peninsula. It was at Hope Bay, an area known to be rich in Adélie penguins, that some of Nordenskjöld's party had wintered. But it was a remote outpost some 140 miles (220 km) to the south and offered only a fleeting chance of sighting a passing whaler. Some called it Hopeless Bay.

Towards night the wind shifted to a strong south-westerly and with the boats tied together, the men endured another appalling night in the open. A tent canvas was stretched over the bodies for a little shelter but few managed any sleep in the damp, freezing conditions. Before turning in, Green somehow contrived to make a warming drink of hot milk. It was the last hot drink they had at sea.

An ethereal film of frost coated the men by dawn. Clothing, said Wild, was like a heavy suit of armour without joints. Most were affected by frostbite and cracked lips, beards were encrusted with ice and some nursed painful saltwater boils. The hollow, drawn faces mirrored the suffering. 'A cold, wet, rotten night,' Worsley wrote.

Breakfast, an unappetising hunk of frozen dog food, was chewed at the oars. To add to the persistent seasickness, many now fell foul of debilitating attacks of diarrhoea and could only relieve themselves by sitting on the gunwales and getting soaked in the process. Some were too sick to eat. Some wept in despair. 'Most of the men,' Shackleton wrote with much understatement, 'were now looking seriously worn and strained.' It was now a question of how much they could take.

Winds changed again and Shackleton, always quick to take advantage of anything in his favour, once more changed course. After a brief discussion with Worsley, the target of Hope Bay was dropped and the boats raised sail and turned for Elephant Island, some 100 miles (160 km) to the north.

Breaking into ice-free water brought a new problem. Helped by the strong winds, the boats had escaped the area of pack faster than expected and they had not found time to collect lumps of ice to melt for fresh water. Men struggling on the edge of survival now faced possible dehydration. Exacerbating their thirst was the increased loss of fluid through diarrhoea and the fact that the cold increases urine flow. To ease the thirst, men chewed slices of raw seal meat.

Entering into heavy swells of open water confirmed Shackleton's worst fears about the vulnerability of *Stancomb Wills*. The sails were too small to keep up and the strength of the rowers was fading fast. At least four of the eight men had virtually collapsed and rowing knee-deep in cold water had become a torturous ordeal. All their feet had turned deathly white.

At first Worsley in the *Docker* fixed a painter to *Wills*, but the *Caird* was better suited and Shackleton took control by attaching a line to the limping craft. Extra food was distributed to raise spirits.

More than ever, Shackleton's presence was the symbol of defiance. The familiar broad shoulders and square-set jaw was a visible demonstration of his determination to get the party to safety. Grasping a stay from the mizzenmast, Shackleton stood resolutely for hours at the rear of the *Caird*, confronting the rolling seas, biting cold and mounting exhaustion. Tormented men looking for inspiration or hope at their darkest hour needed to look no further than the *Caird*'s stern.

'He simply never spares himself if, by his individual toil, he can possibly benefit anyone else,' Orde Lees wrote. Wild said he looked after the men 'just as though they were babes in arms' and added: 'All mothers will understand what I mean.'

Shackleton was not immune to the severe wear and tear of the journey. He was more haggard than anyone could recall and his once strong voice had become husky. Orders had to be whispered and passed on by Wild or Hurley. On one occasion he snapped after a confrontation with the troublesome Vincent. Brushing past the seaman in the crowded *James Caird*, Shackleton felt a hard, round object in his breast pocket. He thrust his hand into Vincent's jacket to discover the gold watch thrown onto the ice months earlier. He snatched the watch from Vincent and hurled it into the sea, shouting: 'No, by God, you shall not have it.'[2]

Shackleton noted that it was the 'old timers' – Crean, Hurley, Wild and himself – who were coping best in the dire circumstances. 'Apparently we were acclimatised to ordinary Antarctic temperatures,' he reasoned. Wild, he noted, was 'unmoved by fatigue and unshaken by privation'. By contrast, Wild estimated at least half the party were 'insane ... simply helpless and hopeless.' Some had collapsed and McIlroy reported from the *Wills* that Blackborow's feet were severely frostbitten.

Dawn on 14 April, the sixth day at sea, produced the first hint that the ordeal was coming to an end. Between the scudding clouds and rolling waves it was possible to pick out the grim mountaintops of Clarence Island and Elephant Island, perhaps 40 miles (60 km) away. The islands were precisely where Worsley had calculated they would be.

Elephant Island, the larger of the pair, was chosen to make landfall because the coastline was thought to be more approachable. But treacherous, lumpy seas and driving snow squalls impeded progress throughout the day and all hopes of making landfall before night disappeared. Hampered by gale-force winds, the boats became separated in the darkness and were only reunited when Shackleton shone a compass light on the *Caird*'s sail to alert Worsley in the *Docker*.

Nightfall brought the gravest crisis since leaving the ice. 'The worst I have ever known,' said Wild. The storm hurled malevolence at the boats with unrelenting fury, soaking the men as they bailed frantically to avoid being swamped. Temperatures dropped sharply to -20° (-28 °C) and the men, still battling with thirst, found it impossible to swallow even a mouthful of cold dog food. Many were shivering uncontrollably after days without proper rest. The only moment of relief came from lighting their pipes for a smoke.

Worsley, who had been at the tiller in the same position for 18 hours, was so cramped that he had to be straightened out like a pocketknife being opened. Amid the tumult Orde Lees showed a fine touch of humanity by calmly reviving Greenstreet's frostbitten foot by placing the deathly cold appendage on his bare stomach.

Shackleton, desperately worried about losing the *Wills,* stayed awake all night on the *Caird* gripping the painter. The *Wills* would have disappeared into the windswept darkness had Shackleton let the painter slip from his grasp. At times the vessel disappeared completely behind a wall of black, rolling seas as men strained their eyes to catch a glimpse of the boat in the darkness. On board the *Caird*, Hurley remembered how, when all seemed lost, 'against the white spume would come, faint but cheering, Tom Crean's reassuring hail, "All well, sir".'

Dawn broke on 15 April to find the *Caird* and *Wills* close to the bleak perpendicular cliffs of Elephant Island and mercifully able to ease their thirst with lumps of ice which had broken away from a nearby glacier. But they had become separated from the *Docker*.

Following the coastline, the two boats passed the eastern end of the island and turned westwards to run along the menacing cliffs of the northern shore, greatly relieved to be passing under the lee of the land where the seas were noticeably calmer. It was possible to release the painter linking the *Wills* and *Caird*.

Shackleton's priority was to get ashore as fast as possible. Alongside him Wild's grisly judgement was that 'at least half the party' would have perished if they stayed another 12 hours in the boats. Shortly after passing

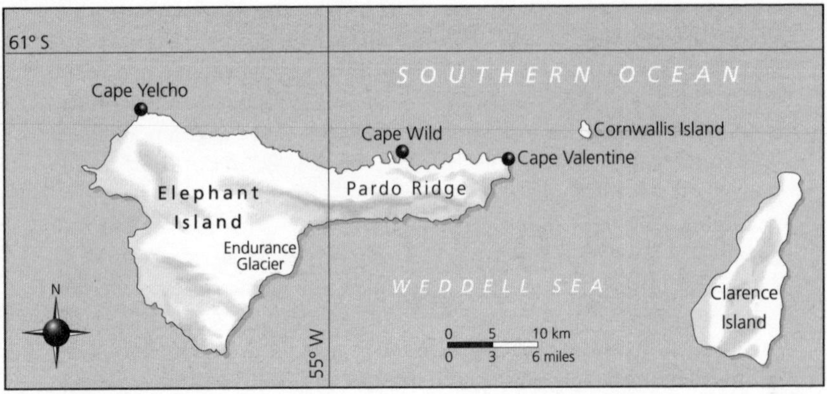

Elephant Island, the tiny refuge in the Southern Ocean reached by the crew of **Endurance** *in 1916.*

the island's eastern cape, a narrow beach was spotted, partly sheltered by an outlying fringe of rocks jutting from the sea. It was not ideal, but there was no time to delay.

As the smallest craft, the *Wills* was best suited to pilot through the unknown approaches to shore and Shackleton went aboard for the manoeuvre. As the boat was eased into position, the *Docker* suddenly came into view.

Rowing was painfully hard work for the exhausted men as Shackleton threaded the *Wills* through jagged rocks and narrow channels towards the beach. Catching the top of an incoming wave, the little boat was carried ashore and ground to a halt on the stony beach.

It was 497 days since anyone had last felt the ground beneath their feet. Against the odds, Shackleton's men had survived the loss of *Endurance*, months of captivity on drifting floes and escaped from the ice. And not a life had been lost.

chapter 32

A Dark Episode

The relief of standing on the terra firma of Elephant Island was in stark contrast to the events engulfing the Ross Sea party, the beleaguered men on the other side of the Antarctic continent waiting in vain for Shackleton's march into McMurdo Sound.

'Thank God I haven't killed one of my men,' Shackleton told Worsley moments after landing. Unknown to them one member of the Ross Sea depot-laying party was already dead and two more would perish within a matter of weeks. And that *Aurora*, after getting trapped by ice like *Endurance*, had spent 10 months at the mercy of the pack. *Aurora*, unlike *Endurance*, had survived.

The Ross Sea party was the darkest episode of Shackleton's Imperial Trans-Antarctic Expedition, a catastrophic combination of poor preparation, bad management and terrible misfortune. The seeds of disaster were sown in Shackleton's hurried and haphazard planning in England, though he could not have foreseen events that led to Mackintosh's party of 10 being marooned at McMurdo Sound.

Mackintosh had landed with the aim of placing tons of supplies along a chain of provision depots – at 80°, 81°, 82°, 83° and 83° 30′ – on a 400-mile (640 km) route across the Barrier from Hut Point to Mount Hope at the bottom of the Beardmore Glacier. It was a hugely ambitious target involving more than 1,000 miles (1,600 km) of sledge journeys with inadequate equipment and a group of mostly inexperienced men.

Without a charismatic and authoritative figure like Shackleton at the helm the party struggled to cope with the isolation of winter. This was partly because of Mackintosh's uneasy grasp of command and partly because of tension between the men. Joyce, the only man with experience of the ice, had little confidence in Mackintosh's leadership and after one clash

Joyce wrote: 'I have never in my experience come across such an idiot in charge of men.'

The commitment to Shackleton bore down on Mackintosh and he doubted it was possible to lay all the provisions intended. In a letter written to Shackleton before embarking on the sledge journeys, he wrote: 'I should not like to predict how far it can be carried out.'[1]

To meet the demanding schedule, Mackintosh began hauling equipment south on 1 September, the moment *Endurance* was in its death throes in the Weddell Sea. He began with nine men in teams of three at times dragging weights of over 200 lb (90 kg) a head. By now the party was down to only four dogs and the major burden of the task fell to man-hauling.

The main thrust to Mount Hope began on the first day of 1916 at the time Shackleton had abandoned the march west with the boats and was spinning out his days at Patience Camp. The bad luck that dogged the operation from the start surfaced soon after beginning and three men – Cope, Gaze and Jack – were sent back to Hut Point after the failure of a primus stove, which itself had been scavenged from Scott's hut at Cape Evans.

Further misfortune arrived as the remaining six men pressed south. Mackintosh was hobbling because of problems with his knee and Arnold Spencer-Smith, on his first expedition, was struggling to cope with the heavy labour of man-hauling. As the group neared Mount Hope, Spencer-Smith collapsed.

Spencer-Smith, who was suffering from exhaustion and the onset of scurvy, was left behind in a tent as the five others hauled the last miles to the slopes of Mount Hope, which they reached on 26 January. A 15-foot (4.5 m) cairn of snow was erected over the store. A sledge, discarded by Scott at the bottom of the Beardmore Glacier four years earlier, was used to mark the spot. Ernest Wild left a personal letter for his brother Frank, which he assumed would be collected when the transcontinental party descended the Beardmore. At Patience Camp floe on the same day, Shackleton signalled the formal end to his hopes of making the overland crossing when he ordered most of the dog teams to be shot. The two parties, over 2,000 miles (3,200 km) apart, would never be any closer.

The return over the Barrier from Mount Hope was a harrowing ordeal for Mackintosh's men. Rations were short, the daily marches long and, like Shackleton's 'furthest south' party in 1909, the body temperatures of the men dropped below the normal 98.4° (37 °C) in the bitter cold. Scurvy also took hold.

Spencer-Smith's condition deteriorated rapidly and he had to be carried on a sledge. Worse followed when Mackintosh was unable to pull and limped alongside the remaining men, Joyce, Richards, Hayward and Wild. The men frequently stopped to look back towards the south in hopes of seeing Shackleton emerge from the wilderness.

Battling through appalling weather, increasing hunger and the growing effects of scurvy, the group was finally pinned down by a storm that lasted 11 days. Spencer-Smith and Mackintosh, the two weakest, were passing blood and fuel had run out. It was cruelly reminiscent of Scott's last days bogged down by blizzards in the same area in 1912.

Leaving Wild to nurse the two invalids, Joyce, Hayward and Richards staggered to the next depot for food and returned to find that Mackintosh had sunk into despair. Fearing the end, he had written a series of farewell letters to his family. Soon after, Hayward, once a strapping figure, succumbed to scurvy and became the third passenger.

After struggling to within 30 miles (48 km) of Hut Point on 7 March, the strength of Joyce, Richards and Wild gave out. It was decided to leave Mackintosh behind while they pressed on to the old *Discovery* hut with the desperately ill Spencer-Smith and Hayward. In the early hours of 9 March, Spencer-Smith fell into a coma and died. The 32-year-old teacher, who was ordained a priest only five days before leaving London, died adjacent to White Island, the spot where 14 years earlier an exhilarated Shackleton had enjoyed his first taste of exploration.

After reaching Hut Point and resting for a few days, the three others left Hayward to recuperate and returned to Barrier where they found Mackintosh barely alive. Summoning up the last reserves of strength, the men eventually congregated in the old *Discovery* cabin at Hut Point on 15 March.

Helped by copious slices of freshly cooked seal steaks, the five survivors from the depot-laying party slowly regained their strength. But they remained cut off from base camp by miles of dangerously unstable sea ice between Hut Point and Cape Evans. The days passed slowly and conditions in the hut were shockingly bad. Apart from seal, the only available food was a few musty biscuits left over from *Discovery* 15 years before. Full winter darkness had descended by late April and for the following weeks, said Richards, they lived a life of 'primitive troglodytes'.

After seven weeks of monotony in the cramped squalor, a frustrated Mackintosh decided to risk a dash across the sea ice to Cape Evans. Despite Joyce's severe warnings, Mackintosh and Hayward left Hut Point in total darkness on 8 May. They were never seen again.

The deaths of Mackintosh, Hayward and Spencer-Smith inevitably overshadowed the extraordinary feats of the depot-laying party. Despite a catalogue of setbacks, the group managed to dump 4,000 lb (1,800 kg) of provisions for Shackleton and somehow travelled about 1,500 miles (2,400 km) back and forth across the Barrier in nearly six months of gruelling sledging. 'A task almost beyond human endurance,' said Joyce. It would prove to be the last great man-hauling expedition of the Heroic Age of Antarctic exploration.

For the men at Cape Evans, the tragic loss of three colleagues was assumed to be part of a far wider disaster to strike the whole expedition. They assumed that Shackleton's overland party had also perished, while the general belief was that *Aurora* had gone down somewhere in the Southern Ocean.

Shackleton's instructions to Mackintosh included a warning that the party should be considered 'unable to cross or dead' if they were not in sight of Hut Point by 20 March. On 7 April, two days before Shackleton manhandled his boats into the water from Patience Camp, Ernie Wild gave up scanning the horizon in search of his brother, now presumed dead. Hayward, who had only just survived the Barrier, said it would be 'nothing short of miraculous' for Shackleton to have completed the coast-to-coast trek.

The ordeal of *Aurora*, though less arduous than Shackleton's or Mackintosh's, provided a third dimension to the expedition's overall tale of woe. After being ripped from her moorings in May 1915, *Aurora* drifted slowly north, away from the continent and encased in the pack for some 1,600 miles (2,500 km). The ship came dangerously close to being crushed on several occasions and the rudder was smashed during the prolonged drift. *Aurora* somehow survived the ordeal and was released from the ice in March 1916. Escape came a few weeks before Shackleton launched his boats from Patience Camp and only days after the death of Spencer-Smith on the Barrier.

As *Aurora* broke into open water in late March, wireless operator Lionel Hooke was able to make contact with a New Zealand station. In the short stabbing taps of the Morse code transmitter, Hooke revealed news of *Aurora*'s drift and that Mackintosh was marooned at Cape Evans. It was the first word of the Imperial Trans-Antarctic Expedition in well over a year.

Hooke's message, understandably brief and limited in detail, posed more questions than answers. Most notably, the transmission carried no information about Shackleton's endeavours in the Weddell Sea. For all the outside world knew, Shackleton had completed the historic transcontinental crossing and was even now sitting contentedly in Scott's old hut at Cape Evans awaiting the fanfare of fame.

chapter 33

Bleak Refuge

Some men staggered around like drunks in the first few moments after landing on the rocky beach at Elephant Island, their legs unable to cope with land after 16 months at sea. Others sat shivering uncontrollably while some ran stones through their fingers as though needing reassurance that they were standing on solid ground. Some laughed uproariously, others sobbed silently into their hands.

Shackleton reported that at least 10 of the 28 men were 'off their heads' as the party stumbled ashore and assembled around the blubber stove for a vital hot drink. Some had to be carried from the boats and others were 'half crazy' according to Wordie. The worst casualties came from the *Docker* and *Wills*, including Hudson who had suffered some form of mental breakdown.

Even Shackleton looked gaunt and haggard. But amid the suffering, he was still able to conjure up a moment of touching compassion. As the *Wills* approached the beach, he decided that Blackborow, crippled by frostbitten toes, should be carried ashore and have the honour of being the first person to land on Elephant Island.

Crean was one of only two men from the *Wills* still standing and Wild, seemingly unaffected by the ordeal, came ashore with the ease of someone out for a casual stroll. Apart from Hurley, McCarthy, McNish and Vincent, few were capable of much. The normally equable Green released his pent-up emotions by launching a frenzied assault on basking seals, slaughtering 10 animals with an ice axe. Green, said Orde Lees, displayed 'all the primitive savagery of a child killing flies'.

Shackleton, taking Wild and Hurley, made a swift inspection of the rocky cove which lies at Cape Valentine on the narrow eastern shore of the island. It was no place to shelter. The cove was only 100 feet (30 m) wide and ran back from the waterline by little more than 50 feet (15 m). Clear

After a harrowing boat journey, exhausted men savour a hot drink on the desolate Elephant Island. (L–r) Orde Lees, Wordie, Clark, Rickinson, Greenstreet, How, Shackleton, Bakewell, Kerr, Wild.

marks on the cliff face showed that the spring tides swamped the area and there was little prospect of the men climbing higher up the cliff face in search of shelter. To confirm the worst fears, Orde Lees and Wordie, two men with climbing experience, somehow scrambled 300 feet (100 m) up the cliff, but found nothing remotely habitable. Wordie slipped and almost plunged to his death before concluding: 'In the neighbourhood of Cape Valentine there is no safe camping place.'[1]

Shackleton moved quickly, sending Wild west along the coastline to find a more suitable site for camp. Wild, taking Crean, Vincent, McCarthy and Marston, sailed the *Wills* to probe every indent in the coastline for a safe haven. After about 7 miles (11 km), a narrow rocky spit of land was seen where, despite the lateness of the season, ample numbers of seals and penguins were found. It was, said Wild, 'a paradise' compared with Cape Valentine.

Getting back into the boats was an appalling prospect for most but it was clear they could not linger at Cape Valentine. Pack was already mobilising out to sea and the fear of being trapped on the barren wedge of land outweighed all else. By 11 a.m. next morning the three boats were back in the water sailing west towards the 'paradise' found by Wild. In an effort to ease the burden, 10 cases of Beveridge's sledging rations were left behind to be recovered a little later. They never were.

Almost immediately, a gale struck from the south-west, leaving the rowers struggling heavily in the lumpy seas. All strength had been drained from their bodies by their exertions in the open sea and Shackleton was forced to seek protection in the lee of rocks. Rations were eaten cold.

Darkness was closing as the *Caird* and *Wills* reached their destination. It had taken six hours to travel just 7 miles along the coastline and the *Docker* had disappeared in the storm. Once again, the *Wills* went ashore first, followed by the *Caird*, although men had to stand waist deep in the incoming tide to unload the vessel before it could be run up the beach. Lewis Rickinson, the chief engineer, turned white and staggered in the surf after suffering a heart attack.

Fortunately, the *Docker* emerged from the squalls soon afterwards and by nightfall all hands, three vessels and most supplies and equipment were installed safely above the high-water mark. It was only a fragile hold on life.

Breaking light next morning revealed the bleak and inhospitable spit. Hurricane-force winds assailed the beach, flattening one tent and ripping another apart. Items of clothing and cooking pans simply disappeared. At times men could not stand upright under the onslaught. Shackleton named it Cape Wild, though most preferred Cape Bloody Wild.

Cape Wild was about 100 yards (91 m) long and 40 yards (36 m) wide, backed by a sheer cliff face about 1,000 feet (300 m) high. 'Like a courtyard of a prison,' said Hurley. Although there was no vegetation, the island offered unlimited fresh water from nearby glaciers and a seemingly generous number of elephant seals and Gentoo and Chinstrap penguins. But the price for a bountiful hunting ground was the all-pervasive, gut-wrenching stench of guano.

Elephant Island is no place to be marooned. The island, which is about 29 miles (47 km) in length and 16 miles (27 km) across at its widest point, is little more than a mountainous chunk of rock and glaciers protruding out from the Southern Ocean with an uninviting climate to match. It lies at the eastern end of the South Shetlands Islands where dense fogs are common and winds can screech to a damaging 100 mph (160 km/h). During winter months, Elephant Island is enveloped in pack ice. Port Stanley in the Falklands and Cape Horn at the tip of South America, both around 600 miles (960 km) from the island, were the nearest habitable landfall.

Elephant Island was also way off known shipping routes and without a radio it was impossible to signal for rescue. 'The world was as completely cut off from us as though we had come from another planet,' Worsley said.

The men's condition, even after landing at Cape Wild, was a cause of deep concern for Shackleton. Many were unable to work without being dragged from their bags and some appeared to have given up hope. An unforgiving Hurley reckoned a 'fair proportion' of the castaways would starve or freeze to death if left to their own devices. With an uncharitable swipe he dismissed the weakest as 'unworthy of gentlemen and British sailors'.

Shackleton was now faced with the most difficult decision of the entire expedition. All along he had maintained morale and commitment by persuading the men that salvation turned on sticking together. But now, with no hope of rescue possible and the condition of the men in serious decline, he was forced to split the party. The only realistic option was to leave the worst cases at Cape Wild and take a single boat through the Southern Ocean to fetch rescue. Sitting out the winter on Elephant Island ran against the grain for Shackleton and, in any event, he was concerned that some might not survive another long spell of captivity. Crossing the Drake Passage to the Falklands or Cape Horn was impossible, however. The small boats were incapable of beating against the powerful westerly winds and hard-driving currents. The only realistic option was South Georgia.

At roughly 800 miles (1,200 km), South Georgia was further than the Falklands or South America, but the island lies to the north-east and with skilful piloting it would be possible to take advantage of the prevailing westerlies to reach the island. The chances were slim and even Shackleton, resolutely optimistic, conceded: 'The perils of the proposed journey were extreme.'

Shackleton, in discussions with Wild and Worsley, recognised that speed was essential. The pack would probably close in by May, shutting off any chance of escape, while gales in the Drake Passage were known to be at their most tempestuous from that time onwards.

On 20 April, two days after setting up camp at Cape Wild, Shackleton called all hands together to announce that a party of six would take the *Caird* and try to reach South Georgia's whaling stations. It was a sombre occasion as the weary, bedraggled company considered Shackleton's audacious plan and pondered whether the castaways on the beach or the crew of the *Caird* faced the greater challenge. 'I'm afraid it's a forlorn hope,' he said, 'and I don't ask anyone to come who has not thoroughly weighed the chances.'

Some volunteered to sail, but others recoiled at the prospect of another long boat journey. Orde Lees was reluctant to chance his luck on the high seas while McIlroy and Macklin, the doctors, generously offered to remain behind to tend the weakened men, especially the crippled Blackborow. Examinations showed he needed an operation to remove his frostbitten toes and Shackleton briefly considered taking him on the *Caird*. But there was no room for a passenger in the Drake Passage and instead Shackleton chose the fittest and most capable men available.

Worsley, the most accomplished seaman and navigator, was the outstanding man to take command of the vessel. Worsley, assuming that Shackleton would remain behind to take charge of the 22 men left on Elephant Island, even volunteered for the task. But Shackleton's approach was to lead from the front. When Worsley volunteered, Shackleton clapped him on the shoulder and said: 'No, that's my job.'

Wild was another who stood out as a member of *Caird*'s crew. But Shackleton recognised the importance of leaving a strong-willed and dependable character to take control of those on Elephant Island. More importantly, it would require someone who commanded respect from all sides. Wild was such a man and he agreed to remain in charge of the castaways.

For the remaining four, Shackleton chose the fittest and best sailors to crew the *Caird*, regardless of previous issues. Significantly, the four men – Crean, McCarthy, McNish and Vincent – had performed outstandingly on the difficult journey to Elephant Island.

Wild had initially asked for Crean to remain on Elephant Island as his deputy. But Crean was an undiluted seaman and preferred to take his chances with the ocean. Crean, whose resolve in commanding the vulnerable *Wills* was widely admired, literally begged Shackleton for the chance to join the *Caird*. McCarthy, another Irishman, was among the best handlers of a small boat in the entire company and McNish, despite his tetchiness, was a robust character whose carpentry skills were invaluable. Although he was a bullying troublemaker, Vincent's 20 years at sea, including time spent on square-riggers, earned him a berth.

Much now depended on whether McNish could make the *Caird* more seaworthy for the Southern Ocean. No one else could match the shipwright's deft skills, particularly with the scarce resources available on Elephant Island, a barren outcrop of mountains, rocks and glaciers without a trace of vegetation. It was an ironic twist that McNish had gone from being threatened with execution to being indispensable.

McNish's determination to succeed was also fuelled by self-preservation. He volunteered for the *Caird* because he saw little hope for the men staying at Cape Wild. 'I don't think there will be many survivors if they have to put in a winter here,' he wrote.

The only timber at his disposal was what the party carried onto the beach. They could find no driftwood. All McNish could lay his hands on were the lids of a few packing cases, four sledge runners and a bolt of canvas. On the floe, McNish had stripped timbers from the stricken *Endurance* to raise the gunwales of the *Caird* and *Docker* and he now cannibalised the *Docker* to increase the *Caird*'s sides by a precious 10 inches (25 cm). In the absence of enough wood to make a deck covering, he improvised with sledge runners and a stretch of canvas. Nails were plucked from old Venesta food cases and gaps in the frame were caulked by an unlikely concoction of Marston's oil paints, strands of lamp wick and seal's blood. To prevent the craft buckling in high seas, the mast from the *Wills* was jammed along the keel from bow to stern.

Conditions could hardly have been worse as the men toiled to make the *Caird* ready in freezing temperatures and high winds. The frozen canvas was held over the blubber stove until each yard became workable and men took turns to hunch over the decking to sew lengths of fabric with cold, brittle needles that had to be pulled through with pliers. Only full-blown blizzards stopped the work.

Shackleton's anxiety, which he had successfully concealed for months, was now plain to see. A line of pack ice was forming on the horizon and the risk of the escape route being closed off grew with every day. Another anxiety was Shackleton's niggling fear that he might be accused of abandoning his men by dividing the party. Even if the *Caird* managed to reach South Georgia, the encroaching pack meant it might be months before a relief ship returned and he was haunted by the fear that some men would not survive a long confinement on the desolate beach. Worsley understood Shackleton's concern and tried to reassure him by declaring: 'Nobody who knew you would ever say, or think, that.' According to Worsley, Shackleton was not reassured.[2]

The weather on 24 April was fine and, with McNish's handiwork complete, Shackleton could wait no longer. The *Caird* was taken 100 yards (90 m) offshore and, using the *Wills* as a tender, the vessel was loaded with ballast and supplies. To Worsley's experienced eye, Shackleton had made a serious mistake placing too much ballast in the bowels of the *Caird*. Using old blankets, Shackleton had ordered around a ton of rocks and shingle to be bagged up and loaded onto the vessel. Worsley urged him to dump at least half the ballast, fearing the vessel would sit too low in the water and move awkwardly through the waves. Shackleton refused to budge, but later, as the *Caird* lumbered uneasily and shipped vast quantities of water, Shackleton did acknowledge that Worsley was correct.

At least the *James Caird* was fairly well provisioned, taking enough food to last six men a month. In addition, they took lumps of ice for cooking and two caskets of drinking water. Besides sea charts, the craft also carried a sextant, prismatic compass and binoculars. They also carried sleeping bags, a primus stove, matches and a rifle.

By contrast, the men were hopelessly under-equipped for a long open-boat journey. Sea boots and oilskins, the basic outfit for sailors, had long since disappeared. Each man wore a layer of heavy woollen underwear, two pairs of socks, a pair of trousers and a sweater. They wore two pairs of gloves and boots made from reindeer skin. A loose Burberry outer garment and helmet was worn on top, though neither was waterproof. The crew of the *James Caird* were dressed for sledging, not the sea.

The departure began badly and then deteriorated. McNish and Vincent fell overboard while loading the *Caird* and, without the luxury of a change of clothes, both had to return to shore in search of men prepared to swap a wet outfit for dry clothing. Next it was discovered a plug had been dislodged and that the *Caird* was leaking badly. What no one spotted was that the *Caird* struck a rock during the process, breaking open a water casket and tainting the contents.

Shackleton spent his final moments on shore pacing around the weather-beaten spit offering a brisk handshake and a few words of encouragement to the men. The burden of responsibility for the lives of the 22 men weighed heavily on Shackleton's shoulders. He told Worsley at one point: 'Skipper, if anything happens to me while those fellows are waiting for me, I shall feel like a murderer.'[3]

Shackleton smoked a last cigarette with Wild and ran through the only realistic option if the *Caird* was lost in the Southern Ocean. If no ship returned by the spring, Wild should attempt to reach Deception Island in the *Docker*. This was a prospect even less promising than sailing the *James Caird* to South Georgia. It was over 200 miles (320 km) to Deception Island and the *Docker*, which had no proper mast and was down to just five working oars, would have to beat against the strong prevailing winds and currents that had caused so much grief in the escape from Patience Camp. 'I have every confidence in you and always have had,' he told Wild.

Launching the James Caird *before the epic open-boat voyage to South Georgia, Easter Monday, 24 April 1916.*

In the brief pause before leaving, Shackleton also took time to tie up a few loose ends of business. He asked Wild, Orde Lees and Hurley to fulfil the book-writing contract if he was lost and for Wild and Hurley to undertake lecture tours in Europe and America. In a separate note he invested all responsibility for exploiting the expedition's photographs and moving footage in the hands of Hurley.

Surprisingly, there was no personal message for Emily or his family. In the note left with Wild he ended with a stiff-sounding parting, which said: 'You can convey my love to my people and say I tried my best.'

The forlorn gathering of men on the beach at Cape Wild cut a pathetic sight as the *Caird*'s jib sail was hoisted and the vessel turned into the breakers. A few lusty cheers were easily swallowed by the strident wind. Some were in tears. 'She is our only hope,' Wordie wrote.

Shackleton could be seen waving hopefully before the *Caird* disappeared behind a wall of heaving dark grey seas. It was around 12.30 p.m. on 24 April, which happened to be Easter Monday, 1916. In Shackleton's country of birth on the same day, Irish republicans launched the Easter Rising against centuries of British rule.

Ahead lay 800 miles (1,200 km) of the most hostile waters on earth. The *Caird*, constructed to Worsley's specifications, was more lightly built than regulations required, making the vessel more 'springy and buoyant' than most. Perhaps this influenced Shackleton's decision to be liberal with ballast. At 22 feet 6 inches (7 m) long, the *Caird* was little more than 7 feet across (2 m) and offered a freeboard of just 2 feet (0.7 m) against the mountainous swells of the Southern Ocean. It was this flimsy protection that most worried Worsley.

Soon after sailing, Shackleton made an astonishing admission. Turning to Worsley, he remarked casually: 'Do you know, I know nothing about sailing?' Worsley laughed either at the misplaced joke or the poor timing of the confession, replying: 'All right, Boss, I do.' Shackleton was not joking. Looking squarely at Worsley, he insisted: 'I'm telling you, I don't.'[4]

chapter 34

Scattered to the Winds

Shackleton's dream, the Imperial Trans-Antarctic Expedition, was in disarray and scattered to the winds by the middle of 1916. Men were dead, survivors were separated across the continent and clinging to life, *Endurance* lay in pieces at the bottom of the Weddell Sea and the *James Caird* was embarking on a seemingly hopeless rescue mission. What began as the 'last great polar journey' was now a fight for life.

On Elephant Island, Wild's first priority was to arrange a permanent shelter against the ferocious winds. After trying unsuccessfully to dig a cave from a nearby snow slope, the men assembled a makeshift hut by turning the *Docker* and *Wills* upside down on top of a few flat stones and stretching canvas over the gaps. Measuring 16 feet x 10 feet (approximately 5 m x 3 m), it was a hideously cramped living space for 22 men. Using the boats as shelter meant the 10 cases of sledging rations left at Cape Valentine could not be recovered. Survival depended largely on finding seals and penguins until Shackleton returned.

It was anybody's guess if Shackleton would come back. By any realistic measure, the chances of successfully navigating an open boat through the Southern Ocean in midwinter were faint. The nearest comparison was Captain William Bligh's open-boat journey following the mutiny on *Bounty* in 1789. In an extraordinary feat of seamanship, Bligh navigated a 23-foot (7 m) open boat containing 19 men for over 4,000 miles (6,700 km) on a 47-day voyage to Timor in the East Indies, but the more temperate waters of the Pacific's south-western region could hardly be compared with the violent seas of the Southern Ocean.

Shackleton's best hope was that the *Caird* would reach South Georgia and return with a relief ship within a month. It was impossible to gauge whether this was meant to reassure those at Cape Wild or whether Shackleton truly believed this was feasible.

Either way, his optimism rubbed off on some. 'Should all go well,' said Wordie, 'we expect relief in a month's time.' Hurley had full confidence in the 'six proven veterans, seasoned by the salt & experience of the sea' who he believed would reach South Georgia in just 14 days. 'How we shall count the days,' he added.

Others were less convinced and sensed that, quite apart from the perils of the Southern Ocean, the growing pack ice of winter would block any chances of getting back to Elephant Island for months. Shortly before the sun set on 24 April, Wild caught his last glimpse of the *Caird* through binoculars before the boat disappeared into the maw of the pack ice to the north. The boat, he said, looked 'pathetic.'

Orde Lees was among those not expecting Shackleton to make a quick return. 'What with the difficulty of getting a [relief] ship,' he told his diary, 'I don't expect he will be able to relieve us much before next spring, say September.'

Uncertainty also gripped the men on the other side of the continent at McMurdo Sound. The original party of 10 had splintered into three groups, the fate of Mackintosh and Hayward was unknown and no one knew if *Aurora* had survived. Since there was no sign of Shackleton, it was assumed the overland party had perished on the crossing.

Conditions for Joyce, Richards and Wild in the small *Discovery* cabin at Hut Point were primitive. No food had been stored there, seals were scarce and, without fresh blubber for the stove, meals were eaten cold. The men spent most days in their sleeping bags.

Joyce, Richards and Wild waited until mid-July before they considered the ice strong enough for the crossing to Cape Evans where four expedition members – Cope, Gaze, Jack and Stevens – were camped. Hoping to take advantage of a full moon, the three men moved tentatively across the sea ice and were astonished when the moonlight was suddenly blotted out by a rare lunar eclipse. At Cape Evans they discovered that Mackintosh and Hayward had never arrived while Cope was suffering mental problems and Stevens was struggling to deal with the isolation. Soon after arriving, Richards complained of heart problems.

The regrouped party of seven now faced a wait of at least six months to learn whether *Aurora* had survived to reach New Zealand and if a relief ship was coming to pick them up. Joyce, now in command, calculated there were sufficient rations – including Shackleton's stockpile at Cape Royds – for 18 months to go alongside any wildlife they could muster in the spring. All they could do was wait.

The only news of the expedition brought back by *Aurora* was that 10 men were stranded at Cape Evans. There was no sign of Shackleton. Nor had *Endurance* reappeared in South America. Joseph Stenhouse, *Aurora*'s captain, launched an immediate call for funds to mount a rescue operation for the Ross Sea party. But nothing was straightforward in the affairs of the Imperial Trans-Antarctic Expedition.

Cables flew back and forth between New Zealand, with Frederick White, the expedition's secretary in London, pleading for money to refit *Aurora* for a relief voyage. At around the time Shackleton's boats were leaving the Patience Camp floe, White finally admitted the truth. 'No news Endurance,' he reported. 'Unable send sum required as no funds available.' White advised Stenhouse to seek free facilities for the ship and drum up support where he could find it.[1]

In fact, he did manage to obtain £500 (about £20,000/€24,000 today) but it was clearly inadequate and Stenhouse was left to his own initiative to raise the funds. A realistic assessment for refitting, provisioning and staffing *Aurora* was around £20,000 – more than six times what Shackleton had paid for the vessel.

The brutal truth was that the expedition was penniless. Nor did newspaper accounts of lost explorers count for much with the general public, who were reeling under the weight of shocking news bulletins and the mounting casualty lists of war. *Aurora* had returned to civilisation shortly after the end of the calamitous Gallipoli campaign. For the first time in history Britain had introduced full-scale conscription in a prelude to the slaughter on the Somme.

In London the Royal Geographical Society, the usual port of call for distressed explorers, had virtually washed its hands of Shackleton. A meeting of the RGS Council in April refused to offer financial assistance or accept any responsibility beyond dispensing advice to any private relief expedition. Douglas Freshfield, the well-known mountaineer and RGS President, insisted the 'speculative syndicate' running Shackleton's affairs should find the money.

However, the syndicate did not exist in any meaningful sense. In the muddle Shackleton left behind in 1914, the ITAE had no spare funds, bills were left unpaid and barely any arrangements had been made to deal with emergencies. Sir James Caird, the expedition's main sponsor, had died a month before Shackleton left Patience Camp and the rump of contributors was an assorted group of personal friends or supporters like Janet Stancomb-Wills and Elizabeth Dawson-Lambton whose resources were limited.

No one appeared to be in charge in London and events took an odd turn in late April when White mysteriously disappeared. Shackleton's official business was now in the hands of a man called Alfred Hutchison at the London firm of Hutchison & Cuff. Before sailing, Shackleton had decided to stop using the services of Emily's brother at Kingsford, Dorman. Also involved was Ernest Perris, whose *Daily Chronicle* owned the exclusive contract to publish Shackleton's story and had a vested interest in keeping track of events. Beyond that nothing was clear.

One of Perris's executives also raised the sensitive issue of raiding the large memorial fund set up after the Scott tragedy to meet some of Shackleton's commitments to ITAE members during his absence. Robert Donald from the *Daily Chronicle* wrote to Reginald McKenna, the Chancellor of the Exchequer, claiming that £10,000 of the £75,000 (over £4 million/€4.8 million today) raised by the Mansion House Fund for the dependants of the five dead explorers remained undistributed. 'It might be possible to devote some of this money to the maintenance of those left behind by the members of the Shackleton expedition,' he said. McKenna offered no sympathy and also dismissed the prospect of the government paying Shackleton's debts. He told Donald: 'I do not think that the Treasury could agree to your proposal that the state should give financial assistance to the dependants of the Shackleton Expedition.'[2]

These were troubled moments for Emily as she struggled with not knowing. At best her husband was marooned in the ice and at worst he had long since died. Among Shackleton's final letters written from South Georgia in December 1914 before disappearing into the ice was the unhappy note complaining about *Endurance* and worrying about the dependability of Worsley. This and the uncertainty were all she had to go on.

Any rescue for the ITAE, like the expedition itself, would have to be a costly two-pronged undertaking. Searching the Weddell Sea meant penetrating the same waters that had swallowed *Endurance,* and another ship, presumably *Aurora*, was needed to find the castaways at McMurdo Sound.

John King Davis, a veteran of *Nimrod* and Mawson's Australian expedition, happened to be in London at the time and gave Freshfield his frank assessment of the situation. By chance, the two men met on Shackleton's first full day on the voyage to Elephant Island. To Davis it was clear that *Endurance* had been lost in the Weddell Sea. By implication, Shackleton was also lost.

While Freshfield was anxious to keep the RGS out of Shackleton's affairs, he accepted that something had to be done. He turned to Davis, urging him to lead the Weddell Sea relief. Davis accepted on condition that he was given sole charge of the relief.

Tall and gaunt-looking, Davis had the demeanour of a man weathered by a life of unending crises. He was popularly known as 'Gloomy Davis' and had a reputation as a taciturn, firm disciplinarian with a streak of arrogance. But he was probably the finest ice pilot on the high seas and a skilled mariner who placed the safety of his ship above all else. 'One sleeps better for his presence,' a shipmate said of Davis.

Davis was a down-to-earth character whose reservations about Shackleton centred on the peculiar way he attracted his oddball friends and itinerant adventurers to the serious business of exploration. To Davis the essence of exploration lay in finding a team of tough, experienced and capable men. Like his friend Mawson, he felt Shackleton was more adventurer than serious explorer. As he prepared to go in search of Shackleton he told Freshfield that *Endurance* was full of people 'without any qualification or knowledge' who had merely signed up for the escapade.

Raising money to fund the two relief missions was a huge challenge and carried an uncomfortable reminder of the messy affair in relieving Shackleton at Cape Royds in 1909. Emily appealed to the Prime Minister Herbert Asquith and the Australian High Commissioner in London. Perris went further by telling MPs the government was partly to blame for Shackleton's plight.

'The Government have some responsibility in this matter,' a senior executive of Perris's *Daily Chronicle* wrote on 11 May, 'because without their advice Shackleton would never have started.'[3]

A working committee was formed at the Admiralty under the chairmanship of naval grandee Sir Lewis Beaumont, which also included Mawson and Darwin from the RGS. Among those also eager to assist were Adams and England from *Nimrod*, Lieutenant Evans and Cherry-Garrard from Scott's last expedition and Shackleton's old friend, Bruce. 'I do not quite like the look of things as a whole,' Bruce wrote when *Aurora* first reappeared from the ice. Bruce knew the Weddell Sea and in other circumstances, of course, he might have been the one seeking relief.

In the event, the committee agreed to purchase either *Discovery* or *Terra Nova* for a voyage through the Weddell Sea in search of Shackleton somewhere along the coast around Vahsel Bay. On the other side of the world, Stenhouse was still anxiously searching for funds to send *Aurora* to McMurdo Sound.

On Elephant Island, Wild faced the first real test of his leadership at the same moment as the relief expeditions began to take shape. Soon after the

Caird sailed from the island, it was discovered that cuts of meat and some biscuits had been pilfered from the store of provisions. Fearing a potentially disastrous breakdown in discipline, Wild assembled all hands and in an echo of Shackleton's determined leadership calmly declared that he would shoot any man caught stealing food. Food was not stolen again.

chapter 35

Epic Journey

The 'ordeal by water', as Worsley called it, began in sunshine and a brisk breeze. As the small boat pulled away, the snowy peaks, towering cliffs and glacial slopes of Elephant Island provided a majestic panorama from the stern of the small craft and a scattering of seals and penguins in the water was a reassuring hint that the men left behind would not go hungry.

The *James Caird* made a creditable 3 knots towards the line of pack ice in the distance, though Shackleton did not allow the optimistic start to obscure the very severe difficulties that lay in wait in the Southern Ocean. Shouting above the roar of the seas, Shackleton told Worsley: 'We've had some great adventures together, Skipper, but this is the greatest of all. This time it really is do or die, as they say in the story-books.'[1]

The pack, which had glowered menacingly offshore in the days before sailing, was the first major obstacle. To minimise the risk of collision, the men frequently took to the oars and towards nightfall, after strenuous efforts, the *Caird* nosed out of the pack. Entering open water, the boat was met by very strong swells and waves breaking over the sides. Worsley's fear that the *Caird* sat too low in the water was well placed. It also meant they would be wet for long periods during the journey.

The plan was to take the *Caird* northwards for a time, away from the general direction of South Georgia, to escape the immediate area of pack. Once beyond the pack, it would be possible to pick up the prevailing strong westerly winds and alter course for South Georgia.

The task proved far harder than anyone imagined. First they were halted by a strong northerly gale, which threatened to drive the craft back into the ice. When the gale abated they found themselves in an area of dangerous cross seas where currents came from different directions and the boat was tossed around violently. In the words of Worsley, the cross seas found the *Caird*'s 'weak spots' and only he and McCarthy escaped being sick in the rolling, pitching seas.

On the third day out, the *Caird* had travelled far enough from the pack to change course for South Georgia and, with more favourable winds at their back, the boat made over 80 miles (130 km). An observation by Worsley placed the vessel about 145 miles (225 km) from Elephant Island.

The *Caird* had now entered the fearsome Drake Passage, the 500 mile (800 km) wide bottleneck channel between Antarctic mainland and Cape Horn, widely regarded as the most dangerous waters on earth. It is an area of powerful westerly winds where waves, the infamous Cape Horn Rollers, frequently climb to over 40 feet (13 m) or more. Worsley called them 'blue water hills' and these walls of solid water, unchecked by land in any direction, are propelled along at up to 25 mph, occasionally faster. Rogue waves at times are known to reach a height of 100 feet (30 m).

By now Shackleton had established a fixed routine, ever mindful that ships perform best to order. Four-hour sea watches were set, with Shackleton, Crean and McNish taking one and Worsley, McCarthy and Vincent the other. One man took the helm as the other two trimmed sails or pumped out the constant deluge of water with a makeshift pump cobbled together by Hurley. Sleep was vital, but desperately difficult to manage. In the tiny space of 7 feet by 5 feet (2 m x 1.7 m) three muscular, soaking wet and cold seamen were jammed together on top of food cases, bags of shingle and lumps of rocks in search of a crucial few hours' rest. 'Indescribably uncomfortable' said Worsley.

Experience on *Discovery* and *Nimrod* had demonstrated that regular hot drinks and solid food were essential to those under great strain and Shackleton knew how important it was to instil new life into tired bodies. If he saw someone struggling he ordered hot drinks all around, anxious not to isolate out any individual as a passenger.

The main item of food was the Beveridge sledging ration, which consisted of a compressed dark brown lump of beef protein, lard, oatmeal, sugar and salt, eaten with clockwork precision every four hours. It was followed by a nutty nougat-like food with a few biscuits and hot tea. It was noticeable how they all learned to swallow drinks at scalding temperatures.

Crean was the regular cook and soon devised his own method of preparation. Deploying Worsley as scullion, the pair sat facing each other, bent almost double in the cramped confines below the canvas decking, with the primus stove jammed between their feet to prevent the contents spilling over. While Worsley held the pot steady in one hand, Crean broke off lumps of ice and brought the rations to the boil. A ring of aluminium mugs eagerly formed around the pot and Crean dutifully poured out the thick porridge-like mixture, ensuring that each cup was filled to the same mark. To add to the scars of frostbite, Crean and Worsley's hands were soon marked with burns from the stove.

The men were constantly wet from waves lashing over the sides of the *Caird* and it was impossible to keep warm. The damp, penetrating cold of the ocean was different from the dry icy chill of the Weddell Sea's pack ice or the lacerating bitterness of the windy Polar Plateau.

Numbed by the cold, wet conditions, the men discovered their feet had turned a ghostly white and lost all feeling. On one occasion a man removed his socks and did not notice when a pin was stuck into his numbed big toe. Further jabs followed, but he felt nothing until the pin was stuck into his leg just below the knee.

A severe south-westerly gale forced the *Caird* to heave to on the fourth day and for a time the craft was in danger of turning sideways to the rolling seas and being swamped. Next day the gale intensified from the south, blown from the Antarctic mainland itself and driving down temperatures to near freezing.

In the raging storm, the mainsail was lowered and an improvised sea anchor put out. Although the anchor, a triangular bag attached to the painter, kept the boat's nose dead ahead, the vessel continued to ship huge quantities of water. Spray froze against the canvas covering, dusting the deck with a layer of ice. 'A thousand times it seemed as if the *James Caird* must be engulfed,' Shackleton wrote, 'but the boat lived.'[2]

The layer of ice was initially welcomed because it contrived to make a shield against the relentless waves washing over the sides. But at night, as temperatures plunged below freezing, the *Caird*'s movements became noticeably sluggish and an alarmed Shackleton clambered forward in the dark to see why the vessel was labouring so badly. What he found was a heavy sheet of ice accumulating across the canvas decking. The *Caird*, weighed down by the extra weight, was dangerously low in the water. *James Caird*, said Shackleton, was 'more like a log than a boat' and at risk of capsizing.

To counter the threatening 15 inch (38 cm) thick coating of ice, the men were forced to crawl along the slippery canvas decking in the rolling seas and chip off the ice with an axe. Despite being almost paralysed by a mixture of cold and fear, each man took turns to inch along the decking. The limit of endurance was barely four minutes. It needed two hours of cold, arduous work in pitch darkness to hack away at the ice and when the last man crawled back to safety Shackleton brewed a hot drink.

It was, said Worsley, as though Shackleton had his 'fingers on our pulse'. Shackleton's inspiration, he added, was that even if things got worse, 'he would devise some means of easing their hardships'. To the hardened sailors, said Worsley, there was an almost feminine touch about how he cared for each man.

Ice formed again after daybreak and twice more the men were forced to crawl forward to break off the ice. Shackleton noticed that the oars, which were lashed to the sides of the boat when not in use, were acting like magnets to the ice. Despite the risk, he took the brave decision to throw all but two oars over the side.

By the seventh day the wind had relented and the sun poked through odd breaks in the clouds. Seas were no longer breaking over the craft with the same ferocity and for a brief moment there was an air of relaxation on board the *Caird*. Sleeping bags were laid out to dry and the men seized the opportunity to dry sodden footwear and clothes. 'Able to reduce some parts of our clothing from wet to damp,' Worsley's log recorded.

Overhead they saw an albatross, like the *Caird*, another isolated wanderer in the vastness of the Southern Ocean. Or was the albatross, awkward on land but graceful and commanding at sea, a symbol for Shackleton himself?

The sun's appearance gave Worsley another opportunity to fix their position. It was a complicated manoeuvre in lumpy seas that involved the efforts of four men. While Vincent and McCarthy held him tightly around the waist, Worsley took aim at the sun with his sextant and Shackleton crouched beneath the canvas with chronometer, pencil and the sodden navigation book. When the sun was obscured by the weather, Worsley estimated the direction and plotted a course by dead reckoning or at times simply used the direction of the wind as a guide. On clear nights he fell back on the ancient method of steering by the stars.

Accuracy, as Worsley understood, was vital since the *Caird* had only one opportunity to find South Georgia on the broad expanse of the Southern Ocean. If they missed the island at the first attempt, the boat would be carried into the interminable waters of the South Atlantic, somewhere between South America and Africa, with no prospect of beating back against the winds and currents.

Worsley's 'fix' put the *Caird* at 56° 13' S, 45° 38' W, which was about 500 miles (800 km) from Elephant Island and more than halfway to South Georgia. It was another moment of optimism.

Shackleton happened to be at the tiller when the Southern Ocean struck back. At around midnight on 5 May he noticed a clear line of sky to the south-south-west and called out below that the clouds were lifting. After a brief moment Shackleton realised the foaming white line was a tidal wave approaching the craft at high speed. 'It was a mighty upheaval of the ocean,' he wrote.

As he shouted for the men to hold on, the *Caird* was struck by the massive wave, which hurled the boat around like a toy. Miraculously, the boat survived the assault, though it was half-filled with water and dangerously low in the water. As Shackleton held the vessel up to the wind, the others grabbed anything they could lay their hands on and bailed frantically. After what seemed an age, the *Caird* slowly began to rise in the water.

It was thought the tidal wave was caused by an iceberg calving from the Antarctic mainland but as Shackleton recalled: 'During twenty-six years' experience of the ocean in all its moods I have never seen a wave so gigantic.'

Gales continued next day, but the *Caird* was getting nearer to the goal. A fresh sighting put them just over 100 miles (160 km) from South Georgia, suggesting they would reach land within two days. It could not come soon enough for the men. Vincent, once considered the strong man of the outfit, had broken down and had ceased to be an active member of the crew, while McNish was struggling badly from the effects of prolonged exposure. McCarthy, though weakening, remained cheerfully optimistic throughout. All were constantly wet and suffering from raw and bleeding sores, saltwater boils and frostbite.

Shackleton was also suffering. He was struck by acute pain from sciatica, though he tried to keep all signs of discomfort hidden. Showing any sign of weakness, he appeared to be saying, might damage the essential belief that they would survive the ordeal. A curious Worsley noticed that the pain seemed to ease as the *Caird* neared South Georgia. But he could not fathom whether Shackleton's condition had improved or whether he was more successful at disguising it. 'I have never been quite sure which,' he added.

It was Worsley and Crean who seemed to cope best with the exhaustion and constant soakings. Worsley appeared almost at ease with the turbulent conditions and was composed and proficient in everything. It was as though he relished the chance to test his seamanship in the most challenging waters on earth.

Crean was unbreakable, standing imperturbably against everything the violent forces of nature hurled at him. Almost oblivious to the roaring winds and crashing waves, he could be seen at the tiller puffing on his pipe and singing songs in the Irish language that passed unrecognised by his shipmates. Tryggve Gran, a member of Scott's expedition, once characterised Crean as a man who 'wouldn't have cared if he'd got to the Pole and God Almighty was standing there, or the Devil. He called himself the Wild Man of Borneo and he was.'[3]

In the wild seas of the Southern Ocean the fate of the *James Caird* now rested on the three contrasting characters: Crean, the indestructible Irishman, Worsley, the light-hearted New Zealander with a touch of navigational genius and Shackleton, the Anglo-Irish dreamer, adventurer and peerless leader of men.

Thirst became the latest problem when it was discovered that seawater had seeped into the last water cask. What remained was brackish and Shackleton ordered the daily supply to be cut to half a pint each. Even the drinks of hot milk became fewer. 'Thirst took possession of us,' he wrote. Fearing that a change in wind direction might blow the *Caird* off course and drive them out to sea without water, Shackleton reverted to his role as 'Cautious Jack'. The water rationing was strictly imposed, even when some begged for a drink.

The morning of 8 May broke with squalls and heavy seas as the *Caird* edged closer to the island. Someone spotted lumps of floating kelp, a sure sign of land. Two shags, which Worsley said never flew more than 15 miles (24 km) from land, were observed perched on a piece of kelp.

All eyes peered into the grey distance, desperate for a glimpse of land between the scudding clouds and rolling seas. At around 12.30, McCarthy yelled 'land ho!' and almost dead ahead the bleak, forbidding cliffs of South Georgia appeared briefly between a break in the skies. It was Cape Demidov, near King Haakon Bay on the southern shores of the island.

Worsley's navigation had been impeccably correct. The cheerful grins confirmed that, against unimaginable odds and hardship, the *James Caird* had done it. However, Worsley's skills were now more important than ever. Initially the aim was to sail around the west coast of the island before running along the northern shores to one of the whaling stations in Stromness Bay. But Shackleton was concerned about the fitness of Vincent and McNish and was anxious to land as fast as possible.

The other concern was that Worsley had sensibly left a 10-mile (16 km) margin of navigational error in his course plotting and, in the poor visibility, Shackleton was not prepared to risk missing the island altogether. Plunging into the wide open spaces of the South Atlantic without hope of retreat was as fearful a prospect as the Southern Ocean itself.

The clock was against them. The afternoon light was fading as the boat approached the craggy, broken shoreline and soaring cliff faces of South Georgia. King Haakon Bay, a long, angular inlet on the island's south-west corner, was the most likely spot to land but the mouth of the bay was guarded by a hazardous combination of uncharted reefs and blind rollers sweeping into the narrow inlet. Attempting a landing in the semi-darkness was far too risky. Reluctantly, Shackleton decided to remain out to sea for the night.

In a high westerly swell, the *Caird* hove to in the darkness. On board the men were reduced to straining the final drops of water through a scrap of medical gauze to remove sediment and stray reindeer hairs from the rotting sleeping bags. The penetrating cold, said Shackleton, seemed to strike right through their bodies.

Soon after dawn the wind grew in strength and again the *Caird* was caught by mountainous swells threatening to drive the boat to destruction on the rocky shore. Shackleton reacted quickly and ordered the *Caird* to make for Annenkov Island, about 20 miles (32 km) to the east where they might find a lee shelter.

The struggle lasted all morning, with the *Caird* shipping vast quantities of water in the raging tumult and Annenkov Island seemingly no nearer. By noon winds had screeched to hurricane force and the men had to find new reserves of strength to bail frantically to stay afloat. Thirst was forgotten in the struggle.

The *Caird*, rising and falling under the onslaught, shuddered with the impact of each blow. Striking the great rolling waves was like running into a brick wall and it seemed only a matter of time before the vessel buckled and broke. Bow planks each side opened and closed from the pounding, sending fresh torrents of water flooding into the craft. In the boat's logbook, a businesslike Worsley simply wrote: 'Mountainous westerly gale and swell. Wind rose to hurricane force. Mast nearly lost.'

The Southern Ocean refused to release its grip as though the seas were raging against the *Caird*'s impudent challenge. In the dying light of day, hopes of a landing began to fade and the *Caird*, having come so far, appeared on the brink of being dashed against the cliffs or swamped by a mighty wave. 'The chance of surviving the night seemed small,' Shackleton recalled. 'I think most of us felt that the end was very near.'

After nine hours of being pummelled by the hurricane, the miracle they wanted came at around 9 p.m. when the winds suddenly eased and shifted. 'So thin is the line which divides success from failure,' Shackleton wrote. By a mixture of brilliant seamanship, sheer bloody-minded determination and outrageous good fortune, the *Caird* had strayed onto the right side of the slim margin between life and death. Reaching out to Browning, he also wrote that 'just when things looked their worst, they changed for the best'.

However, no one at the time quite appreciated the incredible stroke of good luck that saved the *Caird* from foundering in the high seas. As Crean was crawling from his sleeping bag after the storm, he knocked the thwart

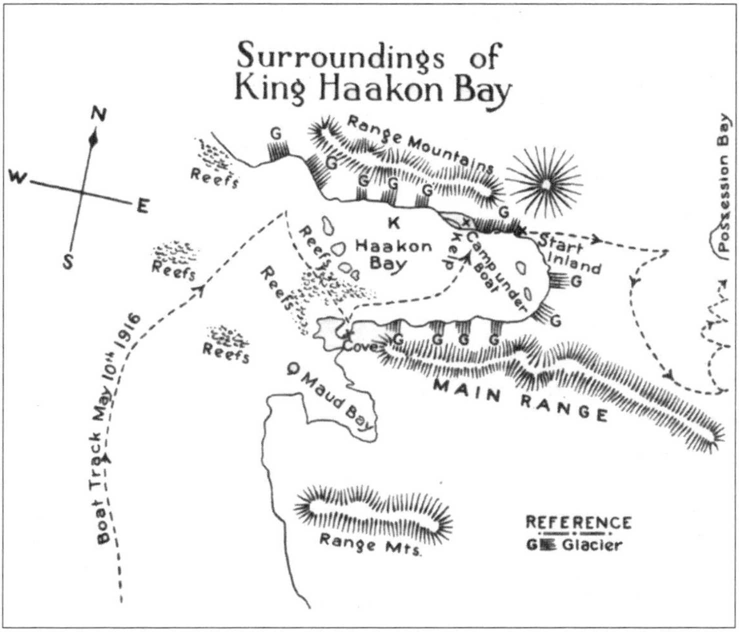

A rough sketch map drawn of King Haakon Bay, South Georgia. It was drawn from memory and although not strictly accurate, it appeared in Shackleton's 1919 book, South.

and dislodged the pin holding the mast clamp in place. It was a trifling incident and McCarthy casually caught the mast and re-secured the pin. But, as Worsley later recalled, the pin must have worked loose during the hurricane until the point alone held. No one had spotted it. 'Had it fallen out in the hurricane,' Worsley explained, 'the mast would have snapped like a carrot and no power on earth could have saved us.'

In the same seas to the north, the steamer *Argos* was less fortunate. The 500-ton vessel, bound for South Georgia from Buenos Aires with a cargo of coal, was caught by the hurricane and sank. There were no survivors.

Although the storm had passed, *Caird*'s misery continued. Unable to make land in the darkness, the vessel stood offshore for another night. A meagre pint of tainted fluid was the only remaining water. Their tongues were so dry and swollen that the men could chew only small morsels of food.

Conditions by dawn were mercifully good and the boat resumed course for King Haakon Bay. But winds soon picked up and once again they were halted as a gale swept down the channel in a last act of malice. For four hours the *Caird* hovered at the mouth of the bay, while the men waited for the winds to drop and their raging thirst to subside.

King Haakon Bay is a weather-beaten inlet about 8 miles (13 km) long and 2½ miles (4 km) at its widest. It is an area flanked by mountains rising to over 3,000 feet (1 km) and laced with glaciers, outcrops and scree slopes. The narrow east-to-west-facing fjord is brutally exposed to the region's strong westerly gales and landing, even today, is a perilous business.

Shackleton was now growing desperate for a break in the weather. Not all would survive another night at sea. Dusk was falling by the time conditions improved enough to risk a landing. It was 10 May 1916 and the 17th day since leaving Elephant Island.

All eyes strained for any reasonable inlet or cove. Under Worsley's guiding hand, the little boat somehow clawed slowly into the bay. In fast-failing light, the exhausted men took to the oars and rowed towards a small cove on the southern headland. It was little more than a notch in the rocky shoreline, but there was no time to look elsewhere.

Edging closer it was possible to pick out jagged reefs jutting above the rollers like the blackened teeth of a crazed monster. Shackleton seized the moment. Standing in the *Caird*'s bows, he carefully guided the little craft through the reefs and, propelled by a combination of swell and the last dregs of strength from exhausted rowers, the *Caird* ran ashore. A curtain of darkness fell soon after.

Shackleton leapt out of the boat and held the painter while the others clambered ashore. After so long at sea they were unsteady on their rubbery legs. Nearby was a pool of icily cold water. Sinking to their knees, the men swallowed their first proper drink in over 48 hours.

chapter 36

South Georgia

Shackleton took the first watch. It was another demonstration of being visibly in charge. After devouring a hot meal, he watched as the exhausted Worsley, Crean, McCarthy, McNish and Vincent sank into a deep sleep. In fact, he took a double watch to allow Worsley, next on duty, to snatch a little extra rest.

Watches were needed because of their own fatigue. Soon after landing, the gear and ballast were removed from the *Caird* and they tried to haul the vessel to safety above the waterline. Seventeen days in the Southern Ocean had drained their strength and it was necessary to ensure the boat was not carried away. The importance of a watchman was shown only hours later.

Crean was on guard at around 2 a.m. when a huge incoming wave caught the *Caird* and threatened to carry the vessel away in the darkness. Crean unhesitatingly plunged in up to his neck and grabbed the painter before the vessel was lost. His shouts alerted the others and he was quickly pulled ashore, still gripping the rope. All hands were summoned to cling onto the painter for the rest of the night.

Daylight showed that the small, shallow cove, backed by steep cliffs, offered only a tenuous foothold on dry land. A hollow, perhaps 10–12 feet (3 m) deep, found in the cliff face was the only shelter. Without the strength to haul the boat up the shore, it was necessary to lighten the load by removing the decking and supports. While McNish and McCarthy laboured, slowly undoing the important modifications done on Elephant Island, Shackleton, Crean and Worsley levelled out the floor of the cave. A carpet of tussock grass created a brief illusion of comfort. Vincent remained in his bag, too weak to assist. It was late afternoon before the *Caird* was finally manhandled out of the water.

Although the small cove was fit only as a temporary shelter, Shackleton insisted the men needed rest and fresh meat before moving. Some nearby albatrosses were slaughtered for food and a few pieces of driftwood allowed them to make a warming fire. Almost unbelievably, it was possible to dry clothes and sleeping bags for the first time in weeks.

Shackleton's aim from the start was to sail around the island to one of the whaling stations on the northern shore. It was perhaps 150 miles (240 km) to the works at Husvik, Stromness or Grytviken, but another sea journey was almost certainly beyond McCarthy, McNish and Vincent. The doughty *Caird,* too, was something of a useless hulk. During the landing and unloading, the craft's rudder had broken loose and drifted out to sea. Rowing for 150 miles was beyond all possibility.

Shackleton now came up with his most daring piece of improvisation. Instead of sailing around South Georgia, he decided to cross the island on foot.

Although he was instinctively reluctant to divide his party again, Shackleton understood that the weakest men would not survive the trek. It was decided to leave McCarthy, McNish and Vincent at King Haakon Bay and march overland with Crean and Worsley, the two strongest. Once again the fate of the expedition hung on the indomitable resolve of two Irishmen and a New Zealander.

After a few days' rest, Shackleton decided the group should move to the head of King Haakon Bay where it was hoped they would find better shelter and a suitable area to ascend into the mountainous interior. Good fortune, once again, smiled on the group. McCarthy was gazing idly at the breakers one day when he spotted the *Caird*'s apparently lost rudder bobbing up and down in the waves. With the entire Southern Ocean to choose from, the lost rudder had miraculously washed up at his feet.

Six days after landing at the cove, Shackleton ordered the *Caird* back into the water and loaded for the short trip deeper into the fjord. 'A great day,' Shackleton wrote. A fresh westerly wind carried them easily into the upper reaches of the bay. 'We felt happy and excited,' said Worsley. Somehow they mustered the spirit to sing a few songs on the way. Flanked on either side by snow-capped peaks and large glaciers disgorging into the bay, the *Caird* made good progress on the 8-mile (12 km) run to the head of the inlet. By midday a gently sloping beach covered in pebbles and countless seals was spotted. Taking to the oars, the party was ashore within an hour.

Although the wildlife was enormously helpful for food and fuel, the beach was more open and did not offer the cove's natural shelter. With little hesitation, Shackleton ordered the *Caird* to be upturned onto walls of rocks as a makeshift camp. Tussock grass and moss provided modest flooring and it was christened Peggotty Camp after the family who lived under a boat in Dickens' *David Copperfield.*

Shackleton was anxious to get away. A little of the old impatience had returned. It was 15 May, over three weeks since leaving Elephant Island and the image of the men at Cape Wild was etched ever more firmly in his mind. Midwinter was only a month away and some might have chosen to sit out the winter at Peggotty Camp before attempting the crossing. But Shackleton felt every day counted and wanted to begin immediately.

By a stroke of good fortune it happened to be a full moon; the moonlight, Shackleton decided, would be very useful. He wanted to travel light, without a tent or sleeping bags, and make the crossing in a night and day.

The trip to the whaling stations was estimated to be about 30 miles (48 km), but this was only a guess. No one had crossed the interior of South Georgia before and the only reference was a sketchy map drawn by Filchner in 1911. The map contained a few notable coastal features, but the interior of the island was completely blank.

As final preparations were being made, the weather closed in and the men were driven back under the *Caird*. The frustrating delay continued next day with a fresh bout of foul weather. It was hardly surprising, being midwinter. But Shackleton, fearing that they might be pinned down for days or weeks, became moody and depressed. Suddenly the weight of responsibility was almost too much to bear. Pessimism and despair was a side of Shackleton they had not seen before. 'Skipper,' he suddenly announced, 'I'll never make another expedition.'[1]

The weather on South Georgia is notoriously changeable and frequently harsh. Strong winds blow continuously and temperatures, particularly in the depths of winter, are mostly below freezing. South Georgia is a high, mountainous island with three-quarters of the wilderness covered with glaciers, ice caps and snowfields. Conditions on the heights, which Shackleton, Crean and Worsley had now to cross, would be at their most severe.

The equipment at hand was primitive and, after the traumatic events of the previous months, the men were physically drained. Each man took three days' food wrapped in a spare sock, a filled primus stove to heat up to six meals and a cooking pot. They also carried matches, binoculars, two compasses, the carpenter's adze and 50 feet (15 m) of rope. Their shabby clothing, frayed by the events of the past few months, was threadbare and offered only a flimsy shield against the penetrating cold.

By the early hours of 19 May conditions had improved. Shackleton, now at fever pitch, could wait no longer. Worsley also noticed how Shackleton's mood had changed with the improved weather. 'He seemed to tauten and gain strength,' Worsley wrote.

After a hot meal, the trio began the crossing at around 2 a.m. in the morning. The moon lit the path over the beach and up to the first slope. McCarthy and McNish, now partially recovered, went along for the first few hundred paces. With due solemnity, the men shook hands and parted company.

In McNish's diary, Shackleton had scribbled a short note placing the carpenter in charge of the three men. As he pointed out, there was ample food and wildlife to support them for 'an indefinite period' and a gun with 50 cartridges. Shackleton's destination, he wrote, was Husvik in Stromness Bay on the island's north coast. 'I trust to have you relieved in a few days,' he wrote.

Appropriately enough, Shackleton led the way as they picked a path up the first slope, reaching a height of a few thousand feet in a short time. The climb was helped by two ingenious pieces of improvisation by McNish who had pulled nails from the sides of the *Caird* and knocked them through the soles of their soft boots as a crude form of crampon. As 'Alpenstocks', the canny carpenter had found three lumps of driftwood that he fashioned into makeshift walking sticks.

From the first vantage point, even in the pale moonlight, it was evident the crossing would be more difficult than expected. Ahead lay a formidable expanse of broken ground, fields of ice and to the east a line of peaks clustered together like the knuckles on a clenched fist.

A damp mist swept down towards daybreak, obliterating the moonlight and plunging the area into darkness. At first they walked on, eager not to lose time. Suddenly the men found themselves on the edge of a precipice. No one had remembered to rope up.

Chastened by the encounter, the trio were roped together as they walked cautiously in single file, led by Shackleton, followed by Crean and with Worsley bringing up the rear. Worsley, navigating as though at sea, directed the course with calls of 'starboard' or port' as they plodded through the darkness, often sinking up to their knees in soft snow.

Daylight was breaking as the three men drew towards the crest of a rise where they saw a large lake spread out before them. The flat, glassy surface seemed to offer faster travel than the soft snow and they hurriedly made for the area. But as dawn broke, it was soon clear that the 'lake' was a bay and they were marching out to sea. It was Possession Bay, a sizeable inlet on the north coast almost opposite King Haakon Bay. Without realising it, the men had crossed the island at one of its narrowest points. However,

Possession Bay was uninhabited and the route along the coastline towards the whaling stations in the east was considered far too dangerous.

The trio retraced their steps to the original course and stopped to prepare the first hot food in six hours. The steaming sledging ration once more injected new life into them and they marched out towards the imposing line of mountains barring the route ahead. With Worsley's nose for navigation, he suggested the right-hand pass was the lowest and they began to climb.

The wear and tear of the *James Caird* journey was soon apparent as the men struggled forward, gasping for air and fearful of unseen crevasses. It was significantly colder as they climbed higher and the men, desperately out of condition, were forced to stop for a rest every 20 minutes. 'We would throw ourselves flat on our backs with our legs and arms extended and draw in big gulps of air so as to get our wind again,' Worsley wrote.

Shackleton and Crean had all the credentials for the formidable task of crossing the peaks and glaciers of South Georgia's interior. The weather-beaten faces of the two Irishmen were etched with the hard-won experience of years in the ice fields. Each was making his third trip south. Both Shackleton and Crean had overcome harrowing ordeals to survive when, at times, it seemed easier to die than live. In addition, both men radiated extraordinary mental strength and a cast-iron determination. Experience had shown that psychological strength was often a more potent force than raw muscle power.

The unknown quantity, of course, was Worsley. The New Zealander was 44 years old and had spent a life at sea. Although Worsley was thought to have once climbed in the Alps, crossing South Georgia was his first significant trek on the ice. According to Macklin, Worsley had 'no experience of sledging in any shape or form'. Yet no one could question his resilience after the *Caird* voyage and it was apparent that, crucially, he also possessed the same mental strength of Shackleton and Crean.

Hacking steps on the ascent, the men finally found their way to the top of the pass where a frightful sight greeted them. Below stretched a sheer precipice that fell away around 1,500 feet (500 m). 'There was no way down for us,' a disappointed Shackleton said. It had taken three hours of climbing and fatigue was starting to affect them all. The only relief was that South Georgia's volatile weather had stayed fine throughout.

Again they were forced to retrace their steps and resume the search for another route. But at the next summit they were again greeted by a precipitous drop. In the distance they could see the majestic Allardyce Range, a 30-mile (48 km) chain of mountains running like a spine through the centre of South Georgia and extending from 6,000 feet to Mount Paget's 9,623 feet (1,800 m – 2,935 m). Huge glaciers draped the landscape. No one had seen the range before and Worsley, who had discovered the euphoria of exploration, wrote: 'We were in a solitude never before broken by man.'

At the bottom of the rise the men were confronted by a yawning chasm about 200 feet (65 m) wide, chiselled out of the ice and snow by centuries of South Georgia's climate. 'Two battleships could have hidden in it,' said Worsley. Carefully skirting the chasm, the group moved slowly to the top of the third pass after another draining climb up to around 5,000 feet (1,500 m).

The chill on the heights cut them to the bone. But still the weather held. From the ridge the terrain ahead appeared better than the others and Worsley, growing increasingly frustrated at the delay, wanted to risk a descent. But Shackleton's caution took over. He sensed it was too dangerous. For the fourth time the weary men turned back the way they had come.

The going was very hard on the way down, the soft snow leaving them up to their knees with each step. Suddenly, without warning, wisps of fog drifted up the slope and threatened to throw a blanket over the area. The men tried to hurry towards the fourth and final pass before the fog descended, but exhaustion in their legs made it impossible. They reached the top of the rise in fading light and an eerie mist cast a near impenetrable gloom over the area. All visible features of the land ahead dissolved into the hazy greyness.

Crean, a jovial soul with robust humour, smiled at Worsley and said: 'You won't be able to do much navigating in this, Skipper.' For once Shackleton was not amused by Crean's humour. 'I don't like it all,' he snapped. 'We shall freeze if we wait here till the moon rises.'

The men were stranded at a height of around 4,500 feet (1,375 m) and Shackleton feared that temperatures might sink to at least -30° (-34 °C) during the night. Without sleeping bags or a tent they would freeze to death.

Another precipitous slope cut off the descent and fog was drifting up the pass. 'Darkness in front, fog behind,' said Worsley. 'There was not much choice.' It was the moment Shackleton abandoned his caution. 'We'll try it,' he announced. Although they could not see clearly ahead, he decided they would make a rapid descent down the slope in gathering darkness. 'We've got to take a risk.'

Shackleton, leading from the front with typical endeavour, guided the men down by cutting steps with the carpenter's adze. Although breaking a trail was more taxing, Shackleton refused to allow Crean and Worsley to take the lead. Progress was painfully slow and exhausting, taking 30 minutes to descend just 100 yards (30 m). 'I could see it telling on him,' Worsley reported.

Shackleton realised the descent was taking too long and had no faith the weather would stay calm. Getting caught in the no-man's land between the summit and the valley meant certain death. They had to descend faster. Pausing for breath, Shackleton suddenly declared: 'We'll slide.'

His idea was to coil the length of rope into three 'mats' and toboggan down the slope. 'It's a devil of risk,' he said. 'But we've got to take it.' Crean and Worsley, astonished at the audacity of the idea, were stunned for a moment but quickly realised there was no alternative. 'It seemed to me an almost impossible project,' said Worsley.

Crean had seen it all before. In 1912, shortly after leaving Scott on the Polar Plateau, he had tobogganed down the crevasse-lined Shackleton Ice Falls above the Beardmore Glacier with Lieutenant Teddy Evans and seaman Bill Lashly. It was a hair-raising descent of around 2,000 feet (600 m) and Evans later admitted: 'It makes me sweat, even now, when I think of it.' The difference was that Crean, Evans and Lashly had ridden a sledge.

Shackleton once again took the lead. Worsley came next, wrapping his feet and arms around Shackleton, and Crean adopted the same position with Worsley. All three kicked off and accelerated into space, yelling with a mixture of fear and excitement as the improbable-looking ensemble slithered noisily downhill.

The terrifying slide came to an abrupt halt after a couple of minutes when they crashed into a soft snowy bank. Any other obstacle might have killed them. They had somehow careered safely down at least 1,000 feet (300 m). Rising to their feet, the men shook hands and smiled at another incredible slice of luck.

There was no time to celebrate. It was now pitch dark, temperatures had plunged and the path ahead was uncertain. A quick hot meal briefly instilled fresh vigour and splashes of moonlight provided a shadowy sight of the landscape. The silvery sea could be seen between the mountain peaks and the route to the east was a moderately gentle plain of snowy uplands cutting through the outfalls to the south and glaciers to the north. To Shackleton, the moon, rising in the east, appeared to 'pilot our weary feet'.

The only sound was the heavy plod of feet through the snow or the distant echo as lumps of glaciers calved into the sea. By 1 a.m., after nearly 24 hours on the march, the men paused to prepare more hot food and drink. Somewhere deep in their inner reserves, they managed to shrug off the cold and tiredness to make light of conditions. Perhaps humour was all they could cling to. 'Worsley and Crean sang their old songs when the primus was going merrily,' Shackleton recorded. 'Laughter was in our hearts, though not in our parched and cracked lips.'

Fighting off the fatigue, they resumed the slow march and their spirits improved as they reached a modest decline, which they believed led down to one of the three whaling stations to be found in Stromness Bay. But any hope of a gentle decline to the bay was soon dashed when they realised the path led into a tangled field of menacing crevasses hidden within another glacier. One feature they remembered from the last visit to South Georgia was that there were no glaciers leading down to Stromness Bay. In the darkness, they had turned too early and were heading into Fortuna Bay, the inlet next to Stromness. 'The disappointment was severe,' Shackleton wrote.

Wearily retracing their steps, the men resumed course with an almost mechanical gait. Waves of tiredness swept over them and the icy wind sliced through their ragged clothes. Bodies are often at their lowest ebb in the early hours before dawn and Shackleton, Crean and Worsley were plumbing the depths of human endurance.

At around 5 a.m. Shackleton ordered a brief rest and both Crean and Worsley immediately sank into deep sleep. Shackleton, by some inner power, managed to resist the temptation to shut his eyes, realising that sleep would swiftly merge into death. After five minutes he woke his companions and told them they had slept for half an hour. It was a lie that saved their lives.

Moving slowly forward the men ascended another ridge and in the twilight before dawn could pick out some vaguely familiar rocky features which indicated being near to Stromness Bay. Below was the harbour at Husvik, which lies in the most southerly reaches of the bay. The three men stood in silence for a moment, each contemplating the enormity of what they had done. Warm handshakes and gentle grins were a mark of the respect each felt for the others.

As breakfast was being cooked, Shackleton went ahead to scout the lie of the land. Somewhere amid the blasts of wind he thought he heard the sound of a whistle. Tiredness plays tricks on the mind and he could not be sure. But it was around 6.30 a.m., the time of day when the whaling stations roused workers from their beds. At 7 a.m., he knew, the same whistle summoned the men to work.

Breakfast was quickly swallowed and the three men gathered around Worsley's chronometer, waiting for the hands to reach 7 a.m. Right on time the shrill sound of a steam whistle cut through the morning air, the first noise of the outside world they had heard in over 17 months.

Having established their bearings for the first time, the three men began to descend a snowy slope towards the head of Fortuna Bay from where they would cross the ridge and descend into Stromness Bay. Once in the bay, Shackleton could choose between the works at Leith Harbour on the northern extremity, Husvik to the south and Stromness itself in the centre. Stromness was Shackleton's choice.

Shackleton had by now abandoned all caution. Getting down from the higher levels was imperative since food was low and there was no knowing how long the weather would hold. Only one hunk of sledging ration and biscuits remained; the primus was dumped.

A field of deep, soft snow and a steep gradient of blue ice on the descent soon confirmed that the final steps to Stromness would be hard won. At one stage it took two hours of painfully slow work to descend just 500 feet (150 m), with Shackleton secured by the flimsy length of rope as he cut steps down the ice face. One slip would have been fatal.

They slid down the final yards of the slope on their backsides, inflicting fresh damage on threadbare trousers. Soon afterwards, the men came across scattered tufts of tussock grass and the deserted sandy beach which lies near the head of Fortuna Bay. After overcoming soft snow and hard glassy ice, they were now forced to trudge ankle-deep through stretches of clogging glacial mud. But the sight of a recently slaughtered seal was a clear sign of human activity in the vicinity.

The going was very hard but, at around 1.30 p.m., the men finally approached the last ridge between Fortuna Bay and Stromness Bay. Summoning reserves of strength, the men flogged their muscles for another climb to the top of the rise. From the crest of the hill the masts of whaling ships could be seen going about their business 2,500 feet (650 m) below. Minute figures moved around the quays and workshops like ants. Once more they shook hands.

Exhilarated by the sight, the men waved and shouted to the diminutive figures below, innocently forgetting that the cries were devoured by the high winds. Besides, no one was looking back up the hill from Stromness. No one had ever approached Stromness from the interior of the island.

Anxious not to lose momentum in the final hours of daylight remaining, Shackleton drove them down the last descent to Stromness. At one point Crean broke through the ice and sank up to his waist in freezing water. After being hauled out, he resumed the slow march in soaking wet clothes, seemingly impervious to the dunking.

Hurrying as fast as tired legs would allow, they came to a ravine cut by water which appeared to offer a quick descent. With icily cold water

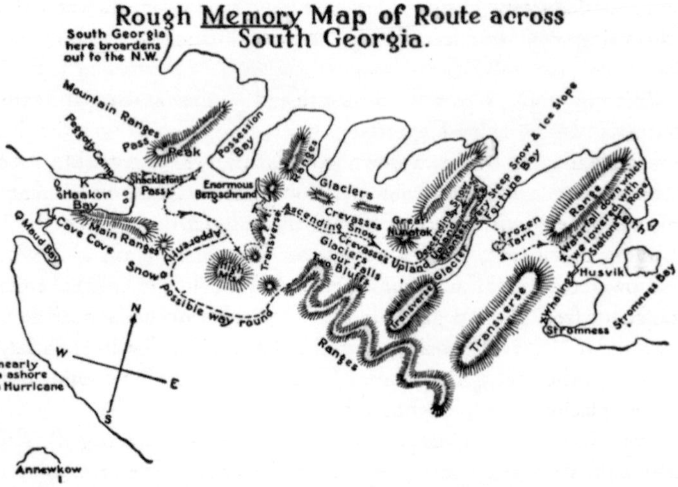

A rough outline of the trek across South Georgia which was drawn from memory and included in Shackleton's 1919 book, South.

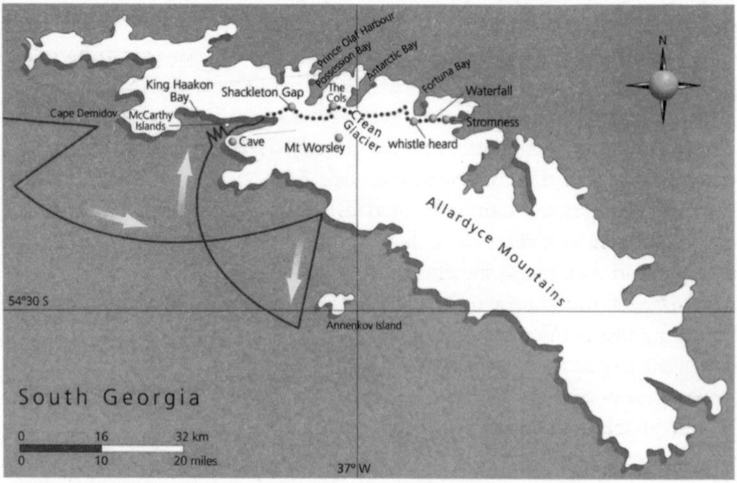

The James Caird *reached South Georgia in May 1916. Shackleton, with Tom Crean and Frank Worsley, crossed the unmapped interior to the whaling station in Stromness.*

lapping at their feet, the men trod wearily downhill through the stream until a sudden precipice stopped them in their tracks. It was a waterfall with a sheer drop of 25–30 feet (10 m) and with impassable ice cliffs on both sides.

Retracing their steps was unthinkable. The men were on the brink of collapse and, with only a few precious hours of light remaining, the chances of finding an alternative way down before dark were improbable. All food was now gone. Shackleton knew that going back was a death warrant. The only option was to climb down through the waterfall.

Tying the rope around a nearby boulder, Shackleton and Worsley first lowered Crean, the heaviest, through the cold cascade. He emerged drenched, freezing and gasping for air. Shackleton went next and slid down the rope into the steadying arms of Crean. Worsley, the lightest, had no faith in the line holding for a third time and slid down sailor-fashion without placing his full weight on the rope.

Something instinctive, perhaps it was superstition, urged them to recover the rope. But nothing would dislodge it from the rock. The length of rope, which had saved their lives on two separate occasions, was left for the ages twirling in the icy waterfall.

Shivering with the cold, the men set off for the sheds and buildings of the whaling station, perhaps 1½ miles (2 km) in the distance. The brass screws McNish had implanted in their boots were now worn flat and they slipped and slithered down the final slopes, the bruises providing a last painful souvenir of the trek. Almost incredibly, the weather had remained calm for a day and a half.

The men cut a pathetic, almost ghostly, sight as they shuffled like sleepwalkers over the last few steps. Their faces were black from blubber smoke, thick matted hair fell down to their shoulders and their filthy clothes were in rags. After more than 12 months without a decent wash, the men gave off a shocking stench. Improbably enough, Worsley was worried what impression they would make on any women they encountered. Fumbling inside his clothing he found some safety pins and patched up a few of the largest tears in his tattered trousers.

On the outskirts of the station the men bumped into two small children. When Shackleton asked the way to the station manager's office, the children were momentarily stunned into silence by the shock of hearing the grotesque-looking scarecrows speak. They turned and fled. An elderly man they encountered soon after scuttled away even before Shackleton opened his mouth.

Matthias Anderson, the station foreman at Stromness, was helping to unload a whaler when he first caught sight of the three unkempt men walking slowly towards him. Shabby clothing, dirty faces and foul smells were hardly uncommon on a whaling station. What surprised Anderson was that the figures wore anoraks and were not dressed in oilskins like most seamen. He politely led the trio to the steps of the manager's office. Understandably, Anderson was taking no chances with the strangers and left Shackleton, Crean and Worsley standing outside while he spoke to the manager, Thoralf Sørlle. 'There are three funny-looking men outside,' he told Sørlle, 'they say they know you.'

Sørlle, a burly Norwegian with a heavy moustache, knew Shackleton, having entertained him before *Endurance* sailed in 1914. But the dirty, ragged, hollow-cheeked figure before him was unrecognisable. Sørlle asked: 'Who the hell are you?' 'My name is Shackleton,' came the reply. 'We have lost our ship and come over the island.' Sørlle was staggered. The expedition, out of touch for so long, was presumed lost. 'Come in, come in,' said Sørlle, almost dragging the men over the threshold.

Shackleton had the presence of mind to ask Sørlle to take a photograph of the men before they were cleaned up. But there was no film readily available and, as Worsley said, 'the world lost a picture of its three dirtiest men.'

The manager's house, a wooden two-storey building called the 'Villa', was a rare haven of luxury amidst the reeking squalor of the whaling station. Sørlle's steward prepared hot coffee, bread and jam, and cakes, ran a bath and dug out clean clothes for the men. The steward, Worsley remembered, looked after the men 'like a hen with three chicks'.

It was around 4 p.m. on 20 May 1916 and Shackleton, Crean and Worsley had been on the march without rest or shelter for over 36 hours. The *Endurance* expedition, which had left South Georgia almost 18 months earlier, had turned 360°.

Entering the ice well-provisioned and equipped, *Endurance* had been shredded by the experience. All that Shackleton, Crean and Worsley carried out of the Antarctic were the soiled, frayed clothes they stood in, the ship's logbook and a carpenter's adze. Luck with the weather had played a significant part in their safe arrival. According to Norwegian whalers, there was not another day during the rest of the winter when the weather was fine enough to have lived through a mountaintop crossing.

Above all, though, it was Shackleton who made the impossible possible. Strikingly visible in leading from the front like a warrior king going into battle, it was his inspired leadership and astute judgement which had

(L–r) Crean, Shackleton and Worsley pictured a few days after crossing the interior of South Georgia. COURTESY: ROBERT BURTON

successfully steered them off the ice, across the South Ocean and over South Georgia.

If there were touches of genius about his leadership, they could be found in the way that Shackleton held together a disparate group of men in appalling conditions, making sure that disruptive cliques were not formed and that everyone was treated equally. He never took unnecessary risks, was able to adapt to the constantly changing circumstances and never asked a man to do something he would not do himself. But Shackleton's supreme achievement was that he instilled hope and the belief that they would all survive.

'We had pierced the veneer of outside things,' Shackleton said. 'We had seen God in his splendours, we had heard the text that nature renders. We had reached the naked soul of man.'

chapter 37

Rescue

A heavy storm struck Stromness two hours after Shackleton, Crean and Worsley staggered into the whaling station, blanketing the area with a deep layer of snow. It is unlikely they would have survived had the storm arrived 12 hours earlier. 'Providence had certainly looked after us,' Worsley wrote.

Despite the exhaustion, Shackleton could barely sleep, even after a hot bath and the unaccustomed comfort of Sørlle's bed. The disturbing news of the war in Europe, where, in Sørlle's words, 'millions are being killed,' had a chilling impact. 'Europe is mad,' said Sørlle. 'The world is mad.'

Like travellers from a different time, Shackleton, Crean and Worsley were among the few people in the civilised world who knew nothing about the horrific slaughter on the Western Front. To men who had expected the war to be over around the time *Endurance* sailed from South Georgia in December 1914, Sørlle's alarming account of millions of men locked in a deadly war of attrition was almost impossible to comprehend. 'No other civilised men could have been as blankly ignorant of world-shaking events,' Shackleton said.[1]

Closer to home, Sørlle was also able to give Shackleton the first hint of trouble with *Aurora*. It was all very sketchy and revealed only that *Aurora* had broken away from winter quarters in McMurdo Sound and drifted back to New Zealand, leaving some men marooned at Cape Evans.

Shackleton's priority was lifting the 22 men off Elephant Island. He was unaware of all other rescue plans because there was no cable head on South Georgia. However, conditions under the boats at Elephant Island were significantly more perilous than in the huts at McMurdo Sound where ample provisions were stored. The men at Cape Wild were heavily dependent on finding a regular supply of seals and penguins.

The first step was to retrieve McNish, McCarthy and Vincent sheltering under the *James Caird* at King Haakon Bay. Sørlle ordered the steam whaler *Samson* to be despatched and Worsley agreed to give up his first night in a soft bed to show the way. As *Samson* pulled out of Stromness Bay a fresh gale hit the area, but Worsley slept undisturbed on the 11-hour trip around the island. McCarthy, seeing rescuers walking up the beach, complained that Worsley should have come to rescue them. Clean, shaved and dressed in borrowed Norwegian clothes, Worsley was unrecognisable to his colleagues.

Shackleton took only minimal rest before embarking on the Elephant Island relief mission. He went to Husvik with Sørlle and Crean in search of a ship where they found the *Southern Sky,* a steam whaler moored in the harbour for the winter. The ship was four years old and belonged to Britain's Southern Whaling and Sealing Company. But there were no company representatives on the island to arrange a charter and it was impossible to send a cable.

To Shackleton, being cut off from the outside world was oddly welcome. It avoided any messy discussions about his non-existent security or finding money for the vessel's charter. Seizing the opportunity, Shackleton went straight to Søren Bernsten, the local magistrate, who had the authority to release the ship. Shackleton promised to take full responsibility for the ship and began arranging for local suppliers to provide gear and provisions.

There was no difficulty in finding a crew for *Southern Sky*. The Norwegians, grizzled veterans of the sea, were in awe of the daring seamanship that had brought Shackleton to South Georgia and volunteers were plentiful. When Worsley returned from King Haakon Bay with McCarthy, McNish and Vincent and the *James Caird*, the Norwegians insisted on carrying the little boat ashore, refusing to allow Worsley or anyone else to lay hands on the vessel. The spontaneous gesture, said Worsley, was 'quite affecting'.

One man in particular who stood out among the eager volunteers was Captain Ingvar Thom, the skipper of a transporter, who also knew Shackleton from 1914. Thom, broad, assured and another experienced hand, offered to sail in any capacity and was given command of the *Southern Sky*.

While Norwegian volunteers worked flat out to get the ship ready for sea, Shackleton and his companions were entertained at a reception thrown in their honour. In a room thick with hard-boiled seafarers and heavy with tobacco smoke, Shackleton briefly recounted the saga of losing *Endurance*, sailing the *James Caird* across the Southern Ocean and traversing South Georgia. One by one, the Norwegians stepped forward to shake hands with Shackleton, Crean and Worsley. One white-haired old campaigner said he had never heard of such a feat after 40 years at sea and finished with a dramatic gesture: 'These are men!'

Shackleton was accustomed to warm speeches of congratulation. After *Nimrod*, he was feted by royalty and politicians across the breadth of Europe and America. But the touching sincerity of the Norwegians exceeded virtually anything before. 'Princes of the ice and sea,' Teddy Evans, Scott's deputy, called Norwegian sailors. Worsley spoke for them all when he said: 'Coming from brother seamen, men of our own cloth and members of a great seafaring race like the Norwegians, this was a wonderful tribute and one of which we all felt proud.'

Next morning, just three days after the men stumbled into the whaling station, *Southern Sky* steamed out of Stromness Bay bound for Elephant Island. Cheers rang out from the quayside. On board were Shackleton, Crean and Worsley. Separate arrangements had been made to ship McNish, McCarthy and Vincent back to Britain.

Southern Sky, very heavily laden with coal, made good progress at the outset. But the ship, a 200-ton steel-built vessel, was not strengthened against the ice and unlikely to fare well if they ran into heavy pack. *Southern Sky* carried only 10 days' coal and would have little spare time to joust with the ice.

Pressing south, the ship soon encountered a sharp drop in temperatures and a line of threatening ice on the horizon. With coal limited, Shackleton reluctantly abandoned the quest. *Southern Sky* had been within 75 miles (120 km) of Elephant Island when the retreat was ordered.

Shackleton turned for Port Stanley in the Falkland Islands, about 500 miles (800 km) to the north, where he expected to find a wider choice of ships. With cable facilities available there, he also had the opportunity to wire the first word of the expedition to the outside world.

Shackleton entered Port Stanley on 31 May in cloak-and-dagger fashion, refusing to give his name to customs officers who feared at first he was a German spy. Even after the traumas of the past 18 months, Shackleton loyally remembered his exclusive contract with Perris at the *Daily Chronicle*. After swearing the two officers to secrecy, he hurried to the cable office to unleash the first flurry of messages announcing the expedition's return from the dead.

Perris was the conduit for information. It was Perris who first broke the news of her husband's safety to Emily. He rang her at home at around midnight to announce that Shackleton was alive, only hours before *Daily Chronicle* hit the streets with its spectacular exclusive story.

Shackleton was under immense strain, exhausted by the ordeal and thwarted by the ice in his attempt to rescue the men from Elephant Island. It was perhaps why he waited a little time before making direct contact with Emily. When he did write to her, three days after reaching Port Stanley, his emotions were under full control. 'I have had a year and a half of hell,' he said. 'And [I] am older of course but no lives have been lost, though we have been through what no other Polar Expedition has done. It was Nature against us the whole time.'[2]

However, he did release his emotions in letters to Perris, which contained personal comments about individuals on the expedition. The remarks are considered so sensitive that, almost a century after they were written, the Shackleton family will not allow the letters to be published in full. The only hint of Shackleton's outburst was given in the 1957 book *Shackleton* by Margery and James Fisher, which revealed that 'some of the men wept and wished to die' in the boats and after landing at South Georgia. Shackleton, said the Fishers, wrote the letter in a state of 'nervous excitement' but he made no mention of these incidents or criticism of individuals in later accounts of the expedition.[3]

Dealing with official channels was more straightforward. Contact was made with the Admiralty in London and Shackleton also sent a personal cable to King George. The King, breaking off from war duties, wired an immediate response: 'Rejoice to hear of your safe arrival in the Falkland Islands and trust your comrades on Elephant Island may soon be rescued.'

By chance, the Admiralty received news of Shackleton's return on a momentous day for the navy: 31 May happened to be the day the Battle of Jutland began, the largest naval engagement of the war, involving 250 ships and the most significant naval battle since Trafalgar. But before news of the encounter filtered through to London it was Shackleton's return from the ice which made the headlines.

Initially, at least, Shackleton's gamble of finding a ship at the Falkland Islands was fruitless. There were no vessels on hand at Port Stanley and the Admiralty indicated the most suitable was *Discovery* but, after allowing for refitting and the long journey south, the ship could not be expected to reach the South Atlantic until October. This was too late for Shackleton, already anxious that some of the weakest men on Elephant Island would not survive more months of isolation. His patience was at breaking point as he stalked the cable office in search of a ship. Shackleton, said Worsley, was in a 'fever of impatience'.

In London the Foreign Office was asked to seek help from the authorities in Argentina, Chile and Uruguay. One possibility was *Uruguay*, the Argentinian gunboat sent to lift Nordenskjöld off the ice a decade earlier. But the most attractive offer came from Montevideo where the Uruguayan government offered the use of a steam trawler, *Instituto de Pesca No 1*. Equally attractive was the offer of free provisioning, crew and the ship's commander, the 28-year-old Lieutenant Ruperto Elichiribehety. Shackleton readily agreed and *Instituto de Pesca No 1* sailed for Port Stanley.

A stout 280-ton vessel built in Aberdeen and operated by the country's fisheries authority, *Instituto de Pesca No 1* made heavy weather of the journey south in very stormy seas. Shackleton, Crean and Worsley were on board.

At dawn on the third day the peaks of Elephant Island, which rise to 2,799 feet (853 m) behind Cape Wild, appeared on the southern horizon. Edging tentatively forward, *Instituto de Pesca No 1* immediately ran into an impenetrable line of pack ice about 20 miles (32 km) from the island and Elichiribehety was reluctant to risk steaming further.

The ship, as Worsley understood, was poorly equipped for the task. The steel-built vessel was in mortal danger if nipped by the ice, the engines were playing up and coal was running out. *Instituto de Pesca No 1* was supposed to travel at 10 knots and on 6 tons of coal. But as Worsley dryly noted, the craft did 6 knots on 10 tons of coal.

Shackleton, in Worsley's words, was 'nearly heartbroken' when the order was given to retreat. 'It was a dreadful experience to get within so short a distance of our marooned shipmates and then fail to reach them,' Worsley wrote. Fortunately, a screen of fog blanketed the island and obscured the ship's smoke from the men at Cape Wild.

With coal virtually exhausted and engines stuttering badly, *Instituto de Pesca No 1* only narrowly made it back to the safety of Port Stanley. Although the generous Uruguayans offered to refit the ship, Shackleton felt it would take too long and graciously declined, quietly hoping to find a more suitable vessel.

HMS *Glasgow*, a navy cruiser, happened to be in port when Shackleton reached Port Stanley and Captain John Luce, the ship's commander, was ready to assist. Luce, a 46-year-old veteran of the battles of Coronel and the Falklands in 1914, signalled the Admiralty for permission to take Shackleton down to Elephant Island. But the Admiralty was reluctant to take *Glasgow* out of the theatre of war and delivered a brusque reply to Luce's request: 'Your telegram not approved.'

Shackleton was on his own and he decided that the chances of raising a ship in the Falklands had disappeared. The most obvious place was South America. On 1 July, nearly six weeks after leaving Elephant Island, he took

Crean and Worsley on the mail ship *Orita* to the port of Punta Arenas in Chile.

Something in Shackleton's instinct drew him to Punta Arenas, the main port along the Straits of Magellan. Punta Arenas, once a penal colony, was just the type of lively, freewheeling community where Shackleton felt most comfortable. It had a certain frontier spirit and the thriving shipping and sheep farming had attracted a sizeable number of British colonialists to the region. The enclave supported three English-language newspapers, a British school and a number of cricket teams. The Rev. Joseph Cater, an old associate from the Royal Scottish Geographical Society in Edinburgh, happened to be serving in Punta Arenas when Shackleton arrived.

Shackleton went straight to see Charles Milward, the amiable British Consul in Punta Arenas. Milward was a man cut from the same cloth as Shackleton and not a typical minor diplomat. He was an adventurous 57-year-old who had survived being shipwrecked in Antarctic waters to build a prosperous business and represent his country at one of its most distant outposts.

Milward was quick to realise Shackleton's plight and took him to the British Association of Magallanes, known as the British Club. The Club, a plush gentleman's-only meeting place for rich sheep farmers and businessmen, was a small haven of influence and Shackleton was greeted with open arms by the President, Allan MacDonald.

A large crowd, mostly British settlers, gathered at a government building in the city on 9 July to hear Shackleton stress the urgency of returning to Elephant Island. With typical generosity, he donated all proceeds from the event to the British Red Cross and Hospital de la Caridad, the French military health service.

Within a short time, MacDonald and his associates at the Club had raised £1,500 (£65,000 today/€78,000) and a further £500 came from a wealthy Chilean businessman, Carlos Campos Torrablanca. With the money Shackleton was able to rent the schooner *Emma* for the third attempt to reach Elephant Island.

Shackleton was confident that *Emma* would succeeded where *Southern Sky* and *Instituto de Pesca No 1* had failed. 'I feel that we are going to rescue them,' he told one crowd. His confidence was wishful thinking. *Emma*, an oak-built vessel of 70 tons with a small auxiliary engine, was almost 40 years old and needed help to get south. To conserve coal, the Chilean authorities provided the steamer *Yelcho*, free of charge, to tow *Emma* on the first stage of the voyage towards Cape Horn.

Emma had a questionable pedigree as a seal poacher and boasted a makeshift crew from various nationalities, including a seaman recently released from prison for poaching. In command was Chilean pilot León Aguirre Romero.

Once at sea, *Emma* struggled to cope with the lusty swells of the Drake Passage. The engine was unreliable and the sails were soon coated with ice. A line of pack ice stopped the vessel about 100 miles (160 km) off the coast of Elephant Island. After three days' searching for a passage through the ice, the quest was abandoned.

The disappointment for Shackleton was acute. For once the voluble character was driven to silence. 'He did not speak of the men on the island now,' Worsley wrote. 'It was a silence more eloquent than words.'

The journey north was a nightmare of storms and rolling seas as the *Emma* tried to beat up to Cape Horn against the prevailing westerly gales in midwinter. It took almost three weeks and Worsley reported that the 'wear and tear' of the voyage was dreadful. He noted how lines were now scored on Shackleton's face. There was a hint of a stoop about the once familiar square-set figure. Worsley also noticed that Shackleton's thick dark wavy hair had turned silvery grey. For the first time he noticed that Shackleton had begun drinking whiskey to cope with the stress. 'His days were bad,' Worsley explained. 'What his nights were like I can only imagine.'

Emma made for Port Stanley again where it was learned that *Discovery* was finally ready to leave England under the command of Captain James Fairweather, a 63-year-old Scot from the whaling fleet. The 8,000-mile (12,000 km) journey would take at least six weeks, adding to Shackleton's increasing despair. According to Worsley, Shackleton feared the authorities were 'winding his men in a shroud of red tape'.

The costs of polar expeditions had a way of inflating beyond all recognition and the government was wary of making an open-ended commitment with resources so stretched by the war. The cost of *Discovery*'s first expedition in 1901 was originally estimated at around £90,000. But because of the expensive relief operation in 1904, the eventual bill for the expedition was £160,000 with the government contributing directly and indirectly some £100,000 (£5.7 million/€6.9 million today) of the final bill.[4]

An unspoken fear was that *Discovery*'s commanders would take control of the rescue operation once the ship arrived. This was out of the question for Shackleton and his anger increased when the Admiralty later confirmed that the navy would assume command of the relief mission. The rescue of his men was a deeply personal quest and Shackleton was now determined to press ahead before *Discovery* reached South America.

From Port Stanley he asked the Chilean authorities to send *Yelcho* to tow *Emma* back to the Magellan Straits. After enduring another horrendous voyage in a strong north-westerly gale, Shackleton arrived at Punta Arenas on 14 August. It was four months since the *James Caird* had left Elephant Island and the strain was intensifying. It was noticeable how Crean watched over Shackleton like an older brother, even persuading him to moderate his drinking.

The choice of vessels available at Punta Arenas was unimpressive. Only two coastguard vessels – *Yanez* and *Yelcho* – were anchored in the port and neither was suitable for the pack ice. But Victor Speranza, the British naval attaché for Chile, nonetheless approached Admiral Hurtador, Director General of the Chilean navy, with a request to release *Yelcho*. Hurtador, too, felt *Yelcho* was unsuitable but later relented.[5] His only condition was that Shackleton must not take *Yelcho* into the ice. Although he accepted the condition, Shackleton knew it was a pledge that would not be kept if there was even a remote chance of reaching Elephant Island.

Yelcho, the fourth attempt to relieve the castaways, sailed on 25 August, carried on a tide of goodwill and the high hopes of the local community. The crew of 23, all from Chile, were volunteers and Shackleton, Crean and Worsley were crammed on board for a round trip of 1,600 miles (2,400 km). The weather was slightly better with the approach of spring and the ship was well stocked with provisions eagerly donated by locals.

Shackleton, said Worsley, was a different man once the voyage was under way. 'Vigorous and alert,' he said, 'urging the engineers to drive the little ship hell-for-leather.'

Yelcho was a measure of Shackleton's desperation. *Yelcho*'s normal role was the humble task of running routine tender services to the area's lighthouses. The ship, built in Scotland in 1906, was hopelessly ill-equipped for the rigours of the journey. A single-hull steel vessel, *Yelcho* was not strengthened against the ice and did not have a proper heating system. Top speed was 11 knots but the ship's boilers, which had not been serviced for three years, were something of an unknown quantity.

By chance, Francisco Miranda, *Yelcho*'s usual commander, was ill and Luis Pardo, a 34-year-old pilot from the Chilean navy, volunteered to take his place. Pardo was also a Freemason. In support, Pardo appointed *Emma*'s former commander, Aguirre, as his deputy and rounded up more experienced volunteers from Chilean navy vessels.

The voyage south was unnervingly smooth. By 29 August *Yelcho* was still luxuriating in open water and barely 60 miles (100 km) from Elephant Island. But a dense fog descended around midnight and Shackleton was uneasy. Directly ahead he knew was a shoal of semi-submerged rocks and violent breakers.

Reluctantly, Pardo ordered the ship to slow steam at half speed as they approached an area of ice. Shackleton, desperate to avoid a fourth disappointment, spent the night on the bridge anxiously peering into the haze for any sign of a passage through the stretches of ice. The fog eased a little after daybreak on 30 August and the ice ahead had scattered. In the distance it was possible to pick out the mountains of Elephant Island.

Yelcho closed on the area around Cape Wild shortly before noon. Through binoculars Shackleton, Worsley and Crean could make out the camp, almost invisible under a layer of snow. Small dark figures could be detected waving frantically from the beach.

Shackleton counted the little figures, hoping they totalled 22. 'There are only two, Skipper,' he began. 'No, four. I see six, eight ... and at last ... they are all there. They are all saved.' His face, said Worsley, showed more emotion than he had ever seen before. 'It sounds trite, but years literally seemed to drop from him as he stood before us,' Worsley added. For the last time, Shackleton, Crean and Worsley solemnly shook hands. 'We were all unable to speak,' said Worsley.

Moments earlier Hurley and Marston were idly shelling limpets on the seashore. As Hurley glanced out to sea, a ship suddenly rounded the point and they yelled: 'Ship O!' Pandemonium broke out as the men rushed out of the camp yelling and screaming hysterically. The cooking pot was sent flying and Wild put an axe to one of the remaining tins of paraffin to light a signal.

Pardo navigated *Yelcho* to within 150 yards (140 m) of the shore and a small boat was lowered. Shackleton, taking Crean and four Chilean sailors, leapt aboard and pulled towards the beach. The castaways, who expected to see an ice-breaker, were puzzled at the sight of a small Chilean navy ship. 'We noticed the great happiness and emotion of the shipwrecked men,' Aguirre's logbook stated in a matter-of-fact entry.[6]

Shackleton stood upright in the boat as he and Crean were taken towards shore. It was 128 days since the *James Caird* sailed. Shackleton, once again visibly in command, yelled to Wild: 'Are you all well?' Wild, who was close to tears, replied: 'We are all well, Boss.'

chapter 38

The Ross Sea Party

Shackleton did not set foot on Elephant Island. This was no superstition or sign of fear. A heavy sea was running and a sudden change of wind might easily unleash the pack, trapping the vulnerable *Yelcho*. It was a race against time and Shackleton was not taking unnecessary risks.

In two rapidly executed manoeuvres lasting no more than an hour, the men were lifted off the beach and ferried out to *Yelcho* a short distance offshore. Shackleton, supervising the loading and unloading, never left the boat.

All the men took with them from the crude encampment under the *Dudley Docker* and *Stancomb Wills* were essential items of equipment, Hurley's precious films and the tattered log of *Endurance*. Inside an hour all hands were jammed below deck and Pardo headed north, anxious not to push his luck too far. The ice was still open and the throb of *Yelcho*'s engines was curiously satisfying to men whose only sound in the past four and half months was the rage of howling gales.

Yelcho, it emerged, had arrived at precisely the right moment. Two days earlier the pack ice in the area was impenetrable. As the ship drove north in a furious gale, Shackleton could see that after their sojourn at Cape Wild some men were nearing the end of their tether. 'Some hands,' he wrote, 'were in a rather bad way.'

Listening intently to Wild's account of the isolation and hardship, Shackleton discovered that some had abandoned all hope of being rescued and others had simply grown apathetic and resigned to their fate as ennui took hold. Towards the end of August, Hussey reported that 'everyone except Wild had become listless'. Although Wild never lost faith in Shackleton's returning, breaking point was fast approaching in the days before *Yelcho* hove into sight. Months later Wild would write: 'I admit things certainly did look rather bleak at this time.'[1]

Wild had followed Shackleton's example and stuck to a simple practice of maintaining strict discipline and consistently nurturing the belief that, despite the agony of waiting, the Boss would come back. In particular, Wild gave the men hope.

It was a remarkable act of leadership on the part of Wild who achieved the near impossible feat of being respected and admired by almost everyone regardless of the privation and fear of being stranded. Macklin reported Wild as 'scrupulously fair in everything' and he rose each day with the cry: 'Lash up and stow, boys, the Boss is coming today.'

Even Orde Lees, who had challenged his decision to follow the example set by Shackleton and not to stockpile food, spoke of the debt they owed to Wild's 'buoyant optimism, dogged determination and calm demeanour'. Shackleton went further, declaring that they would not have survived without Wild's measured and thoughtful command. 'I think without doubt that all the stranded party owe their lives to him,' he said.

Wild's chief support came from the doctors, McIlroy and Macklin, who tended the sick and needy with great care. In mid-June, at around the time *Instituto de Pesca No 1* was blocked by ice just 20 miles (32 km) off the coast of Elephant Island, McIlroy amputated the frostbitten toes of Blackborow in a 55-minute operation carried out in dim light under the boats.

Food was a constant problem, being heavily dependent on finding a fresh supply of seals and penguins. By midwinter, the supply had slowed to a trickle and stocks were very low in the weeks before *Yelcho* arrived, and hope of rescue was fading. The night before rescue Orde Lees wrote that the 'idea of a ship ever coming is more and more remote ...'

By mid-August, some four months after the *James Caird* sailed, Wild was forced to start preparing for the alternatives if Shackleton did not return. The only option was for a party of five, led by Wild, to reach Deception Island against the currents in the barely adequate *Dudley Docker*. It was a voyage probably doomed to failure but Wild felt something must to done to avoid another year on Elephant Island. It was 200 miles (320 km) to Deception Island and the *Docker* had been reduced to only five oars and did not have a proper mast. An old tent cloth had been rigged as a mainsail. Wild planned to sail on 5 October if Shackleton had not returned but, as Hussey suggested, it would be a 'hopeless journey'.

As *Yelcho* struggled north in a gale, Shackleton asked Pardo to pull into Rio Seco, just a few miles from Punta Arenas. At Rio Seco he telephoned ahead to the Governor of Punta Arenas to announce the successful rescue and waited a few hours while a welcoming reception was arranged. In

Safe. The Endurance *party at Punta Arenas after being lifted from the beach at Elephant Island. Shackleton (centre, with hat) stands next to Luis Pardo (in uniform), captain of the Chilean vessel* Yelcho, *which rescued the 22 men.*

anticipation of a rapturous welcome and a momentous photo opportunity, he ordered the castaways not to shave or cut their hair before landing.

Yelcho steamed into Punta Arenas on 3 September to find almost the entire population lining the quays cheering and waving enthusiastically. Bells were rung, fire alarms sounded and a brass band played a series of jubilant tunes, including a rough-and-ready version of *God Save The King*. In a temporary suspension of hostilities, German and Austrian ships in the harbour also flew flags in celebration.

Outside the city's Royal Hotel, the weather-ravaged, shabby and foul-smelling group posed uncomfortably for the historic photograph which meant so much to Shackleton. The grainy image of the shipwrecked crew was more than a simple record of a momentous day. It was graphic proof that Shackleton alone had rescued his men. The image was a declaration of defiance against the bureaucrats and administrators in England.

Amid the hullabaloo Shackleton scribbled a brief letter to Emily. 'I have done it,' he wrote. 'Damn the Admiralty. I wonder who is responsible for their attitude to me. Not a life lost and we have been through Hell. Soon I will be home and then I will rest.'[2]

A month-long fiesta of boisterous South American receptions, dinners and celebratory speeches followed. In the middle of the carnival *Discovery*

(L–r): A fully recovered Worsley, Shackleton and Crean in a posed studio photograph taken after the crossing of South Georgia. Courtesy: Athy Heritage Museum

limped into Montevideo after a difficult voyage south to find rescue was not needed.

The Chilean authorities were eager to bask in the reflected glory of the occasion and placed *Yelcho* at Shackleton's disposal for a trip to Valparaiso and Santiago where the party was engulfed by huge crowds. At Valparaiso it took the men half an hour to walk the short distance to the Naval Club because of the throng. After meeting the President, Shackleton crossed the Andes in a special train provided by the Chilean railway department for another round of receptions in Buenos Aires and Montevideo.

By now, two years after *Endurance* first sailed down the River Plate, it was time to bring celebrations to an end. Several men had already made their passage home to join the war effort and on 8 October the last remnants of the *Endurance* expedition assembled together on a railway platform in Buenos Aires. There were no witnesses and no formalities beyond a few simple handshakes.

Shackleton took time to clarify the important issue of appointing Wordie as the expedition's chief of scientific staff. *Endurance* had sailed without anyone in charge of science, but Shackleton was anxious to salvage something from the disaster by ensuring that official reports were handled reliably.

What Shackleton did not tell his men was that he had changed his mind about paying wages. During McNish's mutiny on the ice, Shackleton had declared that all hands would be paid up to the moment they reached England. But the expedition had run out of money some months before and the chances of raising fresh funds in wartime were remote.

In a confidential note to Perris in London, he sent instructions to pay wages to dependants only up to the time *Endurance* entered the ice which was January 1915. He also chose the most loyal men – he singled out Crean and How – who he deemed would eventually be paid in full. It was a backhanded compliment to Crean and How that Shackleton did not make promises over wages he might not be able to keep.

Relieving the men of the Ross Sea party at McMurdo Sound was now Shackleton's priority. Taking Worsley, he hurried north to Panama to find a ship bound for New Zealand to pick up *Aurora* for a return to McMurdo Sound. Events, however, had moved out of his control.

Shackleton naturally assumed that he would take command of the Ross Sea operation in the same way that he alone rescued the men from Elephant Island. He saw 'no anxiety' for the men, even though he had no knowledge of the circumstances in McMurdo Sound beyond *Aurora*'s entrapment and the stranding of Mackintosh and nine others. Shortly after reaching Punta Arenas, Shackleton told a public audience that 'all their stores were landed and they have sufficient food to keep them for three or four years.'[3]

But control of affairs had now shifted firmly into the hands of the authorities in England, New Zealand and Australia who were collectively funding the relief operation. Although Shackleton resented the 'outside' influence, there was no choice because of the haphazard preparations and lack of funding from the outset.

'On general principles it is right that the relief be a Government relief, as distinct from a Shackleton relief,' Mawson wrote. 'Especially in view of the extremely small sum contributed by the Shackleton expedition to the cost of the Ross Sea enterprise.' Mawson reported 'very strong feeling' in support of a government operation in Australia and saw Shackleton as a disturbing example of reckless preparation: '... all that explorers in future will do is to raise enough money to get away to where they want to do their work, then call out to the Government to complete the job.'[4]

Mawson was echoing the view of many in Australia. Some wanted nothing to do with Shackleton. William Ferguson Massey, the Prime Minister, cabled Perris in London with the blunt message that there was 'no reason' for Shackleton to go to Australia. Mawson added that Shackleton's 'crooked dealings have brought it on himself.'

Costs had ballooned to around £20,000 (over £850,000/€1 million today) and the governments were insisting on placing their own man in charge of the rescue. Shackleton wanted Stenhouse, who had skippered *Aurora* on the first journey. But Stenhouse was blamed for *Aurora*'s captivity and ruthlessly bypassed. The man they appointed was John King Davis, the most proficient of all ice navigators. Davis was given 'absolute and undivided' control of the ship and when he offered to resign in place of Shackleton, the Australians refused to accept his decision.

However much Shackleton admired Davis as a seafarer, his emasculation was painful. *Aurora*, after all, was his ship and Davis had been appointed without his consent. He simply could not understand why he was not allowed to lead the rescue and made another abortive attempt to stop *Aurora* sailing under Davis's command even before he reached New Zealand. In a cable to his agent Tripp, Shackleton demanded that an embargo be placed on the ship to prevent departure. It did not work.

Shackleton and Worsley finally reached Wellington on 2 December in belligerent mood. Tripp took him to see Robert McNab, New Zealand's shipping minister, who immediately fell under Shackleton's charm and casually announced that *Aurora* would not sail south without his presence on board. Worsley, back on home soil and brazenly facetious, suggested an act of piracy to wrest control of affairs.

However, the charm did not work on the implacable Davis, who remained impassive and uncompromising. Davis, despite his misgiving about Shackleton, still considered him a friend but he was also a straight-talking man who cared little for hollow flattery.

Davis, gangly, spare and sombre with sharp, piercing eyes, quietly explained that the carnage of war was significantly more important to Australians and New Zealanders than a botched polar expedition. While Shackleton was lost in the ice, over 10,000 Australians and New Zealanders had died at Gallipoli alone and among the 1 million casualties on the Somme in 1916 the two countries suffered 30,000 dead or wounded. These were huge losses for nations with small populations and gave a painful perspective to the concern for a handful of missing explorers.

During talks together Davis sensed that Shackleton had succumbed to the recent adulation and somehow lost touch. He seemed unable to realise that the world had changed. 'He had emerged,' said Davis, 'into a strange, embattled world that bore small resemblance to the world he had left behind in 1914.'

Davis also noticed that Shackleton was showing signs of wear and tear. He was tired, frustrated and increasingly moody as control of events slipped further from his grasp. 'I am old and tired,' Shackleton had told Emily even before leaving South America. It was six months since he had emerged from the ice and yet he was no nearer to returning home.

'I must settle down and I want to,' he told her. 'I have seen nothing of you or our children really for years ... I still feel certain that when this is all over there will be money enough to make things comfortable.' In a letter to his eldest son, Edward, he wrote that Emily was a 'mother in a million' and that she had 'not had an easy time' over the past years. He signed the letter as 'your loving, wandering father'.

Finally, he repeated the recurring promise of giving up exploration. 'I don't suppose for a moment that the Antarctic will ever see me again,' he wrote.[5]

Shackleton had little choice but to back down. He tried to wring the concession of agreeing to Davis as skipper of *Aurora* provided Worsley and Stenhouse joined them on the voyage south. However, Davis saw the obvious danger of four commanders on the bridge and rejected the notion. It was not until late December, with *Aurora* ready to sail, that a compromise was found and Shackleton finally agreed unconditionally to sail under Davis's command. As part of the deal, the New Zealanders provided first-class tickets to England for Worsley and Stenhouse.

On 20 December *Aurora* finally left Port Chalmers with a full crew of 25 men firmly in the hands of Davis. Shackleton, as supernumerary officer, mucked in as usual and began to shake off the moody irritability. Rediscovering his old verve, Shackleton soon emerged as the most popular man on board.

There was an inescapable feeling of going back in time to a half-forgotten age as *Aurora* drove south in foul weather. Leaving behind a world consumed by war, *Aurora* seemed to be returning to more ordered times when Antarctic exploration was a more straightforward way of having a bad time. They were, as Davis put it, 'receding into the past' and in no one was this 'seeming reversal of the time-space equation' more marked than in Shackleton.[6]

The old haunts and familiar peaks and glacial slopes around McMurdo Sound came into view during the first week of 1917 and on 10 January *Aurora* steamed alongside Shackleton's old hut at Cape Royds. A whole lifetime seemed to have passed in the eight years since *Nimrod* had pulled away in 1909 and yet nothing had changed.

While Davis fired a flare to announce the ship's arrival, Shackleton went ashore to inspect the hut which was largely as he had left it. Inside he found a few signs of recent activity and a note explaining that the Ross Sea party had overwintered a few miles to the south in Scott's old hut at Cape Evans.

A few dark shapes began to emerge from the direction of Cape Evans shortly after and Shackleton, accompanied by two men from *Aurora*, hurried across the ice to meet them. As the figures approached, the hollow eyes, drawn faces and long hair, filthy faces and ragged clothes were stark evidence of their ordeal. Davis said they were the 'wildest looking gang of men that I have ever seen in my life'. To Shackleton, the men were an uncomfortable reminder of his arrival at the Stromness whaling station a few months before.

Within moments of meeting, Shackleton and his two companions stepped aside and lay motionless on the ice. It was a prearranged signal to Davis, watching through binoculars from *Aurora*, to reveal the number of deaths among the party.

The seven survivors – Cope, Gaze, Jack, Joyce, Richards, Stevens and Ernest Wild – were a pitiful sight and able to give only an outline of the terrible two-year struggle and deaths of Mackintosh, Hayward and Spencer-Smith. Their speech, the rescuers noticed, was jerky and almost unintelligible and it would be some time before the men were able to provide a more coherent account of events.

Over the next few days, details of the extraordinary mileages achieved by the depot-layers began to emerge. In particular, Shackleton saw how critical Joyce and Wild had been to their survival when the parties were struggling or separated and how Mackintosh and Hayward had needlessly thrown their lives away in the dash to reach Cape Evans over the sea ice. 'I wish to heavens that they had kept together,' he said. To compound his distress, the remarkable achievements of the Ross Sea party were in vain.

The relief at being rescued did not obscure a certain tension between Shackleton and the survivors who were looking for someone to blame for the two-year ordeal. The Australians – Gaze, Jack and Richards – were reportedly 'rather hostile' to Shackleton and particularly his appointment of Mackintosh as leader. Stevens, who had suffered temperamentally during the isolation, said he was 'disgusted' with Shackleton's 'general behaviour and attitude'. Despite an old friendship, Joyce castigated the recruitment of inexperienced men who were 'only fit for drawing room tea parties'.

The deaths cast a shadow across Shackleton. *Aurora*'s doctor, Frederick Middleton, reported that Shackleton was 'greatly affected' by meeting the survivors and 'very much disturbed' by the loss of three men. He noted

Survivors from the marooned Ross Sea party heading home on Aurora. *(L–r) Jack, Stevens, Richards, Ernest Wild, Gaze, Joyce, Cope, Shackleton and Captain John King Davis*

in his diary: 'Sir EHS is not at all well and I don't think he is in too fit a condition.'

'Though I was thousands of miles away, the responsibility still lay on my shoulders,' Shackleton told Joyce. For all the talk of always putting his men first, Shackleton could no longer claim never to have lost a soul. As Davis said, Shackleton had enjoyed a triumph for his boat journey 'but certainly not for his organisation'.

While Shackleton could not be held directly responsible for the three deaths on the Barrier, he had conceived, planned and executed the expedition in his own name. As overall commander the responsibility was clear.

Shackleton, perhaps haunted by guilt, decided to mount a search for the bodies of Mackintosh and Hayward before *Aurora* sailed north. However, it had been nine months since the two men disappeared and the search was soon called off.

A memorial cross to the dead men was erected at Wind Vane Hill overlooking Cape Evans and Shackleton placed a personal message in a copper tube. As always in search of emotional expression, Shackleton reached out to the poets. He began with his own version of lines taken from Swinburne:

Things done for gain are nought
But great things done, endure.

But it was to Browning, as ever, that Shackleton turned for the fullest expression. The paraphrased words of the original 'Prospice' he left behind were probably as much for himself as for the dead. He wrote:

I ever was a fighter so one fight more
The best and last
I should hate that death bandaged
my eyes and bid me creep past
Let me pay in a minute's life
arrears of pain darkness & cold.

Shackleton returned to *Aurora* on 16 January 1917. It was almost 15 years to the day since he had first set foot on the continent. It was also the last trek he made over the Antarctic ice.

Davis was fearful that *Aurora* would again be snared by the ice gathering in the basin of McMurdo Sound and on 17 January the ship turned north. From the stern Shackleton caught his last glimpse of McMurdo Sound, the familiar smoking beacon of Mount Erebus and towering amphitheatre of snow-capped mountains and vast glaciers falling into the ice-clogged strait.

chapter 39

Adrift Again

Any fears that Shackleton had about the ill-fated preparations for the Ross Sea party were dispelled from the moment *Aurora* anchored at Wellington, New Zealand on 9 February 1917. Local dignitaries poured on board to greet the explorers, newspapermen clamoured for interviews and the quay was packed with noisy well-wishers. 'Everyone is very kind to us,' wrote one survivor, 'too kind in fact.'

Despite the expedition's overall failure, Shackleton once more found himself a popular hero of the time. Even the criticism he feared over sailing south at the outbreak of war was drowned out by the applause. Shrugging off talk of mismanagement, Shackleton swept all before him with his customary bravado. Richards, one of the initially critical Australian survivors from the Ross Sea, came around with the declaration that Shackleton was like Churchill – 'a great man'. One speaker said Shackleton was 'British of the best stamp from the crown of his head to the soles of his feet'.

Shackleton spent a month in New Zealand, touring the country and delivering a series of lectures to packed houses. Told with his familiar flourish, the talks drew thunderous applause and offered a brief respite from the waves of shocking news from the Western Front. With now customary generosity, all proceeds went to causes like the Red Cross or a special fund set up for the widow of Mackintosh.

The warmth of the New Zealand reception coincided with news that, almost without his lifting a finger, Shackleton's money problems in Australia and New Zealand had been resolved. The key figure, working quietly behind the scenes, was the thoughtful, meticulous Tripp, helped by supportive shipping minister McNab.

Tripp, 55 years old and well connected, had taken control of the expedition's financial affairs and somehow extricated Shackleton from any liability over the relief expedition's £20,000 costs, placated creditors over debts dating back to 1914 and raised extra funds to meet most debts in the region. All this was achieved while patiently managing the combustible and impulsive figure of Shackleton himself.

Tripp tapped into his circle of acquaintances to raise a loan of £5,000 and began to sell everything connected with the expedition, including *Aurora*, which alone generated £10,000 (about £425,000/€512,000 today). This was over three times what Shackleton had paid Mawson three years earlier but shipping's value had rocketed since the outbreak of war and Tripp sold at the top of the market. Other debts were cleared and members of the Ross Sea and *Aurora* parties were all paid in full, unlike some unfortunates from *Endurance* who were still waiting for their wages.

Thanks to Tripp's thrift and expertise, Shackleton was able to send £200 to Emily. Fearing that other creditors might descend, he asked that she keep the matter private. No one could recall the last time he had sent money home and it was unclear how Emily was managing.

Shackleton had arranged for his wife to receive £83 a month from expedition funds to meet bills during his absence. He took no money from the expedition for himself. But the payments stopped within nine months when the expedition effectively ran out of money in April 1915.

Aside from her inheritance, it is likely that her family helped out and Janet Stancomb-Wills, kind, supportive and sympathetic, had paid a few bills. There was also speculation that a little money came from Caroline Oates, mother of the tragic Captain Lawrence Oates, who sacrificed himself on the return from the Pole with Scott in 1912.

Tripp recognised that Shackleton had been very lucky and only narrowly avoided being swamped by bankruptcy proceedings. To Tripp, the appalling mess meant that never again could Shackleton mount an expedition without securing adequate funds in advance, especially a contingency fund for emergencies. After twice calling on government help, raising money from official sources was unlikely, he felt.

'It seems to me that it will be impossible for you to do any exploring anyhow for many years,' he said to Shackleton. 'It would be unwise for you ever to take on another expedition unless you not only had sufficient money to pay your way, if everything went alright, but you would have to have money in hand to provide for accidents.'

Shackleton swept imperiously past Tripp's sound logic and travelled to Australia. It was meant to be another round of celebratory speeches and receptions and to thank the Australians for their crucial support. The Australians were Shackleton's fiercest critics, sensing they had been bounced into paying for the Ross Sea rescue and feelings were still running high. Mawson noted that 'Shackleton's sun has really set.'

But, as Tripp observed, Shackleton 'evidently loves a fight'. Never one to shirk a battle, Shackleton decided to confront the committee set up to arrange the *Aurora* relief. The weighty body of experts was led by Rear Admiral Sir William Creswell, considered to be the father of the Australian navy, while two serving naval captains had also been co-opted. One of the scientists was Thomas Griffith Taylor, the geologist from Scott's last expedition who spent a year at McMurdo Sound. Taylor, by coincidence, wore a ring containing a fragment of rock that Shackleton hauled back from the Beardmore Glacier in 1909.

Shackleton, eager to face down his critics, pulled no punches in heated exchanges with the committee. While he accepted overall responsibility for the expedition, Shackleton unkindly saw Mackintosh as the main cause of the party's troubles. Everything on the Ross Sea operation, he told Emily, was in a 'state of chaos' and that it was a mercy Mackintosh was no longer around to account for his actions. Mackintosh had made a 'very bad impression' in Australia but 'for that he is dead through his own carelessness,' he said.

As tensions rose, Shackleton suddenly stood up and left the room. He returned soon afterwards with a broad grin and shook the hand of each committee member in a gesture of reconciliation. Before anyone properly realised what had occurred, Shackleton had disarmed the committee.

It was much the same elsewhere in Australia as Shackleton hurried through a series of hugely popular public engagements, milking the applause and preferring to dwell more on the triumph of *Endurance* than the calamity of the Ross Sea party. At one meeting in Sydney his stirring rhetoric was welcomed by a crowd of 3,500 who, according to newspaper reports, swung from wild enthusiasm to shedding tears. Richards admitted that 'we became staunch admirers' after experiencing the full force of Shackleton's personality.

By late March 1917 Shackleton was on his own and the Imperial Trans-Antarctic Expedition had reached a natural close. The round of public events in Australia had finished and most of the expedition's personnel had scattered, many into uniform. Worsley and Stenhouse were travelling back to England on a steamship, Wild and Crean were serving in the navy and Cheetham, Clark, Greenstreet, Macklin and McIlroy were among those who had signed up. Cheetham and Ernest Wild were later killed and McIlroy and Wordie were among those wounded.

On 16 March, shortly before Shackleton confronted the Australian relief committee, Tim McCarthy, the likeable Irish seaman from the *James*

Caird, was killed off the coast of Ireland when a German U-boat sank the oil tanker *Narragansett*. 'A big brave, smiling, golden-hearted merchant service jack,' said Worsley in tribute. 'We, his shipmates who truly learned his worth on that boat journey, are proud of his memory.'

Shackleton, however, remained oddly reluctant to return home. Rather than catch a mail boat to England and Emily, he headed to America for another round of lectures. Ostensibly the lectures were to repay Tripp's loan. But, after almost three years away, no one would have argued against his going home to the family. Raymond, his eldest son, was in his 13th year, his daughter Cecily was close to passing from being a child to a young woman and Edward, only three when Shackleton sailed south, had few memories of his father.

Yet Shackleton was not ready. Perhaps a return to domesticity was a more frightening prospect than the Antarctic. The lined face, grey hair and rounded shoulders told an outward tale of a man prematurely aged by his experiences, but it was impossible to gauge the full impact of the mental anxiety. In a reflective note home, he wrote: 'I have battled against great odds and extraordinary conditions for more than three years and it is time that I should have a rest from it all. I would not alter or have changed one bit of the work and all its trials, for there is a feeling of power that I like, but at times I have grown very weary and lonely.'

One man who saw beyond the immediate fatigue and emotional strain was Richards who understood the effect of two years in the Antarctic as the *Aurora* retreated from McMurdo Sound for the last time. To Richards the signs were ominous and he felt that the sinking of *Endurance* had, in effect, saved Shackleton's life because he was unfit for the overland crossing. Writing half a century later, he concluded: 'Since my return I believe he would have collapsed on the journey.'[1]

Emily was already well prepared for the difficulties of integrating her husband into the family fold after so long. Eastbourne was smaller, quieter and off the beaten track and she sensed he would be unhappy there. 'I know it would bore Ernest to be here for any length of time,' she told Tripp.

Another significant factor which Shackleton overlooked was that sailing home from Australia through the Suez Canal and by train through France was likely to be safer than crossing the North Atlantic from New York. At the start of 1917, Germany unleashed unconditional war on all shipping in a bid to sever Britain's supply lines and starve the country into submission. Among the earliest casualties of the U-boat onslaught was Tim McCarthy. Remarkably enough, passenger and freight shipping still ran the gauntlet of U-boat patrols without the safety of naval protection in early 1917. In April alone, as Shackleton embarked on his American tour, German submarines sank over 850,000 tons of shipping.

After crossing the Pacific, Shackleton went to San Francisco to begin four weeks of speeches, receptions and dinners. While he was on the high seas, America finally entered the war.

Although the big cities celebrated Shackleton's appearances in style, the tour had been hastily arranged and the turnout at some events was poor because little publicity had been arranged. At Tacoma, under the shadow of Mount Rainier in Washington State, an elderly drunk carrying a poster and covered in scraps of cotton wool to simulate snow was the only apparent sign of promotion. Hardly anyone turned up. Shackleton generously reduced his fee to prevent the theatre losing money and added: 'There has been a mistake in the name Tacoma – the T and A should come off and it should read Coma.'

Audiences grew as he reached the big metropolitan venues in Chicago, Philadelphia and New York and Shackleton eagerly fulfilled the rôle as unofficial British ambassador for war. The packed Carnegie Hall in New York seemed to bring the best out of Shackleton.

Among the audience was Sir Shane Leslie, the well-known Anglo-Irish diplomat and writer who was part of the more formal ambassadorial team desperately trying to douse the flames of anti-British feeling in America. The executions of the leaders of Ireland's Easter Rising in 1916 had caused an outcry in America and Leslie welcomed Shackleton's appearance as a sign of improving relations. Leslie, a cousin of Winston Churchill, watched Shackleton deliver a magnificent performance. 'I've never felt the audience played on like an organ by a man talking, except by Winston and Shackleton,' he said. 'On both occasions it hardly mattered what they said.'[2]

It was something of an anticlimax when Shackleton, having avoided the U-boats, finally landed in England at the end of May. Quite by chance, he crossed the Atlantic in the same week the British government introduced a navy-protected convoy system to halt the appalling loss of merchant shipping.

It was almost a year to the day that Shackleton's cable from the Falkland Islands announced his escape from the ice and approaching three years since he had last set foot in England. However, there were no fanfares or jostling crowds to match the stagey homecoming after *Nimrod* and Shackleton slipped quietly into the country almost unnoticed.

In contrast to the pulsating drama and lively celebrations, Shackleton went tamely into the semi-detached suburban anonymity of Eastbourne. It was a neat family retreat in a quiet road and remote from anything

Shackleton had experienced in recent times. Only the occasional muffled rumble of distant guns in France disturbed the tranquillity.

To the surprise of no one, Shackleton found it difficult to adjust. Three years was a long time to be away and it was expecting too much for him to pick up the threads. 'I only hope he will get something to do that will interest him' Emily wrote, 'as he could never be happy in a quiet domestic life.'

Emily understood the problems because they were a repeat of what had happened after *Discovery* and *Nimrod*. Yet again Shackleton found himself with no employment and no tangible idea of what to do next.

Initially he was summoned to Buckingham Palace to give a personal account of the expedition to King George but little else came from the meeting. Over the next few weeks he returned to speak at the Browning Settlement and lectured at Ramsgate as a way of thanking Janet Stancomb-Wills for her valuable assistance. The Dowager Queen Alexandra was another old acquaintance for him to meet. Alexandra, now into her seventies, had taken to wearing heavy make-up and elaborate veils to obscure the march of time, but she had lost none of her unflagging interest in Shackleton's exploits.

Elsewhere, he found himself drawn back into settling the expedition's muddled financial affairs. While Shackleton was embroiled in the Ross Sea relief, Wild had briefly taken responsibility for sorting out bills and dealing with unanswered correspondence. But in early 1917 Wild joined the naval reserve forces and Shackleton now had to pick up the pieces.

It was almost impossible, as ever, to get a clear picture of his affairs. Money was expected from the deal over Hurley's memorable photographs and there was also a promise of funds from a book. As before, the book was being ghostwritten by Edward Saunders. But since Shackleton was reluctant to accept any fees for lecturing in wartime, his other sources of income were doubtful. Nevertheless, in July he told Tripp the expedition was 'now paid off and there are no liabilities.'

Shackleton was still able to exert some influence with the authorities, regardless of the questions which continued to hang over the expedition. In 1917 he proved a valuable ally to Tom Crean when the Irishman was trying to win promotion from petty officer to warrant officer to improve his naval retirement pension. He was also on the brink of getting married. But as a poorly educated farmer's son, Crean did not expect to pass the written examination and Shackleton approached the senior government minister, Arthur Balfour, for help. To Crean, Shackleton wrote: 'You are not frightened of any seafaring job so don't let a little exam beat you.' At the same time he sent Crean £100 in unpaid wages and promised another £100 (£4,250/€5,100 today), although less than the £332 he was owed. Crean passed the examination and was promoted to the rank of Acting Boatswain. He married a month later.[3]

Arranging his own affairs was proving significantly more difficult for Shackleton, who, within months of coming home, had reverted to a familiar pattern. He was restless and looked to the war to find an outlet for his energy. Within six weeks of his return, Emily reported to Tripp that he was 'chaffing to be off' and added: 'For his sake, I shall be glad when he gets his billet.'

Shackleton was 44 years old but the lined face, grey hair and rheumy eyes again hinted at a man years older. He was drinking and smoking heavily and shrugging off niggling bouts of 'indigestion' and back pain. In a letter to his daughter Cecily, he signed himself 'Your tottering aged Daddy.'

He was rarely at home and Rosalind Chetwynd was still on the scene. In fact, Rosa had found a contentment seemingly beyond Shackleton by clinching a role on the London stage under the name Rosa Lynd.

Finding a suitable niche in the colossal British apparatus of war was Shackleton's next target. He was too old for a call-up – conscription applied to 18- to 41-year-olds – and he was reluctant to take a desk job. He was once offered an administrative post coordinating food supplies to Allied forces and told Emily: 'I would have my own staff and secretaries and about £1,000 a year.' The proposal fell through shortly after. 'The question is whether it might in some quarters be thought that I was avoiding the active side of war,' he explained to Emily.

The idea which appealed most was a proposal to arrange transportation for Russian forces, particularly those bogged down in the winter snows. 'I have applied to get the transport work, especially the winter work,' he told Tripp. 'It is right in my line.' The longer-term possibilities in Russia, he said, were 'beyond belief'. But for reasons that never became clear, the Foreign Office was reluctant to send him east and after months of indecision the idea dissolved into nothing.

Something prompted Shackleton to resurrect an idea first mooted by Tripp to exploit his recognition in South America and lead a propaganda delegation to the area. Nations like Argentina and Chile were resolutely neutral in the war but their sea ports were an obvious attraction to the German navy and British standing in the region was generally unsound.

After passing through various hands, the idea eventually came to rest on the desk of Sir Edward Carson, the formidable Anglo-Irish politician and barrister who successfully led Ulster's Protestant community in the fight against Irish Home Rule. Carson had been First Lord of the Admiralty for a while but as the new Minister Without Portfolio he was responsible for censorship, news management and propaganda at the Department of Information.

Carson, another oratorical powerhouse, warmed to Shackleton and decided he was someone who could cut through the diplomatic red tape and protocol to provide ministers with a clear insight into the state of British relations in the region. Carson felt a sense of vindication at picking an outsider for the role when civil servants tried to block Shackleton's posting.

Shackleton, finally endowed with a wartime role, sailed to Buenos Aires with all his usual hopes and optimism. In his haste, he did not bother to arrange a salary from Carson's department. 'I have the ball at my feet now,' he told Emily shortly before sailing. En route he ran into an obscure businessman with an idea to make money and cheerfully told Emily that, as a result, there were no longer any financial concerns. The business arrangement sank without trace.

Little about the posting appeared new to Emily. The relationship was more distant than before, but the talk of loneliness and missing the family was familiar. 'I miss you more than ever I have done Sweeteyes,' he wrote, adding, 'I suppose darling that I am a funny curious sort of wanderer.'

Shackleton's job was as much fact-finding as spreading goodwill. On his travels he found British propaganda was ineffective and much of the work seemed to end up in the quicksand of diplomacy. In one storehouse he uncovered 900 bales of documents that had not been delivered. Although Shackleton's personal popularity was intact, the mission made very little impression and his report subsequently disappeared into the innards of the Foreign Office.

Shackleton returned to London in late April 1918 having survived a dangerous encounter with U-boat raiders off the west coast of Ireland whose attacks were repelled by naval destroyers. At the height of the U-boat threat Shackleton was placed in charge of a lifeboat for 60 passengers because, as the captain explained: 'You know more about boats than any of us.'

He came home to find that Carson, his political champion, had resigned over the poisonous issue of Home Rule and the war in Europe had entered a new dark and threatening phase. After the 1917 October Revolution the Bolsheviks signed the Brest-Litovsk peace treaty with Germany and withdrew Russia from the war. This freed hundreds of thousands of battle-hardened German troops for a fresh assault on the Western Front before up to 1 million trained American soldiers arrived in the field. On 21 March,

Germany launched a massive offensive in Belgium and France in an attempt to land a decisive blow before America's 'doughboys' were in place. Churchill, who was visiting the front, only narrowly escaped with his life in the onslaught and James Wordie was wounded near Armentières.

The residual affairs of the Imperial Trans-Antarctic Expedition continued to haunt Shackleton. He needed to consider the question of Polar Medals for his men and finalise publication of the expedition book, entitled *South*. He had been curiously indifferent to the book and left it almost entirely in the hands of ghostwriter Saunders. Perhaps he found reviewing the affair difficult, or perhaps he knew there would never be any money to be made from *South*.

During the scramble to raise money for *Endurance*, Shackleton had persuaded the businessman Sir Robert Lucas-Tooth to guarantee a sum of £5,000 (about £220,000/€265,000 today) in return for future earnings from the expedition's book. Lucas-Tooth, brewer, banker and politician, was a generous man with an interest in humanitarian causes who once gave £50,000 to Baden-Powell's Boy Scout movement. He died suddenly in 1915 leaving an estate worth £1.2 million but all three of his sons were killed in the war and Lucas-Tooth's executors subsequently chased Shackleton for repayment of the debt. Shackleton settled by handing over the rights to *South* to the rich man's estate. The book, first published in 1919, remains in print to this day.

Saunders spent about a year working on the manuscript, whereas Shackleton's input was brief. But as happened on *The Heart of the Antarctic*, Saunders insisted on remaining anonymous and his true role in compiling the popular book was not disclosed until later. 'The books should stand without any attempt being made now to explain how they were produced,' Saunders explained.

Shackleton spent only three weeks in Australia and New Zealand dictating the story to Saunders at a series of hurriedly arranged meetings at Tripp's home or on boats and trains as he dashed from one engagement to another. Shackleton's first sight of *South* was the largely finished manuscript and Hussey, fresh from the experience of Elephant Island, helped with the final edit.

Saunders proved once again that he was the perfect foil for Shackleton, although working conditions were not ideal. 'Shackleton's method,' said Saunders in a letter to Hugh Mill, 'was to tell me the story, often under conditions that made even the roughest notes difficult.' He took down Shackleton's flowing dialogue with great accuracy – Shackleton rarely hesitated or stumbled over his words – but was confident enough in his writing ability to make suggestions and polish a few phrases with occasional touches of thoughtful editing.

One story to emerge from the sessions with Saunders was a reference to the presence of a 'fourth person' during the crossing of South Georgia with Crean and Worsley. 'When I look back,' Shackleton wrote in *South*, 'I do not doubt that Providence guided us ... it often seemed to me that we were four, not three.'

Among those listening as Shackleton unburdened himself was Tripp, whose home at Heretaunga outside Wellington was used for the occasion. 'I watched him and his whole face seemed to swell,' Tripp recalled. 'After about half an hour he turned to me and with tears in his eyes he said: "Tripp, you don't know what I have been through and I am going through it all again, and I can't do it".'

Tripp remembered that Shackleton would suddenly break off from his speech and walk out of the room. He would return five minutes later after composing himself and start again as if nothing had happened. 'You could see that the man was suffering,' Tripp said. 'And then he came to this mention of the fourth man and he turned to me and said, "Tripp, this is something I have not told you".'[4]

According to Shackleton's account, he did not share his recollection of the mysterious fourth person with Crean or Worsley. But afterwards, he recalled Worsley saying: '"Boss, I had a curious feeling on the march there was another person with us." Crean confessed to the same idea.' Crean did not keep a diary or write a book about his exploits, but would later tell friends: 'The Lord brought us home.'

It would be reasonable to dismiss the episode as either a minor publicity stunt or a case of utterly exhausted men hallucinating from effects of fatigue and hunger. There have been numerous instances down the ages of an inexplicable presence emerging during traumatic experiences. Two decades before the crossing of South Georgia, the sailor Joshua Slocum reported an 'invisible helmsman' while making the first solo circumnavigation of the globe and aviator Charles Lindberg encountered vague 'disembodied beings' as he fought to stay awake on his epic non-stop flight across the Atlantic in 1927.

Without evidence the mystery of Shackleton's 'fourth man' will remain forever unsolved, except to say that Shackleton himself believed it to be true. To the three men on the peaks and glaciers of South Georgia, he said, it was a subject 'very near to our hearts'.

However, the story struck a chord with the poet, T.S. Eliot, who was inspired to incorporate the episode in his acclaimed work, *The Waste Land.*

Eliot was intrigued by what he called the 'constant delusion' of a mysterious presence on the march and when the poem was published in 1922 it included the lines:

> *Who is the third who walks always beside you?*
> *When I count, there are only you and I together*
> *But when I look ahead up the white road*
> *There is always another one walking beside you*[5]

Shackleton was notably more certain when it came to issuing Polar Medals for the men of *Endurance* and the Ross Sea party. Initially the Admiralty baulked at the idea of issuing peacetime medals in the middle of war but Shackleton persevered and a list was drawn up. Missing from the *Endurance* roster were the names of Holness, McNish, Stephenson and Vincent.

This was a deliberate snub and especially vindictive towards McNish whose carpentry skills had been essential to the *James Caird* voyage and who was deserving of the honour. But McNish had fallen short in the total loyalty demanded by Shackleton and was not to be forgiven.

Shackleton, by now frustrated at his failure to join the war effort, had become, in his own words, 'bitterly restless' and sensed that time was running out in his attempts to serve the country. Even more painful was the knowledge that most of his old colleagues were in service and some were dead or wounded.

Another casualty was the old warhorse, *Aurora*. After 40 years of service in the ice, *Aurora* returned from the Ross Sea and was assigned to carry coal across the Pacific from Australia to Chile and return with valuable war materials. On 20 June 1918 *Aurora* left Newcastle, New South Wales bound for Iquique and was never seen again. Among those killed was James 'Scotty' Paton, a veteran polar sea dog who had been a crew member on board *Morning*, *Nimrod*, *Terra Nova* and *Aurora*.

Shackleton continued to press for a job in Russia at the moment Germany's huge spring offensive stuttered to a halt, the army exhausted by over four months of intensive fighting to break the deadlock on the Western Front. They called it *Kaiserschlacht* (Kaiser's Battle) but by August the casualty rate was so enormous the German high command had accepted the war could never be won. *Kaiserschlacht* alone cost both sides some 1.5 million casualties.

Shackleton spent more time in London during the summer of 1918 busily trying to persuade the authorities to allow him into Russia.

Emily was a distant figure and there were other interests besides Rosa Chetwynd. In August he met an old flame, Belle Donaldson. After a meeting in London, he told Donaldson that she had 'chased away my worries and made me feel better'. He also gave Donaldson a hint of making one more trip to the Antarctic. He was, he said, still capable of doing 'good things' in the south and promised to find 'another and higher Mount Donaldson'.[6]

As the war entered its final phase, Shackleton was suddenly drawn into a shadowy enterprise heading to Spitsbergen, high above the Arctic Circle. The task was to lead a team of prospectors from the private Northern Exploration Company (NEC) to search for gold, coal and other valuable minerals. But the voyage was a cover to investigate a possible German presence on the island.

Shackleton, who was also offered shares in NEC and allowed to recruit Wild and McIlroy to the venture, would have relished the peacetime opportunity of mixing treasure hunting with exploration. It did not turn out that way.

Shackleton met *Ella*, the NEC's ship, at Aberdeen in mid-July and headed towards the Arctic Circle. But when the vessel docked at the Norwegian port of Tromsø there was a message from the War Office recalling Shackleton to London. This was just as well as, during the stop-over at Tromsø, Shackleton suffered another disturbing bout of illness. McIlroy, who knew Shackleton's symptoms well, feared more heart problems but was not allowed to listen to his heart. Having avoided another medical examination, Shackleton headed back to England with the true state of his health still unclear.

Shackleton's recall was leading him to the turmoil of post-revolution Russia. Bolshevik Red Army forces were struggling to retain power across the country in a bitter civil war and a small contingent of British and French troops had occupied the northern ports of Murmansk and Archangel to protect Allied interests in the area and assist the counter-revolutionary White Russians. It was also vital to keep Murmansk, the only port in the region that remains ice free throughout the year, out of German hands. The Germans had over 50,000 troops stationed across the border in Finland and viewed Murmansk as an important base for its U-boats.

With temperatures around Murmansk plunging sharply from October onwards, the War Office wanted Shackleton to arrange supplies and equipment, particularly warm clothing and transportation, for troops overwintering 150 miles above the Arctic Circle. On 22 July he was appointed temporary Major in the army, giving him the uniform he craved. 'I'm a sailor really,' he told someone. 'I'm only dressed up like a soldier.'

The appointment coincided with further upheaval in Russia. Five days before, at Yekaterinburg in the Urals, Tsar Nicholas and his family were herded into a small cellar and shot. The Bolsheviks were assuming wider control and it was far from clear how long the British troops could be kept in Russia.

Nevertheless, Russia was a job after Shackleton's heart, offering risky adventure, some sledging trips and the hint of a fight at the end. The recruitment of several old Antarctic hands heightened his interest and gave the campaign the feel of an old-boy's reunion. The Admiralty had released Worsley and Stenhouse from active duty and they were joined by Hussey and Macklin. Eric Marshall from *Nimrod* and Captain Victor Campbell and Dr Edward Atkinson, members of Scott's final expedition, were also in the region. 'The old gang was on the warpath!' Worsley wrote.

To round off the sense of déjà vu, Shackleton also had to contend with sceptical higher authority. Major General Charles Maynard, who was in command of the Murmansk operation, was a Sandhurst-trained career soldier and veteran of almost 30 years of campaigning who saw no role for amateurs in the serious matter of war. Maynard was already struggling to cope with a scratch collection of troops – including eight different nationalities under his command – while he shared the traditional unease of a soldier placed in a quasi-political role. To complicate matters, Maynard had been lobbied by Campbell, a man firmly on Scott's side in the rivalry with Shackleton.

Maynard, like many others, was quickly impressed with Shackleton's breezy style and wholehearted commitment. Any fears that Shackleton liked to run things his own way and would not accept orders were dispelled and Maynard reported his loyalty 'from start to finish was absolute'. What Maynard did not realise was that Macklin, who had been in Murmansk for some time, warned Shackleton of the undercurrents and encouraged him to be on his best behaviour. Before long he was, as usual, the most popular man at the station.

Two weeks after Shackleton's arrival in Murmansk the war finally ended. On 11 November 1918, an armistice was signed, though the fighting in northern Russia continued. Maynard was recalled to London in December to discuss the post-war strategy in Russia and Shackleton, under the cloak of needing to get fresh equipment, accompanied him. It was, said Maynard, 'like schoolboys starting home for the holidays'.

Shackleton hurried to London for a series of meetings and went to Buckingham Palace with Maynard for a brief audience with the King. One night he turned up unannounced on the doorstep of the family home in Eastbourne.

By early 1919 it was clear that Britain would begin winding down the Russian operation and Shackleton's role was coming to an end. Bolshevik forces had seized the initiative, foreign support for the White Russians was evaporating and the mood in London was to bring the 6,000 British troops home. While Churchill trumpeted the Russian campaign as a means to 'strangle the Bolshevik state at birth', public opinion was summed up by the *Daily Express* which claimed 'the frozen plains of Eastern Europe are not worth the bones of a single grenadier'.

Shackleton resigned his temporary commission in early February after just six months in uniform. He was now free to exploit what he regarded as a spectacular new business deal that would, after so much failure, provide the fortune that had eluded his grasp for two decades.

The proposition, which dwarfed the humble aspirations of Celtic Investments or the Nagybánya gold mine, was to exploit the economic development and regeneration of the entire region around Archangel and Murmansk. The proposal, to mobilise the industrial, shipping and natural resources of the region, was his most audacious scheme yet. Shackleton's imagination conjured up visions of an El Dorado-type bonanza emerging from the mud, snowfields and chaos of war in the frozen outpost of northern Russia.

Murmansk was the last city founded under the Romanovs and established as recently as 1916. It had been an obscure fishing port and after only a brief period in the area Shackleton believed it was ripe for lucrative development. What he proposed was taking a stranglehold on much of the region's vital infrastructure and potentially money-spinning businesses. He proposed setting up a private company to hold exclusive fishing, timber and mineral rights, to acquire the key Murmansk–Sorosky railway and to lead the relief effort bringing provisions and supplies to people in the beleaguered area.

'The trading alone is worth £250,000 p.a.,' he told Emily, 'so at last all is well.' (In today's terms, £250,000 a year is worth well over £5 million/€6 million.) She would never again have to worry about money, he promised.[7]

It was another venture which seemed too good to be true. The White Russian authorities in the area supported the idea in the absence of anything else and there was vague backing in London on the grounds the scheme might conceivably help the long-term interests of Britain.

Shackleton, of course, had no money to get the business started and raising funds to invest abroad in a country torn apart by civil war was always

PLEASE TAKE THIS WITH YOU.
PHILHARMONIC HALL
GT. PORTLAND STREET, W.
(Near Oxford Circus).
By arrangement with Mr. ANDRE CHARLOT
TWICE DAILY
2.30 and 8.30
The EVENING STANDARD says:
Both the lecturer and the pictures provide one of the finest entertainments that have ever been known in London.
SIR ERNEST
SHACKLETON
HIMSELF shows the
Marvellous Moving Pictures
and tells the story
OF HIS LATEST ANTARCTIC EXPEDITION
The Times says—"This entertainment has become one of the most popular in London."
The Daily Telegraph says—"Everybody who goes will have a good time."
The Daily Chronicle says—"Those who miss it will miss one of the finest things which London can give us at the present day."
The Daily Mail says—"Easily the best picture show in London."
The Westminster Gazette says—"A remarkable entertainment which all London should see."
The Daily Express says—"Shackleton held the audience spellbound."
The Daily Mirror says—"The film is among the wonders of the world."
The Evening News says—"One of the best entertainments in London."
Reserved 7s. 6d. 5s. and 4s. Unreserved 3s., 2s. and 1s. (Tax Extra)
From the BOX OFFICE at the Hall (Telephone: Mayfair 3003) and the usual Libraries

A poster promoting one of Shackleton's expedition lectures in 1920. To raise money after the **Endurance** *expedition, Shackleton launched into an exhausting schedule, addressing audiences twice a day, six days a week, for five months.*

going to prove difficult. In addition, the overwhelming priority was to rebuild at home after four years of death and destruction.

Shackleton had also joined the majority of observers in underestimating the strength of the Bolshevik revolution, which threatened to leave the counter-revolutionary White Russians badly exposed when the Allied troops inevitably withdrew. By mid-1919 the Allied retreat was in full swing and the region quickly fell into the dark age of Bolshevik rule.

To *Potentia*, Celtic Investments, Nagybánya and the other stillborn schemes of his, Shackleton now added the most ambitious commercial failure of his life.

In the absence of any other source of income, Shackleton was forced to return to the public arena to make a little money. Towards the end of 1919, *South* was published to general acclaim and Hurley's fine moving film of the *Endurance* expedition was shown to enthralled crowds. But because of complex contractual arrangements, Shackleton took only a modest share of the income. Even then, he often gave away the takings. After one successful showing of Hurley's film at the Albert Hall he donated the proceeds to the Middlesex Hospital.

Shackleton pictured around 1920 while he was searching for funds to mount a new expedition.

The most lucrative vehicle was a long season of public lectures delivered in the grand setting of the Philharmonic Hall in central London. Twice a day, six days a week for over five months, Shackleton's booming rhetoric about Antarctic escapades kept audiences gripped. Each session lasted two hours, though at times audience numbers were disappointing. After a draining season of around 250 lectures, the hard work came to an end in May 1920. 'It is a strain,' he told a friend, 'but then all my life is a strain and I would not have it otherwise.'

It happened that the speaker booked into the Philharmonic Hall in the weeks before Shackleton's season opened was Lowell Thomas, the American war correspondent. Thomas was the man credited with creating the legend of Lawrence of Arabia, a shy man, he said, with a 'genius for backing into the limelight'.

There were unmistakable similarities between Shackleton and the enigmatic T.E. Lawrence, including an Anglo-Irish ancestry. Both, single-minded and highly motivated, were men of incredible vision. Lawrence, in fact, unknowingly captured the likeness in a memorable phrase about his own extraordinary life when he said: 'All men dream – but not equally.'

Throughout the long dreary days on stage at the Philharmonic Hall, Shackleton was again dreaming. In quiet moments away from the spotlight he was visualising the moment he could escape and return to the ice. He wanted to mount one last expedition.

chapter 40

The Last Quest

The icy wilderness was the last refuge for Shackleton in the early months of 1920. One by one all other options and ambitions had evaporated in a series of broken business deals, failed opportunities and fading hope. Rows of empty seats in the half-filled Philharmonic Hall were an uncomfortable reminder that the ice no longer commanded public attention. Perhaps the stories brought home by millions of returning troops were more meaningful.

Shackleton was a jaded, almost spent figure. A few old debts from *Endurance* still hung over him. Once more he was drinking and smoking heavily and his health was irregular. The old restlessness which seemed to haunt his life at home had returned. He was moody and quick tempered. Reginald James, who had seen the best of Shackleton in the Weddell Sea, once said that 'Shackleton afloat was a more likeable character than Shackleton ashore.'

The demanding lecture circuit and his questionable health had sapped Shackleton's strength. He was also uncomfortable with continually living in the past. What mattered most to him was the next big adventure.

He was also disturbed by a curious sense of failure and lack of fulfilment in his life. He was oddly dissatisfied with his accomplishments as an explorer and nursed a feeling that, whatever his achievements, the world had not seen the best of him. 'I will make good,' he said on a number of occasions.

The uneasy relationship with Emily did not help. By now Shackleton had largely detached himself from home and was seeing Rosa Chetwynd on a regular basis. He was also in touch with Belle Donaldson and Hope Paterson. He sent a copy of *South* to Paterson at Christmas 1919 with the inscription: 'To Hope, with love and Christmas thoughts.' It was signed 'Mike', the nickname he normally reserved for personal letters to Emily.[1]

Although Shackleton could never be settled at home, he was tortured by the pain he inflicted on Emily. 'I think you are a wonderful girl and woman to have stood my erratic ways all these years,' he told her. 'I am no good at anything but being away in the wilds just with men,' he insisted. 'I feel I am no use to anyone unless I am outfacing the storm in wild lands.'

Emily stayed stoically loyal and somehow came to terms with the fact that her husband preferred the company of younger women. As she had done for so many years, Emily took comfort from the family. Raymond, now 16, was attending Harrow and Cecily was installed along the coast at the Roedean school for girls. How the fees were being met was a mystery. Janet Stancomb-Wills probably helped and Mrs Caroline Oates was friendly with Emily and quietly supportive.

To add to his worries, Shackleton's father, Henry, was seriously ill. Frank Shackleton, too, had resurfaced in Sydenham under the assumed name of Frank Mellor, an awkward echo of a sleazy past which Shackleton preferred to forget. (Frank later opened an antiques shop in Chichester and lived with their sister Amy Vibert until his death in 1941. His headstone carries the name Mellor.)

In a state of near desperation, Shackleton searched for a new goal, any place that would release him from the discomfort of a conventional life. It was a search which took him from the South Pole to the North Pole.

His plan was to explore the Beaufort Sea, the largest unexplored area in the Arctic. A frozen ocean covering about 180,000 square miles (475,000 sq. km) above Alaska and Canada's Northwest Territories, it is choked with impenetrable ice for much of the year and was thought to contain tracts of unexplored land. To Shackleton it also offered a potential route to the North Pole itself.

However, Shackleton had stumbled into the sensitive issue of Canadian territorial rights to the Arctic regions. Canada had been quietly working on a strategy for sovereignty in the Arctic since 1918 because of fears that America or Denmark wished to establish a foothold in the territory.

While the Canadian authorities were prepared to consider the idea, Shackleton naively interpreted the non-committal response as a firm endorsement and hurriedly launched wholeheartedly into the project. In his mind, the expedition would be ready to sail in a matter of months, forgetting that few administrations or bureaucracies around the world moved at the same pace as impulsive explorers.

There was much to consider, including the enormous cost and the acceptance that his wide-ranging plan went far beyond simple exploration of the uncharted seas and unknown islands. He also wanted to search for 'missing' Eskimo tribes thought to inhabit tracts of the ice and undertake a major scientific programme of research, particularly the painstaking study of magnetism in the area. If possible, he would also strike out for the North Pole itself, a journey of 1,000 miles (1,600 km). To Shackleton it was a case of filling the 'great blank' of the Beaufort Sea and solving 'once and for all the mystery of the North Pole',

But the Canadians were hesitant. This was partly because the authorities were already in advanced talks about a similar scheme proposed by Vilhjalmur Stefansson, the Canadian explorer. Stefansson had over 15 years' experience in the Arctic and keen interest in self-promotion. But his reputation was badly damaged by the disastrous *Karluk* expedition between 1913 and 1918 when 11 men died. Among the dead were Alistair Forbes Mackay and James Murray from Shackleton's *Nimrod* expedition.

Stefansson saw Shackleton as a rival and although they met for a round of convivial drinks at a fashionable London club, the Canadian was not impressed. At one stage he offered his services to Shackleton, but he emerged from the meeting to claim that Shackleton was an 'Antarctic man who cared for nothing but outdoing Scott and Amundsen'.[2]

What Stefansson failed to see were the powerful forces pulling Shackleton towards one last expedition. The destination was irrelevant. Wordie, now assembling the remnants of scientific data salvaged from *Endurance*, said Shackleton was 'willing to explore anywhere'.

Shackleton's most pressing problem was the habitual shortage of money. He had no regular income beyond lectures, a few more speculative business ventures had come to nothing and his father's illness was adding strain to his personal finances. The expedition, he estimated, would need at least £50,000 (over £1 million/€1.2 million today), though nothing had been properly assessed. As the search for the next Beardmore or Caird began, the final cost of Shackleton's ambition was anybody's guess.

An official approach to the British government yielded little, despite Shackleton's supreme confidence that he had already accumulated funds from major interests in Canada. Although no backing had yet been agreed, he vaguely claimed support from the Canadian government, the Hudson's Bay Company, Canadian Pacific Railway and wealthy private individuals.

It was much the same with personnel. Shackleton was fully confident of rounding up old Antarctic comrades like Crean, Wild and Worsley for one last hurrah on the ice and submitted a list to the Admiralty of nine men from *Endurance* or *Aurora* who were ready to sail. It is unlikely he checked with the individuals before submitting their names.

In the event, neither Crean nor Wordie agreed to return to the ice. Wordie was now more interested in geology elsewhere in the Arctic and considering plans for a return to Spitsbergen with Bruce. 'Impress on him [Shackleton] the need for doing any amount of oceanography,' Wordie told Mill, 'he has a very hazy idea of what it is and hates water samples.'[3]

Crean had contemplated returning to the ice and had written as recently as 1918: 'I have now fulfilled three expeditions but will look forward to a fourth.' But by 1920, he was 43 years old, married and the father of two young children in his native County Kerry. With a touch of gentle Irish humour, Crean told Shackleton: 'I have a long-haired pal now.'[4]

In the hunt for funds, Shackleton approached Captain Teddy Evans, Scott's old deputy from *Terra Nova*. Shackleton possessed a nose for other people's money and knew from experience that Evans had played a significant role in raising funds for Scott a decade earlier. Thanks to Evans' connections in Wales, the people of Cardiff made the largest single private donation to *Terra Nova* and Shackleton unashamedly wanted Evans to pull the same strings on his behalf.

He wrote to Evans asking for personal letters of introduction to 'any of your Cardiff or other friends' who might be prepared to help. 'If you have 10 friends who might put up £3,000 each I would be all right,' he casually declared. Nothing came of the approach.

To Shackleton's disappointment, the vague and ill-defined scheme to explore the Beaufort Sea carried little popular appeal. The eye of many adventurers, including the RGS, was turned to the 'Third Pole,' the unclimbed Mount Everest. While Shackleton was assembling his new expedition, the Anglo-Irishman Charles Howard-Bury was leading the first major reconnaissance of Everest. Guy Bullock and George Mallory reached almost 23,000 feet (7,000 m) and subsequently returned with firm plans to mount a major attempt on the summit in 1922. Among those who applied to join the 1922 expedition was Wordie, but his application was turned down.

Shackleton had better luck when he ran into John Quiller Rowett, a school friend from Dulwich College. Rowett, who was two years younger than Shackleton, was the prosperous managing director of Rowett, Leakey & Co., a thriving business which controlled a large slice of the world market in rum. There was a little of Longstaff and Caird in the way Rowett channelled some of his wealth into philanthropic interests. Among the best known was the Rowett Research Institute at Aberdeen University, a nutritional research body which exists to this day.

With Canadian money still proving elusive, Shackleton persuaded Rowett to pump some money into the expedition. Initially, the sums were modest but as the Canadian interest wavered, Rowett changed his mind and agreed to fund almost the entire operation. It was a piece of generosity which cost Rowett around £70,000 (about £1.5 million/€1.8 million today) and possibly more. Rowett committed suicide four years later after running into serious financial difficulties and there was vague speculation that his downfall was caused in part by funding Shackleton's expedition.

In a hasty trip to Norway, Shackleton found a ship which, more or less, suited his purposes. The wooden vessel, named *Foca 1*, was less than four years old and built by the reputable Lindstol shipyard near Risør for the whaling fleet. With a strongly built oak frame and steel-sheathed bow, *Foca 1* was just 111 feet (34 m) long and capable of doing up to 7 knots. In the rush to secure the deal, Shackleton paid almost £11,000 and changed the ship's name to *Quest*. It was said the new name was proposed by Emily.

Shackleton was still hoping to catch the 1921 season by sailing in the middle of the year and his preparations were advancing even before approval was secured from Canada. Mill was asked to draw up a scientific programme and supplies and equipment were ordered, including more than 100 dogs from the Hudson's Bay Company. One source of provisions he hoped to arrange on the cheap was the war surplus left over from the campaign in northern Russia. Amid the preparations his father died, aged 74.

Several trips to Canada failed to speed up official approval and Shackleton was increasingly concerned that he would miss the 1921 season. The aim was to cross Baffin Bay, penetrate Lancaster Sound and find a passage through the ice-choked channels around Axel Heiberg Island, which were open for only a few weeks during the summer.

By May, with Shackleton desperate to sail, the Canadian government was facing the unhappy prospect of fighting a general election in a few months and decided that a costly expedition would not be popular. While the Canadians only wanted to delay the venture for a year, it was clear that a new government might be in power by 1922 and Shackleton could not wait. With characteristic improvisation he promptly switched attention from the Arctic to the Antarctic.

Amundsen had performed the same volte-face in 1910 with stunning results. Shackleton's proposal, however, was huge in its scope but notably less eye-catching. There was no obvious target like the Pole or a continental crossing. It was simply the vehicle for Shackleton to escape. 'I am mad to get away,' he told Stancomb-Wills.

The undertaking, now officially called the Shackleton–Rowett expedition, involved circumnavigating the Antarctic continent and mapping a 2,000-mile (3,200 km) stretch of uncharted territory in Enderby Land. He also threw in the possibility of establishing the precise position of various islands in sub-Antarctic waters.

Finally, he had the fanciful notion of searching the South Atlantic archipelago of Trindade and Martim Vaz (known as South Trinidad in Britain) for the buried treasure of 17th-century pirate, Captain William Kidd. Shackleton's dreamy longing for treasure had occupied his thoughts since childhood and this was an opportunity to play out his fantasy. Among his possessions was *The Cruise of the Alerte*, a little-known book by an eccentric character called Edward Knight which gave intricate details of his own personal search for Kidd's long-lost booty.

Shackleton, anxious to fortify the expedition's credentials with the authorities, promised to undertake a substantial scientific programme to study the oceans, weather patterns and the glacier formations. He also wanted to fulfil another long-term ambition of exploiting what he believed were rich deposits of minerals waiting to be found in the Antarctic wastes. 'I do pray we will make good,' he told Janet Stancomb-Wills.

The expedition was a peculiar mixture of the old and the new. The sense of familiarity was provided by the roll call of so many old Antarctic hands, all eager to join Shackleton in one final adventure and the typically unorthodox recruitment process. It was like a reunion for ageing polar explorers.

Wild and McIlroy, who had been in Africa trying their hand at cotton planting in Nyasaland (now Malawi), did not hesitate after receiving Shackleton's invitation to join *Quest*. Also on board were Hussey, Kerr and Macklin, while the veteran McLeod and Green, the cook from *Endurance*, also volunteered, as he had promised he would while adrift in the Weddell Sea. Dell, who was well into his 40s and had been on *Discovery* with Shackleton 20 years before, eagerly signed up as wireless operator. Dell told Shackleton he was unable to operate a wireless but Shackleton said: 'That's alright.'

Worsley, as skipper of *Quest*, was the crucial appointment. The journey, which was likely to last two years, would cover a distance of some 30,000 miles (48,000 km) at sea and Worsley's expertise would be vital.

So eager was he to recruit his old colleague that, when told that Worsley was being pressed for an outstanding mortgage of £150 on a ship, Shackleton promptly sat down and wrote out a cheque from the expedition's funds, declaring. 'It is worth it to have you free from anxiety and to take that glum look off your old face.'

The gloss of newness came from Shackleton's willingness to exploit the latest technological advances. As he demonstrated on *Nimrod*, he was never afraid to experiment. *Quest*, he decreed, would have an electrically heated crow's nest and an instrument for automatically measuring a ship's course, called an odograph.

But most innovative of all was the plan to take an aircraft. The germ of the idea came from George Hubert Wilkins, an Australian aviator who had survived Stefansson's disastrous Arctic expedition and was keen to explore from the skies. While in New York, Wilkins received a telegram from Shackleton inviting him join *Quest* at a salary of £600 (£13,000/€16,000 today) a year and immediately dropped plans to mount his own Antarctic expedition.

The aircraft was a single-seater seaplane developed by A.V. Roe & Company of Manchester, one of the world's first plane makers. Shackleton also recruited New Zealander Roderick Carr as a further pilot.

However, the idea never got off the ground. A change of *Quest*'s route south meant that vital parts were never retrieved from storage in South Africa and the aircraft was never deployed. Shackleton, as he discovered with the disappointing Arrol-Johnson motor vehicle in 1908, was ultimately frustrated in his ambitious attempts to make the transition to the mechanical age of polar exploration. (Wilkins made the first ever flight across Antarctica in 1928.)

One initiative which did catch on was a plan to take young Boy Scouts on the expedition. With an inspired piece of showmanship, Shackleton persuaded the *Daily Mail* to run a competition to find two youngsters prepared to go south. More than 1,700 boys applied and Sir Robert Baden-Powell, founder of the scout movement, drew up a shortlist and eventually picked two candidates: 18-year-old James Marr and Norman Mooney, who was 17.

As a publicity stunt, the idea aroused much attention from the press and public. For this, Shackleton could thank his wife. Since 1917, Emily had thrown a large amount of her time into the Girl Guides and Boy Scouts. With the children at school, it was a means of usefully filling her time. Baden-Powell later invited her to take control of the Guides in Eastbourne and, as her interest developed, Emily encouraged scout companies around the world to adopt the Shackleton name.

The diversion only added another burden to the hurried scramble to get away. Mill, who watched with quiet fascination, said preparations were made with 'fevered haste'.

Shackleton with his wife, Emily, and Frank Wild on board Quest *in 1921 shortly before departing on his last voyage.* COURTESY: SEAMUS TAAFFE

Shackleton summoned as much energy as possible, though he was visibly tired and his health was increasingly fragile. 'Old friends,' said Mill, 'saw in his face signs of the wear and tear of his long years of unceasing hardship and toil.' Shackleton had also put on weight and developed an irksome case of flat feet.

The biggest issue, of course, was his heart, but Shackleton was determined to keep the doctors at bay. The intermittent chest pains, he decided, were simply indigestion or rheumatism. Emily persuaded him to see a specialist shortly before *Quest* sailed, though he fared little better than so many other doctors down the years. As McIlroy recalled, Shackleton 'examined the specialist instead of the specialist examining him'.

After refitting at Southampton, *Quest* came to London in mid-August with Shackleton conscious that the expedition would be sailing very late in the year. As a polite gesture, Shackleton had been elected to the Royal Yacht Squadron and he could fly the White Ensign. At an audience with King George, he was presented with a silk Union Jack.

Another reminder of happier times was a brief meeting with Queen Alexandra. She was now 77 years old, a frail, elderly woman in poor health.

Quest *sails under Tower Bridge in London at the start of the expedition in 1921.*

But she had lost none of her interest in Shackleton's activities. It was almost 20 years to the day since the pair first met on the decks of *Discovery* and Alexandra had been a feature on all his voyages. It was inconceivable that Shackleton would sail without her personal blessing. She gave him a personal talisman to take south.

Quest finally left St Katherine's Dock on the Thames on 17 September. Emily, as was her custom, did not come down to watch as the little vessel ducked under Tower Bridge and moved slowly downriver. Shackleton left the ship at Gravesend in his usual attempt to tie up the many loose ends of his affairs. Before rejoining *Quest* at Plymouth, he spent his final moments with Emily.

In a farewell message carried by the *Daily Mail*, Shackleton told the country: 'The lines are now cast off and over the horizon lies the goal of our ambition.' On 24 September, as *Quest* slipped out of Plymouth Sound, he wrote in his diary: 'At last we are off. Providence is with us even now.' He was cutting ties with the old world and entering his own domain. Three days later he ordered the wireless operator to stop taking the daily news bulletins as they were, in his own words, 'of little importance to us now in a little world of our own'.

Quest, with 18 men on board, was overcrowded and cramped. Once in open seas, the little vessel's flaws were readily apparent. Top speed was barely 5 knots and Shackleton was already revising his plans, concerned that the *Quest* would not reach the ice on schedule by December. The ship sat very low in the water and was regularly swamped by waves, the engine was knocking – the crankshaft was out of alignment – and the boiler had developed a worrying crack. Labouring in the heavy, rolling seas, *Quest* was forced to put into Lisbon for repairs, the first of many irritating stops on the way south. When the ship stopped at Madeira for further running repairs, Mooney, the scout, left the expedition because of acute seasickness.

Worsley had been unhappy with the ship from first sight. He considered the vessel too small for an ocean voyage and difficult to handle. 'The voyage appeared ill-starred from the beginning,' he wrote. Shackleton's health was a source of further concern for Worsley. 'At the outset Shackleton did not appear to me to be physically the man he was when he led the old expedition,' he wrote. Before leaving, he discovered, Shackleton had suffered from some unspecific pains. 'In the light of later knowledge, I realised [it] must have been a heart attack,' Worsley added. At St Vincent in the Cape Verde Islands he went down with an attack of 'suppressed influenza'. Macklin noticed that he was occasionally drinking champagne 'in the hope of staving off anginal attacks'.

Shackleton seemed unusually downbeat. The familiar swagger had disappeared and for once Shackleton at sea was more reminiscent of Shackleton ashore. 'This is a lonely life after all,' he wrote to Emily. 'I miss you more than I can put into words. Your old Micky ... not so bad after all and I love you.'

In a bid to solve the engine problems once and for all, Shackleton decided to abandon plans to call into Cape Town – where important aircraft parts were waiting – and head straight to Rio de Janeiro for repairs. On 21 November, after two months of interruptions, *Quest* finally anchored in Rio.

The damage proved far worse than anticipated and the expedition was delayed for a month in the stifling heat. Almost everything seemed to go wrong and the anxiety was starkly apparent to all on board. 'All his hopes and ambitions seemed centred in that little ship,' one observer wrote, 'and she seemed to let him down so much that I got to hate the damned boat.'[5]

To Emily he wrote that he was feeling the strain 'especially with the eyes of the world' on the expedition. 'I am doing my best,' he added. 'Darling I am a little tired but all right. You are rather wonderful.'

One of the last photographs of Shackleton, taken on board Quest *in 1921.*

On 17 December Macklin received an urgent message that Shackleton had been taken ill from an apparent heart attack while staying on shore overnight. Shackleton would not allow himself to be examined and never complained. But Macklin was now convinced that Shackleton 'must have heart trouble'.

Quest sailed from Rio next day, with Shackleton lethargic and ill at ease. He was plainly tired and Worsley noticed that, uncharacteristically, he spent much of his spare time in his little cabin where a single porthole was his only window on the world. He seemed unusually preoccupied with the past. But in a letter to Rowett, Shackleton finished with a defiant, Browning-like quotation:

Never for me the lowered banner,
Never the lost endeavour![6]

After deciding against Cape Town, Shackleton took *Quest* directly to South Georgia to obtain fresh coal supplies before entering the Antarctic pack ice sometime in January. But on the way a new problem emerged with the discovery of a leak in the furnace. Until the fires were drawn and the furnace examined closely, the scale of the damage was unclear.

This was another huge blow, which Shackleton thought serious enough to imperil the entire undertaking. 'If this crack in the furnace proves serious I may have to abandon the expedition,' he wrote. 'My reputation will stand it – but I am not beaten.'

Storms battered *Quest* as the ship lumbered southwards through heavy seas. Shackleton seemed depressed and irritable. He was also in pain but ignored the advice of Macklin to spend less time on the bridge. To Macklin he was unusually docile and subdued. 'I grow old and tired,' he wrote, 'but must always lead on.' Overhead an albatross could be seen, another wanderer.

Quest closed on South Georgia on 4 January, with Shackleton suddenly revived by the coves, peaks and glaciers he remembered so well during exploits with Crean and Worsley. As the ship entered Grytviken, he wrote in his diary: 'The old familiar smell of dead whale permeates everything. It is a strange and curious place.'

Shortly before leaving England, Shackleton had given an interview to the *Daily Graphic* newspaper in which he was asked to explain why he had chosen a life of exploration. In reply, Shackleton said: 'I go exploring because I like it and because it's my job. One goes once and then one gets

Quest moored in the harbour at Grytviken, South Georgia, in January 1922. Shackleton died on board.

the fever and can't stop going. So I return to the wild again and again, until I suppose in the end the wild will win.'

He went ashore, chatted with a few old friends and returned to the ship invigorated for the challenge ahead. He was happy and content that the expedition was about to begin in earnest.

Before going to bed, Shackleton scribbled a few lines in his diary. His last entry was: 'A wonderful evening. In the darkening twilight I saw a lone star hover gem-like above the bay.'

At around 2 a.m. Macklin was called to Shackleton's cabin where he was told that he was suffering from back pains and neuralgia. He took three aspirin and asked Macklin to explain the cause of his problems. 'I told him as I had told him many times before that he had been overdoing things,' Macklin recalled. He asked what he should give up and Macklin replied: 'Chiefly alcohol, Boss, I don't think it agrees with you.'

Soon afterwards, Shackleton suffered a massive heart attack and died at around 3 a.m. on 5 January 1922. He was 47.

chapter 41

At Rest

Macklin and McIlroy, two of Shackleton's closest disciples, had the unpleasant task of arranging affairs after his sudden death. During the embalming of the body, Macklin performed a rudimentary examination of the heart and confirmed that Shackleton had died from massive heart failure. 'We found fatty extensive atheroma of the coronary arteries,' Macklin wrote, which suggested that Shackleton must have summoned huge reserves of willpower to keep going during his final months.[1]

Shackleton was dressed in silk pyjamas, sewed in a sheet and wrapped in a piece of canvas. The coffin was lined with galvanised zinc and hermetically sealed. A White Ensign was placed on top.

The long funeral procession began on 19 January when the body was placed on board the rugged old whaler *Professor Gruvel* for shipment to Montevideo before being transported to London in the care of Hussey who, with Shackleton gone, had decided to return home. Wild, reluctantly in charge for the first time in his life, had decided to continue with the *Quest* enterprise, though the expedition's heart and soul had long since departed.

During the 10-day voyage to South America word reached Emily that Shackleton was dead. Emily always read Shackleton better than anyone, particularly the sharp contrasts between the man at home and the man in the wilds. She decided, without much hesitation, that it would be appropriate to bury him in South Georgia where he fell. It was where he was happiest, overlooking the sea, surrounded by snow-topped mountains and glaciers and among the peripatetic whalers, drifters and adventurers with whom he bonded so well. Emily understood.

Shackleton was given full military honours in Montevideo, the body lay in state for two weeks and his life, which had touched so many South Americans during the Elephant Island rescue, was commemorated at a

Last respects. Old hands from **Endurance** *gather at Shackleton's graveside in May 1922. Frank Wild, his most loyal companion, is second from right.*

memorial service in the city's English church. Baltasar Brum, Uruguay's President, described Shackleton as a 'magnificent type of humanity'.

From Montevideo, Shackleton was placed on board the steamer *Woodville* and carried back to South Georgia. *Woodville* had served Shackleton nobly before, carrying the little *James Caird* back to England in 1916 after the open-boat journey. Appropriately, a blinding snowstorm was blowing on 27 February as Shackleton made his final landing in South Georgia.

Shackleton was buried in the graveyard of the small wooden Lutheran church at Grytviken on 5 March 1922. With no priest available on the island, the service was conducted by the local magistrate, Edward Binnie. Only Hussey from Shackleton's loyal band of men was able to attend. Six ex-servicemen from the Shetland Islands – Willie Sandison, Geordie Manson, Magnus Leask, John Byrne, Jeemie Brown and James Leask – carried the coffin and a scattering of whalers, seamen and port workers gathered at the graveside. Mrs Aaberg, the only woman on the island, placed a bunch of flowers from her conservatory on the coffin. He was laid with his head facing south.[2]

It was as though Shackleton had choreographed his own departure, determined to find a resting place by the sea and icy slopes where his restless spirit at least found some measure of peace. Before leaving England, Shackleton reportedly told someone that he 'did not mean to die in Europe'.

Macklin said Shackleton would have wanted to be 'standing lonely in an island far from civilisation, surrounded by stormy tempestuous seas and in the vicinity of one of his greatest exploits'. Hussey said the simple grey granite tombstone overlooking the bay 'borrows dignity from the grandeur of the surroundings'. Wild, a man with the same itchy feet and who spent two decades as Shackleton's most faithful companion, recognised that South Georgia was the 'ideal resting place' for the Boss. He wrote: 'I have not the least doubt that had Sir Ernest been able to decide upon his last resting place, it is just here that he would have chosen to lie.'[3]

A month after the funeral, *Quest* returned to Grytviken where the ageing hands from *Endurance* – Wild, Worsley, Macklin, McIlroy, Green, McLeod and Kerr – gathered to pay their final respects. Wild dusted snow off the wreath sent by Emily. (The model of a polar wife, Lady Emily Shackleton lived on the income from her father's estate and accepted help from friends to complete the education of the three children. She lived for a while in a grace-and-favour apartment at the palatial Hampton Court and died in June 1936 at the age of 68.)

Wild abandoned the *Quest* voyage, his fifth expedition, a few months later and effectively drew a line under the Heroic Age of Antarctic exploration, which was moving rapidly from geographical discovery to scientific study. He later drifted to South Africa in search of work where he died in 1939, aged 66. After a long search by the writer Angie Butler, Wild's remains were discovered in a vault in Braamfontein and were buried alongside Shackleton at Grytviken in 2011.

At home, the nation paid a far more elaborate tribute to Shackleton with a memorial service in the magnificent arena of St Paul's Cathedral, London. Emily led the solemn family group and old comrades from *Discovery*, *Nimrod* and *Endurance* were also seen among the large crowd. Representatives of the King, the Admiralty, Royal Geographical Society and other public bodies, whose support was often lacking over the years, bestowed an official veneer to the ceremony. Queen Alexandra, a trusty devotee for over two decades, was also represented.

Shackleton was known to royalty and politicians across the world and during his lifetime received more than 50 medals and other decorations from governments and institutions in Britain and over a dozen other nations. These included America, Austria, Chile, Denmark, France, Norway, Russia and Sweden.

The small quarters on Quest *(bottom left) where Shackleton died on 5 January 1922. Measuring 7 ft x 6 ft (2.13m x 1.82m), the cabin stood opposite the wheelhouse and was described as a 'glorified packing case' (top left).*

Quest *was sold to Norwegian shipowner and respected ice pilot Ludolf Schjeldrup in 1923 for a modest £1,740 and was later involved in several Arctic expeditions. Schjeldrup took* Quest *north in 1928 to locate the missing Italian explorer, Umberto Nobile, a search which also resulted in the death of Roald Amundsen.* Quest *sank in the ice off Newfoundland in 1962.*

During refitting in Norway in the 1920s, the shipyard owner Johan Drage removed Quest*'s cabin and had it towed by horse-drawn sledge to his home 6 miles (10 km) away where it was kept in his garden for many years (bottom right). Drage (top right) and Schjeldrup preserved the cabin to commemorate Shackleton's memory and thanks to the efforts of his descendants, Karl Bakke and Ulf Bakke, it remains in the family of Johan Drage to this day.* COURTESY: ULF BAKKE

Yet Shackleton was ever the restless outsider, who fell tantalisingly short of the ultimate accolade of greatness because he failed at almost everything he attempted. Roland Huntford, an earlier biographer, said he 'lacked the winning touch'. However, Shackleton's pioneering feat up the Beardmore Glacier and across the Polar Plateau in 1908–09 is an achievement of exploration to rank alongside those of Columbus or Cook. Amundsen and Scott, in particular, owe much to Shackleton.

Shackleton was the great paradox. Restive, impatient at home, he was measured, cautious and inspirational on the ice. Money ran through his hands like water and on the rare occasions it stuck he gave it away to charity. He spent a life in the futile pursuit of riches, but left behind a trail of debts estimated to be around £40,000 (almost £900,000/€1.1 million today), though the real figure is impossible to determine. He possessed an exceptional knack of selecting the right sledging companions from a medley of misfits, adventurers and itinerant sailors but could not spot a charlatan in a business suit. Shackleton was an optimist with great vision, but haunted by a fear in later life that he had somehow failed.

Shackleton's great flaw was an unfortunate lack of technique – specifically the failure to embrace dogs and skis – and a ruinous lack of patience which played to his great strength of masterful improvisation, but left him cursed by a shortage of money and the pitfalls of hurried preparation. Few explorers cut corners as cleverly, but ultimately there were only a few extra pounds of pemmican and biscuits standing between Shackleton and the South Pole.

His finest qualities were a remarkable gift for leadership and an unrivalled instinct to survive. Those with a touch of genius look at most things in the same way as everyone else, but at critical moments they have a vision and insight which is beyond ordinary people. Shackleton was such a man.

Shackleton did not have to die to become a hero; he earned the unswerving loyalty of his men because he always put their lives first. The safety of his men was more important than the Pole itself. Sir Raymond Priestley, one of Shackleton's eminent scientists, said: 'For scientific leadership, give me Scott. For swift and efficient travel, Amundsen. But when you are in a hopeless situation, when there seems to be no way out, get on your knees and pray for Shackleton.'

He was a warrior who feared nothing and no one. He fought battles all his life, from the new schoolboy with the thick Irish accent standing up for himself in the playground to the anti-establishment outsider struggling for acceptance. He won most battles, except the fight for inner peace with himself.

Sir Ernest Shackleton's grave at Grytviken, South Georgia.
COURTESY CON COLLINS

For most of his life, Shackleton leant heavily on poetry for inspiration and expression. Tennyson, Swinburne and Browning were his particular favourites. However, it was to Browning he turned most, especially as he summoned up the blood at moments of great endeavour or when communicating with Emily in their private code.

The optimistic defiance of Browning echoed Shackleton's unquenchable spirit, endearing optimism and a relentless drive forward. In *Epilogue to Asolando*, Browning said:

One who never turned his back but marched breast forward
Never doubted clouds would break,
Never dreamed, tho' right were worsted, wrong would triumph,
Held we fall to rise, are baffled to fight better,
Sleep to wake.

Browning's verse became synonymous with the essence of Shackleton. He once said that polar explorers needed a mixture of optimism, patience, imagination and courage, which at times could also be found in the themes of Browning. Hugh Mill, who doubtless heard Shackleton's deep brogue reading the same lines aloud, regarded 'Prospice' as the most fitting of all Browning's poems.

I was ever a fighter, so one fight more,
The best and the last!
I would hate that breath bandaged my eyes, and forebore,
And bade me creep past

No! Let me haste the whole of it, fare like my peers
The heroes of old
Bear the brunt, in a minute pay glad life's arrears
Of pain, darkness and cold;

For sudden the worst turns the best to the brave

Another poem, which might easily apply to Shackleton, was written by Robert Service, another outsider who was born exactly one month before Shackleton and someone who, like Shackleton, was never fully accepted by the establishment of the day. In 'The Men Who Don't Fit In', Service successfully captured the adventurous spirit that drove men into the wilderness. He might well have been writing about Sir Ernest Shackleton:

There's a race of men that don't fit in,
A race that can't stay still;
So they break the hearts of kith and kin,
And they roam the world at will.
They range the field and they rove the flood,
And they climb the mountain's crest;
Theirs is the curse of the gypsy blood,
And they don't know how to rest.[4]

Notes

Abbreviations used

ML Mitchell Library, Sydney, Australia
NMM National Maritime Museum, London, UK
RGS Royal Geographical Society, London, UK
SPRI Scott Polar Research Institute, Cambridge, UK

Introduction

1. For a fuller explanation of the association between Ireland and Antarctic exploration, see: Michael Smith, *Great Endeavour – Ireland's Antarctic Explorers.*
2. Hugh R. Mill, *The Life of Sir Ernest Shackleton.*
3. Margery & James Fisher, *Shackleton.*
4. Jonathan Shackleton & John MacKenna, *Shackleton: An Irishman in Antarctica.*
5. Roland Huntford, *Shackleton.*

1: Touching History

1. There are numerous sources for information about the ancestry of Ernest Shackleton and the Shackleton family. They include: H.R. Mill, *The Life of Sir Ernest Shackleton;* J. Shackleton & J. MacKenna, *Shackleton: An Irishman in Antarctica;* Margery & James Fisher, *Shackleton*; Jonathan Shackleton, *The Shackletons of Ballitore: A Genealogy (1580–1987);* M. Rosove (ed.), *Rejoice My Heart*; Mary Leadbeater, *The Leadbeater Papers*; Caroline Jacob, *The Shackletons of Ballitore;* Frank Nugent, *In Search of Peaks, Passes & Glaciers*; Bingley & District Local History Society.
2. Rosove, *Rejoice My Heart*, p. 6.

2: The Lonely Sea and the Sky

1. Hugh R. Mill, *The Life of Sir Ernest Shackleton*, p. 24.
2. *Ibid.*, p. 24.
3. *The Captain*, April 1910.
4. John Masefield, 'Sea Fever', 1902. Masefield was 16 years old in 1894 when he sailed as an apprentice on North Western Shipping Company's *Gilcruix.*

3: Love and Ambition

1. Leonard Hussey, *South With Shackleton*, p. 179.
2. Hugh R. Mill, *The Life of Sir Ernest Shackleton*, p. 51.
3. *The Captain*, April 1910.
4. Mill, *op. cit.,* 56,
5. The full title of the book is *OHMS: An Illustrated Record of the Voyage of SS* Tintagel Castle, *conveying Twelve Hundred Soldiers from Southampton to Cape Town, March 1900.* The shorter title on the cover reads *OHMS: or How 1200 Soldiers Went to Table Bay,*

4: Laying the World at Her Feet

1. Beau Riffenburgh, *Nimrod*, p. 52.
2. *The Captain*, April 1910.
3. Hugh R. Mill, *The Life of Sir Ernest Shackleton*, p. 57.
4. J. Scott Keltie & H.R. Mill, *Report of the Sixth International Geographical Congress,* 1896.
5. Sir Clements Markham, *The Lands of Silence*, p. 455.

5: Fortune Hunting
1. David Swain, Navy Lodge History.
2. Ernest Shackleton to Emily Dorman, 30 April 1901.
3. M. & J. Fisher, *Shackleton*, p. 21.

6: A Hunger
1. Hugh R. Mill, *The Life of Sir Ernest Shackleton*, p. 61.
2. Michael Rosove, *Antarctica 1772–1922*, p. 269.
3. Hugh Robert Mill, *Hugh Robert Mill: An Autobiography*, p. 151.
4. T.H. Baughman, *Pilgrims on the Ice*, p. 66.
5. Louis Bernacchi, *Saga of the 'Discovery'*, p. 218.

7: Baptism by Ice
1. Robert Scott, *The Voyage of the 'Discovery'*, p. 170.
2. Louis Bernacchi, *Saga of the 'Discovery'*, p. 40.
3. T.C. Fairly, *Sverdrup's Arctic Adventures*, p. 33.
4. M. & J. Fisher, *Shackleton*, p. 37.
5. Bernacchi, *op. cit.*, p. 64.
6. Reginald Koettlitz to Maurice Koettlitz, 21 March 1904, Koettlitz Family Papers.
7. Koettlitz to Fridtjof Nansen, 8 December 1900, Koettlitz Family Papers.
8. George Seaver, *Edward Wilson of the Antarctic*, p. 104.
9. Edward Wilson diary, 12 June 1902.
10. Seaver, *op. cit.*, p. 106.

8: A Step into the Unknown
1. M. & J. Fisher, *Shackleton*, p. 59.
2. Louis Bernacchi, *A Very Gallant Gentleman*, p. 221.
3. Louis Bernacchi, *Saga of the 'Discovery'*, p. 63.
4. Louis Bernacchi, *A Very Gallant Gentleman*, p. 227.
5. Frank Debenham, *Antarctica: The Story of a Continent*, p. 183.
6. Reginald Koettlitz, letter to Maurice Koettlitz, 21 March 1904.
7. Aubrey Jones, *Scott's Forgotten Surgeon*, p. 146.
8. Hugh R. Mill, *The Life of Sir Ernest Shackleton*, p. 78.

9: A Beeline
1. David Yelverton, *Antarctica Unveiled*, p. 196.
2. Robert Scott, *The Voyage of the 'Discovery'*, p. 481.
3. Hugh R. Mill, *The Life of Sir Ernest Shackleton*, p. 79.

10: Rejection
1. Aubrey Jones, *Scott's Forgotten Surgeon*, p. 160.
2. Edward Wilson, The Medical Aspects of the *Discovery*'s Voyage to the Antarctic, *British Medical Journal*, 8 July 1905.
3. Ranulph Fiennes, *Captain Scott*, p. 101.
4. Beau Riffenburgh, *Nimrod*, p. 88.
5. David Crane, *Scott of the Antarctic*, p. 222.
6. Hugh R. Mill, *The Life of Sir Ernest Shackleton*, p. 286.
7. Lord Mountevans, *Adventurous Life*, p. 67.
8. Ernest Shackleton, telegram to Emily Dorman, March 1903, SPRI.

11: Two Characters
1. M. & J. Fisher, *Shackleton*, p. 80.
2. Cecily Shackleton, interview with James Fisher, SPRI.
3. David Yelverton, *Antarctica Unveiled*, p. 326.
4. Arthur Conan Doyle, *Arthur Conan Doyle*, p. 181.

5. Hugh R. Mill, *The Life of Sir Ernest Shackleton*, p. 95.
6. The result of the Dundee election, 1906 (2 seats): Edmund Robertson (Lib) 9,276; Alexander Wilkie (Lab) 6,833; Henry Robson (Lib) 6,122; Ernest Shackleton (Lib Un) 3,865; A. Duncan Smith (Con) 3,183.
7. Mill, *op. cit.*, p. 97.

12: Finding a Niche
1. M. & J. Fisher, *Shackleton*, p. 97.
2. *Ibid.*, p. 99.
3. Ernest Shackleton to Emily Shackleton, 12 February 1907, SPRI.

13: Looking South
1. Hugh R. Mill, *The Life of Sir Ernest Shackleton*, p. 99.
2. John Scott Keltie to Robert Scott, 8 March 1907, RGS.
3. Robert Scott to Ernest Shackleton, February 1907, SPRI.
4. M. & J. Fisher, *Shackleton*, p. 110.
5. Scott to Keltie, 20 February 1907, RGS.
6. Scott to Keltie, 1 March 1907, RGS.
7. Keltie to Scott, 1 March 1907, RGS.
8. Edward Wilson to Ernest Shackleton, 28 February 1907, SPRI.
9. Fisher, *op. cit.*, p. 113.

14: Dreams and Realities
1. Ernest Shackleton to Elspeth Beardmore, 13 May 1907, NMM.
2. Jon Sörensen, *The Saga of Fridtjof Nansen*, p. 249.
3. *Pearson's Magazine*, March 1904.
4. Ernest Shackleton, *The Heart of the Antarctic*, p. 13.
5. Aubrey Jones, *Scott's Forgotten Surgeon*, p. 181.
6. Ernest Shackleton to Arthur Schuster, 14 May 1907, SPRI.
7. M. & J. Fisher, *Shackleton*, p. 125.
8. Ernest Shackleton to Emily Shackleton, 14 August 1907, SPRI.

15: Broken Promise
1. Ernest Shackleton to Elspeth Beardmore, 15 October 1907, NMM.
2. Shackleton to Elspeth Beardmore, 20 January 1908, NMM.
3. Shackleton to Elspeth Beardmore, 5 November 1907, NMM.
4. Shackleton to Emily Shackleton, 26 January 1908, SPRI.
5. Leif Mills, Polar Friction.

16: Ice and Men
1. Ernest Shackleton to Rupert England, 18 January 1908, *The Shackleton Letters*, p. 127.
2. Shackleton to Emily Shackleton, 15 February 1908, SPRI.
3. David Crane, *Scott of the Antarctic*, p. 390.

17: Making Ready
1. Ernest Shackleton to Emily Shackleton, 18 February 1908, SPRI.
2. Shackleton to Emily Shackleton, 22 February 1908, SPRI.
3. Leif Mills, Polar Friction.
4. Eric Marshall, diary entries: 23–27 February 1908, SPRI.
5. Leif Mills, *op. cit.*.

18: South
1. The quotations of Shackleton are taken from diary of Ernest Shackleton published in *Heart of the Antarctic.*
2. Frank Wild, Diary of Southern Journey, SPRI.

3. Ernest Shackleton to James Murray, 23 October 1908, SPRI.
4. M. & J. Fisher, *Shackleton*, p. 105.

19: Penniless
1. Charles Herbert Dorman to Emily Shackleton, 12 June 1908, SPRI.
2. Dorman to Emily Shackleton, 14 July 1908, SPRI.
3. Dorman to Emily Shackleton, 4 November 1908, SPRI.
4. Dorman to Emily Shackleton, 29 December 1908, SPRI.

20: Gateway
1. The quotations of Shackleton are taken from: diary of Ernest Shackleton published in *Heart of the Antarctic;* the diary of Frank Wild, SPRI; the diary of Eric Marshall, SPRI.
2. Leif Mills, Polar Friction.
3. Roald Amundsen, *The South Pole*, p. 114.
4. Roald Amundsen, *My Life As An Explorer*, p. 66.
5. Frank Wild, Memoirs, ML.

21: *'Death on his pale horse ...'*
1. The quotations of Shackleton are taken from: diary of Ernest Shackleton published in *Heart of the Antarctic;* the diary of Frank Wild, SPRI; the diary of Eric Marshall, SPRI.
2. M. & J. Fisher, *Shackleton*, p. 218.

22: Home is the Hero
1. Ernest Shackleton to Leonard Darwin, 23 July 1909, SPRI.
2. Sir Clements Markham to Scott Keltie, 28 March 1909, RGS.
3. Scott Keltie to Ernest Shackleton, 1 April 1909, RGS.
4. Ernest Shackleton to Hugh Mill, 5 May 1909, SPRI.
5. Markham, Memorandum to RGS, (undated) 1909, RGS.
6. E.A. Reeves, Report into Southern Party's Latitudes to Royal Geographical Society, 14 September 1909, RGS.

23: Arise, Sir Ernest
1. Ernest Shackleton, *The Heart of the Antarctic*, Vol. 2, p. 414.
2. Ernest Shackleton to Emily Shackleton, 25 April 1909; 15 May 1909, SPRI.

24: A Man of Parts
1. Douglas Mawson, *Mawson's Antarctic Diaries*, p. xxxv.
2. Mawson, *op. cit.*, p. xxxvi.
3. Tom Clarke, *My Northcliffe Diary*, p. 216.
4. David Crane, *Scott of the Antarctic*, p. 390.
5. Edward Wilson to Shackleton, (precise date not given) 1909, SPRI.
6. M. & J. Fisher, *Shackleton*, p. 289.

25: Unrest
1. Ernest Shackleton to Leonard Tripp, 24 May 1911, SPRI.
2. Emily Shackleton to Hugh R. Mill, 29 August 1922, SPRI.
3. Tor Bomann-Larsen, *Roald Amundsen*, p. 111.
4. Ernest Shackleton, *South*, p. 77.
5. John King Davis, *High Latitude*, p. 186.
6. Roald Amundsen, *My Life As An Explorer*, p. 71.
7. Hugh R. Mill, *The Life of Sir Ernest Shackleton*, p. 187.

26: Towering Ambition
1. M. & J. Fisher, *Shackleton*, p. 297.

2. Roland Huntford, *Shackleton*, p. 374.
3. Peter Speak, *William Speirs Bruce*, p. 124.
4. Sir Clements Markham, Memo to Royal Geographical Society, 1914, RGS.
5. Peter Speak, *William Speirs Bruce*, p. 123.
6. Royal Geographical Society, Report on Meeting with Sir Ernest Shackleton, 4 March 1914, RGS.
7. *Geographical Journal*, Vol. 43, p. 318.
8. Hugh R. Mill, *The Life of Sir Ernest Shackleton*, p. 198.
9. Dame Janet Stancomb-Wills, *James Caird Society Newsletter*, October 2000.
10. Eric Marshall letter, 15 September 1950, RGS.
11. Frank Worsley, *Endurance*, p. 12.
12. Ernest Shackleton to Scott Keltie, 2 February 1914, RGS.
13. Stephen Haddelsey, *Ice Captain*, p. 21.
14. Robert Burton, private research.
15. Robert Burton, private research.
16. Martin Gilbert, *The First World War*, p. 297.
17. M. & J. Fisher, *Shackleton*, p. 327.
18. Mill, *op. cit.*, p. 203.

27: Into the Pack

1. Robert Burton, Endurance at South Georgia, *Nimrod Journal*, 2013.
2. Robert Burton, unpublished manuscript, 2013.
3. Quotations are taken from the *Endurance* diary of Sir Ernest Shackleton and his book *South*.
4. Prospectus: The Imperial Trans-Antarctic Expedition, Oldham Council Archives.
5. Ian B. Hart, *Pesca*, p. 148.

28: Imprisoned

1. Quotations are taken from Ernest Shackleton's diaries, his book *South*, and the diaries of other members of the Imperial Trans-Antarctic Expedition including Frank Hurley, Henry McNish, Thomas Orde Lees, Frank Wild, James Wordie and Frank Worsley.
2. Aeneas Mackintosh diary, 21 June 1915, SPRI.
3. William Barr, Antarctic Debacle, *Nimrod Journal* 2013, p. 41.
4. Sir Leopold McClintock, *The Voyage of the Fox in the Arctic Seas*, p. 47.

29: Death of a Ship

1. Quotations are taken from Ernest Shackleton's diaries, his book, *South*, and the diaries of other members of the Imperial Trans-Antarctic Expedition including Frank Hurley, Henry McNish, Thomas Orde Lees, Frank Wild and Frank Worsley.

30: Defiance

1. Quotations are taken from Ernest Shackleton's diaries, his book *South*, and the diaries of other members of the Imperial Trans-Antarctic Expedition including Frank Hurley, Henry McNish, Thomas Orde Lees, Frank Wild and Frank Worsley.
2. Hugh R. Mill, *The Life of Sir Ernest Shackleton*, p. 291.
3. Leonard Hussey, Interview with James Fisher, November 1955, SPRI.
4. Frank Worsley, Paper on Animals Killed in Weddell Sea.

31: Into the Boats

1. Quotations are taken from: Sir Ernest Shackleton, *South;* Frank Worsley *Shackleton's Boat Journey* and *Endurance;* the diaries and papers of Sir Ernest Shackleton, Frank Worsley, Henry McNish, Thomas Hans Orde Lees, Frank Wild and other members of the Imperial Trans-Antarctic Expedition.
2. Geoffrey Hattersley-Smith, personal recollection of Walter How, interview with author 2003.

32: A Dark Episode

1. Aeneas Mackintosh, letter to Ernest Shackleton, August 1915, SPRI.

33: Bleak Refuge

1. Quotations are taken from: Sir Ernest Shackleton, *South;* Frank Worsley *Shackleton's Boat Journey* and *Endurance;* the diaries and papers of Sir Ernest Shackleton, Frank Worsley, Henry McNish, Thomas Hans Orde Lees, Frank Wild and other members of the Imperial Trans-Antarctic Expedition.
2. Frank Worsley, *Endurance*, p. 87.
3. *Ibid.*, p. 104.
4. Frank Worsley, *Shackleton's Boat Journey*, p. 54.

34: Scattered to the Winds

1. Frederick White, cable to Joseph Stenhouse, 1 April 1916, SPRI .
2. Correspondence between Robert Donald and Reginald McKenna, May 1916, National Archives.
3. Robert Donald, *Daily Chronicle*, to Reginald McKenna MP, 11 May 1916, National Archives.

35: Epic Journey

1. Frank Worsley, *Endurance*, p. 99.
2. Quotations are taken from: Sir Ernest Shackleton, *South;* Frank Worsley *Shackleton's Boat Journey* and *Endurance;* the diaries and papers of Sir Ernest Shackleton, Frank Worsley, Henry McNish.
3. Michael Smith, *An Unsung Hero*, p. 168.

36: South Georgia

1. Quotations are taken from Sir Ernest Shackleton, *South*; *Shackleton's Boat Journey* and *Endurance* by Frank Worsley.

37: Rescue

1. Quotations are taken from Sir Ernest Shackleton, *South*; *Shackleton's Boat Journey* and *Endurance* by Frank Worsley.
2. M. & J. Fisher, *Shackleton*, p. 390.
3. *Ibid.*, p. 390.
4. O. Locker Lampson MP, letter to David Lloyd George, 25 April 1911, National Archives.
5. V.E. Speranza, re *Yelcho*, 30 November 1936, Seamus Taaffe Collection.
6. Alfonso Filippi Parada, Shackleton Versus Pardo, *James Caird Journal*, 2012.

38: The Ross Sea Party

1. Leif Mills, *Frank Wild*, p. 265.
2. Ernest Shackleton to Emily Shackleton, 3 September 1916, SPRI.
3. *Magellan Times*, 13 July 1916.
4. Douglas Mawson memo, National Archives, T/1/12012.
5. M. & J. Fisher, *Shackleton*, p. 415.
6. John King Davis, *High Latitude*, pp. 257–60.

39: Adrift Again

1. Richard McElrea & David Harrowfield, *Polar Castaways*, p. 265.
2. M. & J. Fisher, *Shackleton*, p. 424.
3. Michael Smith, *An Unsung Hero – Tom Crean*, p. 300.
4. Hugh R. Mill, *The Life of Sir Ernest Shackleton*, p. 245.
5. T.S. Eliot, *The Waste Land, Collected Poems.*
6. Ernest Shackleton to Belle Donaldson, 2 August 1918, Seamus Taaffe Collection.
7. Ernest Shackleton to Emily Shackleton, 4 March 1919, SPRI.

40: The Last Quest

1. Seamus Taaffe, personal collection.
2. Vilhjalmur Stefansson, *Discovery*, p. 238.
3. James Wordie letter to Hugh Mill, 6 July 1921.
4. Michael Smith, *An Unsung Hero*, p. 308.
5. M. & J. Fisher, *Shackleton*, p. 469.
6. Research by Jan Piggott indicates the source of the lines was an unfamiliar poem by Fiona Macleod in *The Hour of Beauty* in 1907.

41: At Rest

1. Corbishley, Dr Cathy, The Death of Shackleton on South Georgia, *South Georgia Association Newsletter*, November 2013.
2. Robert Burton, *Shackleton at South Georgia*, p. 12.
3. Frank Wild, *Shackleton's Last Voyage*, p. 70.
4. The Spell of the Yukon and Other Verses, Robert Service. *Collected Poems of Robert Service,* Warner Books, 1993.

Select Bibliography

This book arose from a lifetime's interest in the history of polar exploration and it would be impossible to record all the items of published or unpublished works that have contributed to it. The list below represents the names of books, magazines, diaries, correspondence, online outlets and visual sources which have been most useful. It is an entirely personal selection and because of the vast array of material available, the list cannot be considered complete. Any omissions are unintentional and errors or oversights can be remedied in due course.

Books

Aldridge, Don, *The Rescue of Captain Scott*, Tuckwell Press, 1999
Alexander, Caroline, *The Endurance*, Bloomsbury, 1998
Altick, Richard, *The English Common Reader: A Social History of the Mass Reading Public 1800–1900*, University of Chicago Press, 1957
Amundsen, Roald, *My Life As An Explorer*, Wm Heinemann, 1927
Amundsen, Roald, *The South Pole*, Hurst & Co., 1976
Armitage, Albert, *Cadet to Commodore*, Cassell & Co., 1925
Armitage, Albert, *Two Years in the Antarctic*, Edward Arnold, 1905
Bakewell, William L., *The American on Endurance* (ed. Elizabeth Anna Bakewell) Dukes Hall Publishing, 2004
Barczewski, Stephanie, *Antarctic Destinies: Scott, Shackleton and the Changing Face of Heroism*, Hambledon Continuum, 2007
Barnett, Corelli, *The Collapse of British Power*, Eyre Methuen, 1972
Barrie, David, *Sextant*, William Collins, 2014
Bartlett, Thomas, *Ireland: A History*, Cambridge University Press, 2011
Baughman, T.H., *Pilgrims on the Ice*, University of Nebraska Press, 1999
Begbie, Harold, *Shackleton: A Memory*, Mills and Boon, 1922
Bennett, Laura & Emily Dorman, *The Corona of Royalty*, Blackwood, 1902
Bernacchi, Louis, *A Very Gallant Gentleman*, Thornton Butterworth, 1933
Bernacchi, Louis C., *Saga of the 'Discovery'*, Blackie & Son, 1938
Bernacchi, Louis C., *To the South Polar Regions: Expedition of 1898–1900*, Hurst and Blackett, 1901
Bickel, Leonard, *In Search of Frank Hurley*, Macmillan, 1980
Bickel, Leonard, *Shackleton's Forgotten Men*, Pimlico, 2001
Bickel, Leonard, *This Accursed Land*, Macmillan, 1977
Bomann-Larsen, Tor, *Roald Amundsen*, Sutton Publishing, 2006
Borchgrevink, Carsten, *First on the Antarctic Continent*, George Newnes, 1901
Bowman, Gerald, *From Scott to Fuchs*, Evans Brothers, 1960
Browning, Robert, *The Poems of Robert Browning*, Wordsworth Poetry Library, 1994
Bruce, William Speirs, *Polar Exploration*, Williams & Northgate, 1910
Bryan, Rorke, *Ordeal by Ice: Ships of the Antarctic*, The Collins Press, 2011
Burton, Robert & Stephen Venables, *Shackleton at South Georgia*, Robert Burton, 2001

Butler, Angie, *The Quest for Frank Wild*, Jackleberry Press, 2011
Cameron, Garth James, *From Pole to Pole: Roald Amundsen's Journey in Flight*, Pen & Sword, 2013
Campbell, Mary, *Curious Tales of Old West Yorkshire*, Sigma Leisure, 1999
Carpenter, Kenneth J., *The History of Scurvy*, Cambridge University Press, 1986
Cavill, Janice & Jeff Noakes, *Acts of Occupation: Canada and Arctic Sovereignty 1918–25,* University of British Columbia Press, 2011
Cherry-Garrard, Apsley, *The Worst Journey in the World*, Penguin, 1983
Clarke, Tom, *My Northcliffe Diary*, Gollancz, 1931
Crane, David, *Scott of the Antarctic,* Harper Collins, 2005
Daly, Regina *The Shackleton Letters: Behind the Scenes of the Nimrod Expedition*, Erskine Press, 2009
Davenport-Hines, R.P.T., *Dudley Docker: The Life and Times of A Trade Warrior*, Cambridge University Press, 2004
David, Edgeworth, *The Life of Sir T.W. Edgeworth David*, Edward Arnold, 1937
Davis, John King, *High Latitude*, Melbourne University Press, 1962
Davis, John King, *Trial By Ice: the Antarctic Journals of John King Davis*, Bluntisham Books, 1997
Day, David, *Antarctica – A Biography*, Oxford University Press, 2013
Debenham, Frank, *Antarctica: The Story of a Continent*, Jenkins 1959
Debenham, Frank, *The Quiet Land*, Bluntisham Books, 1992
Dooley, Terence, *The Decline of the Big House in Ireland,* Wolfhound Press, 2001
Doorly, Gerald, *The Voyage of the Morning*, Smith, Elder, 1916
Doyle, Sir Arthur Conan, *Memories and Adventures: An Autobiography*, Wordsworth Literary Lives, 2007
Dunnett, Harding, *Shackleton's Boat: The Story of the James Caird,* Neville & Harding, 1996
Eliot, T.S., *Collected Poems 1909–62*, Faber and Faber, 2002
Evans, E.R.G.R., *South With Scott*, Collins, 1924
Fairley, T.C., *Sverdrup's Arctic Adventures,* Longman, Green & Co., 1959
Fiennes, Ranulph, *Captain Scott,* Hodder & Stoughton, 2003
Fisher Margery & James, *Shackleton*, Barrie Books, 1957
Ford, Charles Reginald, *Antarctica, Leaves from a Diary Kept on Board an Exploring Vessel,* Whitcombe & Tombs, 1908
Fuchs, Sir Vivian & Sir Edmund Hillary, *The Crossing of Antarctica: The Commonwealth Trans-Antarctic Expedition 1955–58,* Cassell, 1958
Geiger, John, *The Third Man Factor*, Canongate, 2009
Gilbert, Martin, *First World War*, Weidenfeld & Nicolson, 1994
Gran, Tryggve, *The Norwegian With Scott*, HMSO, 1984
Gurney, Alan, *Below the Convergence: Voyages Towards Antarctica*, Pimlico, 1998
Gwynn, Stephen, *Captain Scott*, Bodley Head, 1929
Haddelsey, Stephen, *Ice Captain: The Life of J.R. Stenhouse,* The History Press, 2008
Harris, C.J. & Brian Ingpen, *Mail Ships of the Union Castle Line*, Fernwood Press, 1994
Harrowfield, David, *Icy Heritage: Historic Sites of the Ross Sea Region,* Antarctic Heritage Trust, 1995
Hart, Ian B, *Pesca: A History of the Pioneer Modern Whaling Company in the Antarctic,* Aidan Ellis, 2001
Hayes, J. Gordon, *The Conquest of the South Pole: Antarctic Exploration 1906–1931,* Thornton Butterworth, 1932
Herbert, Kari, *Heart of the Hero*, Saraband, 2013
Herbert, Wally, *The Noose of Laurels*, Hodder & Stoughton, 1989
Hobsbawm, Eric, *The Age of Empire: 1875–1914*, Weidenfeld & Nicolson, 1987
Huntford, Roland, *Nansen*, Gerald Duckworth, 1997
Huntford, Roland, *Scott & Amundsen*, Hodder & Stoughton, 1979
Huntford, Roland, *Shackleton*, Hodder & Stoughton, 1985
Hurley, Frank, *Shackleton's Argonauts*, Angus & Robertson, 1948
Hussey, Leonard, *South With Shackleton,* Sampson Low, 1951
Huxley, Elspeth, *Scott of the Antarctic*, Weidenfeld and Nicolson, 1977

Jacob, Caroline, *The Shackletons of Ballitore*, Friends General Conference, 1984
James, Lawrence, *The Rise and Fall of the British Empire,* Little, Brown & Co., 1994
Jeal, Tim, *Stanley: The Impossible Life of Africa's Greatest Explorer*, Faber and Faber, 2007
Johnson, Anthony M., *Scott of the Antarctic*, University College Cardiff Press, 1984
Jones, A.G.E., *Polar Portraits,* Caedmon of Whitby, 1992
Jones, Aubrey, *Scott's Forgotten Surgeon – Dr Reginald Koettlitz,* Whittles Press, 2012
Jones, Max, *The Last Great Quest,* Oxford University Press, 2003
Jones, Tom, *Patagonian Panorama*, Outspoken Press, 1961
Joyce, Ernest, *The South Polar Trail*, Duckworth, 1929
Kee, Robert, *Ireland: A History*, Weidenfeld & Nicolson, 1980
Kennedy, Paul, *The Rise and Fall of the Great Powers*, Unwin Hyman, 1988
Korda, Michael, *Hero: The Life & Legend of Lawrence of Arabia*, Aurum Press, 2012
Kruger, Rayner, *Goodbye Dolly Gray*, Pan Books, 1974
Lansing, Alfred, *Endurance*, Granada Publishing, 1984
Larson, Edward J., *An Empire of Ice: Scott, Shackleton and the Heroic Age of Antarctic Science,* Yale University Press, 2011
Lashly, William, *Under Scott's Command: Lashly's Antarctic Diaries* (A.R. Ellis ed.), Victor Gollancz, 1969
Leadbeater, Mary, *The Leadbeater Papers: A Selection from the MSS. and Correspondence of Mary Leadbeater,* Bell and Daldy, 1862
Leadbeater, Mary, *Memoirs and Letters of Richard and Elizabeth Shackleton,* J.B. Gilpin, 1849
Leake, Bernard E., *The Life and Work of Professor J.W. Gregory*, The Geological Society, 2011
Leake, W.R.M., *Gilkes and Dulwich*, The Alleyn Club, 1928
Longstaff, Llewellyn W., *The Kingston Masonic Annual*, M.C. Peck & Son, 1871
Loomis, Chauncey, *Weird & Tragic Shores*, Macmillan, 1971
Lopez, Barry, *Arctic Dreams*, Pan Books, 1987
McClintock, Sir Leopold, *The Voyage of the Fox in the Arctic Seas: Fate of Sir John Franklin*, John Murray, 1875
McConville, Michael, *Ascendancy to Oblivion: The Story of the Anglo-Irish*, Phoenix, 2002
McElrea, Richard & David Harrowfield, *Polar Castaways: The Ross Sea Party (1914–17) of Sir Ernest Shackleton*, McGill-Queen's University Press, 2004
McGhee, Robert, *The Arctic Voyages of Martin Frobisher*, British Museum Press, 2002
McKinlay, William Laird, *Karluk*, Weidenfeld & Nicolson, 1976
Mackintosh, A.L.A., *Shackleton's Lieutenant; the Nimrod Diary of A.L.A. Mackintosh, British Antarctic Expedition 1907–09* (Stanley Newman ed.) Polar Publications Ltd (1990)
Markham, A.H., *The Life of Sir Clements Markham*, John Murray, 1917
Markham, Clements, *Antarctic Obsession: The British National Antarctic Expedition 1901–04,* Bluntisham Books, 1986
Markham, Clements, *The Lands of Silence*, Cambridge University Press, 1921
Marr, J.W., *Into the Frozen South*, Cassell & Co., 1923
Mason, Theodore K., *The South Pole Ponies*, Dodd, Mead & Co., 1979
Mawson, Douglas, *Mawson's Antarctic Diaries* (Fred & Eleanor Jacka eds.), Unwin Hyman, 1988
Mawson, Douglas, *The Home of the Blizzard*, Hodder and Stoughton, 1930
Mawson, Paquita, *Mawson of the Antarctic*, Longman, 1964
Maxtone-Graham, John, *Safe Return Doubtful*, Patrick Stephens, 1989
Maynard, Sir Charles, *The Murmansk Venture*, Naval & Military Press 2010
Mill, Hugh Robert, *Hugh Robert Mill: An Autobiography*, Longman, Green, 1951
Mill, Hugh Robert, *The Life of Sir Ernest Shackleton,* William Heinemann, 1923
Mill, Hugh Robert, *The Siege of the South Pole*, Alston Rivers, 1905
Mills, Leif, *Men of Ice,* Caedmon of Whitby, 2008
Mills, Leif, *Frank Wild,* Caedmon of Whitby, 1999
Morrell, Margaret & Stephanie Capparell, *Shackleton's Way*, Nicholas Brearly Publishing, 2001
Mountevans, Lord, *Adventurous Life*, Hutchinson, 1946

Murphy, D.T., *German Exploration of the Polar World: A History 1870–1940,* University of Nebraska Press
Murray, James and George Marston, *Antarctic Days: Sketches of the Homely Side of Polar Life by Two of Shackleton's Men*, (Introduction: Joe O'Farrell), Erskine Press, 2012
Nansen, Fridtjof, *Farthest North,* Constable, 1904
Nansen, Fridtjof, *In Northern Mists: Arctic Exploration In Earliest Times*, Frederick A. Stokes, 1911
Nasht, Simon, *No More Beyond: The Life of Hubert Wilkins,* Birlinn, 2006
Niven, Jennifer, *The Ice Master*, Macmillan, 2000
Nugent, Frank, *In Search of Peaks, Passes & Glaciers,* The Collins Press, 2013
Nugent, Frank, *Seek The Frozen Lands*, The Collins Press, 2003
Pakenham, Thomas, *The Boer War*, Abacus, 1992
Pakenham, Thomas, *The Scramble for Africa*, Weidenfeld & Nicolson, 1991
Piggott, Jan, *Shackleton: The Antarctic and Endurance*, Dulwich College, 2000
Piggott, Jan, *Dulwich College, a History, 1616–2008*, Dulwich College, 2000
Ponting, Herbert, *The Great White South*, Duckworth, 1921
Pound, Reginald, *Evans of the Broke*, Oxford University Press, 1963
Pound, Reginald, *Scott of the Antarctic,* World Books, 1966
Preston, Diana, *A First-Rate Tragedy*, Constable, 1997
Probert, Laura, *A Life in History: Ramsgate's First Lady Mayor*, Millicent Press, 2008
Quartermain, L.B., *Antarctica's Forgotten Men,* Millwood Press, 1981
Queen Alexandra, *Queen Alexandra's Christmas Gift Book: Photographs From My Camera*, Daily Telegraph, 1908
Richards, R.W., *The Ross Sea Party 1914–17,* Scott Polar Research Institute, 1962
Riffenburgh, Beau, *Nimrod*, Bloomsbury, 2004
Riffenburgh, Beau, *Racing With Death: Douglas Mawson*, Bloomsbury, 2008
Riffenburgh, Beau, *The Myth of the Explorer*, Bellhaven Press, 1993
Roberts, David, *Alone On The Ice*, W.W. Norton, 2013
Ross, James Clark, *A Voyage of Discovery and Research in the Southern and Antarctic Regions, during the years 1839–43*, John Murray, 1847
Ross, M.J., *Ross in the Antarctic*, Caedmon of Whitby, 1982
Rosove, Michael, *Antarctica, 1772–1922*, Adélie Books, 2001
Rosove, Michael, *Let the Heroes Speak*, Naval Institute Press, 1999
Royal Irish Academy, *Dictionary of Irish Biography*, Royal Irish Academy, 2009
Savours, Ann, *The Voyages of the 'Discovery',* Virgin Books, 1992
Scott, Robert, *The Diaries of Captain Scott 1910–13* (facsimile edition), University Microfilms, 1968
Scott, Robert, *The Voyage of the 'Discovery'*, John Murray, 1905
Seaver, George, *Edward Wilson of the Antarctic,* John Murray, 1933
Seaver, George, *Scott of the Antarctic*, John Murray, 1940
Sefi, Alexander J., *King Edward Land: A History of the Special Postage Stamp Issued in the Antarctic Regions for Sir Ernest Shackleton's Expedition of 1907–09*, D. Field, 1912
Shackleton, Emily & Hugh R. Mill, *Rejoice My Heart* (Michael Rosove ed.), Adélie Books, 2007
Shackleton, Ernest (ed.), *Aurora Australis*, Airlife Publishing, 1988
Shackleton, Ernest & W. McClean, *O.H.M.S. An Illustrated Record of the Voyage of the S.S.* Tintagel Castle, Hazell, Watson and Viney, 1900
Shackleton, Ernest, *South*, Wm Heinemann, 1919
Shackleton, Ernest, *The Heart of the Antarctic*, Wm Heinemann, 1910
Shackleton, Jonathan, *The Shackletons of Ballitore: A genealogy (1580–1987)*, Shackleton, 1989
Shackleton, Jonathan & John MacKenna, *Shackleton: An Irishman in Antarctica*, Lilliput Press, 2002
Shaw, C.D. & W.R. Winterton, *The Middlesex Hospital*, The Middlesex Hospital Journal, 1967
Skelton, J. & D.M. Wilson, *Discovery Illustrated: Pictures from Captain Scott's First Antarctic Expedition*, Reardon Publishing, 2001
Smith, Michael, *An Unsung Hero: Tom Crean Antarctic Survivor*, The Collins Press, 2000
Smith, Michael, *Great Endeavour: Ireland's Antarctic Explorers,* The Collins Press, 2010

Smith, Michael, *I Am Just Going Outside: Captain Oates, Antarctic Tragedy,* The Collins Press, 2002
Smith, Michael, Captain *Francis Crozier: Last Man Standing?*, The Collins Press, 2006
Smith, Michael, *Polar Crusader: Sir James Wordie*, Birlinn, 2004
Smith, Michael, *The Boss: Shackleton*, The Collins Press, 2006
Solar, Rosamaria (ed.) *Traces of Antarctica: Around Punta Arenas and the Straits of Magellan*, Instituto Antártico Chileno, 2013
Solomon, Susan, *The Coldest March*, Yale University Press, 2001
Jon Sörensen, *The Saga of Fridtjof Nansen,* Allen & Unwin, 1932
Speak, Peter, *Deb: A Biography of Frank Debenham*, Polar Publishing, 2008
Speak, Peter, *William Speirs Bruce,* National Museums of Scotland Publishing, 2003
Speight, Harry, *Chronicles and Stories of Old Bingley*, Elliott Stock, 1898
Spufford, Francis, *I May Be Some Time: Ice and the English Imagination*, Faber & Faber, 1996
Stefansson, Vilhjalmur, *Discovery*, McGraw-Hill, 1964
Straithie, Anne, *Birdie Bowers: Captain Scott's Marvel,* The History Press, 2012
Stump, Edmund, *The Roof at the Bottom of the World*, Yale University Press, 2011
Summers, Julie, *The Shackleton Voyages,* Weidenfeld & Nicolson, 2002
Taylor, Griffith, *With Scott: The Silver Lining*, Bluntisham Books, 1997
Taylor, S.J., *The Great Outsiders: Northcliffe, Rothermere and The Daily Mail,* Weidenfeld & Nicolson, 1996
Thomas, Lowell, *Sir Hubert Wilkins*, Arthur Barker, 1961
Thompson, E.P., *The Making of the English Working Class*, Pelican, 1975
Thomson, David, *Scott's Men*, Allen Lane, 1977
Thomson, John, *Elephant Island and Beyond: The Life and Diaries of Thomas Orde Lees,* Bluntisham Books, 2003
Thomson, John, *Shackleton's Captain: A Biography of Frank Worsley*, Hazard Press, 1998
Turner, J. Horsfall, *Ancient Bingley: Bingley, Its History and Scenery*, Thomas Harrison & Sons, 1897
Tyler-Lewis, Kelly, *The Lost Men: The Harrowing Story of Shackleton's Ross Sea Party,* Bloomsbury, 2006
Weems, John Edward *Peary: The Explorer and The Man*, Eyre & Spottiswoode, 1967
Wheeler, Sara, *Cherry: A Life of Apsley Cherry-Garrard,* Jonathan Cape, 2001
Wild, Frank, *Shackleton's Last Voyage,* Cassell & Co., 1923
Wilkins, Hubert, *Sir Hubert Wilkins: His World of Adventure,* Arthur Barker, 1961
Williams, Isobel, *Captain Scott's Invaluable Assistant: Edgar Evans,* The History Press, 2012
Williams, Isobel, *With Scott in the Antarctic: Edward Wilson*, The History Press, 2008
Wilson, David, *Nimrod Illustrated*, Reardon Publishing, 2009
Wilson, Edward, *The Diary of the Discovery Expedition to the Antarctic Regions 1901–04,* Blandford Press, 1966
Worsley, Frank, *Endurance*, Philip Allan & Co, 1933
Worsley, Frank, *Shackleton's Boat Journey*, Hodder & Stoughton, 1940
Worsley, Frank, *The Great Antarctic Rescue: Shackleton's Boat Journey*, Times Books, 1977
Yelverton, David, *Antarctica Unveiled*, University Press of Colorado, 2000
Young, Louisa, *A Great Task of Happiness*, Papermac, 1996

Newspapers, Magazines, Journals

Anon., Dash for the South Pole, *Shipping World*, 8 February 1908
Anon., Dulwich College Form and Class Lists
Anon., How Sir Ernest Shackleton Proposes to Drag His Sledges, *The Sphere*, 10 January 1914
Anon., Edward Saunders, The Shy Ghost Writer (publication unknown)
Anon., The Antarctic Bubble, *John Bull*, 22 July 1916
Anon., The Imperial Transantarctic Expedition's ship, 'Endurance', *Shipbuilding and Shipping Record,* 30 July 1914
Antarctic Heritage Trust, Shackleton's Hut at Cape Royds, Ross Island, Antarctica, *James Caird Journal*, No 3, 2007

Barr, William, Antarctic Debacle: Wilhelm Filchner's Second German South Polar Expedition 1911–12, *Nimrod: The Journal of the Ernest Shackleton Autumn School,* 2013

Barczewski, Stephanie, The Changing Face of Heroism, *James Caird Journal,* No 4, 2008

Blackborow, Perce, Text of Talk by Perce Blackborow to Bolt School, Newport and YMCA (undated) *James Caird Journal,* No 6, 2012

Board of Trade, Board of Trade (British Wreck Commissioners) Public Enquiry into loss of SS *Titanic,* 1912

Burton, Robert, Endurance at South Georgia, *Nimrod: The Journal of the Ernest Shackleton Autumn School,* 2013

Burton, Robert, The Endurance Dogs, unpublished manuscript

Burton, Robert, Shackleton, Robert Mossman and the Weddell Sea, unpublished manuscript

Campbell, Duncan and Clark, Robert S., Marooned on Elephant Island, *Aberdeen Grammar School Magazine,* March 1920

Cockram, Roy, Charles Green – the Antarctic Chef, Hull History Centre

Cooper, A.B., How I Began: Sir Ernest Shackleton, *The Captain,* April 1910

Corbishley, Dr Cathy, The Death of Shackleton, South Georgia Association, 2014

Daly, Regina Wilson, Shackleton's Affinity for the Poetry of Robert Browning, *Nimrod: The Journal of the Ernest Shackleton Autumn School,* 2012

Fagan, Patrick, Retracing Shackleton's Crossing of South Georgia, *James Caird Journal,* No 1, 2003

Ferris, Christine, D.H. Lawrence and the Heroic Age of Polar Exploration, *James Caird Journal,* No 3, 2007

Freedman, Bernard, M.R.C.P., Dr Edward Wilson of the Antarctic, Proceedings of the Royal Society of Medicine, Vol. 47, March 1954

Gibbs, Sir Philip, Sir Ernest Shackleton's Lecture, January 1921, Publication unknown

Gilkes, Michael, It Ain't Necessarily So: South Georgia Loose Ends, *Polar Publishing* 2007

Gordon, W.J., Shackleton's Furthest South, *The Boy's Own Paper,* 1909

Greene, Martin L., Aurora Australis: A New Description of the First Book Published on the Antarctic Continent, *Booktalk,* 2006

Hooper, Meredith, The Arrol-Johnston Motor Car, *James Caird Journal,* No 2, 2004

Jones, A.G.E., Frankie Wild's Hut, *Falklands Islands Journal,* 1982

Keen-Hargreaves, H., Sir Ernest Shackleton's Great Expedition, *Mayfair,* 3 January 1914

Keltie, J. Scott & H.R. Mill, Report of the Sixth International Geographical Congress, John Murray, 1896

Larson, Edward J., Did Shackleton Care About Science? *Nimrod: The Journal of the Ernest Shackleton Autumn School,* 2013

Lewis, Dr H.E., Medical Aspects of Polar Exploration: Sixtieth Anniversary of Scott's Last Expedition, Proceedings of Royal Society of Medicine, Vol. 65, January 1972

Locke, Stephen, George Marston – Shackleton's Antarctic Artist, Hampshire County Council, March 2000

Lucas, Anna, Launching Mawson's Australasian Antarctic Expedition 1911/14 – Shackleton's Role Explored, *James Caird Journal* No 6, 2012

McAdam, Professor Jim, Coins Issued to Commemorate Sir Ernest Shackleton, *Nimrod: The Journal of the Ernest Shackleton Autumn School,* 2013

McAdam, Professor Jim, Sir Ernest Shackleton and Fur Sealing in the Falkland Islands, *Nimrod: The Journal of the Ernest Shackleton Autumn School,* 2010

McAdam, Professor Jim, Shackletonia in the Falklands, *Nimrod: The Journal of the Ernest Shackleton Autumn School,* 2011

McAdam, Professor Jim, The Shackletons in the Falklands, *Nimrod: The Journal of the Ernest Shackleton Autumn School,* 2007

McAdam, Professor Jim & Geraldine McDonald, Shackleton's First Two Public Lectures on his Return from the Endurance Expedition, *Nimrod: The Journal of the Ernest Shackleton Autumn School,* 2009

Macaya, Carlos Gonzalez, The British Presence in Magallanes, Chileno, UK (undated)
MacInnes, Margaret, Endurance Bible, Stornoway Historical Society, undated
Markham, Sir Clements, Memo to Royal Geographical Society 1914, RGS
Mill, Hugh Robert, Ernest Shackleton, *Travel & Exploration Monthly*, July 1909
Mills, Leif, Polar Friction: The Relationship Between Marshall and Shackleton, *Polar Publishing*, 2011
Murphy, Sean J., *Irish Historical Mysteries: A Centenary Report on the Theft of the Irish Crown Jewels in 1907*, Centre for Irish Genealogical and Historical Studies, 2008
Murphy, Shane, The Endurance Photographs, *James Caird Journal*, No 5, 2010
Nethery, James W., James Graham: 6th Duke of Montrose, *Clan Graham News*, 2010
Ormiston, Thomas, Dulwich College Register 1619–1926, Dulwich College
Parada, Alfonso Filippi, Shackleton in Chile – Events Between July and September 1916, *James Caird Journal*, No 6, 2012
Pardo Luis A., Rescue from Elephant Island – Official Chilean Navy Report, 5 September 1916, Patagonia Bookshelf
Perkins, Dennis, Leading at the Edge: Leadership Lessons from the Extraordinary Saga of Shackleton's Antarctic Expedition, Net Library, 2000
Piggott, Jan, Charles Sargeant Jagger and the Shackleton Memorial Statue, *James Caird Journal: The Journal of the Ernest Shackleton Autumn School*, 2003
Piggott, Jan, Shackleton's Men: Life on Elephant Island, *James Caird Journal*, No 2, 2004
Piggott, Jan, Shackleton Plays Truant in the Silverdale Wood, *Nimrod: The Journal of the Ernest Shackleton Autumn School*, 2013
Piggott, Jan, Shackleton, Reader and Writer, *James Caird Society Journal*, No 1, 2003
Poulton, Professor Edward, The National Antarctic Expedition, *Nature*, Vol. 64, May 1901
Pugh, Dr L.G.C., The Logistics of the Polar Journeys of Scott, Shackleton and Amundsen, Proceedings of the Royal Society of Medicine, Vol. 65 January 1972
Raban, Jonathan, Journey to the End of the Night, *New York Review of Books*, 10 June 1999
Reeves, E.A., Report into Southern Party's Latitudes to Royal Geographical Society, 14 September 1909, RGS
Robinson, Robb, Blundell Spence & Company: The Longstaff Family and Exploration, Maritime Historical Studies Centre, University of Hull, 2008
Sarolea, Charles, Sir Ernest Shackleton: A Study in Personality, *The Contemporary Review*, March 1922
Savours, Ann, Clements Markham: Longest Serving Officer, Most Prolific Editor, *The Hakluyt Society*, Vol. 183, 1996
Savours, Ann, The Diary Dr A.H. Macklin Kept During the Imperial Trans-Antarctic Expedition 1914–17, *James Caird Journal*, No 2, 2004
Savours, Ann, From Greenland's Icy Mountains to India's Coral Strand, *History Today*, March 2001
Scott-Fawcett, Stephen, Endurance and Harry McNish, James Caird Journal, No 4, 2008
Scott-Fawcett, Stephen, Walter How, *James Caird Journal*, No 3, 2007
Shackleton, Ernest, In the Days of My Youth, *M.A.P.*, No 572, July 1909
Shackleton, Sir Ernest, The Imperial Trans-Antarctic Expedition, *Geographical Journal*, Vol. 43, 1914
Shackleton, Ernest, Life in the Antarctic, *Pearson's Magazine*, 1903
Shackleton, Ernest Sir, Transcript of Evidence to Board of Trade Tribunal on the Loss of SS *Titanic*
Stenhouse, J.R., Log of the *Aurora*, 1914–16, SPRI
Stephenson, Robert, Shackleton in Boston, *James Caird Journal*, No 5, 2010
Swain, Captain David, Navy Lodge History
Wilson, Edward A., Medical Aspects of the 'Discovery' Voyage, *British Medical Journal*, July 8, 1905
Wood, Michael J., Meteorologist's Profile – Thomas Griffith Taylor, *Weather*, Royal Meteorological Society Vol. 63, No 12, 2008
Wordie, James, Depths and Deposits of the Weddell Sea, Royal Society Edinburgh, Vol. 52, Part 4, No 30, 1921

Wordie, James, The Drift of the Endurance, *Geographical Journal*, Vol. 51, April 1918
Wordie, James, Geological Observations in the Weddell Sea Area, Royal Society Edinburgh, Vol. 53, Part 1, No 2, 1921
Wordie, James, The Natural History of Pack-ice As Observed in the Weddell Sea, Royal Society Edinburgh, Vol. 52, Part 4, No 31, 1921
Wordie, James, Ross Sea Drift of the Aurora in 1915–17, *Geographical Journal*, Vol. 58, September 1921
Wordie, James & Brian B. Roberts, The Scientific Results of the Shackleton Antarctic Expeditions, *Polar Record* Vol. 4 No 26, 1943
Wordie, James M., Obituary: Sir Ernest Shackleton, *Geographical Journal*, No 3, 1922
Wordie, James, Frank Wild – An Obituary, *Polar Record*, Vol. 3 (19), 1940
Worsley, Frank, Shackleton's Expedition to the Antarctic – The Rescue by Chile, *The Chilean Review*, 1928
Yelverton, David, Shackleton's First Sledging Journey, *Polar Publishing*, 2004

Newspapers, Magazines, etc.

British Medical Journal
John Bull
Canterbury Times
Daily Chronicle
Daily Graphic
Daily Mail
Daily Mirror
Daily Telegraph
Dundee Advertiser
Dundee Courier
Geographical Journal
Glasgow Herald
Illustrated London News
Lyttelton Times
Magellan Times
Mayfair
Morning Bulletin
Morning Post
National Geographic
News Chronicle
Pall Mall Gazette
Pearson's Magazine
Scotsman
Shipping World
Sydney Morning Herald
The Boy's Own Paper
The Captain
The Contemporary Review
The Press
The Star
The Sphere
The Times
Travel & Exploration Monthly
Wanganui Chronicle
Weekly Press
Westminster Gazette
Yorkshire Post

Unpublished Sources

Alfred Wegener Institute, Germany (AWI)
Athy Heritage Museum, Ireland
Dulwich College, London, UK
Edinburgh University Library (EUL)
Kerry County Library, Tralee, Ireland (KCL)
Kerry County Museum, Tralee, Ireland (KCM)
Library and Museum of Freemasonry (LMF)
Mitchell Library, Sydney, Australia (ML)
National Archives, UK (NA)
National Library of Australia (NLA)
National Library of Scotland (NLS)
Royal Geographical Society, London, UK (RGS)
Scott Polar Research Institute, Cambridge, UK (SPRI)
South Georgia Museum-South Georgia Heritage Trust (SGM)

Unpublished material

Adams, J.B., Correspondence, SPRI

Admiralty Records, *Discovery* expedition; British Antarctic Expedition; Imperial Trans-Antarctic Expedition; *Quest* expedition; NA

Anon., Letter to (Lady) Emily Shackleton, 10 August 1915, Seamus Taaffe

Armitage, Albert, Correspondence, SPRI

Aurora Log book, 1914–16, SPRI

Bakke, Ulf, Artefacts, correspondence re: *Quest*

Beardmore, William, Correspondence, SPRI

Bernacchi, Louis, Correspondence, SPRI

Corbishley Michel, Dr Cathy, The Death of Shackleton on South Georgia, South Georgia Association Newsletter, November 2013

Crean O'Brien, Mary, Interviews with author, 1997

Crean, Thomas, Papers, KCM, SPRI

David, T.W.E., Correspondence, SPRI

Duncan, James, *Discovery* diary, 1901–03, Dundee Art Galleries & Museum

Dunlop, Harry, Correspondence, SPRI

England, Rupert, Correspondence, SPRI

Falklands Islands Government, Agreement with Sir Ernest Shackleton for Lease of Fur Seal Rookeries, Falkland Islands, 14 May 1914, Falkland Islands Archives

Fisher, M. & J., Correspondence and Papers, SPRI

Gregory, John Walter, Obituary Notices of Fellows of the Royal Society, December 1932, Vol. 1, No 1, 53–59

Harboard, Derek, Letter to Raymond Priestley, 2 February 1963, Seamus Taaffe

Hattersley-Smith, Geoffrey, Interview with author, 2003

Hinks, Arthur, Correspondence, RGS

Hurley, Frank, Journals, 1914–16, (ML)

Imperial Trans-Antarctic Expedition, Prospectus, Oldham Local Studies & Archives

James, Reginald, Journals, Imperial Trans-Antarctic Expedition 1914–16; *Endurance,* Final List of Noon Positions, 1914–16; Correspondence; SPRI

Joyce, Ernest, Correspondence, SPRI

Koettlitz, Reginald, Papers, documents, photographs, Koettlitz Family

Leech, Herbert W., Notes on The Northern Exploration Company, Private

Mackay, A.F., Nimrod Diary, SPRI

Mackellar, Campbell, Correspondence, SPRI

Macklin, Alexander, Letters and papers; Letter to James Wordie, 10 June, 1933; Letters to James Wordie; Shackleton: As I Knew Him, speech to Rotary Club, 1959

McNish, Henry, Diary of Endurance Expedition, NLA

Mann, John, *Endurance Dogs*, Endurance Obituaries (Website)

Markham, Clements, Correspondence, Report to Council of Royal Geographical Society re Imperial Trans-Antarctic Expedition, 1914 RGS; SPRI

Marshall, Eric, Correspondence; Diary of British Antarctic Expedition, SPRI

Marston, George, Correspondence: Hampshire Record Office; SPRI

Mawson, Douglas, Letters to Lady Shackleton November 4, 1915; 25 November 1915, Seamus Taaffe

Mill, Hugh R., Correspondence, SPRI; Letter to unnamed person, 30 May 1922, Seamus Taaffe

Petrides, N., Correspondence, SPRI

Priestley, Raymond, Diaries of British Antarctic Expedition, SPRI

Sarolea, Charles, Papers and correspondence re: Ernest Shackleton, EUL

Shackleton, Aimee, Correspondence, SPRI

Shackleton, Alice, Correspondence, SPRI

Shackleton, Eleanor, Correspondence, SPRI

Shackleton, Emily, Correspondence, SPRI

Shackleton, Sir Ernest:
Correspondence and papers. Admiralty, Ref: *Quest* expedition, ADM 1/8595/162;
Correspondence and papers, National Archives: Ref: Quest acquisition, *Quest* survey, ownership papers CUST 148/129; Ref: Death, burial arrangements of Sir Ernest Shackleton, ADM 1/8621/39; Ref: Correspondence with David Lloyd George 1911, T 172/51; Ref: Documents relating to Russian campaign, WO 32/5664; Papers T 1/12579; Ref: Correspondence regarding *Endurance* and *Aurora* relief operations 1915–16, T 1/12012; Correspondence for Beaufort Sea expedition 1920–21, ADM 1/85959/162; Correspondence Hutchison & Cuff regarding Imperial Trans-Antarctic Expedition, MT 9/977
Correspondence and papers, Royal Geographical Society;
Correspondence and papers, Scott Polar Research Institute; Diary of British National Antarctic Expedition; Diary of British National Antarctic Expedition: Southern Journey; Diary of British Antarctic Expedition; Diary of British Antarctic Expedition: Southern Journey;
Shackleton letter to Isobel Donaldson, 2 August 1918, Seamus Taaffe
Shackleton, Kathleen, Correspondence, SPRI
Skelton, Reginald, Journals of British National Antarctic Expedition, SPRI
Skinners, The Skinners' Company Records, Guildhall Library
Smith, Mark K., Francis Herbert Stead, Browning Hall and the Fight for Old Age Pensions, *The Encyclopaedia of Informal Education*
South Georgia Museum, Correspondence
Speranza, V.E. Letter to W. T. C. Smith, 30 November 1936, Seamus Taaffe
Stancomb-Wills, Dame Janet, Correspondence, SPRI
Stenhouse, Joseph, Diaries, Logs and Papers, SPRI
Sweeney, Michael, *From the Front: The Story of War*, National Geographic Society, 2002
Tripp, Leonard, Correspondence, SPRI
Wild, Frank, Correspondence and papers, SPRI; Diary of British Antarctic Expedition: Southern Journey, SPRI, Memoirs, ML
Wild Island, South Georgia's Cemeteries, Pat and Sarah Lurcock
Wilson, Edward, Journal of British National Antarctic Expedition: Southern Journey, SPRI
Wordie, James, Weddell Sea log, 4 vols. 1914–16, Wordie Family
Wordie, James, Papers, correspondence, diaries and papers 1889–1962, NLS, RGS, SPRI
Wordie, Peter, Interviews with Author, 2001–03
Worsley, Frank, *Endurance* journals 1914–16; Correspondence, papers; SPRI; Paper on Animals Killed in the Weddell Sea, 1914–16

Online Sources

Antarctic Circle: www.antarctic-circle.org
Endurance Obituaries: www.endurancebituaries.co.uk
James Caird Society: www.jamescairdsociety.com
British Association of Magallanes: www.patbrit.org
Sydenham Society: www.sydenhamsociety.com

Visual Sources

Butler, George, *The Endurance: Shackleton's Legendary Antarctic Expedition,* White Mountain Films, 2000
Crossing the Line Films, *Tom Crean – Kerryman on the Ice*
Hurley, Frank, *South: Sir Ernest Shackleton's Glorious Epic of the Antarctic,* British Film Institute, 2002
Making Movies, *Shackleton's Captain*, 2011
Ponting, Herbert, *90° South*, National Film & Television Archive

Index

Note: Numbers in *italics* refer to photographs or maps